THE FOURFOLD

Northwestern University
Studies in Phenomenology
and
Existential Philosophy

THE FOURFOLD

Reading the Late Heidegger

Andrew J. Mitchell

Northwestern University Press
Evanston, Illinois

Northwestern University Press
www.nupress.northwestern.edu

Printed in the United States of America

10 9 8 7 6 5 4 3 2 1

Library of Congress Cataloging-in-Publication Data

Mitchell, Andrew J., 1970–
    The fourfold : reading the late Heidegger / Andrew J. Mitchell.
        pages cm. — (Studies in phenomenology and existential philosophy)
        Includes bibliographical references and index.
    ISBN 978-0-8101-3076-0 (paperback) — ISBN 978-0-8101-3077-7 (cloth) —
ISBN 978-0-8101-3078-4 (ebook)
    1. Heidegger, Martin, 1889–1976.   I. Title.
    B3279.H49M4988 2015
    193—dc23
    2015006105

In memory of
Mary Barbara Mitchell
1915–1995
Beloved grandmother
Trusted friend

Contents

Acknowledgments

My interest in the fourfold began in 1996 with a reading group on the Bremen lectures organized by Peter Trawny of the Bergische Universität Gesamthochschule Wuppertal while I was an exchange student there under the supervision of Klaus Held. Prior to that I was dismissive at best. That awakened interest led to a dissertation at SUNY Stony Brook in 2001 entitled *The Fourfold and Technology: Heidegger's Thinking of Limit,* under the direction of Edward S. Casey, with Peter Manchester, François Raffoul, Peter Trawny, and Krzysztof Ziarek as committee members. I am grateful to each of these for their time and effort on my behalf. François and Peter in particular have shaped my understanding of Heidegger in more ways than I can tell or thank them for.

The present volume is a complete rewriting of that dissertation after a decade's worth of reflection, experience, and thought. Over that period there have been so many people who have helped me see this through with encouragement, support, inspiration, and good cheer. I marvel at their generosity, both at how much I need and how much they give, and believe philosophy itself to depend on people like these: David Allison, Dan Dahlstrom, Tom Flynn, Hans Ulrich Gumbrecht, Robert Harrison, Stuart Kendall, Sean Kirkland, John Lysaker, Eduardo Mendieta, Malek Moazzam Doulat, Mary Rawlinson, John Sallis, Tom Sheehan, John Stuhr, Alejandro Vallega, Daniela Vallega-Neu, Cynthia Willett, Jason Winfree. More immediately, Lily Levy and Chris Merwin were kind enough to serve as proofreaders for the text. Amy Alexander has lived with this project as long as I have, unwavering in her support.

I am appreciative of the confidence shown in me by Northwestern University Press, especially director Jane Bunker and also series editor Tony Steinbock. Thanks, too, to their anonymous reviewers whose attentive comments were not only beneficial in preparing the final manuscript, but uplifting as well.

A portion of chapter two, "Animals (*Getier*)," was published as "Heidegger's Later Thinking of Animality: The End of World Poverty" in the inaugural issue of *Gatherings: The Heidegger Circle Annual.* At the Heidegger Circle I had the opportunity to respond to lectures on the fourfold by Rex Gilliand and Jussi Backman at meetings in 2005 and 2010 respectively. Critically engaging with their ideas helped me identify failings in my own.

I am fortunate to be at Emory University, where a grant from the Fox Center for Humanistic Inquiry and Dean Robert Paul allowed me to pursue archive work at the Deutsches Literatur Archiv in Marbach, Germany, during the summer of 2008.

Lastly, at least four cats have been involved with this: Torte, Lucy, Kit Marlowe, and Phoebe. Any remaining typos are theirs.

A Note on Abbreviations and Conventions

References to the works of Martin Heidegger are provided parenthetically in the text by the volume number of Heidegger's complete works (*Gesamtausgabe*, abbreviated *GA*), with German pagination provided first, followed by a slash and the English pagination of published translations where they exist. The only exception is *Being and Time* (*GA* 2), where no English pagination is provided; instead the *Gesamtausgabe* pagination is followed by the German pagination of the single edition published by Niemeyer (included as marginal pagination in all three of the English translations of *Being and Time*). Other works by Heidegger—single editions and English translations—are also abbreviated, as well as some frequently cited texts by other authors. All abbreviations are given in the bibliography alongside full publication information; see page 351.

Modifications to published translations are indicated by the abbreviation "tm"; the addition of emphasis by "em." Where no English translation pagination is provided, translations are my own.

THE FOURFOLD

The Fourfold: On the Relationality of Things

The fourfold (*das Geviert*) is a thinking of things. The fourfold names the "gathering" of earth, sky, mortals, and divinities that comes to constitute the thing for Heidegger. In the late 1940s, operating under a teaching ban imposed by the French authorities in the wake of World War II, Heidegger ventures "the boldest statement of his thinking" in announcing the fourfold.[1] First named in the 1949 lecture cycle *Insight Into That Which Is*, held at the private Club zu Bremen, developed and refined over the next decade, and remaining with Heidegger until the end of his life, the fourfold is nothing less than the inauguration of Heidegger's later thinking. The fourfold brings together the poetic sensibility of Heidegger's Hölderlin interpretations of the 1940s with the esoteric rigor of his notebooks from the 1930s, into a new figure of thought: the thing. The simple things around us—indeed, the things themselves—become the focus of his attention, lending to his work of the period a unique phenomenological density disencumbered of all formal transcendentalism. The fourfold provides an account of the thing as inherently relational. Thanks to the fourfold, these things unfold themselves ecstatically, opening relations with the world beyond them. Unlike the self-enclosed object of modern metaphysics, the thing is utterly worldly, its essence lying in the relations it maintains throughout the world around it, the world to which it is inextricably bound. The world becomes the medium of the thing's relations. The fourfold is the key to understanding this streaming, mediated, relationality of finite, worldly existence.

The importance of this new thinking of the thing should not be underestimated. The 1949 Bremen lecture cycle, *Insight Into That Which Is*, where the conception of the fourfold is first forged in its opening lecture "The Thing," stands alongside *Being and Time* (1927), Heidegger's landmark early work, and the *Contributions to Philosophy* (1936–38), the gravitational center of his middle period, as a third, decisive milestone along his path of thought. While such a claim might first appear hyperbolic, Heidegger himself puts great stock in this orientation to the thing. In a 1964 letter reflecting on his path of thought hitherto, he confesses: "*Apart from the thing lecture, I have never once presented my own thinking purely on its own terms in publications,* however far it has come in the meantime, but rather have always only presented it in such a way that, provisionally, I wanted to make my thinking understandable in terms of the tradition."[2] It behooves us then to take up Heidegger's thinking "on its own terms."

The following work consequently focuses on the most distinguishing feature of the "Thing" lecture—the fourfold—and attempts to do so "on its own terms." So much confusion and befuddlement has attended Heidegger's thinking of the fourfold that his basic insights into the thing have largely gone unheeded. Too often commentators have taken flight from the perplexity of thinking through the fourfold in Heidegger's work by assimilating it to some outside framework or set of concerns, be they Platonic, Aristotelian, Ancient Greek more generally, Native American, Chinese, Hölderlinian, or a recasting of Heidegger's own *Being and Time.* But even when this is not the case, commentary has not remained very close to the actual wording of Heidegger's text.[3] In making my case for the fourfold's central place in a Heideggerian thinking of relationality, my intention is to take Heidegger at his word and follow the presentation of the fourfold as given in "The Thing" lecture of 1949, as well as the complementary presentation in the lecture "Building Dwelling Thinking" from 1951.[4] The following chapters devoted to the fourfold thus examine these initial depictions on a word-for-word basis. Instead of explaining away the fourfold, I endeavor to trace out the importance of each term used in these presentations, following their resonances throughout the surrounding texts. Broadly speaking, then, the chapters devoted to the fourfold stake out and survey the terrain of Heidegger's later concerns out from this epicenter of the fourfold. In so doing, I develop a conception of mediation and relationality as operative across Heidegger's thinking of the thing. While such an approach may not grant us comprehensive coverage of Heidegger's later thought, it does allow us an ordered approach to the bulk of his motivating concerns of the period and a point of conceptual purchase for reading the later Heidegger.

What I hope to show through such an exegesis of the fourfold is that Heidegger's thinking taken "on its own terms" is ultimately a thinking of finitude. Obviously, this is no startling claim, but the fourfold pushes the consequences of finitude to their extreme. To think the finitude of a thing is to think it as limited, but for Heidegger this limitation is to be thought positively. To think the finite is to think the limitation of a thing as the surface of its exposure to the world beyond it. The limit of a thing is its interface with that beyond. But this means that to be finite is to extend past oneself and enter into a multiplicity of relations. Finitude is a kind of relational "radiance," we might say. By thinking finitude in this "ecstatic" way, we make the relation to a beyond essential to what the finite thing is. This means that a thinking of finitude is impossible without a concomitant consideration of this beyond (the finite is nothing other than this connection or relation). For finite existence to be ecstatic, then, entails in turn that the "beyond" of the thing be no empty void, but be itself essentially capable of transmitting these radiant relations. That is to say, to be finite is to exist beyond oneself and this manner of existing requires a medium capable of supporting it. This notion of "medium," which I endeavor to unfold in what follows, is endemic to a Heideggerian thought of finitude, and for Heidegger this beyond, this medium, is the world. Simply put, to think the finitude of things is to think the mediacy of the world.

Such a thought requires putting aside a few misconceptions that all too readily assert themselves, most prominently that in speaking of a "medium" we are speaking of something that would lie in between two fixed poles. To begin with, the things in question are nothing so fixed or self-contained. What appears in this world does so in conjunction with everything around it. There is nothing that does not exist in this relational way. To appear is to be exposed and to be exposed is to be opened to a beyond, even to welcome that beyond (to invite it). This is what we might term the "hospitality" of things. From this perspective, then, the things are already beyond themselves and do not stand outside the relation as poles isolated from each other. Second, this likewise means that the medium itself is no present-at-hand third party intervening between two otherwise independent ones, equally present-at-hand. The medium is not simply "between" the things; rather, in some abstract geometrical sense, it surrounds them. The things are immersed in it. It is the field of their interaction, that through which streams the relations that they maintain. The pages that follow will develop this thought in greater detail and follow the various formulations of it across Heidegger's texts of the period. For now it is worth noting that a "medium" is nothing between two otherwise present objects, but is instead the essential attendant of any finite mode of existence whatsoever. To be finite is to implicate such a beyond. Hence the increasing importance and proliferation of names that Heidegger grants to media in his thinking, each of which will be discussed in what follows: the "between" (*das Zwischen*), the "joyous" (*das Heitere*), the "holy" (*das Heilige*), the "aether" (*der Äther*), the "middle" (*die Mitte*), the "dimension" (*die Dimension*), the "element" (*das Element*), the "clearing" (*die Lichtung*), and ultimately even "death" (*der Tod*). It is my contention in what follows that the fourfold names the structural minima for the mediated, finite existence of things. As such, the fourfold grants us insight into what I take to be the the center of Heidegger's later thinking, a thinking of mediation and relationality.

In proceeding, I subscribe to a roughly drawn tripartite periodization of Heidegger's work: early (1912–1932, culminating in *Being and Time*, 1927), middle (1933–1944, centering on the *Contributions to Philosophy*, 1936–1938), and late or "post-war" (1945–1976, taking its orientation from *Insight into That Which Is*, 1949). While the bounds of these are not rigidly fixed, they are not arbitrary categorizations, either. To be sure, good cases could be made for further dividing each of these periods: separating the juvenilia from the works of fundamental ontology, for example, or the rectoral texts from the esoteric notebooks and the exoteric lecture courses of the late 1930s and early 1940s, or, lastly, distinguishing the work of the 1960s—the homeland speeches and aesthetic investigations (signally, of sculpture)—from the immediately post-war period of the fourfold running through the 1950s. The latter will be our concern in what follows. Nevertheless, the heuristic benefits of such a rough division warrant this simplified, tripartitioned approach to Heidegger's remarkable path of thought.

Consequently, I will broadly refer to the "time" or "period" of the fourfold in Heidegger's lectures and essays as extending from 1949–1960, where the majority of references are to be found, with the decisive developments largely occurring between 1949 and 1955. The parochialism of my approach, however, should not lead us to dismiss the fourfold as a fleeting concern of a few years' time for Heidegger. Nothing could be further from the truth. The fourfold remains prominent across Heidegger's thinking of the 1950s as a whole and accompanies his thinking to the very end (it is mentioned in texts from as late as 1973–1975).[5] The fourfold remains a concern for Heidegger into his final years; it is no passing phase of his thought.[6]

In adherence to this periodization, my first recourse in what follows is always to the essays and lectures of the period immediately surrounding the texts of the fourfold (the time of the fourfold). Where broader reference better illuminates the ideas under consideration, however, I also take up texts from the early 1960s as well as the mid-1940s (particularly the readings of Hölderlin and Heraclitus there). I return to the earlier works—the *Contributions to Philosophy* and affiliated notebooks of the middle period, as well as the earlier *Being and Time* and other texts of fundamental ontology—largely by way of contrast, so as to draw attention to the shifts in Heidegger's thought rather than the continuities. In my first chapter, "The Technological Challenge to Things," for example, I show how the later Heidegger's conception of technology in *Insight into That Which Is* (1949) advances beyond the considerations of machination from the earlier *Contributions to Philosophy* (1936–38), and indicates a parallel shift in his conception of being itself. In emphasizing the chronology, I hope to allow Heidegger's later writings to show themselves on their own terms, or at the very least to grant them a certain independence from his earlier writings. I keep to the texts of the time so that the novelty of the period might become more apparent. Consequently this book is not the "genesis" of the fourfold. I am not necessarily providing a developmental account of the fourfold or casting it as a reconfiguration of positions earlier held. Instead, I am attempting to begin with the fourfold and unpack its import through interpretations of the texts that first present it. In so doing I hope to avoid a philosophical anachronism in reading Heidegger, whereby the later work is read solely in terms of the earlier, and as a redundant and ultimately unnecessary confirmation of his own earlier insights.

Against such approaches, I take the crux of Heidegger's later thinking to be preeminently a new concern for the thing. The fourfold names the structure of such things (they are a "gathering" of it), and it is the fourfold that allows things to be opened to relations in the way that they are. I argue that such things cannot be understood apart from the medium in which they are found. For something to be ecstatic is for it to be so essentially tied to what lies beyond it so as to be unthinkable apart from it. The fourfold opens the thing to its beyond in this way. Otherwise put, the fourfold opens that thing to the world. But as so opened, the thing is likewise made addressable by that world in turn. For Heidegger this means that the thing will be addressed by a world given over to the dominance of technology. As relational, the thing will be claimed from the outset by the prevailing demands of technology. It is not a coincidence that the Bremen lecture cycle, *Insight Into That Which Is*, where Heidegger first presents the fourfold, is likewise where he most powerfully articulates these demands of technology, coining the terms "positionality" (*Gestell*) and "standing reserve" (*Bestand*) to identify them. Positionality imposes an infinitely extendable regimen of commodification across the globe. There is no center to this (the United States, for example), nor is this anything like a framework or scaffolding around an otherwise intact world. Technology is a transformation of being, it frames nothing. Inseparable from thinking the thing is therefore a conception of the standing reserve, the mode of existence within positionality.[7]

The first chapter of this work is thus an exploration of Heidegger's views on technology. Heidegger understands technology as a drive toward replaceability and "commodification" (which I oppose to the emphasis on "objectification" that worried his work of the 1930s) whereby all that is becomes replaceable "standing reserve." Technology thus poses a threat to the singularity and uniqueness of things. But this is unavoidable. Technology does not befall things from outside, it is itself a way of being.

Being is what threatens things with their replacements. A proper understanding of technology will attune us to the basic tension in Heidegger's later thought between the singular and the replaceable and keep us from construing the fourfold as a second world somehow superior to this one. The ultimate transformation into replaceability is the process whereby everything becomes so much energy. Heidegger's consideration of technology culminates in a thinking of the annihilatory threat of the atomic bomb, which he understands as effecting an ontological change in the nature of things (all that is now exists as destroyable in principle). My intention in all this is to lay the foundation for an appreciation of how the technological challenge to things is necessary for the very singularity and relationality of things enacted by the fourfold (the topic of my conclusion). Without standing reserve, no things; without positionality, no fourfold.

The next four chapters each pursue a single member of the fourfold—earth, sky, divinities, and mortals—following Heidegger's formulations through the works of the period. Heidegger's discussions of the earth finds it to be the very "matter" of existence. What this matter is, however, is nothing that we normally associate with earth. It is neither solid nor grounded. Instead, the earth names the sensuous. In keeping with earlier insights from "The Origin of the Work of Art," the earth names a kind of non-quantifiable sensuous appearing. It is not a substantial basis that would ground all things. Instead, what is of the earth is ungrounded and free to "shine" or "radiate." All appearance is earthly in this sense, qualitatively dense.

Yet there would be no such shine or radiance of things without a medium through which they might appear. Heidegger's thinking of the earth unsettles the thing, it unseats it. But in so doing, it releases it into the space around it. The earth is thus an entry to sky. The sky is consequently the earth's medium. And it is crucial to this whole thinking of mediation to note that this medium of the sky is no empty void, but instead a space traversed by weather patterns and variable lighting, a medium that is likewise temporally disposed into night and day and the seasonal changes of the year. What appears in a medium (what is of the earth) is affected by that appearing. The sky under which it appears "weathers" it.

Heidegger makes earth and sky constitutive of the thing. This means that all things are earthly, i.e., ungrounded, sensuous, and apparent, and as such move through a medium capable of receiving them, a medium that is itself nothing stable, void, or self-same. Things effect a movement into their medium, which in turn rubs back on them.

But Heidegger will go further than this in his thinking of the thing. Through the divinities he comes to understand the exposure of finite, mediated appearance as essentially meaningful. Things are inherently meaningful for him, and the participation of the "divinities" in the constitution of the thing is meant to indicate this. Meaning is a kind of relation, a connection between things. Such relating and connecting would not be possible without the opened thing exposed to a beyond and addressable by it. This is why the divinities are understood by Heidegger as "messengers." By incorporating them into the things themselves Heidegger is ensuring that existence be understood as always already invested in what I will call a "hermeneutics of the message." To say that the divinities are gathered into things is to say that all things are exposed to the surprise of grace and that such exposure is the condition for any meaningful existence at all.

What is more, these things could not appear to us, appeal to us, if we were not likewise exposed to them. There is no relation of one. The mortals are those who are capable of death and thus have their being in the world. In *Being and Time*, Heidegger showed how death is most our own, in that no one can die our deaths for us, but that death is nevertheless nothing we possess (when it is here, we are gone, and when we are here, it is not). Existence was thus defined by this non-possession of one's own. What is most our own is no possession and this frustrates the attempts of the ego to seclude itself in isolation. To be mortal is to be defined by just such a dispossession, by a death we can never have. What is most my own remains outside of me, and this fact draws me out of myself, and is thus my fundamental opening to world. Mortals exist as members of a community that participates in world.

Following chapters two through five on the members of the fourfold, the sixth chapter treats of the "thinging" of the thing, recomposing this from out of the analyses of the fourfold, so as to take up the thing's relation to world more directly. Here I pay particular attention to the way in which Heidegger describes the belonging together of the four (which he casts in the puzzling terms of a "mirror play") as well as to his remarks on the nature of the things so constituted (that they are "slight," that they "abide," that they are "in-finite," properly understood).

Lastly, the conclusion returns to the question of how the technological threat of replaceability is involved in the very singularity of the thing itself. Here I explore the broader repercussions of the fourfold in Heidegger's latest thinking (notes and sketches from the early 1970s). Signal among Heidegger's claims of the time is that the fourfold would effect a break with the thinking of ontological difference that had so profoundly marked Heidegger's earlier work of fundamental ontology. The abandonment of the ontological difference shows exactly how much is at stake in a thinking of the simple thinging of things.

At this point, however, one might object that a thinking of things is nothing completely novel for Heidegger. Undoubtedly one of the major breakthroughs of *Being and Time* (1927) was its reconsideration of the beings around us and the discernment of a distinction within their mode of existence, as either present-at-hand or ready-to-hand. The theoretico-scientific approach to beings, predominant across the history of philosophy, presents itself as an unprejudiced regard for the entity, "when concern holds back from any kind of producing, manipulating, and the like" (*GA* 2: 82/*SZ* 61). In comporting toward beings in this way, the being is understood in terms of presence-at-hand (*Vorhandenheit*). But this presumed objectivity of beings is itself founded upon a more primordial pragmatic relationship where we are already engaged with these beings, where they are themselves matters of our concern (*pragmata*; cf. *GA* 2: 92/*SZ* 68). Such beings are defined as equipment—"We shall call those entities which we encounter in concern 'equipment,'"—where "the kind of being which equipment possesses—in which it manifests itself in its own right—we call *'readiness-to-hand [Zuhandenheit]'*" (*GA* 2: 92, 93/*SZ* 68, 69). This fundamental mode of existence is nothing substantial, but located within an underlying context of use and application through which Dasein as a being-in-the-world pre-conceptually organizes and evaluates beings in the service of its always ongoing projects. Dasein is always in a world, always ahead of itself, always engaged in projects, and always comporting to beings within a context of its concerns (an equipmental context) whereby these beings are useful to it. This pragmatic basis underlies any objective regard for a present-at-hand object. When there is an interruption in the work, when the hammer we have been using, for example, is inadequate for the task at hand, then it comes to our attention and leaps into focus as something present-at-hand. But when the work flows on and the hammer serves as we expect, then it disappears from sight as a piece of the equipmental context of the ready-to-hand. In other words, the objection would go, beings—or "things"—appear in *Being and Time* in terms of either presence or utility.

Further, if we were to respond to this objection by insisting on the term "thing" (*Ding*) as distinct from the present-at-hand or the ready-to-hand, to claim that Heidegger does not think "things" in *Being and Time*, our interlocutor could simply point to the text, to wit, Heidegger's analysis of the worldhood of the world. This investigation begins from a conception of the "world of everyday Dasein," the environment: "We shall seek the worldhood of the environment (environmentality) by going through an ontological interpretation of those entities within-the-environment which we encounter as closest to us" (*GA* 2: 89/*SZ* 66). In the "Analysis of Environmentality and Worldhood in General" Heidegger wonders what sort of entities these may be (entities that will grant us access to Dasein's understanding of being as displayed in its concernful dealings). His response tells us all we need to know about the role of "things" in *Being and Time:*

> One may answer: "Things." But with this obvious answer we have perhaps already missed the pre-phenomenal basis we are seeking. For in addressing these entities as "Things" (*res*), we have tacitly anticipated their ontological character. When analysis starts with such entities and goes on to inquire about being, what it meets is thinghood and reality. Being as substantiality, materiality, extendedness, side-by-sideness, and so forth. But even pre-ontologically, in such being as this, the entities which we encounter in concern are proximally hidden. When one designates things as the entities that are "proximally given," one goes ontologically astray, even though ontically one has something else in mind. What one really has in mind remains undetermined.
> (*GA* 2: 91/*SZ* 67–68)

Being and Time would thus already think the particular beings of the world and rebut any attempt to simply cast these beings as "things" as itself overlooking their fundamental status as ready-to-hand.

But it is precisely for this reason that we cannot speak of any "things" in *Being and Time* at all—not in the sense that Heidegger will develop the thing in his later work. A thing is no simple presence, nothing that can be understood as an independent and relationless unit of objective presence. Things concern us and appeal to us, we care for them and live with them. We leave our marks upon them, even wear them out, and they leave their marks upon us. They are nodes of a relation, not inert and dumb objects. Yet when *Being and Time* recognizes this and offers the ready-to-hand as an alternative to such objective presence, it changes nothing. To think of things in terms of tools is only to subordinate them to the purposes of a user. They serve as means to an external end. But things do not serve, they *are.* Heidegger's reflections through the thirties lead to an understanding of the history of philosophy as a history of the will (as a 1945 dialogue expresses it, "with the word 'will' I do not in fact mean a faculty of the soul, but rather that wherein the essence of the soul, mind, reason, love, and life is based, according to a unanimous yet hardly thought through doctrine of occidental thinkers," *GA* 77: 78/49). Approaching the world in terms of use and utility, in terms of tools, is part and parcel of this metaphysical world of the will. It culminates in Nietzsche, or more precisely in that last avatar of Nietzsche, Ernst Jünger, who understands all of reality in terms of the worker (*Der Arbeiter*). The worker makes the world an unworld, a "workshop landscape."[8] There is no place for things in such a workshop, only tools that serve purposes outside of themselves and are utterly replaceable in an endless mobilization.

For all its transformation of our conceptions of "subjectivity," *Being and Time* remains wedded to an inadequate conception of "objectivity" or thinghood. To change our understanding of the subject, it is not enough to rethink human existence as Dasein. Humans do not exist alone, as no one knew better than Heidegger; they exist in a world, one replete with things. To transform the human through a thought of being-in-the-world is to likewise transform the world, and so long as the hard, philosophical work of transforming the conception of the thing in that world remains outstanding, nothing changes at all. To change the "subject" while retaining the "object" is to change nothing. The project of *Being and Time* demands more. The thinking of the fourfold provides this rethinking of thing and world and in this regard arguably could be read as the consummation of *Being and Time's* effort to think being-in-the-world. But from another perspective, and this is the perspective adopted in what follows, *Being and Time* participates in the general ignorance of things endemic to the history of philosophy. Heidegger's later thought corrects for this.

The "Essence" of Things

The members of the fourfold name the conditions by which the thing extends into a world of relations (as appearances, as mediated, as meaningful, as with others), they coalesce in the emergence of the thing into this world. But this relationality would not be possible for "objects" as self-contained pieces of material, as the sturdy "furniture" of a pre-existing world. Things are not the building blocks of reality, they are never solid enough for this. For the thing to be a thing of the sort described, it must surrender itself into a play of relations, exist as a cluster and conglomeration of relations. The fourfold allows Heidegger a way of articulating the desolidification or dis-closure of the thing, the interruption of the thing's self-presence and self-identity whereby that thing passes into the world. Rather than an underlying substantial existence, things are thought in terms of a "gathering" (*Versammlung*) of the fourfold.[9] The fourfold is "gathered" (*versammelt*) into things.

As a gathering, the thing is desubstantialized, it is no longer construed as a present and self-enclosed entity, but instead as the intersection of earth, sky, mortals, and divinities. Considering the thing a gathering thus precludes any conception of the thing as a steady presence. The fourfold gathers around the thing in a tenuous convergence. There is nothing everlasting or monumental about such things, they tarry ephemerally (Heidegger's term is *weilen*). The thing abides. The same gathering that unites the four in the thing is equally a disaggregation of that thing. What is gathered is not a homogeneity, but a spaced parting of assembled members. The fourfold disaggregates the thing by releasing it from the bounds of an encapsulated self-identity into the streams of relation. Heidegger calls this "thinging" ("The thing things"; *GA* 79: 17/16). The thing in its thinging is telescoped out beyond itself. The thing is not only gathered but disassembled at once, and through this disassembly it enters the world. The extrapolated thing extrudes beyond itself, billowing through the four members of the fourfold. Each of these grants the thing a place within a particular cluster of relations and supportive connections. The thing is nestled within a context.

The things that appear in Heidegger's lectures emphasize this contextual, relational character as well. A thing is a jug ("The Thing"), a vessel that holds and retains, gives and pours out (Heidegger speaks of a "gift of the pour [*Geschenk des Gusses*]"; *GA* 79: 11/11).[10] This thing the jug is determined by its pour, "the pour [*Guß*] determines the jughood of the jug" (*GA* 79: 11 n. a/10 n. 1). But this pour is itself never simply contained or retained without further ado, the sharing of it is an ineradicable and constitutive possibility. The pour is then always at the same time a pouring out: "What is authentic of the pour is nevertheless the outpouring [*Ausgießen*]" (*GA* 79: 11 n. a/10 n. 1). The jug as thing is determined by a pouring out. This outpouring exceeds any utilitarian directive. It is a sacrifice: "Sufficiently thought and genuinely said, where it is essentially performed pouring is: donating, sacrificing, and therefore giving [*schenken*]" (*GA* 79: 12/11). The jug is not a jug because it is useful, the jug is a jug because it is capable of sacrificial expenditure.

A thing is a bridge ("Building Dwelling Thinking"), a crossing over two shores that provides passage along a way. Bridges conduct, accompany, and escort us (*geleiten uns*) along a path (and Heidegger does not fail to note that we ourselves, as mortals, are always underway and in the crossing; cf. *GA* 7: 155/*PLT* 150, tm). The bridge brings about a relation between the shores and the surrounding landscape such that "it brings stream and shore and land into a reciprocal neighborliness [*Nachbarschaft*]" (*GA* 7: 154/*PLT* 150, tm). This sort of bond does not occur among the indifference of objects. Instead, when a thing is in place, it transforms its surroundings. The shores are no longer "already present-at-hand shores" (*GA* 7: 154/*PLT* 150, tm), they are transformed by the relations presented by the bridge. The bridge stands in a particular relation to the shores it touches: "In the crossing over of the bridge the shores first come forth as shores" (*GA* 7: 154/*PLT* 150, tm). The relational bridge touches what surrounds it and participates in the building of a particular locale with them.

These are not so many arbitrary facts about jugs and bridges, but essential traits of things, the instantiations of an "ontological" relationality. Things are all jugs, defined by their relation to a giving out (of themselves) determinative for what they are. Things themselves are so many gifts of excess, they gush beyond their bounds as ecstatic existences. Ecstatic existence is no longer a privilege of Dasein, but whatever appears within a world, if there is a world, must appear ecstatically. Things exist within a cluster of relations that draws them out in innumerable directions and in varying degrees. They give themselves out to the world. And in so doing things are all bridges, too. They forge connections between what exists around them, they "throw a bridge" between our surroundings and ourselves. No thing is simply in a position, but already extends beyond itself as part of a context. Things pass from themselves into relations of every stripe—spatial, temporal, affective, associative, etc.—and no relation is foreign to them or impossible for them. They reach across to us, departing from their physical bounds in creating a context, in appealing to us, in providing for us. Things touch us, transform us, and conduct us along a meaningful path through the world. We who are always underway could never be so underway were it not for the things accompanying us in this ecstatic exploration of world. The thing gestures out beyond itself, exposed on all sides, and shaped by nothing it would possess on its own, but instead by a world that ever exceeds it. The fourfold specify the rules of mediation, we might say. Taken together, they desubstantialize the thing and deliver it to world.

In this way, the fourfold could be said to establish the strange, permeable limit of the thing. These limits are the matter of relation. The thing relates to the world at the limit. To properly understand the nature of such a limit means coming to terms with Heidegger's oft repeated claim that "the limit is not where something ceases, but rather, as the Greeks recognized, the limit is that from where something *begins its essencing* [sein Wesen beginnt]" (*GA* 7: 156/*PLT* 152, tm).

The limit is not where something ceases or ends. To end there would mean that this limit completed the thing and encapsulated it. Such a limit would be a solitary confinement, trapping the thing within itself. So construed, the thing would be amputated from the world, locked in a shell. Yet the limit is not the end of the thing (at least not in this conception of "end"), but its beginning. The thing begins where it ends. As a limit, its ending is simultaneously an opening. The end can never eradicate what lies beyond it, what abuts it, rubs up against it and teases it out further beyond itself. No end is conclusive, not even the end of metaphysics, as Heidegger repeatedly stressed. The limit of the thing is where it dissipates into the world. The thing is always only this entering into world (the thing only *is* at its limit). But given the reflexivity of all limits, this is to say that the limit is where the world enters the thing, where it makes its way into it. The limit is consequently where the world begins as well. The thing is not the end of the world, but its beginning. To understand this relationship between thing and world requires giving up the thought of thing and world as object and container. This requires that we think a differential emerging of thing to world, a non-presence no longer indifferent to its surroundings, but claimed by them and participating in their never ending activity of bearing up the world. In so doing, the thing begins.

Beginning is the entry into world. To begin at the limit is to begin where one is exposed. Beginning at the limit extends the thing beyond itself into the surrounding environment that touches it. The thing begins in relation to this environment, called out by it. But for this to be a beginning of the thing, there can be no complete arrival into the world. If the thing were to completely enter into the world it would once again simply take on the status of an object in a container. Or the thing would merge so completely with the world as to lose itself in a seamless absorption into the beyond. In either case there would no longer be a thing. For the thing to begin, it must always be beginning, always entering and arriving at the world. Encapsulation and absorption are possibilities for objects and containers, not things and worlds. The thing begins outside of itself and this already disrupts any idea of a stable or fixed presence. The thing is not present to itself, but already outside and ahead of itself. To begin is to maintain this separation within oneself, this tear between thing and world, this differentiating rift that is nothing other than the limit itself. The thing is limit through and through. For this reason, to begin is not simply to start anew. The thing does not leave itself behind in entering the world. This would be just another form of seamless merger with the beyond. To begin is to be always arriving in the world, to be drawn out and supported by the world and likewise to participate in the buoying up and supporting of the world. This bearing (*halten*) of the world is the gist of the relation (*Verhältnis*) between thing and world. Things begin in this engagement with world. To think things as relational means that no thing exists independent of another and that to ex-ist is already to be held out and supported by a context. The world is borne at the limit.

But Heidegger's statement concerning the limit as a beginning specifies that what begins at the limit is the essence of the thing, its essencing. The conception of essence operative in Heidegger's thinking at the time of the fourfold stems from the middle period of the *Contribu-*

tions to Philosophy, where essence is "an occurrence of the truth of beyng" (*GA* 65: 288/226, tm).[11] As we shall take repeated recourse to this notion of essencing in considering the thing in what follows, a short consideration of its development and determination is in order.[12]

Rather than an eternal nature, essence is an "occurrence" (*Geschehnis*) of the truth of beyng, and is thus historicized in the here and now. The *Contributions* also make clear that the "truth" of beyng is to be understood in terms of the Greek *alêtheia, Unverborgenheit,* unconcealment, but the quality of this unconcealment is thought now in a remarkable way. Rather than the disrobing of something previously hidden, what unconcealment brings to light is concealment itself. That is to say, unconcealment is not simply a matter of revealing something otherwise concealed, it is no longer thought in such rough and ready oppositions. Unconcealment is now capable of letting appear the concealment that is essential to all revelation. The height of unconcealment is this ability to reveal without thereby stripping things of the concealment proper to them. Heidegger's conception of truth brings concealment and unconcealment together and this distinguishes it from Greek *alêtheia,* which, we might suppose, still operated upon a concealment/unconcealment opposition: "Truth as the clearing for concealing is therefore an essentially different project from that of *alêtheia,* although it belongs directly to the memory [*Erinnerung*] of *alêtheia* and *alêtheia* to it" (*GA* 65: 350/277, tm). When things appear in truth they are attended by a peculiar concealment.

If unconcealment is identified with an unveiling that brings something forth into appearance, i.e., if unconcealment is identified with the presencing of something, then this complication of concealment/unconcealment means we are no longer dealing with a being that would be simply or purely present. When concealment is no longer opposed to unconcealment, but intimately involved with it, then the opposition between presence and absence must be abandoned as well. What presents itself to us, what is unconcealed, is nothing utterly present—there remains a concealment. But this concealment is now no longer determinable as a covering over of something otherwise revealed. Instead, the undoing of the concealment/unconcealment distinction (which we might identify in a word with "essencing") requires that we think another way for things to appear, a way that is no longer wedded to purity of presence or absence. What appears is just as much concealed as unconcealed. The two can no longer be separated, not even within the same thing. There is not one "piece" of the thing that is unconcealed, next to another "piece" that would be concealed. Concealment cannot be confined apart from unconcealment. The unsettling combination of concealment/unconcealment permeates the thing as a whole, demanding we think its "presencing" in terms other than those of presence and absence. The unsettling of the thing is an upsetting that agitates any presumed stability or stolidity and inclines the thing into the world.

The truth of beyng as this strange unconcealment of concealment is also thought by Heidegger in terms of a clearing (*Lichtung*). The truth of beyng is a "clearing for self-concealing," and thus "truth is never merely a clearing, but instead essences as a concealing just as originarily and intimately [*innig*] along with the clearing" (*GA* 65: 346/273; 349/276, tm). The convolution of concealment and unconcealment unsettles the sheer presence of a thing *and in so doing ushers that thing into a clearing*. Let us note the expansion of the thing that takes place here: the interruption of self-presence spills the particular being into a clearing beyond it. The idea of a completely encapsulated object is here abandoned in favor of a conception of beings whereby they open onto what lies beyond them *so thoroughly that this beyond, the clearing, is involved in their very essence.*

For something to essence is for it to enter a clearing about it whereby its "concealment" can come to light. In avoiding the oppositional conception of concealment and unconcealment the particular being can no longer be considered as present-at-hand and in place. The concealment endemic to the being in its truth brings that being into the world. Concealment becomes coterminous with (being-in) the world itself. This is not as shocking as it might sound. It means that if the particular being were somehow extracted from this clearing, it would no longer be what it is. This present-at-hand capsule would not be the truth of the thing. The world is what would be "concealed" when we consider the isolated being alone. Now, this world is nothing dark or obscured. It exists just as much as the thing does. But they all exist together in an ebb and flow with one another. Essence as an occurrence of the truth of beyng is thus an occurrence of a clearing that harbors a self-concealing. Essence is an entry into relationality. In the *Contributions to Philosophy (Of the Event)*, concealment names the disruption of stability and self-centeredness that allows the particular being to enter the clearing of truth (*Wahrheit*).

If essence is a bringing of the particular being to a clearing, if it is an entry into world, then this entails an entry into relations. Nothing can appear without relation to anything else, appearance itself is always contextualized and extended through connections it maintains with its surroundings. There can be no relational being for us, without a relation to us. When the thing enters the world, we are called by it. Even our indifference is a way of responding to the world. We participate in the "essencing" of the thing as it reaches out to us. We guard and protect it in its essencing. In the language of truth (*Wahrheit*), the particular true thing (*das Wahre*) is said to be "protected" (*bewahrt*) when it appears in this way. Heidegger's thinking of the thing inherits this conception of essence from his work in the mid-thirties.

The fourfold names the reverberating extent and radiant fringe of the essencing thing, the way it issues out beyond itself and thus belongs to world. Each element or member of the fourfold reverberates through an endless constellation of relations that interweaves and intertwines the thing in world, the woof and warp of which contextualize the thing in place. If the essence of the thing begins at the limit and this limit is where the thing is relationally exposed to the world, then the world is of the essence of the thing. The essence of the thing is no possession, but lies beyond it, in and as the world. This is no more than to say that the essence of things must now be thought as a being-in-the-world, an in-finite belonging to world. This is the thrust of Heidegger's later thought. Ecstaticity is no longer the privilege of Dasein alone.

Heidegger's Lateness, Biographically Considered

In all that I have said, the claim that the fourfold is the inauguration of Heidegger's later thought should not be understood solely in terms of a chronology of works; it is also understandable, and perhaps even better understood, at the level of biography. The "lateness" of the late Heidegger would then consist in a new biographical context for the transformative thinking of the fourfold. To be sure, such a notion of "late" Heidegger would be found repugnant by the man himself, for whom biographical concerns are almost always obscuring distractions from the matter of thought. Nevertheless, and with that acknowledgement, four aspects can be briefly mentioned that situate Heidegger's thinking of the fourfold as "late."

The first of these is World War II. I argue in what follows that Heidegger's thinking of technology undergoes a fundamental shift at this time. This is no small concern or minor adjustment in an otherwise untouched thinking of being, for in the era of technology, positionality (*das Ge-Stell*) is precisely how being gives itself to us today. The shift in Heidegger's thinking of technology provoked by the war, the emergence of a thinking of replaceable, circulating commodities or resources ("standing reserve"), is nothing less than a shift in his conception of being. As this receives more detailed treatment in what follows ("World War II," chapter 1), I will merely note here that the human's relation to technology is dramatically altered in the texts following the war, where the human likewise becomes a replaceable, consumable commodity.

Second, in the wake of the war, Heidegger was subjected to a teaching ban by the French authorities. While this might seem a small, extraneous matter, we should recall Hannah Arendt's characterization of Heidegger as teacher, that "in the opinion of his students at the time, the book's success [*Being and Time*] merely confirmed what they already knew about him as a teacher."[13] Even as early as 1919, the renown of this teacher was growing: "there was hardly anything more than a name, but the name traveled throughout Germany like the rumor of the secret [*heimlichen*] king."[14] Arendt sums up Heidegger's fame with the avowal that "there is a teacher; one can perhaps learn thinking."[15]

Jaspers, too, from whom Heidegger had requested the French denazification committee seek a reference, emphasizes Heidegger's hold over students in his report to the committee of 22 December, 1945. In what Hugo Ott terms "a comprehensive general evaluation of Heidegger's personality,"[16] Jaspers writes:

> In our present situation the education of the younger generation needs to be handled with the utmost responsibility and care. Total academic freedom should be our ultimate aim, but this cannot be achieved overnight. Heidegger's mode of thinking, which seems to me to be fundamentally unfree, dictatorial and uncommunicative, would have a very damaging effect on students at the present time. And the mode of thinking itself seems to me more important than the actual content of political judgements, whose aggressiveness can easily be channeled in other directions. Until such time as a genuine rebirth takes place within him, and is *seen* to be at work within him, I think it would be quite wrong to turn such a teacher loose on the young people of today, who are psychologically extremely vulnerable. First of all the young must be taught how to think for themselves.[17]

Jaspers's recommendation is just as damning and just as focused on his effect in the classroom:

> He should be suspended from teaching duties for several years . . .
> The question that must then be asked is whether the restoration of full academic freedom is a justifiable risk, bearing in mind that views hostile to the idea of the university, and potentially damaging to it when propounded with intellectual distinction, may well be promoted in the lecture room.[18]

The authorities agreed with Jaspers's assessment and the ban was in place from 1945 until 1951.

After the war, issues around education assume a new importance in Heidegger's thinking. The November 1946 "Letter on 'Humanism,'" for example, traces the history of *paideia* from the Greeks to its Roman translation as *humanitas*. At the other end of metaphysics, the 1953 lecture "Who Is Nietzsche's Zarathustra?" treats its subject as a teacher, too, the teacher of the *Übermensch*. Most forcefully, and quite contrary to Jaspers's expectations, Heidegger's first return to the classroom, the 1951–52 lecture course *What Is Called Thinking?*, takes up the issue of teaching in its very first session. The point is elaborated in the transition to the second hour:

> Teaching is more difficult than learning because what teaching calls for is this: to let learn. The real teacher, in fact, lets nothing else be learned than—learning. His conduct, therefore, often produces the impression that we properly learn nothing from him, if by "learning" we now suddenly understand merely the procurement of useful information. The teacher is ahead of his apprentices in this alone, that he has still far more to learn than they—he has to learn to let them learn. . . . If the relation between the teacher and the taught is genuine, therefore, there is never a place in it for the authority of the know-it-all or the authoritative sway of the official. It is still an exalted matter, then, to become a teacher—which is something else entirely than becoming a famous professor. (*GA* 8: 17–18/15)

They are words that seem to respond directly to the concerns of the Jaspers letter. They also stand worlds apart from the inflammatory views of the rectorship, focusing as those did on the institution of the university and its jarring reform, rather than the face to face encounter of teaching. A certain humility seems to have been learned.

Without insisting on the cause, or even the existence, of such a change, a third threshold for the later work is Heidegger's mental collapse in the wake of the war in 1945. The doctor to whom Heidegger was brought might seem the worst choice imaginable for Heidegger, bringing together so many of Heidegger's philosophical *bêtes noires* of the time: Dr. Victor Emil Freiherr von Gebsattel, an anthropological, existential, Christian, psychologist. Heidegger gives his own account of matters to his biographer, Heinrich Petzet:

> When in December 1945 I was brought totally unprepared before the "settlement committee" and was confronted with the twenty-three

> questions of the inquisitorial hearing, and when I subsequently
> collapsed [*darauf zusammenbrach*], the dean of the medical school,
> Beringer (who saw through the whole farce and the intentions of
> the accusers), came to me and simply drove me away to Gebsattel in
> Badenweiler. And what did he do? He hiked for the first time with me
> through the snow-covered winter forest upon the Blauen [one of the
> highest mountains in the Schwarzwald]. Other than that, he did noth-
> ing [*Sonsttat er nicht*]. But as a human being he helped me, so that
> three weeks later I was again healthy and returned home.[19]

We now know that Heidegger's time with Gebsattel was much more extensive than Heidegger lets on (approximately four months, February
to May 1946), that Gebsattel himself developed a therapeutic method
wherein the goal is to appear to "do nothing," and that Heidegger was
indeed treated with a dextrose cure during his stay.[20]

Gebsattel's treatment provides Heidegger his first serious contact
with psychiatry and psychoanalysis; it will not be his last. One of the initial
formulations of the fourfold, the 1950 lecture "Language," will be delivered at a sanatorium in Bühlerhöhe, directed by Dr. Gerhard Strooman.
Even more significantly, in 1947, not long after his treatment, Heidegger
begins his lifelong correspondence with the Swiss psychoanalyst Medard
Boss, occasioning a decade of collaborative seminars with Boss on issues
in existential psychiatry. Such a turn to psychiatry, the psychological, and
the psychoanalytic (existential or otherwise) would be unimaginable for
the vitriolic Heidegger of the 1930s.

Heidegger's first published text after his treatment, the "Letter on
'Humanism,'" composed in November 1946, offers a passing comment on
the break down of thought, which gains a provocative poignancy when
read in light of the biographical circumstances of the time: "'Philosophizing' about a break down [*das Scheitern*] is separated by a chasm from a
broken down thinking. If this should fortunately come to a person, what
would occur is no misfortune. To him would come the sole gift that could
come to thinking from being" (*GA* 9: 343/261, tm). Thinking must be
broken open. Only in this way could it receive any gift at all. The gift of
the break down is a break through into the world. The concluding lecture of the 1949 *Insight Into That Which Is*, "The Turn," again emphasizes
the renunciation of human arrogance and presumption for the gaining
of insight: "Only when the human essence, as what is caught sight of in
the appropriative event of insight, disavows human stubbornness and
casts itself before this insight, throwing its stubbornness away, only then
does the human correspond in his essence to the claim of the insight"
(*GA* 79: 76/71). The point is summed up in Heidegger's contribution to

the 1958 Festschrift for Gebsattel, "The Basic Principles of Thinking" (the first lecture of the five-lecture cycle with that title), a text concerned precisely with the history of human thinking and with the critique of attempts at dialectical reconciliation therein: "Mortal thinking must let itself down into the dark depths of the well if it is to see the stars by day" (*GA* 79: 93/89). Heidegger's thinking after the war could indeed be said to have entered that well, lost its stubbornness, and issued out into a greater welcoming of world.

Lastly, the year of the Bremen lectures, 1949, was the year in which Heidegger turned sixty years old. While this might seem a minor piece of trivia, Heidegger actually puts great stock in this event. Anyone who surveys Heidegger's numerous speeches and missives to his friends on the occasion of their sixtieth birthdays cannot help but be struck by this. Sixty is "the age" (*das Alter*), what we would call in English "old age," the age of maturity.

In 1949, the year of his own sixtieth birthday, in a letter on the occasion of the sixtieth birthday of one of his friends from school, Ernst Laslowski, Heidegger writes: "Now it gets serious. Or is 60 only a number, the sign for something with which we calculate? Unconnected with the number, however, is the transition into the age [*das Alter*]" (*GA* 16: 440). Another 1949 speech on the occasion of the sixtieth birthday of his friend Theophil Rees points out that "the sixtieth birthday is the beginning of something new, namely the age [*des Alters*]" (*GA* 16: 435). The speech goes on to say that "the age that begins with sixty years is the *autumn* of life. Autumn is the filled, settled [*ausgeglichene*] and therefore balancing season [*ausgleichende Zeit*]" (*GA* 16: 436).

A 1951 speech on the sixtieth birthday of a high school friend, Bruno Leiner, explains what is meant:

> *The* age is that time where we have become sufficiently old to recognize of human Dasein how it is, and to treasure of all things, how they are. *The* age is the time where knowing and being have become mature for each other. *The* age is the autumn of life; though autumn is the most gentle season, since everything is balanced by its equivalent, where bliss and sorrow just as essentially belong to Dasein, where the calm of a free superiority [*Überlegenheit*] has come to be at the core of all movement in every deed and allowance. (*GA* 16: 473)

Autumn is the season of balance (we shall return to Heidegger's thinking of the seasons in treating of the sky below in "The Seasons of the Year," chapter 3), the season that tempers the extremes of winter and summer, the season of the middle, of the between. The calm of this age permeates each gesture and movement, a calm that opens the self in the midst of life to the surrounding world.

The text for Rees specifies this openness more provocatively: "Autumn is the superior time which awakens the senses for the concealed harmony of all things" (*GA* 16: 436). From the midst of life, a receptivity is born. At "the age" one senses what is not overtly present. One's very body senses the Heraclitean togetherness of things. The age is consequently an awakening to what we shall term in the following "relationality," the belonging-together of what is, of what is always arriving. The age is an awareness of this and as such it is a way of beginning again. To Laslowski: "In this year, you perhaps stand at a new beginning of a fruitful work. This belongs to the secret art of coming of age [*Altwerdens*], that we are able to ever again be beginners" (*GA* 16: 441).

The age of sixty is the entrance into maturity and with this, the thinking of the fourfold marks the inauguration of Heidegger's "mature" thought, his "late" thought.[21] The pages that follow are devoted to unpacking the mature concerns and issues of this later period of his work. As such, while it is by no means a comprehensive account of these concerns, it could be seen to function as something of an introduction to the core of Heidegger's later thinking, the thinking of relationality found in the interrelation of fourfold, thing, and world. If the thing exists as exposed and limited, as we have indicated, then with the entry of thing to world, the world likewise enters the thing. The technologically determined contemporary reality so unflinchingly detailed by Heidegger comes to permeate the thing itself. And there is no escape from this. For this reason, no treatment of the fourfold can forego a consideration of Heidegger's conception of technology, to which we now turn.

1

The Technological Challenge to Things

Heidegger's thinking of the thing departs from the modern philosophical conception of the object as a discrete and self-standing presence. As we have noted, the thing is no object (*Gegenstand*), but extends beyond itself into the world. As relationally so *disposed,* the thing is always simultaneously *exposed* to world. What relates the thing to the world likewise relates that world to it. And at the time of the fourfold, this world is dominated by the transformative forces of contemporary technology. Indeed, it is in the 1949 Bremen lectures where Heidegger first introduces the fourfold that he likewise first introduces the thought of "positionality" (*das Gestell*), that is, the ineluctable demand placed upon all that exists that it be available to the point of replaceability, that what exist show itself only as so many resources or commodities, as pieces of "standing reserve" (*Bestand*). This standing reserve is the culmination of the metaphysical history of the thing. The relation between the thing and the standing reserve is nothing accidental, however, but tied to the very "essencing" or "thinging" of the thing. A proper understanding of the thing consequently requires a fuller understanding of Heidegger's view of technology at this time.[1]

Heidegger's mature (post-war) conception of positionality as the essence of technology could be said to have its precursor in the considerations of "machination" (*Machenschaft*) operative in his work of the mid- to late 1930s. At this time, machination names a systematic tendency toward objectification in all areas of life. Technology contributes to this process, to be sure (the analysis is obviously indebted to Jünger), though it is not yet identified with the process as a whole, nor even as an essential instance of it. Instead, the objectifying agenda of machination attests to its provenance in the era of philosophical modernity. Machination continues the modern philosophical thinking of objectivity and representation. With the advent of World War II, however, Heidegger finds technology to be far outstripping the objectifying claims of machination, particularly in regards to the human's place within the technological regime. The effect is profoundly evident in the wake of the war, in the 1949 Bremen lectures, and it is here that Heidegger's conception of technology reaches its apogee, for here the analysis moves beyond the machinational understanding of re-presentation from the 1930s to catch sight of a transformation in the very notion of presence itself. Technology is subsequently nothing modern, nor machinational, but instead points to a new epoch in the destiny of beyng, that of "post-modern" positionality (*das Ge-stell*). Under the aegis of positionality all that exists is transformed into standing reserve (*Bestand*), and this is something quite far from the modern philosophical conception of objectivity proffered by machination.

The standing reserve is how beings show themselves in an era of circulative replacement. The standing reserve exists as available, immediate, and orderable, and each of these designations shall be examined in turn in what follows. This examination will grant us purchase on Heidegger's thinking of positionality as an order of being distinct from that of modernist representational objectivity. Heidegger carries this thinking of commodified replaceability to its furthest extreme in his conception of atomic energy, culminating in the atomic bomb. In regards to the bomb, which first arises as an issue of concern for Heidegger at this time, his worry is not so much over atomic destruction as the pervading threat of this and the ontological transformation in the nature of being that this threat has already set into play, even before a single bomb was ever detonated. This threat of being troubles our easy distinctions between presence and absence, and in so doing distinguishes the standing reserve from the metaphysical object at an ontological level. The technological challenge to the thing is thus no simple opposition of representational objectivity, on the one hand, and the relationality of the thing on the other. Instead it is a tension between two departures from objectivity, that of the thing and that of the standing reserve.

As a result, there is a strange alliance between the thing and the standing reserve in their distance taking from modern objectivity as encapsulated self-identical presence. The threat to the thing is not the closure of machinational objectivity, but the unlimited availability of the standing reserve. To understand the ways in which Heidegger's mature conception of technology surpasses a thinking of objectification, we will first examine the objectification at work in machination as it appears in the works of the 1930s, signally the *Contributions to Philosophy* and its cotemporaneous supplement, "The Age of the World Picture." The shift in Heidegger's thinking away from this modernist conception occurs with the outbreak of World War II, and a brief sketch of Heidegger's views on the war and the changes it makes evident provides a transition into his later thinking of technology. This accomplished, we turn to the ontological status of the standing reserve as available for immediate ordering and go on to situate this in an understanding of positionality as circulative replacement. From here, all that remains is to view the culmination of technological replaceability in a thinking of atomic destruction. Such considerations will set the stage for our subsequent investigation of the thing.

§1. Machination as Representational Objectification

Machination is how we experience what Heidegger terms the "abandonment of being [*Seinsverlassenheit*]" (*GA* 65: 107/85, tm). Something is abandoned when it suffers a departure. What abandons it "withdraws" from it (withdrawal being the twin notion of abandonment). But it is crucial to note that what withdraws nevertheless maintains a connection with what remains, and this simple fact prohibits us from casting this withdrawal in terms of a lack or even an absence (as withdrawal always leaves its traces). Abandonment likewise avoids these easy oppositions. Abandonment does not mean that being has fled from beings, that there would only be beings and no being. The abandonment of being is never a discarding of beings. And these beings, for their part, are not missing or lacking being, whatever that could mean. Instead, abandonment names the persistence of a relationship to being in the midst of its supposed departure. To designate something as "abandoned" is to understand it in a relation to something else that is not present—in Heidegger's case, a relation to something that can never *be* present, i.e., being (*Sein*) itself. Abandonment is thus Heidegger's name for the relations between being and beings. Being abandons them.

Abandonment names a relation to something outside of the being, beyond it, but nonetheless not present. To be marked as abandoned is to be left behind, to remain behind, it is to sustain a connection despite all seeming absence. To be abandoned is to enter into a relationship where absence and presence lose their oppositional antagonism. The "absent" stays "present" in the very determination of what remains as "abandoned." The mark of abandonment is nothing other than the very way that beings exist. That is to say, there is nothing that has abandoned the being, there is no agent of abandonment. Instead, abandonment names a way of being whereby the particular being is abandoned to the world. As abandoned, beings are defined not by a relation to any particular present entity, they are defined by relationality as such. This is the effect of abandonment: what remains is left open to something beyond itself, what remains lies exposed. Beyng as relationality abandons beings to the world. Relationally opened by abandonment, the being is left exposed in a world of others. Beings are abandoned to themselves.

Beings are abandoned to the world, and this means they are abandoned into machination. As so abandoned, "the being then appears *thus, it shows itself as object and present-at-hand, as if beyng did not essence*" (*GA* 65: 115/91, tm). Machination names the constellation of forces that struggle for the objectification and presence of the world, performing the continual work of abandonment. As such, beings appear as objects present-at-hand and machination sets in place a whole support system to ensure that they be treated as such ("Machination and constant presence [*beständige Anwesenheit*]"; *GA* 65: 107/85). Machination names "an interpretation of beings in which their makeability comes to the fore, so much so that constancy and presence [*Beständigkeit und Anwesenheit*] become the specific determinations of beingness" (*GA* 65: 126/100).[2]

Despite appearances (". . . as if beyng did not essence"), machination names "a type of essencing of beyng" (*GA* 65: 115/91; 126/99, tm). What appears under the aegis of machination comes forward as objective, but can never fully attain this. Beings ape objective presence in a denial of their condition, as if abandonment had not taken place, as if there were no withdrawal, no essencing, or, in other words, no world. The "as if" that Heidegger includes here points to the ineluctable fact of essencing, that even objectivity remains a way of being, a showing of beings, an exposure in contact with the beyond, and, thus, an openness and irrevocable exchange with world. In the epoch of abandonment, beings put on a performance of objectivity as though all the world were a stage, something duly noted by Heidegger: "*Stage [Bühne]*—the formation of the actual [*des Wirklichen*] as the task of stage-designers!" (*GA* 65: 347/275, tm). The world constructed by the stage-designers is a world of complete, actual, and objective presence. It is a world of objects readied for scientific investigation, and Heidegger does not fail to trace the role of "theory" in modern science back to its Greek source in *thea*, "the look, the outward appearance," emphasizing the very staging of presence that concerns us: "*Thea* (cf. theater)" (*GA* 7: 46/*QCT* 163, tm).

But the "as if" in Heidegger's claim (". . . as if beyng did not essence") entails that machination and objectivity nonetheless remain ways in which beyng essences. Objectification could be seen as the way in which the essencing of being is misconstrued, a way in which the abandoned character of beings is overlooked, but also a way in which this essential abandonment is left intact. Indeed, in this stage play where beings are paraded around as objects, machination can even be seen as a preservation of this essencing of being. In keeping with the theatrical language of the discussion, the objectification of machination could be seen as a "mask" that leaves the face beneath it untouched. Heidegger wonders, "can the negativity of beings and the abandonment by being be preserved better and more surely in the mask of 'true actuality' than through machination and lived-experience?" (*GA* 65: 131/103). Even in the 1930s Heidegger saw that machination was not the annihilation of being, but in a jarring sense its preservation. Machination does not eliminate the essencing of being, only disguises it. It remains behind the (representational) mask to be rediscovered.

At the time of the *Contributions*, machination is thus a term for the forces in society working toward the objectification of beings and our experience of them (*Erlebnis*). It is not merely a social event, however, but an ontological one, the objectification of beings as residue of the abandonment of being. Heidegger sees the process propelled by the determining ground of modernity itself, representation. We have already encountered one way in which machination is an interpretation of beings (machination as "an interpretation of beings in which their makeability comes to the fore, so much so that constancy and presence [*Beständigkeit und Anwesenheit*] become the specific determinations of beingness," *GA* 65: 126/100). Now we should consider a second, "machination, that interpretation of beings as representable and represented [*Vor-stellbaren und Vor-Gestellten*]" (*GA* 65: 108–9/86). The two "interpretations" are not mutually exclusive, but rather compatible, if not ultimately the same: the objectivity of machination is carried out through an agenda of representation. The focus in the *Contributions to Philosophy* is on tracing out the coordinate systems of objectification that cumulatively give rise to this dominance of machination. The machinational worldview belies the fact that beings are not solid and encapsulated entities, but are opened beyond themselves contextually. In being so opened, they are able to reach us and touch us, concern us. For the Heidegger of the thirties, the greatest distress (*Not*) of the modern age is found in our very distresslessness (*Notlosigkeit*) in the face of these changes, and the various machinational systems collude in preventing this distress from coming to our attention by objectifying the beings that would otherwise address us. Machination is thus a modern phenomenon, the work of an age determined by representation, as detailed by another essay of this period, "The Age of the World Picture" (1938), which further elaborates what the *Contributions* identifies as "modern science and its machinationally rooted essence" (*GA* 65: 141/111).

In this provocative and wide-reaching essay, Heidegger inquires into the essence of our age (modernity) by investigating one of its essential formations, modern science and the guiding role of research therein

("The essence of what is today called science is research"; *GA* 5: 77/59). Research within modern natural science has embarked upon a quest for certitude and it is representation that provides the objectification necessary for such certainty: "This objectification of beings is accomplished in a setting-before, a representing [*Vor-stellen*], aimed at bringing each being before it in such a way that the person who calculates can be sure, and that means be certain, of the being" (*GA* 5: 87/66, tm). The objectivity prerequisite for being certain (*sicher*) is thus the result of an act of securing (*sicherstellen*) directed at the being in question: "To represent means here: of oneself to set something before one and to make what has been set in place [*das Gestellte*] secure as something set in place" (*GA* 5: 108/82).

Representation dominates the age to such an extent that only what is represented is admitted as true or extant, "so construed, only what becomes an object *is*, i.e. counts as extant" (*GA* 5: 87/66, tm). This means that existence is now at the disposal of the human as subject of the representation: "Beings as a whole are now taken in such a way that they are first and only extant insofar as they are posed by the representing-producing human" (*GA* 5: 89/67–68, tm). All that is becomes dependent on human representational activity for its validity and, indeed, for its very existence. The human now only encounters what it has represented to itself.

At this point in the stage-play construction of reality, the human steps onto the scene, or rather, through representation, the human becomes that scene itself:

> To represent means here: to bring the present-at-hand before oneself as something standing-over-and-against, to relate it to oneself, the representer, and, in this relation, to force it back to oneself as the standard-giving [*maßgebenden*] domain. Where this happens the human puts himself into the picture in precedence over the beings. But in that the human puts himself in the picture in this way, he places himself in the scene; i.e. in the open horizon [*Umkreis*] of what is generally and publicly represented. With this, the human henceforth makes himself the scene in which beings place themselves before the human, present themselves, i.e. must be the picture. (*GA* 5: 91/69, tm)

When Heidegger discusses the essence of modernity as the emergence of a "world picture" (*Weltbild*), he has in mind precisely this transformation of all that exists into wholly determinable representations at the mercy of a human become subject. The common phrase "to get the picture" means that one understands the situation schematically at a glance, a usage Heidegger himself notes (literally, to "put oneself in the picture about something," see *GA* 5: 89/67). The being becomes its own unambiguous representational double—as a formal geometrical-mathematical figure, for example—where a certainty can be found. This transformation of world into picture determines the age: "The fundamental process of modernity is the conquest of the world as picture. From now on the word 'picture' means: the construct of representational production [*das Gebild des vorstellenden Herstellens*]" (*GA* 5: 94/71, tm).

What is uncanny about the "world picture" is that it is a picture without aesthetic content; we might say, it is more a construction, formation, or schema (in keeping with the sense of the word *Gebilde*) than it is a picture in any simple sense. Heidegger returns to this idea eight years later in treating of the metaphysical nature of Rilke's poetry:

> The objectiveness of the world becomes *steady* [ständig] in representational production [*vorstellenden Herstellen*]. This representing makes a presentation. However, what is present is present in a representation that has the nature of calculation. This representing knows nothing of the intuited [*Anschauliches*]. What is intuited in the look of things, the image [*Bild*] they offer to direct sensible intuition [*Anschauung*], falls away. . . . Facing the intuitable image [*Bild*], deliberate self-assertion, in its projects, places a scheme based only on calculated constructions [*Gebilde*]. (*GA* 5: 304–5/228–29, tm)

The "picture" of the world is not really a picture at all, more a schematized and formal outline of it, a construction. The Cartesian mathematicization of nature would be the prime example.

Ultimately, it is possible to see this representational activity of the human as standing in the service of the will to power. This is already visible in the definition of machination as "that interpretation of beings as representable and represented [*Vor-stellbaren und Vor-Gestellten*]" (*GA* 65: 108–9/86). Even though beings are interpreted as *represented*, where representation is considered a *fait accompli*, they are at the same time interpreted as *representable*, as though they had *not yet been represented enough*. This strange mix of fixation on the one hand (beings as already represented) and increase (beings as still representable) on the other is what Heidegger identifies as the will to power in his almost contemporaneous readings of Nietzsche (see *GA* 6.2: 7/*N3*: 167 and 240–41/196–97, among others). The will to power secures itself only in order to overcome itself, to extend itself ever further beyond itself, securing this newly acquired position only in order to extend itself beyond itself again anew. When Heidegger writes that beings are interpreted as re-presentable and re-presented, then, he is writing about the will: "Everything 'is made' and 'can be made' if only the 'will' to it is summoned up" (*GA* 65: 108/86). This willful "making" is the very *machen* of *Machenschaft*, its connection to the will to power (*Wille zur Macht*) here lies in the "making" of representations.

Heidegger's hyphenated term *vor-stellen* likewise draws our attention to the "vor" character of representation. As represented, the being is "set before" us (*vor-gestellt*), over and against us in the position of an object. But it is also posited in advance, before hand (*vor-gestellt*), and in this way achieves the status of the a priori: "the *a priori* is attributed to the *ego percipio* and thus to the 'subject'; it leads to the precedence *of re-presentation* [*Vorgängigkeit*, des Vor-stellens]" (*GA* 65: 223/174, tm). But the "vor-" of *vorstellen* is also a setting forth, where the representation is set into a peculiar motion from the outset, set to go forth (another sense of its "Vor-gängigkeit").

> In one respect, re-presentable means "accessible to intention and calculation" [constructed in advance to stand over against us as object; the first two senses of *vor* mentioned above]; in another respect it means "advanceable [*vorbringbar*] through production and execution." But thought in a fundamental manner, all of this means that beings as such are re-presentable and that only the representable *is*. (*GA* 65: 109/86)

The representation is "advanceable" and *to be* advanced. As a matter of principle, the representation can be known exhaustively, in complete detail. But as a matter of fact, our knowledge is limited. Yet this limitation has no source in the object itself, but instead only in our mode of access to the representation. This access itself is advanceable and can be ever refined through technology. This is the progress that is written into the representation, a progress that "has no future, however, because it merely takes things that already are and expedites them 'further' on their previous path" (*GA* 65: 113/89). Representation in the *Contributions* names a prior decision concerning all that presences, making this presencing into something that stands over and against the human subject in a manner that is not simply at the disposal of the human for further specification and experimentation, but is posed in such a way as to demand this continuous refinement.

The seemingly privileged position of the human subject in representation leads to a personal and societal emphasis upon lived-experience (*Erlebnis*) that Heidegger identifies as the necessary attendant of machination's extension. Indeed, Heidegger links machination and lived-experience directly as the epoch's transformation of the traditional affiliation between being and thinking: "Machination and lived-experience are formally the more originary version of the formula for the guiding-question of Western thinking: beingness (being) and thinking (as representational conceptualizing [*vor-stellendes Be-greifen*])" (*GA* 65: 128/101, tm).[3] The representational object is a being that is always related back to a subject (the representer), and insofar as this subject is likewise always understood as a "living" subject, then that being is always related back to life: "The being counts first as extant, insofar as and to the extent that it is included in and related back to this life, i.e, is experienced in life [*er-lebt*] and becomes lived experience [*Erlebnis*]" (*GA* 5: 94/71, tm). Life here is understood biologically, which is to say, by a science determined by research and objectification: "The mechanistic *and* the biologistic modes of thinking are always only consequences of the concealed machinational interpretations of beings" (*GA* 65: 127/100). In the *Contributions to Philosophy*, Heidegger connects lived experience with the Roman conception of the human as *animal rationale*: "Why the human as 'life' (*animal rationale*) (ratio—re-presentation! [*Vor-stellen*])" (*GA* 65: 129/102, tm). This brief note avers that in the metaphysical determination of the human as *animal rationale*, the *animal* becomes the subject of lived experience and the *rationale* becomes the representing faculty. They work together in the form of the modern human who has an irrational (animalistic, in this oppositionally determined sense) and addictive craving for lived experiences that are pre-packaged and objectified (represented) for consumption.

Under the reign of machination, experience itself is objectified. The human is delivered over to a sham world of objectified experiences that may be hoarded and possessed. They are available for the taking by the intrepid adventurer. Heidegger mentions "movies" and "seaside spa resorts" in this regard (*GA* 65: 139/109, tm). The drive to possess or have experiences (the Germans tellingly say "make" experiences) can also be seen as the exacerbation of the Greek understanding of the human as *zôon logon echon*, where the *echon*, or "having," is equiprimordial to the definition and institutes a reign of possession in the very definition of the human (we shall return to this in considering the mortals in chapter 5, below). The critique of *Erlebnis* and the life (*Leben*) it fosters is fueled by Heidegger's opposition to biologism, anthropology, psychologism, and culture. The role of the human within the domain of machination is to be driven about as though an animal acting on instinct, from one superficial experience to another (cf. *GA* 65: 98/78). The human as subject of *Erlebnis* becomes the possessor of the world, a status that likewise calls for the further representational objectification of that world. Such a life insulates one from the distress of abandoned being. Within the epoch of modern machination, the human becomes the greedy consumer of objectified experience.

§2. World War II

The shift between Heidegger's theorizing of machination in the mid-1930s and his mature reflections on technology from the late 1940s is coincident with the outbreak and aftermath of World War II. For Heidegger, this war signaled the end of war as hitherto practiced, the end of war as a modernist enterprise, and the end of the idea that the human would only be a consumer of lived-experience, rather than precisely what was consumed.

In the eyes of Carl von Clausewitz, the chief theorist of modern warfare, war was an aggrandized duel that pitted the dueling parties at opposite ends of the battle field.[4] They battled until the opponent either surrendered or was killed. The purpose of war was thus to put an end to war and to restore the peace. Nevertheless, war remained a tool in the pocket of the politician (Clausewitz's continuation thesis). World War II presented Heidegger with a war that could not really be deemed a war as hitherto understood. In a 1939 "Letter to a Solitary Soldier" he writes, "'War' is a name that no longer suffices to name what for a long time already 'is' and which now becomes both more significant and more veiled in its warlike appearances" (*GA* 90: 271). If war is understood in opposition to a condition of peace, then the collapse of this opposition brings an "end" to war. War is no longer an attempt to restore the peace, but an undoing of peace as previously understood; "war doesn't battle for a state of peace, but establishes peace anew" (*GA* 69: 180).

This new state of peace, however, is one that has been made indistinguishable from war. Peace and war are each completely given over to the technologically facilitated consumption of beings. In Heidegger's first publication to address the war, "The Abandonment of Being and Errancy," published in 1951 with an editorial note specifically dating it from "1939/1940, the beginning of the Second World War,"[5] Heidegger quickly sketches what lies beyond this now outmoded opposition: "Beyond war and peace is the sheer errancy of the consumption of beings in a self securing of order from out of the emptiness of the abandonment of being" (*GA* 7: 91/*EP* 104, tm). Instead of war or peace there is now a security agreeable to both parties whereby order is established through the unleashing of unchecked consumption. The consumer consumes beings so as to reduce them to nothing, rather than ever experience them as anything less than full. Such consumers require a supply and this establishes an order in the construction of supply chain relations. Heidegger's consideration of consumption beyond the war and peace distinction makes his later thinking of technology and its relation to the fourfold a truly "post-war" thinking, in a sense stronger than mere chronology. For by the time of World War II, the machinational agenda of objectification is already outdated.

In its place is a conception of replaceability that will play a dominating role in the Bremen lectures of 1949. Heidegger's thinking of substitution and the ersatz, certainly an outgrowth of earlier considerations of total mobilization in the work of Ernst Jünger, comes to the fore during the war: "the 'substitute' and the mass production of ersatz things is not a temporary corrective, but the only possible form in which the will to will, the 'all-inclusive' guarantee of the ordering of order, keeps itself going and thus is able to be 'itself' as the 'subject' of everything" (*GA* 7: 94/*EP* 107, tm). This "will to will" names the Nietzschean will to power carried to its extreme. What is willed is more of the same, more willing. This will is only able to will more willing thanks to the proliferation of the substitute and the ersatz which protect this will from loss. It wills in order to increase itself with more of the same (it wills so as to will again). When all is the same, the will achieves its goal of willing only itself. In so doing, it becomes the "subject" of everything, the quotation marks here already pointing to the fact that when all is the same, the very distinction between subject and object is superseded.

The consumption that Heidegger sees at work in both war and peace, which we today could easily term "consumerism," does not stop with the stockpiling of weaponry or the securing of access to the necessities and pleasantries of life. Instead, the human itself becomes a commodity in the exchange. The essence of the human itself has been targeted, addressed, and transformed: "The 'world wars' and their 'totality' are already consequences of the abandonment of being. They urge toward the securing in place of a constant form of consumption. The human is also drawn into this process and can no longer conceal its character of being the most important raw material" (*GA* 7: 91/*EP* 104, tm).[6] Once the human is considered a "raw material" there is no longer any real distinction to be made between the human and the world at its disposal, everything is rendered disposable. Any residual privileging of the human, any "humanism," even any space between the human as subject par excellence and its object (*Gegenstand*) is now lost.

At the very beginning of the war, Heidegger had already identified the biotechnological ramifications of this transformation. "Since the human is the most important raw material, we can expect that someday factories for the artificial breeding of human material will be erected, based on contemporary chemical research" (*GA* 7: 93/106, tm). The human is here cast as the "most important" raw material because it is the human who conducts and leads (*führt*) the processes of production and consumption. But even these leaders (*die Führer*) are functionaries of the standing reserve. The commodification of the human happens whatever the status that human might pretend to within the circuitry of distribution. The grimmest confirmation of this point, that the role of a leader lies in the orchestration of supply chains, is found in the ovens of World War II. With the war only four years over, Heidegger reports the ugly consequences of commodification: "Hundreds of thousands die in masses. Do they die? They perish. They are put down. Do they die? They become pieces of inventory of a standing reserve for the fabrication of corpses. Do they die? They are unobtrusively liquidated in annihilation camps" (*GA* 79: 56/53). These lines from the 1949 Bremen lecture cycle *Insight Into That Which Is* show just how far the technological grip has extended itself. They are distressing words, spoken to a distressless audience, and they are worlds apart from the earlier critique of the human predilection for *Erlebnis*.

Heidegger nevertheless maintains that World War II has decided nothing, despite these changes in his conception of technology, or rather, on account of them. Decisions and victories dissolve in an unending circulation of the same that transcends war and peace. On the day of Germany's surrender ending the war, Heidegger writes the following:

> Hausen Castle in the Danube Valley, on the 8th of May, 1945
> On the day in which the world celebrates its victory
> and does not yet recognize that for
> centuries already it is the victim
> of its own insurrection. (*GA* 77: 240/157, tm)

The would-be victors of the war are themselves the victims. They are victims of their own insurrection, their own rise to prominence as the leaders of the orchestrated chains of supply and demand that sustain consumerism. From this perspective, victor and victim are necessary complements to the process of consumption. The war would only be the most egregious and harrowing display of this fact, as Heidegger's notes to the same piece state: "The war at its end, nothing changed, nothing new, on the contrary. What has already been long endured must now notably come to the fore" (*GA* 77: 241/157, tm). Wars decide nothing because they bring only more of the same. The shock of wars and the intensity with which they appear only masks their essential redundancy.

We could call it, pace Clausewitz, Heidegger's own "continuation principle," that the war would be a continuation of the history of being, of ontological decisions. It is a sentiment that Heidegger voices some weeks later to a small circle of friends on June 27, 1945, while staying at the Forsthaus von Burg Wildenstein in refuge from the bombing of Freiburg, in his last lecture as a full professor, entitled "Poverty" ("*Der Armut*"): "Wars are not in a position to decide historical destinies, because they already rest upon spiritual decisions and entrench themselves precisely upon these. Even world wars are incapable of this. But they themselves and their exit could give the peoples occasion to bring about a mindfulness."[7] The wars that bring the celebration of the victors are never so powerful as to defeat the need for mindfulness. Wars can never do away with our distress, in other words, and this fact in the midst of and in the wake of the carnage of war can call attention to our very distress-lessness in these conditions.

The ontological condition that World War II follows from is that of the abandonment of being. At the very outset of the war, Heidegger was already committed to this thought. In a section of "The Abandonment of Being and Errancy" internally dated 1938–39, Heidegger writes, "the 'world wars' and their 'totality' [a reference to Jünger's conception of "total mobilization" as well as to the supposed Clausewitzean advocacy of "total war"] are already consequences of the abandonment of being" (*GA* 7: 91/*EP* 103, tm). Insofar as this war is an instance of technological replacement, and that replacement seeks to install an order and persistence in the ceaseless passing away of beings, the war is a response to the abandonment of being, an attempt to cover over that abandonment and its opening of beings. As such, it simply reinforces the supply chains that provide security and identify beings with certainty.

Heidegger's first university lecture after the war, the first after the restoration of his teaching credentials, *What Is Called Thinking?* (1951–1952), is no different on this point than his last lecture in Wildenstein. "What has the Second World War actually decided, to say nothing of its horrible consequences for our fatherland, and particularly the rip down its middle? This world war has decided nothing" (*GA* 8: 71/66, tm). Heidegger is so adamant that the war has decided nothing because no decision can be reached—whether by tanks or by treaties, whether in times of war or of peace—where both parties to the opposition are ultimately allies, joined together in the total mobilization of consumption and replaceability, what Heidegger in the years ahead comes to recognize as the order of "positionality" (*das Gestell*).

§3. The Standing Reserve and the End of the Object

What Heidegger saw in World War II was nothing less than the birth of the commodity, which he names the "standing reserve" (*Bestand*). The war did not just announce the end of the object, but the end of its constant companion, the subject, as well. Now everything is marshaled into the service of what Ernst Jünger termed a "total mobilization."[8] The human, too, is now enrolled in cycles of consumption like any other "raw material," as the war made gruesomely clear. Yet this was by no means simply the enlistment of an otherwise objectively extant being into cycles of consumption, but the birth of an ontologically distinct post-modern age of technological replaceability.

The standing reserve is the mode of presence for all that exists under the dominance of contemporary technology and it is the only permissible mode: "In positionality, the presencing of all that presences becomes standing reserve" (*GA* 79: 32/31). This is so much the case that "even the object disappears into the objectlessness of standing reserve" (*GA* 7: 19/19). Heidegger could not be more clear on this point in "The Question Concerning Technology," where he states that "what stands by in the sense of standing-reserve, no longer stands over against us as object" (*GA* 7: 17/*QCT* 17). The object, as *Gegenstand*, requires an "over and against" (a "gegen") in which to stand. This space of the *gegen*, for its part, names a distance between subject and object, the space of representation. But it is precisely this distance that is put in question by positionality: "Nature is no longer even an object [*Gegen-stand*]" (*GA* 79: 44/41). Instead of a space between subject and object, there is now a suffusion into that space and a smothering of the difference between subject and object in the general transformation into standing reserve. No space is unclaimed or off limits. Nearly twenty-five years later in the 1973 seminar in Zähringen, Heidegger remains true to this insight, describing how the human "has gone from the epoch of objectivity [*Gegenständlichkeit*] to that of orderability [*Bestellbarkeit*]. . . . Strictly speaking, there are no longer objects" (*GA* 15: 388/*FS* 74). In the words of the Bremen lectures, "when the standing reserve comes into power, even the object crumbles as characteristic of what presences" (*GA* 79: 26/25).

While the standing reserve is not an object, Heidegger cautions us against thinking it simply in terms of a resource or stock: "the word here says something more and something essentially other than merely 'stock' [*Vorrat*]" (*GA* 7: 17/*QCT* 17, tm). The point bears repeating: the standing reserve is not simply a group of objects available for delivery, it is an ontological change in the nature of being itself.

The technological reign of orderability, of the standing reserve, is essentially different from the order of objectivity and representation found in modern science. Positionality is not to be identified with machination, however much it may appear to be prefigured by it. The challenge facing the thing as a gathering of the fourfold is not a closure into objectivity, but an explosion into "standing reserve" qua commodity. Only with this thought of the standing reserve does the thing find its basic tension, the relationship that first grants it its essence. Only in an epoch of standing reserve could there be things. Let us then turn now to the dominant characteristic of this standing reserve, its availability for immediate ordering.

a. The Standing Reserve Is Available

The availability of the standing reserve is perhaps its most prominent feature. The availability in question places the standing reserve at the disposal of a general requisitioning (*Bestellen*). This requisitioning demands that the being show itself. It "challenges" it to come forth, but to come forth as solely what it is, devoid of both the concealment and the relations to others that sustain the thing. The standing reserve thus names "the way in which everything presences which is met by an unconcealing that challenges forth [*herausfordernden Entbergen*]" (*GA* 7: 17/*QCT* 17, tm). Availability is the way in which the being discloses itself when challenged forth.

The challenge of this challenging forth is the demand [*fordern*] that all it meets come out [*aus*] from where it is and show itself here [*her*], outside [*heraus*]. It demands that things show themselves in their entirety as arrayed for our disposal. It demands they come out of their hiding, and for Heidegger this entails that they cease their essencing.[9] We have already addressed the role of concealment for essencing in the preceding introduction. Let us recall only that this must be understood as running through the entirety of the thing. The concealment of essencing is nothing partial, but a way of being. Understood ontologically, then, concealment prevents the closure of presence from befalling the thing, and in so doing it opens it to the world. As this negotiating of concealment and unconcealment, essencing establishes a differentiation within the thing itself, a differentiation that allows the thing to exceed itself and thereby grants that thing its relational purchase on world.

Heidegger's consideration of availability takes place in the midst of his engagement with Heraclitus (between the lecture courses of the mid-1940s and the essays of the early 1950s). As availability targets the concealment of essencing, Heidegger's interpretation of Heraclitus fragment 123 is of particular note. This famed fragment reads, *physis kryptesthai philei*, or in Freeman's shamelessly conservative translation, "nature likes to hide."[10] Heidegger's translation is more daring. *Physis* names emergence and *kryptesthai* the concealment endemic to it. *Philei* then names the relation between them and Heidegger sees in *philein* here a favoring or a granting (of one's grace). This granting stands as the pivot of the relation between unconcealment (the emergence of *physis*) and concealment in Heidegger's own translation of the fragment, "emergence (from out of self-concealment) grants its grace [*schenkt's die Gunst*] to self-concealment" (*GA* 7: 279/*EGT* 114, tm).[11] Emergence, the entry into appearance (unconcealment) grants its grace (its appearing character) to self-concealment. That is to say, unconcealment lets concealment show itself. And without this showing of concealment, there would be nothing concealed, for concealment would go unremarked, a lapse into oblivion. For its part, concealment likewise lets emergence conceal itself. Emergence not only needs concealment precisely to emerge from, it also requires the shelter that it provides: "Emergence as such is each time already inclined to self-closure. In the latter the former remains sheltered. The *kryptesthai* as a bringing-oneself-to-shelter [*Sichver-bergen*] is not a mere self-closure, but rather a sheltering [*Bergen*] wherein the essential possibility of emergence remains guarded, a sheltering to which emergence as such belongs. The self-sheltering [*das Sichverbergen*] vouches [*verbürgt*] its essence to self-disclosure" (*GA* 7: 278/*EGT* 114, tm). What essences emerges as sheltered in concealment.

Heidegger sees the affiliation between concealment and unconcealment (the *philein*) as essential to essencing itself, "so then *physis* and *kryptesthai* are not separated from each other, but rather reciprocally inclined to one another. They are the same [*das Selbe*]. In such inclination the one first grants [*gönnt*] to the other its own essence" (*GA* 7: 278–79/*EGT* 114, tm). To essence is to engage with concealment, to emerge in a way not entirely present. Emergence and concealment belong together, and a marginal note stresses this appropriative character of *philein*, translating it not as "it likes," but as "it has to own [*es hat zu eigen*]" (*GA* 7: 278 n. j).[12] Heidegger explains that the fragment concerns *physis*, not as "the what of things" but instead in terms of "the essencing (verbal) of *physis*" (*GA* 7: 278/*EGT* 113, tm). Essencing is impossible without this concealment; what essences only ever does so in concealment (i.e., as non-present).

Now it is this very concealment that is targeted by the standing reserve. What is concealed and withheld is not available. Availability is not primarily a matter of rows and aisles of items arranged in department-store-like fashion, but rather must be understood in terms of an availability that inhabits the item itself. There is nothing of the item that is not turned over to the demands of service. There is nothing "inside" that would be shielded, guarded, or preserved against the demands of supply. The item is "called out" into availability. The demand of *herausfordern* is that everything show itself in the light of day and be what it is. That there be total and complete revelation without obscurity, remainder, or ambiguity: this is the challenge put to nature. Nature must come out of its hiding and stand ready in place, available and at our disposal.

With this, the standing reserve shows a marked contrast with the perceptual object of phenomenology as well. Part of the Husserlian conception of the object—indeed, a basic tenet of phenomenology itself—is that the object is not given all at once, but instead in profiles and perspectives. Husserl is always quite clear that "the perception of a whole does not imply perception of its parts and determinations."[13] True, the "rest" of the object is intended in these profiles, either as retained in memory or protained in expectation, but in each case what is directly given is only a profile. In the *Thing and Space* lectures of 1907 Husserl fastidiously distinguishes between these as "proper" (*eigentliche*) and "improper" (*uneigentliche*) modes of appearing: "the total apprehension and total appearance of the perception divide into the *proper appearance*, whose correlate is *the side of the object* that is perceived in the proper sense and that actually comes to presentation, and the *improper appearance*, the appendage of the proper appearance, which has its correlate in *the rest of the object*."[14] What Husserl makes clear in the *Thing* lectures, however, is that without the impropriety of the appended perceptions, there would not even be a proper one. The proper is dependent upon this horizon. Indeed, when we speak of perceiving only a side of something, this is only possible thanks to these improper non-presenting appearances: "The improperly appearing objective determinations are co-apprehended, but they are not 'sensibilized,' not presented through what is sensible, i.e., through the material of sensation. It is evident that they are co-apprehended, for otherwise, *we would have no objects at all before our eyes, not even a side*, since this can indeed be a side only through the object."[15] The profile we see is only a profile in its connection to a non-present whole of the thing. We are given the thing, in other words, by precisely not being given it in a "proper" fashion.

But with the standing reserve there is no longer any impropriety of appearing. The obscenity of the standing reserve does away with that in a sheer availability. There is neither profile nor part, concealed or otherwise. So construed, the standing reserve in its availability would require us to further reflect upon some of the more basic presuppositions of phenomenology, in particular, those surrounding the nature of objects, wholes, givenness, and even propriety itself. When "that which is" is standing reserve, phenomenology itself suffers a loss of its grip on the world.

The challenge that requisitioning poses for the thinging of the thing is consequently a peculiar one. It targets nothing that would show itself. The thing is not threatened with containment within itself (objectification), but with the externalized utter availability of itself (commodification). In either case (suffocation or evisceration), the thing no longer things. But where the object was discrete, the standing reserve is anything but. Its availability ultimately sends it along chains of replaceability and destruction, as we shall see. Requisitioning turns the thing inside out in order to render it available for immediate delivery.

b. The Standing Reserve Is Immediate

The availability of the standing reserve drives the entirety of the item into the open, to be solely what it is, without concealment. But it is just this concealment that interrupts the self-presence of the being and keeps it from finally identifying itself as merely what it is. The differentiation that this concealment establishes for the being is effectively the constitution of a limit (between concealment and unconcealment), of the thing as liminal, as differential. The concealment of the thing troubles its borders and allows it the seepage into world (and world's seepage into it), the reciprocity of which we term relationality. The being is essentially defined now by relations with what exceeds its bounds. It is *mediated* in that it is now indissociable from the medium through which it essences. Availability destroys the relationality of the being in question by eliminating this mediation. These mediate relations are likewise what grants the thing its identity in the first place, as something different from something else (and not simply as the "opposite" of something). Relational mediation is *essential* to what the thing is, to how it is as *essencing*. At the time of the Bremen lectures, Heidegger thinks this mediation in terms of distance. The standing reserve does not reach beyond itself to relate across distances. It does not participate in a belonging (relationality), which always entails the crossing of distances. It refuses distancing and the mediation this requires. As such, the standing reserve is distanceless, and this means immediate.

The Bremen lectures begin from the "Point of Reference" that "all distances in time and space are shrinking" (*GA* 79: 3/3). The distance in question is the separation by which things are able to reach us. This kind of distance is necessary if there is to be any contact at all. The relational contact of the thing is a bridging of distances, but it does not collapse them. Instead, this distancing allows things to reach us in their mediate approach. They come to us, *geht uns an*, as Heidegger says, where the phrase not only means that the things "go to us," but also that they "concern us." Things reach us in a "concernful approach" (*Angang*). Heidegger remarks:

> What one calls distance [*Abstand*] we know as the interval between two points. If we step outside the house under the tree and in its shadow, however, then admittedly the distance between house and tree does

> not rest in the measurement of the interval between them. The distance consists rather in that the house, tree, and shadow concernfully approach us from their mutual reciprocity, and also in how they do so. Such concerned approach attunes the distance (longinquity) between what is present within presencing. The distance to us of all that presences and absences is attuned by this concerned approach. Whatever has such distance, among themselves and to us, concernfully approaches us precisely by this distancing, be it that something lies far from us, be it that something comes near to us. (*GA* 79: 25/23)

What approaches us does not cross an empty space to reach us (the "longinquity" mentioned above), but instead from the outset populates this space, attuning it and modulating it. Distinct things would modulate this distance differently. Distance is found in the singular things extending beyond themselves and, through their medium, appealing to us. The standing reserve is im-mediate in purporting to a completely available self-presence. In being just what it is, the standing reserve rejects its need for relations with others, refusing the mediation that this requires.

Along with this thought of distance, another way in which Heidegger thinks the immediacy of the standing reserve is through the notion of an "unguarding" (*Verwahrlosung*) of the thing. Indeed, Heidegger views this unguarding as the essence of positionality itself: "Positionality's essence lets the thing go without guard. In our language, where it still inceptually speaks, the word 'guard' [*die Wahr*] means protection. In our Swabian dialect this word 'guard' means a child entrusted to maternal protection [cf. English "'ward"]. Positionality in its positioning lets the thing go without protection—without the guard of its essence as thing" (*GA* 79: 46/44–45). This guarding is the creation of a "safe" space around the thing through the cultivation of a medium in which the thing might grow into its relations. We are not to view this unguarding as simply a matter of neglect (the ordinary meaning of *Verwahrlosung*). Rather, "unguarded" is the way in which beings must show themselves as standing reserve. Unguarding is part of technology's very essence: "Unguarding here does not mean a slipping into neglect, does not signify a decay into disorder. The word 'unguarding' as now used is no term of derision; it entails no value judgment at all. *The unguarding of the thing names what proceeds from the essence of positionality, signaling to us the essence of technology*" (*GA* 79: 47/45, em). The unguarding of the thing is the evaporation of its medium, the dissolution of the element in which it essences. And here the medium in question is truth (*Wahrheit*).

The unguarding of the thing is the ousting of it from its truth. Something is "guarded" or "protected" (*bewahrt*) when it is allowed to essence, i.e., is not challenged forth into a total presentation. This guarded thing is the true (*das Wahre*) when it resides in the medium of truth (*Wahrheit*). And since Heidegger understands truth as un-concealment (*Un-verborgenheit*), in keeping with the Greek sense of truth as *alêtheia*, the thing is only truly the thing when it retains an essential concealment. Simply put, the thing is true when it essences, but it can only essence when sheltered in the medium of truth. What positionality brings about, then, is the unguarding (*Verwahrlosung*) of the thing, its truthlessness, and the challenging forth of its essence.[16] Laid bare in this way, the thing becomes *immediate*. The lecture "The Danger" casts this in terms of an alteration in the nature of being, being become positionality: "Ordering the standing reserve, positionality allows unconcealment and its essence to lapse into full forgetting. Positionality as the essence of being transposes being outside of the truth of its essence, ousts [*entsetzt*] being from its truth" (*GA* 79: 52/50). Here we are dealing with positionality as the face of being itself and it is being that unseats itself from its truth (we shall have occasion to return to this). Consequently, truthless positionality is nothing that could completely sever its connection to being, it remains the way that being gives itself today: "In the essencing of positionality, being itself is ousted from the truth of its essence, without however at any time in this displacement and self-unseating being able to sunder itself from the essence of beyng" (*GA* 79: 52/50). "The Question Concerning Technology" can thus claim that "positionality dissembles the shining and reigning of the truth" (*GA* 7: 29/*QCT* 28, tm).

A consequence of this immediacy of the standing reserve is that it cannot take part in something larger than it, a whole. Rather than parts, the standing reserve is a matter of pieces. Pieces never make a whole, only ever at best a heap. Heidegger distinguishes pieces from parts in just these terms in "Positionality":

> The piece [*das Stück*] is something other than the part [*der Teil*, which one could also translate as "the share"]. The part shares itself with [*teilt sich mit*] parts in a whole. It takes part in the whole [*nimmt am Ganzen teil*, it "participates" in the whole], belongs to it [here Heidegger adds a marginal note (m) that the part "completes its wholeness," *ergänzt seine Gänze*]. The piece on the contrary is separated and indeed, as the piece, is even isolated from the other pieces. It never shares itself with these in a whole. The piece of standing reserve does not even share itself with its own kind in the standing reserve. The standing reserve is much more that which has been shattered into the orderable [*in das Bestellbare Zerstückte*, dispersed into pieces, where again the emphasis falls on *Stück* and not *Teil*]. This shattering does not break apart, but instead precisely

> creates the standing reserve of the pieces of inventory [*den Bestand der Bestandstücke*]. Each of these is loaded into and confined in a circuit of orderability. The isolating of piece from piece corresponds to the confining of everything that has been isolated in an industry of requisitioning. (*GA* 79: 36/34)

Pieces are without relation to a whole, they do not participate with each other in the constitution of this; they are isolated. The pieces are not even pieces because of the breaking apart of any pre-existent whole. On the contrary, parts carry the whole with them. Through this essential exposure to the whole, the separated part nonetheless remains a part, its separation remains a mode of being-with. Such parts belong to what is other to them, to the whole. And this other to them is nothing opposed to them, for the part is so essentially related to the whole lying beyond it as to be permeated by that whole, as Heidegger explains: "My hand, on the contrary, is not a piece of me. I myself am entirely in each gesture of the hand, every single time" (*GA* 79: 37/35). I am the whole that suffuses all of my parts.

In sharing itself with the other parts, the part takes part in the whole. And the whole is inseparable from this sharing. A whole, then, would not name anything closed in upon itself, but would name a configuration, or gathering, of parts. The figure of this configuration follows the contour of the parts, a contour that marks the limits of self-possession. The whole is not a sealed off unit, but the spacing of the parts whose very separation delimits each part such that it opens onto (participates in) the wholeness of the whole. It begins at the limit of the parts, parts irrevocably exposed and opened to the other.

And yet, this talk of pieces makes it sound as though we had inadvertently returned to the closure of objectivity. How can the standing reserve be in pieces if the pieces are closed in on themselves? The question begins from a faulty assumption. The confinement of the piece is due to its presence in a circuit of orderability. The pieces do not share themselves, they do not partake or participate in anything beyond themselves. But this is no longer a thinking of objectivity. They are not closed in on themselves; rather, they are so utterly unveiled as to undermine and destroy relationality as such. Pieces refuse the whole that would mediate their relations.

It is this mediating whole that the standing reserves obliterates. Heidegger explains that "positionality is the essence of technology. Its positioning is universal. It addresses itself to *the unity of the whole* of all that presences. Positionality thus sets in place the way that everything present now presences" (*GA* 79: 40/38, em). This united whole is nothing less than the Greek *hen*, the One that mediates the *panta* that participate within it. The work of positionality, its requisitioning (*Bestellen*) is directed against nothing other than this. As Heidegger states, "requisitioning is only directed at one thing, *versus unum*, namely to position *the one whole* of what presences as standing reserve" (*GA* 79: 32/30). The distanceless, unguarded pieces of standing reserve are relationally detached: immediate. Immediacy is this *decontextualization* of the thing.

c. The Standing Reserve Is Orderable

Requisitioning (*Bestellen*) names the predominance of ordering (*bestellen*) within the technological landscape. As the word *Bestand* is derived from the verb *bestehen*, meaning to persist, exist, or consist of something, it is tempting to hear in standing reserve a similar kind of enduring solidity. Yet it is exactly this understanding that Heidegger cautions against in a marginal note to "Positionality" stating that standing reserve is "meant in the sense of an orderable standing reserve, i.e., not of steady lasting [*stetig andauern*]" (*GA* 79: 28 n. d/27 n. 4). The same idea motivates his comment that the term standing reserve "says something more and something more essential than merely 'stock'" (*GA* 7: 17/*QCT* 17, tm). Rather than understand standing reserve as something stable and, indeed, standing, we should instead construe it from the outset as transitive and mobile, swept up in the movement of requisitioning (*Bestellen*) and the orderability (*Bestellbarkeit*) that this demands.

The standing reserve is requisitioned to be ordered and delivered (*bestellt* and *zugestellt*). To say that the standing reserve is *ordered* is to say both that it is *arranged* in a particular way to facilitate its distribution (it is uniform, already prepared for delivery), and that it is at the *disposal* of a demand that provokes it. The immediate availability of the standing reserve makes this ordering resistanceless, frictionless. There is nothing concealed or opaque about the standing reserve and thus nothing withheld from the delivery. Since there is no differentiation between concealment and unconcealment for the standing reserve, there is consequently nothing of it to resist displacement. Nothing is held back. Availability does not simply place the object at the disposal of future uses that may or may not avail themselves of it; instead availability as transformation of essence cracks the very discreteness of the object itself and mobilizes it for use qua standing reserve. A certain mobility is inalienable from the standing reserve; it is always on the way to and from something else, surreptitiously blending away into what comes next. The immediate orderability of the standing reserve unsettles it from a static position.

Indeed this is so much the case that we would misconstrue the standing reserve entirely were we to think it as simply responding to a previously placed demand. Casting things in this light misses what is most perplexing about the standing reserve. It is always in demand, we might say, it is constituted by demand. It is not an independent entity that occasionally faces a demand from outside to which it subsequently responds. Rather, the imposed demand actually constitutes the standing reserve: "The standing reserve persists [*der Bestand besteht*]. It persists insofar as it is imposed upon for a requisitioning" (*GA* 79: 26/25). The nature of this imposition pushes the standing reserve along chains of transformation. The orderable standing reserve is ordered so that it itself will impose a further ordering. Heidegger contrasts the positioning (*stellen*) of the requisitioned (*bestellt*) standing reserve with the simple poise of the thing. The standing reserve is always imposed upon *for* something:

> But now what is it positioned toward, the coal that is positioned in the coal reserve, for example? It is not poised upon the table like the jug. The coal, for its part, is imposed upon, i.e., challenged forth, for heat, just as the ground was for coal; this heat is already imposed upon to set in place steam, the pressure of which drives the turbines, which keep a factory industrious, which is itself imposed upon to set in place machines that produce tools through which once again machines are set to work and maintained. (*GA* 79: 28/27)

The available immediacy of the standing reserve is nothing static. Rather, the standing reserve is irremediably out of place. Or rather, standing reserve cannot be understood as having a proper place at all as it is itself constituted by an unsettling imposition that sets it underway from the outset. It is imposed upon to serve the purpose of imposing upon something else, seeming to end here in the circularity of machines assisting in the production of more machines. The standing reserve is not simply put to use or applied toward a particular end, but instead is surrendered to endless repurposing.

Heidegger's comments on application make this clear. The exigency of application demands the instability of the standing reserve so as to lead directly to *results of consequence*: "Application positions everything in advance in such a manner that what is positioned follows upon a result. So placed, everything is: in consequence of. . . . The consequence, however, is ordered in advance as a success. A success is that type of consequence that itself remains assigned to the yielding of further consequences" (*GA* 79: 26/25). The positioning of all that is sets everything in place as a follower, as something dependent. Yet this very dependency is lauded as a success. And the successful proves its efficacy by setting up further successions of dependence: "What is ordered is always already and always only imposed upon to place another in the succession as its consequence" (*GA* 79: 29/28). The itinerant standing reserve is nothing that might repose in itself, but instead something that always follows upon something else so as to set up its own successor. Success requires this smearing of its integrity between predecession and consequence. The successful have all surrendered to it. This succession operates within a general circulation of the standing reserve, as we shall consider in the following section.

The endlessness of succession here cannot be construed serially, and if it is a repurposing, it is not that of an otherwise extant object. This is the whole point: repurposing is nothing external to the object that would then "apply" the otherwise untouched object toward an end. Rather, this repurposing comes to permeate the entirety of the object at the level of its essence. The object no longer exists in one place, but is so determined by orderability and availability as to be already driven out along the circuitry of delivery. One thing leads to another in dizzying chains of ordering and consequences, lacking the finality of either origin or end.

This transformation of the world into standing reserve immediately available for the ordering is capitalized on by contemporary science and lies at the heart of its predictive power. Science demands results: "For natural science, something only counts as presencing when it is calculable in advance and only insofar as it is. The predictability of natural processes, standard for all natural scientific representing, is the representational orderability of nature as *the standing reserve of a succession*" (*GA* 79: 43/41, em). What follows from an experiment can only be a success.

But it is not simply that one thing follows on another that is at stake here. Rather, one thing enlists another into the standing reserve. There is an appropriative dimension to the mobility of the standing reserve that Heidegger calls "conscription" (*Gestellung*). He views it in conjunction with the essence of technology: "The essence of technology is positionality. Positionality orders. It orders what is present through conscription. Positionality orders what is present into standing reserve" (*GA* 79: 40/38). Conscription is here the motor of requisitioning. As such, it is directed to all that is: "Requisitioning affects all that presences in respect to its presence with a conscripting" (*GA* 79: 31–32/30). By entering the standing reserve, what exists is not only established as a consequence, but is set the task of providing further consequences as well. Heidegger gives the example of a tract of land:

> A tract of land is imposed upon, namely for the coal and ore that
> subsists in it. The subsistence of stone is presumably already conceived
> within the horizon of such a positioning and even only conceivable in

> terms of this. The subsisting stone that, as such, is already evaluated for a self-positioning is challenged forth and subsequently expedited along. The earth's soil is drawn into such a placing and is attacked by it. It is ordered, forced into conscription. This is how we understand the word "ordering" [*bestellen*] here and in what follows. (*GA* 79: 27/26)

What becomes a piece of the standing reserve does not do so docilely; rather it enters the standing reserve with the task of further converting what exists into inventory.

The paradox is that the so-called standing reserve does anything but stand. It is itinerant and transitive, but simultaneously "in place and at the ready" (*auf der Stelle zur Stelle*), as Heidegger repeatedly observes: "The power station in the Rhine river, the dam, the turbines, the generators, the switchboards, the electrical grid—all this and more is there only insofar as it stands *in place and at the ready*, not in order to presence, but to be positioned, and indeed solely to impose upon others thereafter" (*GA* 79: 28/27, em). Heidegger's phrasing here is quite precise: the "*zur*" of "*zur Stelle*" already imparts a certain departure from the "*auf*" of "*auf der Stelle*." Even when "in" place, the standing reserve is already tending "toward" something else, arriving from somewhere else (it comes "to" this place where it would stand, directed "toward" some further end). The example of assembly line vehicle production demonstrates this:

> The tractors and automobiles are brought out, spewed out, serially piece by piece. But where out there does something put out in this manner stand? Into what standing is it so brought?
>
> The automobile is put out in such a way that it is *in place and at the ready, i.e., immediately and constantly deliverable.* It is not produced so that it would stand there and remain standing there like the jug. The automobile is much more imposed upon *to leave* and indeed as something orderable that, for its part, can be challenged forth and precisely for a *further conducting along*, which itself sets in place the promotion of commerce. (*GA* 79: 35–36/34, em)

The immediate availability of the standing reserve severs the thing from the relations that would ground it. The thing loses its grip on the world, its place, its location in a context. Instead, the standing reserve is ripped away into ceaseless mobility, orderability.

This itinerant standing reserve is nothing locatable or identifiable, so much so as to render it inexplicable: "requisitioning can never be explained by any single item of standing reserve, just as little as it can be conceived from the sum of items of standing reserve at hand as a universal that would just hover above them. Requisitioning cannot be explained at all, i.e., it cannot be led back to something clear" (*GA* 79: 31/30). What exists under this inexplicable requisitioning is standing reserve.

Examining the standing reserve in terms of its availability, immediacy, and orderability reveal the ways in which the standing reserve breaks with the modernist conception of the object. Where the object is represented before a subject, the standing reserve is utterly available. Where that object still stands over and against a subject, the standing reserve is immediate (without medium). And where the object is encapsulated, the standing reserve rushes out in orderability. In what follows we will be led to consider the ways in which the thing as the gathering of the fourfold differs from both modern objectivity and the standing reserve. Where the standing reserve is available, the thing essences; where it is immediate, the thing is mediated; and while the standing reserve is driven out in orderability, the thing abides. For this reason Heidegger can claim to find "something astonishing" in technology, that it "requires of us that we think what one commonly understands by 'essence' in another sense" (*GA* 7: 31/*QCT* 30, tm). He immediately adds, "but which?" The answer, we shall see, lies in the gathering of the fourfold, which grants the thing its singular essencing in contrast to the circulating replaceability of the standing reserve, to which we now turn.

§4. Positionality as Circulative Replacement

The standing reserve marks an epochal break with the objectivity that defines modern metaphysics. The post-modern order defined by the prevalence of standing reserve is what Heidegger calls "positionality" (*das Ge-Stell*), and this can be thought as composed of two processes: "Positionality: the gathering of positioning in the sense of pursuing [*Nachstellens*] and requisitioning [*Bestellens*]" (*GA* 79: 63/60). Pursuing and requisitioning serve to instate the circulative replacement that defines the era as post-modern. Requisitioning establishes the standing reserve as replaceable and pursuing sets it into circulation. Positionality thus inaugurates a regime of circulative replacement that holds sway for existence today. Before turning to these matters, however, a few words on the term "positionality" (*Ge-Stell*) itself are first in order.

Whereas machination is the exacerbation of an age of representation (*Vorstellen*), this *Vorstellen* is only one of many ways of positioning or placing, of the German *stellen*. In the late 1940s Heidegger comes to see *stellen* as the root of technological activity as such and names the collection of these settings or posings "positionality" (*Ge-stell*).[17] In this lineage, then, the solitary dominance of *vorstellen* for the epoch of modern science gives way to a proliferation of settings and positionings at the end of metaphysics in the age of technology. Signal among this constellation around *stellen* are: *bestellen* (to order, to requisition), *zustellen* (to deliver), *nachstellen* (to pursue), *herstellen* (to produce), *darstellen* (to present), *feststellen* (to fix in place), and *verstellen* (to disguise).

Heidegger's usage of the term "positionality" is, of course, unique. As he says in "The Question Concerning Technology," his 1953 report to the Bavarian Academy of Fine Arts in Munich, a text that is something of a revised, redacted, and recontextualized extract from the Bremen lectures of four years prior, "we hazard to use this word ["positionality"] in a completely unusual sense" (*GA* 7: 20/*QCT* 19, tm). As for the customary use of the term, "according to its usual meaning, the word 'Gestell' means a device, for example, a bookcase" (*GA* 7: 20/*QCT* 20, tm). But Heidegger will not think positionality in these terms. The lecture "Positionality," where the name was first announced, explains, "the word now no longer names an individual object of the sort like a bookcase [*Büchergestells*] or a water well" (*GA* 79: 32/31). A marginal note to the text here continues, "still sharper contrast with installation [*Montage*], rod and piston assemblies [*Gestänge und Geschiebe*]; skeleton [*Gerippe*]" (*GA* 79: 32 n. j/31 n. 10). In the 1956 appendix to "The Origin of the Work of Art," Heidegger explains that the term positionality is thought from out of an historical connection with the Ancient Greeks, and explicitly "*not* from bookcase [*Büchergestell*] or installation [*Montage*]" (*GA* 5: 72/54). The conclusion to the third lecture of *Insight Into That Which Is*, "The Danger," is definitive on the point: "The word positionality names the essence of technology. Technology does not essence in the manner of a requisitioning and pursuing [*Bestellens und Nachstellens*] due to the technological process of building and using an apparatus, something that still appears to us as a 'framework' [*Gestelle*] in the sense of scaffolding and equipment" (*GA* 79: 65/61).

Positionality is thus explicitly distinguished from all manner of framing (or "enframing" as the term has previously been translated). We cannot think positionality as some kind of framework or scaffolding thrown over the world. To do so is to persist in the belief that this incursion of the technological would be something that came to us from the outside, that it would remain somehow extrinsic to all that is and would only ever approach this from without, covering over all that is and obscuring it, but leaving our existence ultimately untouched. It is to believe, for example, that nature would still exist outside of technology, even if only as the source from which it draws its materials (an idea that Heidegger excoriates in "Positionality," cf. *GA* 79: 43/40). To think position-ality as a frame casts it as something extractable from all that presences around us, and this is simply not the case. Positionality is no framework or scaffolding, whether as an external casing (a bookcase), a surround-ing apparatus (a waterwell), or even an internally erected structure (a skeleton). More, it cannot be conceived as a collection of devices, like the rod and piston assemblies that Heidegger repeatedly mentions. Po-sitionality is not something distinct from the presencing of beings, but rather is their very way of presencing in a post-modern era of circulative replacement.

a. Circulation, Rotation, Recurrence

"Positionality" is what enables the standing reserve to circulate, "*position-ality is in itself the reaping, impulsive circulation* of the requisitioning of the orderable in the ordering" (*GA* 79: 33/32, em). But positionality "does not name something constant in the ordered standing reserve," rather, "the circuit of ordering takes place in positionality and as positionality" (*GA* 79: 32/31). Positionality is not a structure, but a way of being; "po-sitionality is the being of beings itself" (*GA* 79: 51/49). As such it forms the "essence" of the standing reserve. Where will to power is the essence, what exists does so as eternally recurrent, just as where positionality is the essence, what exists does so as standing reserve, which is to say, as circulative.

Positionality is consequently impulsive. Positionality "never merely piles up inventory. Much more, it reaps away what is ordered into the circuit of orderability. Within the circuit, the one positions the other. The one drives [*treibt*] the other ahead, but ahead and away into requi-sitioning" (*GA* 79: 33/31). Positionality drives the standing reserve ahead through the circuit of orderability. Heidegger goes so far as to define positionality itself in terms of this circular impulsion: "The collected positioning of positionality is the gathering of self-circulating impulse [*Treibens*]" (*GA* 79: 33/31).

Given this "essential" character of positionality, it comes as no sur-prise that the standing reserve depends on the circulatory system of po-sitionality for its very existence. The pieces of the standing reserve are "loaded into and confined in a circuit of orderability" (*GA* 79: 36/34). They could not exist apart from this. Heidegger envisions what would happen if someone tried to remove the standing reserve from its circuits of orderability when considering a fleet of automobiles:

> If one wanted to take away, piece by piece and all together, the pieces of
> inventory in a fleet [*Bestand*] of automobiles and put them somewhere

else, then the pieces would be torn out of the circuit of their orderability. The result would be some kind of automobile graveyard. The parking lot is something different, since there every car in its orderability stands at the ready and is the positioned piece of an ordered standing reserve of ordering. (*GA* 79: 36/34–35)

Removing the cars from their usual functional circuitry does not simply put them aside for future deployment. They are not thereby located in a "parking lot" awaiting their next service. The parking lot is still part of the circuit. Instead, removing the cars from their circuit decommissions them and yields a graveyard.

To say that positionality circulates is to say it is without purpose. This circuitry does not lead any where, it only ever feeds back into itself:

> Again we ask: where does the chain of such requisitioning finally run out to? It runs out to nothing; for requisitioning produces nothing that could have, or would be allowed to have, a presence for itself outside of such positioning. What is ordered is always already and always only imposed upon to place another in the succession as its consequence. The chain of requisitioning does not run out to anything; rather it only enters into its circuit [*Kreisgang*]. Only in this does the orderable have its persistency [*Bestand*]. (*GA* 79: 28–29/28)

The standing reserve cannot exist outside of its circuitry, these chains of requisitioning. The circuit in question is not anything pre-given like a predetermined path or pre-established route, but is instead a conglomeration of positionings. It is the restricted space through which the standing reserve courses. The standing reserve cannot exist outside of this.

By virtue of this defining dependency, the machine becomes the icon of positionality, bearing in mind, of course, that the essence of technology is nothing technological (see *GA* 79: 34/33, *GA* 7: 36/*QCT* 35) and that the conception of the contemporary era as a "machine age" is grossly inadequate to the task of responding to that which is ("one says nothing of the essence of modern technology when one conceives it as machine technology," *GA* 79: 33/32). Positionality is the essence of the machine:

> From the outset, positionality as such imposes upon all standing reserve that it only persist through the machine. To what extent? Positionality is the gathering of the drive's plundering of the constancy of the orderable, which itself is solely imposed upon such that it would stand in place and at the ready. Positionality is the collected requisitioning of the orderable that circulates in itself. Positionality is in itself the

> reaping, impulsive circulation of the requisitioning of the orderable in
> the ordering. Positionality imposes this equality of the orderable upon
> everything, that everything constantly position itself again in equivalent
> form and indeed in the equality of orderability.
>
> Positionality, as this circulation in itself of requisitioning, composes
> the essence of the machine. (*GA* 79: 33–34/32)

The connection between the machine and the circulation of positionality does not stop there, however, for the machine itself is defined by its own brand of circulation, by *rotation*. Heidegger's comments in "Positionality" continue by situating rotation within the circulation of positionality:

> Positionality, as this circulation in itself of requisitioning, composes the
> essence of the machine. Rotation belongs to this, though not neces-
> sarily in the form of a wheel, for the wheel is defined by rotation, not
> rotation by wheels.
>
> Rotation is that revolving which courses back into itself, driving on
> the orderable (propellant) into the requisitioning of the orderable
> (propulsion). The rotation of the machine is positioned, i.e., chal-
> lenged forth, and made constant in the circulation that lies in drive,
> the essential character of positionality. (*GA* 79: 34/32)

Revolving and coursing back into themselves, driven along in requisitioning, all pieces of the standing reserve revolve or rotate in this way, however stable or constant they otherwise appear. Rotation is synonymous with circulation itself, perhaps even the "soul" of technology; an entry entitled "The 'Automobile' (in the Essential Sense)" in a sheaf of notes headed "*Technē* and Technology" (dated only 1940 f.), asks, "to what extent is 'uninterrupted circular motion the soul of technology'? Roller, wheel (that which turns, such that the *middle point moves forward* at the same time—auto tire)" (*GA* 76: 307).[18] Rotation propels the circulation of standing reserve forward along the circuitry of positionality.

Rotation likewise plays a part in rendering the world orderable on a broader, social scale. A note called "*What is called a power producing machine? What is a generator?*" observes "Energy—to be retained in the form of rotational movement (the textile industry)" (*GA* 76: 368). Heidegger views the advent of industrialization and the societal transformations that accompany it as all deriving from the introduction of these rotating generators. The textile industry plays a signal role in this. In a section of the technology notebooks entitled "Positionality and the Steam Engine" we read:

Watt's steam engine, i.e. power producing machine, exists so that another possibility of power propulsion [*Kraftantriebes*], such as weaving and spinning, requires proportionally less power for the propulsion of the individual machines.

In order to position the power machine effectively, and this means as rentable, within an industry [*Betrieb*], weaving stools must be put together in large numbers in one place; thus is required the transplanting of the worker (women and children) from home to the factory, from the country into the city. Textile factories as model for industrial mechanization.

The steam engine was more economic in large firms than in small ones. Positionality and economy (*commodity* [Ware] and *standing reserve*). (*GA* 76: 367)

The rotational effect of the machine extends well beyond any particular device. It transforms the ones who use these machines themselves, subjecting them, too, to the same rotational displacement. Their center moves.

The machine of contemporary technology is thus something quite distinct from the tool. Heidegger is explicit on this point, "the machine is nothing that separately presences for itself. It is by no means merely a more developed sort of tool and apparatus, merely a self-propelled wheel assembly, as distinct from the spinning wheel of the peasant woman or the bucket wheel in the rice fields of China" (*GA* 79: 35/33). Consequently, Heidegger's thinking of the machine would likewise exceed the famed tool analysis of *Being and Time*, some twenty years prior. There, too, the tool stood within an equipmental context. With the standing reserve, however, the situation becomes more aporetic, more paradoxical. There is not even the possibility of removal from the "equipmental context," if the term is to be retained. The interruptions of equipmentality that occupy Heidegger in *Being and Time*—interruptions that served to reveal the *world* to Dasein—are here drawn into the system of replacement and orderability. Functioning is so much the guiding principle of positionality that it is no longer opposed to breakdowns and interruptions, but is even advanced by them. Functioning already includes within it downtime for crashes, upgrades, etc. As Heidegger explains:

The machine does not at all merely step into the place of equipment and tools. The machine is just as little an object. It stands only insofar as it goes. It goes insofar as it runs. It runs in the drive of industry. The drive drives as the bustle of the requisitioning of the orderable. If the machine stands, then *its standstill is a condition of the drive*, of its cessation or disturbance. Machines are within a machinery. But this is no piling up of machines. The machinery runs from the plundering of the drive, as which positionality orders the standing reserve. (*GA* 79: 34/33, em)

What functionality tends to is instant and complete replacement, without remainder, of whatever "breaks." What this means is that there is no "outside" to the circulation of standing reserve, no chance for an interruption, no chance for the world. "Everything functions. That is exactly what is uncanny," Heidegger says in the 1966 *Spiegel* interview (*GA* 16: 669/*HNS* 55).

The endlessness of circulation is of the kind championed across the history of philosophy as the endlessness of the circle. The priority of the spherical, the rotational, the circular, and the recurrent, in Parmenides, Plato, Aristotle, Hegel, and Nietzsche, to name only a few, all of this can be seen in Heidegger's determination of *Ge-stell* as circulation. At the end of metaphysics, this persistent trait of philosophical thought is stripped of all subtlety and crudely installed in the most literal manner as technological circulation: "*Technology is thus the authentic completion of 'metaphysics'*" (*GA* 76: 294). Instructive in this regard are Heidegger's comments on the two figures who mark the start and finish of this completion of metaphysics, Hegel and Nietzsche.[19]

For Hegel, the machine is an object of mechanical repetition. He notes that "*A mechanical style of thinking, a mechanical memory, habit, a mechanical way of acting*, signify that the peculiar pervasion and presence of spirit is lacking in what spirit apprehends or does."[20] Lacking this suffusion of spirit, the mechanical process, i.e., "mechanism," remains an "external" process, one formally abstract, where "the differentiated moments are *complete* and *independent* [selbstständige] *objects* which consequently, even in their relation, stand to one another only as *independent* things and remain *external* to one another in every combination. This is what constitutes the character of *mechanism*, namely, that whatever relation obtains between the things combined, this relation is one *extraneous* to them."[21] As such, mechanism is operative in the various processes of nature: "in nature only the wholly abstract relationships of a matter which is still not opened up within itself are subject to mechanism."[22]

Now Heidegger denies precisely this supposed independence of the mechanical, of the machine. Speaking of "Hegel's definition of the machine as an independent tool," he observes that, "viewed in terms of the tool of handicraft, his characterization is correct. Yet, in this the machine is precisely not thought in terms of the essence of technology, in which it belongs. Viewed in terms of the standing reserve, the machine is unqualifiedly dependent; for it has its status solely from out of the requisitioning of the orderable" (*GA* 7: 18/*QCT* 17, tm). Hegel's independent machine remains at the level of the objective, not the circulative.

Turning to Nietzsche, Heidegger finds machinic rotationality at work in the doctrine of the eternal recurrence of the same. In a notebook entry outlining and considering the main moves of the lecture "The Question Concerning Technology," Heidegger remarks that "without being stated, the steps [of the lecture] already moved outside of metaphysics. Metaphysics is not recognized in its authentic relation to what essences of technology [*das Wesende der Technik*]: in the eternal recurrence of the same as will to power (*will to will*)" (*GA* 76: 361). To be sure, such an association between eternal recurrence and technology is nowhere to be found in the lecture course on Nietzsche's doctrine of the eternal recurrence. That 1937 course, for all its concern with "*constancy* [Beständigkeit] *and presence*" (*GA* 44: 227, cf. *N2*: 200), is simply too early for this shift in Heidegger's thinking from machination to the machinic, i.e., the shift to the reign of the machine as paradigm instance of the standing reserve in an era of technological positionality. The lecture course is still operating under the thought of representational objectivity. It is only after the war, in the technology notebooks leading up to the Bremen lectures, that we first encounter an explicit connection between eternal recurrence and the machine:

> In regard to the requisitioning of the pieces of inventory of the standing reserve into the constancy [*Beständigkeit*] of the replaceably uniform [*Gleich-Förmigen*], the essence of positionality is intimated in Nietzsche's doctrine of the eternal recurrence of the same [*Gleichen*]. Only Nietzsche could not yet comprehend that with this doctrine he thinks the essence of technology and thinks this essence as the essence of being. (*GA* 76: 321)

The thought enters his published work only with the post-war essay on Nietzsche, "Who Is Nietzsche's Zarathustra?," of 1953. This concludes with something of an appendix, a "Remark on the Eternal Recurrence of the Same," where we read: "What else is the essence of the modern power-driven machine than *one* offshoot of the eternal recurrence of the same? But the essence of such machines is neither something machinelike nor anything mechanical. Just as little can Nietzsche's thought of eternal recurrence of the same be interpreted in a mechanical sense" (*GA* 7: 124/*N1*: 233). The point is that the machine is as much informed by eternal recurrence as the latter is instantiated in the machine. Together they agree in a dependence upon technological, rotational, circulation.

Through all of this we must avoid construing technology as some foreign power bearing down on an otherwise intact and "hale" existence. The pieces of the standing reserve are *ontologically* incapable of existing apart from the routing of positionality. Technology is ontology. The work of positionality is the work of being. Being sets itself into circulation, pursuing itself. Heidegger thinks positionality in just this way, literally, as a "setting after," as a "pursuit," *Nachstellen,* a pursuit by the forgetting of the truth that is required for any essencing to occur. We might call it a forgetting of world:

> positionality importunes upon the world with the completion of the forgetting of its worlding. Importuning in this way, positionality sets after the truth of the essence of being with forgetfulness. This pursuit [*Nachstellen*] is the authentic positioning [*Stellen*], which takes place in the essence of positionality. In this pursuit there first rests that positioning of positionality that, in the manner of the ordering of the standing reserve, places all that presences into the state of the unguardedness of the thing. The innermost essence of positioning, as which positionality essences, is pursuit as here characterized. (*GA* 79: 53/50–51)

Positionality pursues the worlding of world, i.e., the medium of appearance, with a forgetting. In so doing, it unguards the thing.

But we do wrong to think positionality as somehow levying an attack on being from outside of it. Positionality is how being shows itself to us in our era, how it has been dispensed to us and is our fate: "being now essences in the manner of positionality. It is the epoch of the completed unguarding of the thing by positionality" (*GA* 79: 51/49). As such, what befalls being does not happen from anywhere outside of it. The danger of technological positionality is self-inflicted. Through its pursuit, being endangers itself:

> In Old High German, to pursue is called *fara.* The positioning gathered in itself as pursuit is the danger [*die Gefahr*]. The basic trait of the essence of danger is pursuit. Insofar as being as positionality pursues itself with the forgetting of its essence, beyng as beyng is the danger of its own essence. Thought from the essence of positionality and in regard to the refusal of world and the unguarding of the thing, beyng is the danger. *Beyng is unqualifiedly in itself, from itself, for itself, the danger.* As this pursuit, which pursues its own essence with the forgetting of this essence, beyng as beyng is the danger. (*GA* 79: 53–54/51, em)

This is the drastic conclusion that Heidegger is led to: beyng is itself the danger. The pursuit that lies at the "innermost essence" of positioning, the pursuit that races headlong into circulation, ultimately derives from a division within being itself. Positionality as immediacy, on the one hand, and "world" or "truth" as medium for relational appearing on the other. Both are aspects of beyng. The "essential danger" is the way that "what is same—world and positionality as the respective differentiation of what essences of beyng—displaces itself from itself in setting after itself" (*GA* 79: 54/51). And insofar as the history of metaphysics has missed the relationality of existence, it too participates in beyng's self-disguise. Metaphysics is the danger: "Beyng, as it has hitherto unfolded itself in metaphysics from the [Platonic] idea up to now and in accordance with its hitherto concealed essence, belongs to the danger that now reigns over beyng" (*GA* 79: 54/51). Beyng disguises itself in various reified forms across the history of metaphysics. The withdrawal of beyng and with this the abandonment of beings are both overlooked, and thereby the distancing that follows from this withdrawal is likewise neglected, the very distancing that opens the field for relational connectivity and touch. Metaphysics threatens beyng with the forgetting of its mediating essence.

The forgetting of being is thus a forgetting of the medium in which beings appear. Without this understanding of mediation, the forgetting of being instantiates itself positively in a reified conception of being, or rather of "beinghood." Instead of mediating beings, positionality establishes their circulation along its circuitry. Being pursues itself and therefore it circulates.

b. Replacement and Consumption

Circulation diffuses the items of standing reserve across its circuitry. Nothing simply is where it is, but is also off somewhere else, further along the circuitry, and immediately available for the ordering. This is the only status or "standing" that the standing reserve is able to achieve, a ghostly kind of constancy through the sheer immediacy of circulation: "Positionality constantly [*ständig*] draws what is orderable into the circuit of requisitioning, establishes it therein, and thus assigns it as *something constant* [*Beständige*] in the standing reserve. The assignment does not place what is constant outside of the circuit of positioning. It only assigns it, but off and away into a subsequent orderability, i.e., back and forth into the requisitioning" (*GA* 79: 32–33/31, em).

The constancy that is achieved, however, is nothing self-same and stable. As rotation is that "revolving which courses back into itself" (*GA*79: 34/32), the standing reserve must be understood as revolving, i.e., as constantly feeding back into itself. But it can only do this if it is not simply where it is. Rather, it must always be arriving into itself and always departing away from itself as well. Revolution, the coming and going of the standing reserve, is ultimately another name for replacement. The stability of the standing reserve is manufactured by such rotations, an ideal produced through the continual repetition of replacement: "The constant consists [*das Beständige besteht*] in an orderable replaceability by an ordered equivalent [*Gleiche*]. . . . What is constant of the standing reserve are the pieces of standing reserve. Their constancy consists in the orderable replaceability of the steadily equivalent [*ständige Gleiche*], which is in place and at the ready" (*GA* 79: 40/38).

But we fail to think replacement and replaceability when we think of one item taking the place of another. This view of replacement which imagines it along the lines of a serial progression still operates on a model of discretion, one item being replaced by another item separate from it. The replacement of the standing reserve is far more uncanny than this. The replaceability of the standing reserve is a replaceability where *the standing reserve is so available as to be already replaced.* The standing reserve is successive, it is in motion, *inclined,* but now we see where this motion points: back to itself, or rather, out ahead to itself. The piece of standing reserve is always already drawn toward its replacement. The stock of items is already here replacing the item, and this whole movement is written into the item itself. The item that is here *is not here* insofar as it is also over there, in the storehouse, over there, on the trucks, and here before the one who orders it. The pieces are so orderable that they have been ordered already in essence. Removing the item from the cycle of replacement deprives the item of its being, because the being of the standing reserve lies only in being-replaced. Everything exists as en route to replacement.

Because the standing reserve is utterly available for immediate ordering, there is no opportunity for concealment with it. The standing reserve is *essentially essenceless,* nothing is withheld from view. As such, the pieces of the standing reserve can be surveilled at a glance and completely known. They are what they are and nothing more. They are fully present and at the ready for our evaluation. Due to their overt presencing we are able to assess them with certainty. There is nothing concealed to escape the assessment. As such, the standing reserve becomes a stock of secured and certain value. At this moment it becomes replaceable by whatever else is of equal value:

> everything is imposed upon for the constant replaceability of the equivalent by the equivalent [*des Gleichen durch Gleiches*]. Only in this way does positionality remain completely reaped into the constancy of its drive. Positionality reaps everything orderable in advance into the equivalence

> of the unrestricted orderability of the complete standing reserve. A constantly exchangeable equivalence holds equally in everything constant. The equivalence of value in everything constant secures for this its constancy through a replaceability that is orderable and in place. The standing reserve consists of the requisitioning of positionality. In the standing reserve everything stands in equal value. (*GA* 79: 44/42)

Where the thing essences, there is an ineluctable withholding, a concealment, an essential relation to the world beyond the thing's own bounds. Simply put, the thing is not all there for the assessment, eluding perfect valuation and evading the surety of replacement. The thing is singular through this essencing, not so the standing reserve. Instead, the pieces are lodged within the circuitry of positionality so as to facilitate their immediate exchange and replacement. As Heidegger states, "piece of standing reserve means: that which is isolated, as a piece, is interchangeably confined within a requisitioning" (*GA* 79: 36–37/35). Indeed this is so much the case that this interchanging and replacing has already taken place: "One piece of standing reserve is replaceable by another. The piece as piece is *already imposed upon* for replaceability" (*GA* 79: 37/35, em).

These thoughts on the replaceability of the standing reserve culminate in the 1969 seminar in Le Thor, France, with the arresting (well-nigh Baudrillardian) claim that "today being is being-replaceable [*Ersetzbarsein*]" (*GA* 15: 369/FS 62). What exists is produced from the very outset to be replaced: "A piece of clothing is no longer changed as soon as and because it has become damaged, but rather because it has the essential character of being 'the outfit of the moment in expectation of the next'" (*GA* 15: 369/FS 62). The outfit of the moment urges toward the next one, itself only a spasm of stock. The replacement found in circulation is so total as to do away with the notion of an original, insofar as the original is held to be a point of distinction, a moment discrete from all those that succeed it.

As always on the way to replacement, the item's replacement is already here—it is the item itself. Replaceability is an ontological determination. "It is essential for every being of consumption," Heidegger writes, "that it *be already* consumed and thus call for its becoming replaced" (*GA* 15: 369/FS 62, tm). To be already consumed is to call for *becoming* replaced, not *being* replaced (the latter entailing a serial movement of replacement). There is no end to replacement, never a final exchange of item for item, only this unending slippage and dispersal. The disintegration (indiscretion) of the standing reserve necessarily leads to this obscene and constant replacing, with each item so available as to almost slip through one's fingers in the constancy of its revolving replacement.

Replacement brings no relief or reprieve; it is a replacement without replacement.

Otherwise stated, the standing reserve is eternally consumed. It is a commodity in this regard, the stuff of constant consumption. Heidegger, too, will think the standing reserve in just these terms. In a marginal note to "The Question Concerning Technology" where the discussion is of the needs or wants (*Bedürfnisse*) that technology serves, Heidegger remarks: "(economy—fulfillment of demand—consumption [*Konsum*]) industry. *An increased consumption potential* [Konsumspotential]" (*GA* 7: 8 n. a). The standing reserve is not a resource in the sense of something that would satisfy a need, but rather something that would maintain it. If it serves at all, the standing reserve serves consumer demand and its increase (beyond all "need" we might say). In some notes on machine technology, the point is more direct: "With the production of force [*Krafterzeugung*, a leading characteristic of the machine for Heidegger] there goes together the production of *needs* [*Bedürfniserzeugung*], not first as a consequence of the production of force but as its essence" (*GA* 76: 308). The needs produced are needs for consumption. In Heidegger's late consideration of technology, the 1969 seminar in Le Thor, this consumptive character of the standing reserve plays a predominant role. Heidegger there remarks of this transformation into commodity that "the further that modern technology unfolds, the more does objectivity transform into standing reservedness (into a holding-at-one's-disposal). Already today there are no longer objects (no beings, insofar as these would stand against a subject taking them into view)—there are now only standing reserves (*beings that are held in readiness for being consumed*)" (*GA* 15: 367–368/FS 61, em). This ontological dimension of consumption leads Heidegger to take a jab at contemporary anti-consumerism as well: "Did the slogans of May 1968 against consumer society go so far as to recognize in consumption the current countenance of being?" (*GA* 15: 369/FS 62).

This shift into commodity claims the human. One does not simply consume commodities and walk away unscathed. One becomes part of the circulatory process, or rather a *piece* of this. Heidegger's example is the radio listener:

> Every radio listener who turns its dial is isolated in the piece character
> of the pieces of the standing reserve, isolated as a piece of the stand-
> ing reserve, in which he remains confined even if he still thinks he is
> entirely free to turn the device on and off. . . . Let us again suppose,
> indeed, a more unlikely case, that suddenly everywhere across the earth
> the radio receivers were to disappear from every room—who would
> be able to fathom the cluelessness, the boredom, the emptiness that

> would attack the human at a stroke and would completely dishevel their
> everyday affairs? (*GA* 79: 38–39/36–37)

Nothing exists outside of the circulation of standing reserve. Without the radio would this humanity exist? Heidegger's answer is cagey, yet clarifying, "they are in their essence already imposed upon with the character of having to be a piece of standing reserve [*Bestandstück zu sein*]" (*GA* 79: 39/36). The temporality of the claim is noteworthy: *already* they are imposed upon *to be* a piece of standing reserve: *already/to-be*. Essentially, humanity is in danger of becoming pieces of standing reserve. Essentially, it always has been. It is already in danger from the start and the danger is likewise what is to come. Already they are to be pieces of the standing reserve—nothing else was ever known.

The circulation of standing reserve is endless. From the outset the standing reserve is made available for immediate ordering, transitioning along supply chains and depending on these for its very existence. This circle may be an endless line, a line that chases itself back into itself and never departs from its track to run out into the space beyond it, but there is a width to that line, the spacing of a limit. The circle does not simply run into itself perpetually, it also runs alongside what lies outside it, brushes against this even, try as it might to deny it. The sides of the circle touch out upon the world. In other words, if a circle is seen as enclosing a circular space, then that same limit of enclosure is equally an interface with the world beyond.[23] Even the circulation of standing reserve in positionality, then, is exposed to what lies beyond it. The tracks of circulation can never be so complete as to eliminate this facet of existence. This fact would seem to motivate an alteration that Heidegger introduces between the lecture on "Positionality" in 1949 and the published essay "The Question Concerning Technology" in 1954. It concerns the way the human is claimed by positionality and the example is that of a forester. In "Positionality" we hear that:

> The forester, for example, who surveys the felled wood in the forest and
> who to all appearances still goes along the same paths in the same way
> as his grandfather is today positioned by the lumber industry. Whether
> he knows it or not, *he is in his own way a piece of inventory in the cellulose
> stock* and its orderability for the paper that is delivered to the newspapers and tabloids that impose themselves upon the public sphere so
> as to be devoured by it. (*GA* 79: 37–38/36, em)

The forester is named a piece of the standing reserve here. By the time the revised version of this lecture was published as an essay, however, we read the following:

The forester, who surveys the felled wood in the forest and who to all appearances still goes along the same forest paths in the same way as his grandfather, is today positioned by the lumber industry, whether he knows it or not. He is arranged into the orderability of cellulose, which for its part is challenged forth by the demand for paper that is delivered to the newspapers and tabloids. These however set upon the public opinion, to swallow what is printed, so as to make orderable an ordered configuration of opinions. Indeed precisely because the human is challenged forth more originarily than natural energy, namely into positionality, *does he never become mere standing reserve. (GA 7: 18–19/ QCT 18, tm, em)*

We need not choose one of these versions over the other. Paradoxically enough, they are not mutually exclusive. The human does indeed become a piece of the standing reserve, but there is no standing reserve so completely challenged forth as to simply be standing reserve and nothing more. This is the nature of the ontological transformation that has taken place through positionality. That the challenge is never complete means there is always more to challenge forth, always the possibility for new breakthroughs and technological developments to challenge existence ever further in unexpected ways. The possibility of such progress is consequently a testament to its own impossible completion. A trace of the thing persists in the standing reserve—otherwise there would be no challenge—just as a trace of the standing reserve will inhabit the thing.

§5. The Atomic Bomb

The most devastating consequence of positionality is the advent of the atomic bomb. With this, destruction is available on command and the attendant threat of destruction hangs over all that is. Its achievement requires an advanced physics operating at the atomic level. It also requires a peculiar brand of energy. For Heidegger, the equation is simple: atomic energy is atomic destruction. This is the consummation of the circulative replacement of positionality. Energy is the ultimate standing reserve, all that is converts to it. The world of energy reserves is no world at all, but an unworld. In the deployment of atomic energy, the world becomes a "desert." In the desert, all that is exists as threatened. Nature becomes energy becomes threatened becomes desert.

The challenge that technology places upon nature to show itself as utterly available, likewise "places the demand on nature that it deliver energy, which, as such, can be expedited along and stored" (*GA* 7: 15/

QCT 14, tm). The conversion into energy is a defining characteristic of positionality. Indeed, nature is so thoroughly relegated into the delivery of energy that it now only exists as "the main storehouse of energy reserves [*Hauptspeicher des Energiebestandes*]" (*GA* 7: 22/*QCT* 21, tm), or as he puts it in "Releasement," a few years later, "a gigantic gasoline station" (*GA* 16: 523/*DT* 50). As a result, we cannot construe nature as somewhere outside of technology, somewhere otherwise safe that is now encroached upon by an over-zealous technology. Rather, nature is already claimed by technology.[24] Nature "does not at all stand over against technology as an object that is opportunely exploited. In the world era of technology, nature belongs in advance in the standing reserve of the orderable within positionality" (*GA* 79: 41–42/39). A marginal note to this claim simply reads "atomic physics" (*GA* 79: 42 n. q/39 n. 15).

Atomic physics is the means by which nature becomes destruction. Indeed, western thinking celebrates "its ultimate triumph" insofar as it has "compelled nature into relinquishing atomic energy" (*GA* 79: 88/84). In "Positionality," Heidegger traces the path of the requisitioning of this energy from the air we breathe to atomic destruction. He states, "even the tending of the fields [*die Feldbestellung*] has gone over to the same requisitioning [*Be-Stellen*] that imposes upon the air for nitrogen, the soil for coal and ore, the ore for uranium, the uranium for atomic energy, and the latter for orderable destruction. Agriculture is now a mechanized food industry . . . the same as the production of hydrogen bombs" (*GA* 79: 27/26–27).[25] The bombs harness atomic energy and embody destruction on demand. All that is empowers its own destruction.

Nevertheless, while Heidegger is cognizant of "the hydrogen bomb, whose detonation, thought in its broadest possibility, could be enough to wipe out all life on earth," he still sees this detonation as a derivative event (*GA* 79: 4/4). In the opening "Point of Reference" for *Insight Into That Which Is* as a whole, he states: "The human is transfixed by what could come about with the explosion of the atomic bomb. The human does not see what for a long time now *has* already arrived and even *is* occurring, and for which the atomic bomb and its explosion are merely the latest emission" (*GA* 79: 4/4). The atomic bomb is the consequence of the shift into positionality. The horror of the bomb has been with us for some time; "what is this clueless anxiety waiting for, if the horrible [*das Entsetzliche*] *has* already occurred?" (*GA* 79: 4/4). The horror of it is precisely its displacing character. The horrible is a shift in the presencing of things: "The horrifying is what transposes [*heraussetzt*] all that is out of its previous essence. What is so horrifying? It reveals and conceals itself in the way that everything presences, namely that despite all overcoming of distance, the nearness of that which is remains outstanding" (*GA* 79:

4/4). The horror of the bomb lies in the transformation of the world into immediate (distanceless) standing reserve. The horrifying is thus ontological. The horrifying (*das Entsetzende*) "ousts" (*entsetzt*) being from the protection of the truth of being into the immediacy of the distanceless. "Ordering the standing reserve, positionality allows unconcealment and its essence to lapse into full forgetting. Positionality as the essence of being transposes being outside of the truth of its essence, ousts [*entsetzt*] being from its truth" (*GA* 79: 52/50). The truth in question here is *alêtheia*, a truth inseparable from the concealment (*lêthê*) endemic to it, a concealment that likewise entails a forgetting (*lêthê*). To oust being from its truth, i.e., from its concealment, is to render it standing reserve, where the impulse of the ousting drives these reserves into circulation.

The atomic bomb would thus culminate the unconcealment of the world, the making availabile of all that is. Without this concealment, the world becomes an unworld, the "technological landscape" that Jünger extols. The world of the bomb lacks the darkness of concealment; all that appears does so in the brightest of lights. Heidegger construes matters in just these terms in the opening lecture of the *Basic Principles of Thinking* lecture cycle. The darkness of concealment, he says, "is perhaps in play for all thinking at all times. Humans cannot set it aside. Rather they must learn to acknowledge the dark as something unavoidable and to keep at bay those prejudices that would destroy the lofty reign of the dark. Thus the dark remains distinct from the pitch-black as the mere and utter absence of light. The dark however is the secret of the light. The dark keeps the light to itself. The latter belongs to the former. Thus the dark has its own limpidity" (*GA* 79: 93/88). This darkness is precisely what the atomic bomb targets, it seeks sheer brightness independent of any darkness: "The light is no longer an illuminated clearing, when the light diffuses into a mere brightness, *'brighter than a thousand suns.'* It remains difficult to guard the limpidity of thinking, i.e., to keep at bay the admixture of the brightness that does not belong and to find the brightness that is alone fitting to the dark" (*GA* 79: 93/88–89, em). The unattributed quotation in the text ("brighter than a thousand suns") is from the *Bhagavad Gita*; Robert Oppenheimer uttered these very words at the detonation of the first atomic bomb.[26] The bomb eradicates the concealment endemic to essencing and shows everything in the stark reality of resource.

For this reason, the bomb need not explode for its effects to be felt. Two results follow from this. First, Heidegger can make the claim (as he does in the 1949 "Thing" lecture) that "within its purview, that of objects, the compelling knowledge of science has already annihilated the thing as thing long before the atomic bomb exploded. The explosion of the atomic bomb is only the crudest of all crude confirmations of an annihilation of things that occurred long ago: confirmation that the thing as thing remains nullified" (*GA* 79: 9/8). In other words, modern science already destroyed the world prior to the first detonation of the bomb. Second, Heidegger can likewise proffer the seemingly incompatible claim that the bomb was already detonated long ago, some 320 years prior, in fact! In the 1951 Zürich seminar he states: "The atomic bomb exploded long ago; namely at the moment that the human stood in insurrection against being and posited being from out of himself and made it the object of his representing. This since Descartes" (*GA* 15: 433). Modern natural science nullified things long before the bomb exploded, though the bomb exploded with modern natural science.[27]

Consequently, Heidegger will claim in the 1966 *Spiegel* interview that "we don't need an atom bomb at all; the uprooting of human beings is already taking place" (*GA* 16: 670/*HNS* 55). But here, the reason we do not need the bomb is because its effects have already been felt as positionality. We do not need the bomb to detonate at all for this. In fact, Heidegger will go so far as to mark the effect of the bomb to lie more in its non-detonation than in its militarized deployment. In the 1955 "Releasement" lecture, in a discussion of new scientific advances whereby chemists are close to synthesizing living substance, he notes: "We do not stop to consider that an attack with technological means is being prepared upon the life and nature of man compared with which the explosion of the hydrogen bomb means little. For precisely if the hydrogen bombs do *not* explode and human life on earth is preserved, an uncanny change in the world moves upon us" (*GA* 16: 525/*DT* 52).

When the bombs do not explode we live under their threat, and it is this threat that effects the grand changes in question. For the atomic bomb unleashes atomic energy, the energy of all that is, and the nuclear destruction that it promises encompasses us and our lives as well. For the Heidegger of the "fundamental ontology" period, this was the mark of a properly metaphysical question, one that calls the self into question as one being amid beings as a whole. With the atomic bomb, the question becomes pressing, threateningly oppressive. Now the very fact that something does indeed exist is testament to the equally brute "fact" *that we have not destroyed it.* That is to say, the entire world, all that exists, now shows itself as *indebted to us in its very existence.* Existence under this threat is its way of being. It flees the threat by running headlong into the circuitry of circulative replacement, guaranteeing itself a ghostly constancy across an unrelenting consumption.

Otherwise put, the atomic disaster that has already happened has been the conversion of all that is into energy. All specificity beyond the quantitative is lost in this, though, to be sure, the mathematics involved well surpasses any simple thinking of discrete "quantities." Everything is capable of rendering energy, as everything is "atomic." The energy that is drawn out of everything is likewise the same energy—there is no qualitative distinction to be had here. The homogeneity of energy renders it without assignable location, place, or home. As we have already noted, energy courses along a network of circuitry and *is* only in this circulation of charge. But this charge permeates the circuit as a whole, is nothing discrete. To localize the charge would be to objectify it. The energetic charge of the standing reserve is everywhere along and throughout the circuitry. Without those circuits, there is no energy. The charge exists only as confined in this circuitry. And this charge is nothing but the mis-named "objects" or "pieces" around us. This energy is homeless in another way, too. As Heidegger remarks, "soon the procurement of the new energies will no longer be tied to certain countries and continents, as is the occurrence of coal, oil, and timber. In the foreseeable future it will be possible to build atomic power stations anywhere on earth" (*GA* 16: 523–24/*DT* 51). There is no regional or local limitation to the obtaining of energy; atoms are everywhere.

Heidegger sees in this seemingly innocuous conversion into energy a devastation of the earth. When he writes that "through such requisitioning the land becomes a coal reserve, the soil an ore depository" (*GA* 79: 27/26), a marginal note to the passage adds, "the soil, land—homelessness [*Heimatlose*] of the standing reserve!" (*GA* 79: 27, n. a/26 n. 1). The *Spiegel* interview carries on the lament: "technology tears people away and uproots them from the earth more and more" (*GA* 16: 670/*HNS* 55). Nothing and no one belong to any particular place any more than to any other place. "We only have purely technological conditions left. It is no longer an earth on which human beings live today" (*GA* 16: 670/*HNS* 55). Instead, it is a desert.

Atomic energy effects the ultimate conversion of all that is into so much distinctionless, suppliable, circulating energy, and in so doing it transforms the world into a desert (*Wüste*). Heidegger terms this a "devastation," *Verwüstung*, literally a "becoming desert" or "desertification": "'Devastation' means for us, after all, that everything—the world, the human, and the earth—will be transformed into a desert" (*GA* 77: 211/136). Heidegger notes in *What Is Called Thinking?* that "the Sahara in Africa is only one kind of desert" (*GA* 8: 31/30, tm). The other is explored in the "Evening Conversation in a Prisoner of War Camp in Russia between a Younger and an Older Man." The younger man explains: "the geographical concept of the desert is just the not yet sufficiently thought-out idea of desolation, which proximally and thus mostly comes into our view only in particular circumstances and conditions of the surface of the earth" (*GA* 77: 212/137, tm). We think the desert of the earth, in other words, on the basis of our concept of desolation, wherein the desert is thought of as a boundless expanse hostile to life. The older man says as much in the conversation: "We are thus transferring the geographical idea of a desert, for example the Sahara, onto the process of the desolation of the earth and of human Dasein" (*GA* 77: 212/137, tm). For the younger man: "The desert is the wasteland [*die Öde*]: the deserted vastness of the abandonment of all life; an abandonment which reaches so deep, that the wasteland does not allow what emerges from itself to unfold itself in its emergence and in this unfolding call others into the co-emergence. The desolation [*Verödung*] reaches so wide, that it likewise allows no more perishing [*Untergehen*]" (*GA* 77: 212/137, tm). What grows does so in an open expanse, as we shall see in the next chapter. The desert qua wasteland prohibits this, allowing only the persistence of what is adapted to its disastrous conditions.

Such devastation "is not exhausted by what is visible and tangible. It can also never be accounted for by an enumeration of instances of destruction and the obliteration of human lives, as if it were only the result of these" (*GA* 77: 207/133). It is something larger than this. Indeed, its effects are so large, in fact, as to encompass World War II: "the World War, for its part, would be already and only a consequence of the devastation [*Verwüstung*], which has undermined the earth for centuries" (*GA* 77: 211/136, tm). As we have already discussed how the commodification of positionality transcends any distinction between times of war and times of peace, it should come as no surprise to find Heidegger averring a few years later, while commenting on Nietzsche's claim that "the desert is growing," that "the devastation of the earth can easily go hand in hand with a guaranteed supreme living standard for man, and just as easily with the organized establishment of a uniform state of happiness for all men" (*GA* 8: 31/30). For all its devastation, life can be quite comfortable in the desert. The desert maintains itself and persists.

Thus we would do wrong to think this devastation as an annihilation (*Vernichtung*) of the world. This is not the becoming of a nothingness; something yet remains. Devastation is a transformation, to be sure, but no annihilation. There is little solace in this, however, as devastation is far more unsettling than annihilation ever could be: "Devastation [*Verwüstung*] is more uncanny [*unheimlich*] than mere annihilation [*bloße Vernichtung*]. Mere annihilation sweeps aside all things including even nothingness, while devastation on the contrary orders [*bestellt*] and spreads everything that blocks and prevents" (*GA* 8: 31/29–30, tm). Devastation is transformative, not annihilative, and it leaves us behind in its wake.

The circulation of the standing reserve is the becoming energy of all that is. The effect of this is consummated in the atomic bomb—not in its detonation, but in its threat. The threat of nuclear annihilation unseats everything, ousts it from its truth, from the mediation that buffers it and eases it into its place in the world. This place is lost in the immediacy of circulation. All that is exists as threatened by a threat that does not fall on it from without, for the bomb was already operative with modernity. At once, it has already exploded and has no need to explode. To annihilate the world would bring a chilling peace. Annihilation brings relief. There would be nothing more to decide, nothing more to defend or protect, no more responsibility of any sort. Annihilation would be the ultimate affirmation of metaphysics, its own reversal, whereby the privilege would no longer fall to presence but to absence, absence in its sheerest form as pure annihilation. But this way is barred to us. Instead, we have entered a state beyond the strictures of modern metaphysics, beyond the opposition of presence and absence. Whatever now exists does so thanks to the fact *that we have not annihilated it.* It exists as utterly at our disposal; i.e., it exists as standing reserve. The bomb brings to light our threatened condition, the condition of the age: "The being (*Sein*) of an age of devastation would then consist precisely in the abandonment of being" (*GA* 77: 213/138).

And yet, we have already seen that abandonment is not isolation, that abandonment names a relation. The acknowledgment of this relationality effects a change in our relation to technology itself. Technology can never complete itself in either annihilation or consummate presence. Heidegger explains this in "The Danger":

> Thus in the essence and reign of positionality, the arrival of the worlding of world is withheld. Yet precisely this event of the withholding of world maintains a hidden distance to the worlding of world.
>
> In positionality as the completed destiny of the forgetting of the essence of being, a ray from the distant arrival of world inconspicuously shines. Insofar as world refuses its worlding, what happens with world is not nothing, but rather from refusal there radiates the lofty nearness of the most distant distance of world. (*GA* 79: 52–53/50)

The abandonment of being that devastates the earth under the threat of atomic destruction, converting all that is into so much standing reserve, cannot eradicate all distance. The distant still shines through it, a point he returns to in "The Turn," the concluding lecture of the Bremen cycle. Heidegger claims here: "And nevertheless—in all this disguising of positionality, the glimmer of world still lights up, the truth of beyng flashes" (*GA* 79: 75/71).

Toward the close of the Bremen lectures, the question is posed as to whether we correspond with this gleam that flashes up in technology. Do we correspond to it "by a glancing that glances into the essence of technology and perceives in it beyng itself?" (*GA* 79: 77/73). To do so would be to cancel the "forgetting of the essence of beyng" cited above. It would be to remember the mediacy of things, that things are not simply present at our disposal, that things begin at their limits, that even the cycles of circulation sketch their own limits, and that all these limits are interfaces with a beyond, with the distant. To comport oneself toward the non-present, to remember, and to think the limit, all of this is contained in that single word of Heidegger's inherited from Hölderlin, *An-denken*, thoughtful remembrance. It is a notion to which we shall have opportunity to return in what follows. Put in terms of the desert with which we have concerned ourselves: "Devastation is no mere turning to sand. Devastation is the high speed expulsion of Mnemosyne" (*GA* 8: 31/30, tm).

Having addressed the technological challenge faced by things, the threat of their transformation into standing reserve, we turn now to the thing in its relationality. More specifically, we turn to each of the four elements that compose the relational thing: earth, sky, divinities, and mortals. Unpacking Heidegger's remarks on these will ultimately unfurl the landscape of the late Heidegger, one in which the thing may be at home, not apart from technology, but in the midst of it. After these necessarily sprawling and far-reaching analyses are complete, we will recompose the fourfold to understand its role in the thinging of the thing. The conclusion of all this will finally address the relation between standing reserve and thing broached in the above. We turn first to the earth.

2

Earth, Bearing and Fructifying

Within the fourfold, the earth names what we might traditionally think of as the "material basis" of the thing. Such a claim can only be maintained if we understand "material" and "basis" in ways quite distinct from their traditional employ in the history of philosophy. That is to say, strictly speaking, the earth is neither "material" nor a "basis." The role of the earth within the fourfold transforms all our usual expectations of what counts as earthen or even earthly, for the "matter" of the earth is nothing other than phenomenality as such. So "earth" does indeed name the constituency of things, but what constitutes the thing is sensuous appearance. The "matter" of experience is phenomenality. This sensuous phenomenality of things, their way of being in the world, is their shine, gleam, and radiance. The earth names nothing burdensome, unless it is the reluctance of this simple shining itself to appear as anything stable and fixed. If we say the earth is material, we must think that "material" as phenomenal radiance.

And similarly for any notion of a "basis" in the earth. Heidegger's sense of earth runs counter to the thought of a present basis, either for the life that would support itself upon it or the forms that would adopt it as their matter. This phenomenal character of the earth is not a basis because it does no work of grounding. The earth refuses this grounding role. If appearance is to shine and radiate through the world, then it cannot be tethered and chained to a ground. The earth as appearance must then be groundless, or, rather, neither grounding nor groundless, but something "between" these two and outside their oppositional polarity. For this reason Heidegger speaks of the earth as an "abyss" rather than a ground. All the earth bears is phenomenal and the phenomenal is all it can bear without becoming ground. The substantive requires grounds, the phenomenal does not. From this conception of earth as phenomenal appearing (no *fundamentum inconcussum*), Heidegger sketches a new vision of nature, encompassing rocks and waters, flora and fauna.

Heidegger famously first introduced a new conception of the earth in his essay "The Origin of the Work of Art" of 1936. (The first elaboration is dated as early as 1931.)[1] This is not to say that the fourfold is already present in the artwork essay—it is not—but the role that the earth plays there prepares it for eventual inclusion in the fourfold in 1949. Before turning to the fourfold, then, some brief remarks on the situation of the earth within this earlier essay are in order.

From the first elaboration of the essay through to its published version, earth is understood in a tense relation with world. Heidegger's breakthrough in this essay—Gadamer called it "surprising"—is to think withdrawal as integral to world and to name that withdrawal "earth."[2] While one of the pillars of *Being and Time* is the interpretation of truth as unconcealment, from the Greek *alêtheia* (*Unverborgenheit*), the shift in Heidegger's thinking around the time of the artwork essay (mid-1930s) could be said to follow from the realization that this "un" of unconcealment is perhaps too strictly demarcated. In place of a simple opposition between concealment and unconcealment, Heidegger's thinking now turns to the idea of "withdrawal" (*Entzug*). The logic of this withdrawal is articulated in the notebooks of the time, *The Contributions to Philosophy (Of the Event)*, but this withdrawal also makes its appearance in the artwork essay under the rubric of the earth.

Here, the earth is the necessary attendant of worldly appearance. Heidegger takes as his example a Greek temple to show how the earth localizes and organizes the space and beings around it. The storm raging around it, the light of day, the breadth of the sky, the darkness of night, the surge of the tide, the raging surf, the trees and grass, the animals and insects, all of this comes forth within the ambit of the temple. This temple is a work and as such it opens a world. But this opening is no longer thought against a *background* of closure or concealment. Instead, what is revealed within the opening of world is closure itself, a paradoxical closure that Heidegger terms the "earth." Paradoxical because this earth *reveals* itself as the sensuous shine of things, a shine that withdraws from all efforts to contain it, as we shall see.

The artwork opens up a world, organizes a cluster of meaningful relationships around it, but does so through the presentation of something that cannot be grasped: the earth as sensuous appearing. This correlation of withdrawal and appearance moves past the simple opposition of concealment/unconcealment to think the destabilization of both of these, their interdependence as well as their antagonism. Heidegger terms it their strife (*Streit*): "The opposition of world and earth is a strife. . . . In essential strife however the contestants [*Streitenden*] raise each other respectively to the self-pronouncement of their essence. . . . In strife *each bears the other* [*trägt jedes das andere*] out beyond itself" (*GA* 5: 35/26–27, tm, em). The earth represents the appearance of a kind of withdrawal at the heart of the world and it is precisely this that the artwork stages. Heidegger goes on to show how the artwork serves to inaugurate or institute the destiny of a historical people.

While the discussions that follow will take recourse to this conception of earth within "The Origin of the Work of Art," it is worth mentioning at the outset some of the major differences between this account and that of the earth within the fourfold. The most obvious difference lies in the earth's relationship to the world. In the artwork essay, the earth is on equal footing with the world, is its partner in the "conflict" that opens a space for the dwelling of a historical people. By the time of the fourfold, the earth has lost this privileged position. It is no longer the sole antagonist of the world, but a participant along with the sky, divinities, and mortals in the worlding of the world. More precisely, it shares in the thinging of the thing, which itself then throws open a world. In short, the earth/world dualism of the artwork essay is abandoned in favor of a more fractured or differentiated conception of worlding. A second point to note is that the relationship of earth and world is no longer that of a "conflict." As we shall see in considering the relationship between thing and world in chapter six, the earth dances in things and these in turn gesture forth the world. Lastly, though such a list could continue, the purview of the earth is somewhat more restricted by the time of the fourfold. In the artwork essay, earth included practically all existence; indeed, the second, Freiburg lecture version of the essay (1935) identifies earth with *physis* as such (UK 2: 26). By the time of the fourfold, the conception of the earth is more refined. Most importantly, it is disambiguated from the sky, which now stands as a separate member of the fourfold, for reasons we will attend to in the next chapter.[3]

Despite these rather large scale differences, it is in the artwork essay that the role of the earth is first broached by Heidegger. Indeed, it is perhaps only a slight exaggeration to say that the rethinking of earth that transpires there ultimately demands a rethinking of finite existence as such. A marginal note to "The Origin of the Work of Art" gestures in this direction. To the statement *"The work lets the earth be an earth,"* Heidegger comments (at the first occurrence of the word "earth"): "meaning? cf. 'The Thing': the fourfold" (*GA* 5: 32 n. c/24 n. c). Remaining true to this earth, then, would require a thinking of the fourfold, to which we now will turn.

The presentations of the fourfold in "The Thing" (1949) and "Building Dwelling Thinking" (1951) are in the earth's case quite similar. In "The Thing" the passage reads:

> earth is the building bearer, what nourishingly fructifies, tending waters and stone, plants and animals. (*GA* 79: 17/16)

and in "Building Dwelling Thinking" it reads:

> earth is the serving bearer, what bloomingly fructifies, spread out in stone and waters, rising up into plants and animals. (*GA* 7: 151/*PLT* 149, tm)

While one might be tempted to see a change to greater activity in the second case—the earth is presented as "blooming" instead of "nurturing," "rising up" instead of "tending"—or perhaps a change to greater passivity—the second text demotes the earth from its role as "building" to one of "serving"—the two presentations are complements of the same earth. The earth is a bearer (*Tragende*), the earth is fructifying (*Fruchtende*), the earth is the inorganic (stones and waters) as well as what we call the flora and fauna (Heidegger's locution, *Gewächs und Getier*, avoids the Latin). We shall examine each of these in turn.

The supposed "material basis" of things is a groundless bearing of fructifying phenomenality. What we would think to be the most fundamental aspect of things is the very *appearing* of these things themselves in all their sensuousness. This groundless or abyssal structure of the earth informs Heidegger's understanding of natural phenomena at the time of the fourfold.

§6. Abyssal Bearing

Fundamentally, the earth is a bearer (*die Tragende*). That which bears lends support, it holds something up or out. But bearing in this case cannot be thought of as a grounding, if by "grounding" one understands what is grounded to rest on solid ground or *terra firma*. Rather, bearing names a "groundless" grounding, and the paradox in this is that each time such a groundless bearing takes place upon the earth. As we shall see, the earth is not thought by Heidegger to be a solid ground, a ground that would be present and accounted for. Instead, the earth is thought in terms of a withdrawal. "Bearing" names an ungrounded presencing, a presencing whose ground has been withdrawn. Bearing designates a complication in the work of grounding such that the borne and the bearer are spotted in their mutual need of each other. A brief survey of Heidegger's deployment of the term and root "*tragen*" will make this evident.

From the time of its introduction, the earth is tied to the notion of ground. All three versions of "The Origin of the Work of Art"—the first elaboration, the Freiburg lecture, and the published version (the Frankfurt lecture)—proclaim the earth a "self-enclosing ground" (*UK1*: 20/344, *UK2*: 40, *GA* 5: 63/47, tm). Indeed, if we understand the earth as holding an intimate relation to *physis*—and the Freiburg lecture "Of the Origin of the Work of Art" identified the earth with *physis,* a claim rather tempered in the published version (cf. *UK2*: 26 and *GA* 5: 28/21)— then we might understand Heraclitus's famed maxim that nature loves to hide in the terms that Heidegger proposes for the earth.[4] Heidegger himself makes the connection, something likewise omitted from the published text: "this is the essence of the earth: the essentially self closing. *physis kryptesthai philei*—what emerges has the urge to keep itself closed" (*UK2*: 32).[5] The key for Heidegger is that it is precisely this concealment that is brought forth as the earth. This touches upon a central tenet of Heidegger's thinking from the middle period onward. What is concealed must announce its concealment. The earth can only be self-concealing by announcing itself as such and it does so in the world. The difficulty here is two-pronged: if the concealed ground is simply revealed, then it would no longer be concealed; and if this ground were to be entirely concealed then one could not speak of it. What is required is a revealing or announcement of this self-concealing ground which, paradoxically enough, allows it to remain self-concealed. The concealed ground must announce itself, and it does so in a particular being, signally a work of art. What this peculiar ground requires, then, is that it itself be grounded.

This reciprocal relationship between grounded and ground, where the ground needs what it grounds in order to be grounding, is what Heidegger means by "bearing."[6] The situation is first explained as one of bearing in the Freiburg lecture (second version) "Of the Origin of the Work of Art," in a discussion of the poetic project that likewise holds for all of art:

> The true poetizing project is much more the opening of that wherein Dasein as historical has already been thrown. And this is the earth and for a people always its earth, the self closing ground that it rests upon with all that which—still hidden from itself—it already is. Thus this endowment must be pulled up here into the project and properly be set upon this ground. In this way *the ground is first grounded as a bearing ground* and pulled into the open of Dasein. (*UK2*: 40–42, em)[7]

The people has been thrown into this self-secluding and closed ground, thrown upon an earth that is its own. What lies in this hiddenness must be taken up into a project, but this cannot be understood as simply making the implicit explicit, for what is taken up out of the earth must nonetheless be set upon this earth as ground. It must remain grounded in hiddenness even while appearing as project. The project of a people is thus not merely a matter of bringing to light what was otherwise concealed;

it is a grounding of what comes to light as project, but a grounding of it upon this concealed ground. As such, it is a grounding of that same concealed ground which is now allowed to appear in the project. (The published version says it comes to appear in the world; cf. *GA* 5: 63/47.) This is what it means for the ground itself to be "grounded as a bearing ground [*tragender Grund*]" (*UK2*: 42).

The ground itself must be grounded, and not by some deeper or more stable ground, but rather in the work. There is no ground prior to the grounding—the ground does not "become" the bearing ground, it is already such *as ground*. What is grounded in the grounding action of the work is the ground itself (as bearing ground). If it is said that the ground grounds the work, then it can just as easily be said that the work grounds the ground. Bearing is the reciprocality of grounding: ground and grounded are held together in a bearing. All grounding is a bearing, where bearing names a grounding whose ground does not precede its grounding in a work.

This non-ground in need of ground provides no footing, not even the comfort of an utter absence of ground. Instead, it is rightly called an abyss (*Abgrund*), as Heidegger explained in the early versions of the artwork essay. These speak of the earth as "a ground which, as it is essentially and always self-secluding, is an abyss [*Ab-grund*]" (*UK1*: 11/335, tm; cf. *UK2*: 32). Bearing names the hold of things in the abyss. Indeed, only on the "basis" of this abyss—neither absent nor present ground—could there be any bearing at all. The ground of the earth, the earth that bears, is an abyss.

The contemporaneous *Contributions to Philosophy* takes up these notions of a self-concealing ground and an abyss. Here Heidegger speaks of Dasein as taking over a place in the midst of beings (similar to what we have previously cited in terms of the formulation of a project for a people) and names this taking over a suffering wherein "the self-closing opens itself as the bearing-binding [*Tragend-Bindende*]" (*GA* 65: 260/204, tm). One must suffer through this bearing and endure its ambivalence as both grounding and grounded. One must suffer the abyss, for as Heidegger writes, "the abyss is the original essencing of the ground" (*GA* 65: 379/264, tm). As we have noted, this abyss is not a ground, but neither is it groundless—indeed the abyss is "fully distorted" when construed as an "un-ground" (*GA* 65: 380/300, tm)—for there is a bearing that takes place upon it. Instead, we have to think this abyss otherwise: "the abyss is the remaining-away [*Weg-bleiben*] of the ground" (*GA* 65: 379/299, tm). To remain away is not to be nothing, assuredly. It names a relationship to a departure. This abyssal remaining-away of ground is the earth as bearer.

Immediately after this claim, Heidegger asks, "and what is the ground? It is that which veils itself and also takes up, because it bears and does so as the protruding of what is to be grounded. Ground: self-concealing in a protruding that bears" (*GA* 65: 379/300). What this passage indicates is that concealment is something that itself must be borne. The same structure is operative here as was the case in "The Origin of the Work of Art": the ground must itself be grounded and what protrudes or towers up from the ground must nonetheless be grounded in a self-concealment of the ground as a bearing. Bearing is a way of letting concealment show itself as such, a way of letting it shine.

The relationship of bearing that Heidegger articulates as central to the earth as bearer is extended to nothing less than the relationship between being and beings in "The Onto-Theological Constitution of Metaphysics" from *Identity and Difference* (1957). In this text *tragen* plays a leading role, though now as part of the *Austrag,* a "carrying out," "execution," or "performance." In these pages, Heidegger seeks to understand a transitive sense of the verb "to be," a transitive sense of the "is" in the statement "Being is beings" (see *GA* 11: 70–71/*ID* 64). He reads this transitive sense of "being" as indicating a "going-over" (*übergehend*) to beings on the part of being itself. This is, of course, not to claim that beings existed prior to being's going-over to them, nor is one to assume that, in its going-over, being leaves its proper place behind. The case is quite the contrary. Being's proper place is in this going-over. Being comes disclosively over that which first arrives at unconcealment through such a coming over. Being comes over beings and beings endure (*ertragen*) this being. What being comes-over are beings, but these beings are not to be thought of as separated from being before this over-coming. Beings must likewise motion toward being, if we are to avoid thinking of them as themselves extant prior to being. Heidegger seeks to articulate this reciprocal relation of being and beings toward each other. For this reason, beings must be described in terms of "arrival": "Arrival means: sheltering oneself [*sich bergen*] in unconcealment: thus sheltered enduring [*anwähren*]: to be a being [*Seiendes sein*]" (*GA* 11: 71/*ID* 64, tm). Thus we have here a disclosive over-coming (*Überkommnis*) on the part of being coupled with a self-sheltering arrival into that disclosure on the part of beings.

This is where bearing arises in the text. Since the two belong so intimately together, Heidegger will talk of them as the differing partners of a differentiation (*Unter-Schied*; *GA* 11: 71/*ID* 65). The space of differentiation between them (which Heidegger designates as the "between"; *GA* 11: 71 n. 92) is where the over-coming of being and arrival of beings "are *born* [*getragen*] apart-from-one-another-to-one-another [*auseinander-zueinander*]" (*GA* 11: 71/*ID* 65, tm, em). *Austrag* names the performance or carrying out of this peculiar separating relation: "The difference of being and beings is, as the differentiation of coming-over and arrival, the disclosive-sheltering carrying out [*Austrag*] of the two" (*GA* 11: 71/*ID* 65, tm). The difference between being and beings, which lets each of them be, must itself be carried out and performed. Heidegger will not fail to name this execution a grounding, bringing us full circle: "Those which are borne apart [*Auseinandergetragenen*] are so in the tension of execution [*Austrag*], such that not only does being ground beings as their ground, but rather that the being for its part and in its way grounds being, brings it about" (*GA* 11: 75/*ID* 68–69, tm).[8] This is precisely the relation that we noted in "The Origin of the Work of Art" more than twenty years earlier, and it is what we should hear in the word "*tragen*" when the earth of the fourfold is named a bearer (*Tragende*).

But what manner of support could such a groundless bearing provide? To answer this we should first ask, what is it that actually needs grounding? If there were ground, if there were that Archimedean point of unmoving ground, all could be derived from it and grounded on it. More, all would *already* be grounded on it. If there were ground, everything would already be on the ground, there would be nowhere else for it to be. If there is ground, everything hangs from and stands upon that ground. There would be the grounded and the ungroundable. The greatest problem would be to distinguish between the two. If there is ground, *then there is no need for grounding*. This needlessness (*Notlosigkeit*) is the greatest need (*Not*), the greatest distress for Heidegger: "The greatest distress [*Not*]: The distress of distresslessness [*Notlosigkeit*]" (*GA* 65: 107/85, tm).[9] Heidegger seeks to preserve the need for ground. In effect, this is what he views as the task of philosophy during the 1930s, it is the necessity (*Notwendigkeit*) of philosophy: "The necessity of philosophy, as mindfulness [*Besinnung*], consists in not pushing aside this distress [*Not*], but rather in enduring and grounding [*ergründen*] it, to have to make it the ground of human history" (*GA* 65: 45/37, tm). The distress of there being no need for grounding, the suffering of this, the distress of the ground, paradoxically, must itself be grounded. If there is ground there is no need for grounding. This no need for grounding is the greatest distress; it is the distress of there being a ground. The task of philosophy is to confront this distress and *to ground this ground in no need of a grounding*. This is the uselessness and futility of philosophy, to ground what does not need grounding; it is also its necessity. This grounding of the ground is, as we have seen, a bearing.

Bearing operates as a technical term for Heidegger; thus it should not be taken lightly that, in the two crucial presentations of the Fourfold, the earth is each time identified as bearing. But what is it that the earth bears? The answer will take us into a consideration of the other modifier used to designate the earth, "fructifying."

§7. Fruition of the Sensible

What could a groundless ground support? The answer seems obvious: nothing. Without ground, nothing can be supported. But to speak of a "bearing" is to speak of something borne. The tension is clear: bearing would seem to require a ground, but there is no ground; the abyss would seem to support nothing, yet there is a bearing. What this abyssal bearing bears can only be something (nothing) very peculiar; something that "is" and "is not." Something that "is" because there is a bearing, something that "is not" because there is no ground. We will take these two together and claim that it is this very "is not," this remaining away which is no absence, but which nevertheless "is," that must be borne. We have seen that the earth is an abyss (*Abgrund*), a withdrawal and departure (*Ab-*) of the ground (*Grund*). We have also proclaimed that this withdrawal must appear as announced. All there is to bear is withdrawal. To ask "what is to be borne?" is to ask "how does withdrawal appear?," which is to ask at the same time "how does the appearance appear?" Given the prevailing groundlessness, the phenomenon in question cannot be anything substantial—to begin with, there is nothing beneath (*sub*) upon which to stand (*stantia*). The announcement of the abyss must take place insubstantially, in a way not tied to any substance. What could this be but a "superficial" appearance? The earth is consequently phenomenality as such, or as Heidegger puts it, the earth is "the massiveness and heaviness of stone . . . the firmness and flexibility of the wood . . . the hardness and gleam of the ore . . . the lightening and darkening of color . . . the ringing of sound" (*GA* 5: 32/24). What comes to fruition upon the bearing earth will be nothing other than the luster of the abyss itself. *Phenomenality is the announcement of the abyss.* Freed from the task of grounding, the earth is let shine.

This shine is not an appearance, if by this we mean something that would ride piggy-back upon a substance. There is no ground beneath it from which to emanate. Its depth is the depth of a refraction, the depth of shimmering color, no depth at all. The world of appearance is therefore superficial—and in a way metaphysics has never said anything other than this, in different registers, with different intents. But in this superficiality lies its profundity. The world of appearance is superficial and befuddlingly so, its sparkling gleam occludes the metaphysical thought of appearance and phenomena where these are held to be the deficient partners of a subtending reality and noumenal basis. The transformation of ground that makes of it a bearer likewise transforms what would rest upon that ground, moving it from derivative appearance to shining radiance.

And this radiance is the fruit of the earth, what comes to fruition upon its bearing ground. Its groundless superficiality is tied to a certain withdrawal and refusal, but a withdrawal that is coordinated with a blooming of phenomenality. A passage from "The Origin of the Work of Art" emphasizes just this in considering the heaviness of stone and the shine of color. As we shall have occasion to return to this passage, it is worth quoting at some length:

> A stone presses downward and announces its heaviness. But while this heaviness presses upon us it denies us any penetration into it. If we attempt such a penetration by breaking open the rock, then it never displays in its fragments anything internal and opened. The stone has instantly drawn back again into the same dull pressure and bulk of its fragments. If we try to lay hold of the stone's heaviness in another way, by placing the stone on a balance, we merely bring the heaviness into the calculation of a weight. This perhaps very precise determination of the stone remains a number, but the press of it has withdrawn from us. Color shines and wants only to shine. When we analyze it in rational terms by measuring its wavelengths, it is gone. It shows itself only when it remains undisclosed and unexplained. The earth thus allows every penetration into it to shatter upon it. It lets every merely calculating importunity upon it to turn into a destruction. (*GA* 5: 33/24–25, tm; see also *UK2*: 30–32)

Let us first note that there is nothing to be found within the earth. There is nothing beneath appearances. Nature may love to hide, but it never holds anything behind its back. All that is to be found in the earth is simply more earth, dig as one might. Yet throughout all the digging, the earth remains depthless. What is dug *up* and drawn *out* is always *in* appearance and *at* the surface. Its superficial gleam does not conceal anything behind itself. It is "pure interiority," to borrow a term from Hölderlin (*"reine Innigkeit"*), a term for *Natur*. And this despite the fact that the earth always gives itself out, always appears (and must, to be earth). The superficiality of the earth undoes these distinctions between in and out. Whatever appears does so outside of itself, as something radiant. But there is ever only appearance; even the inside must appear. The intimacy (*Innigkeit*) of the earth is such that it invites us inside. Nature is entirely superficial, for if nature is everything, then there can be nothing outside of this everything, and thus only the superficiality of a being-in. Nature is pure interiority, shining out to us.

Given this, the shining of the earth cannot be known in the way that one knows an object present-at-hand. It cannot be investigated as something simply present. Its superficiality renders it impenetrable, as there is no interior into which to penetrate. (Otherwise put, all is interior.) The earth is likewise incomprehensible. The weight of the stone, or rather the downward press of it, cannot be comprehended and completely contained in a number or figure. This would belie the radiance that is essential to the earth. What shines radiates. Untethered from ground, its superficial shine is not held in place, but reaches out. It "wants only to shine" and strives for this shining with the world as its witness. It "presses downward," moving to bring us into its relation. The scientific examination must snip this comet's tail of appearing, its radiance. But to lose this is to lose the earth.

This conception of radiant appearance remains with Heidegger in his thinking of the fourfold. The withdrawal of ground that makes of the earth a bearer is the precondition for the fruition of this radiant appearing. But formulating things this way misses the very relationship at stake. The withdrawal is not a precondition for appearing. This would be to make the abyss of the earth into a ground once more, a causal basis for a distinct event. Instead, what appears in radiance is that withdrawal itself. Withdrawal of ground does not happen somewhere behind appearances or in some noumenal realm. It happens in appearance itself. Withdrawal of ground names one side of a relationship. The withdrawal is a distance-taking. It stretches back in such a manner that allows something to come forth: the appearance. Its radiance, its streaming and gleaming, is the other side of that relation, is the same distance instituted by withdrawal. Otherwise put, withdrawal does not leave a discrete presence behind it. Withdrawal by its very nature undoes all discretion in the drawing out of a relationship. Withdrawal grants the space through which the shine of appearance radiates. Withdrawal does not make possible or bring about shining; rather *withdrawal is that shining itself.* What is borne upon the groundless ground of the abyss is nothing—the abyss can support nothing substantial. It cannot even support the announcement of the withdrawal of ground; rather, it is that announcement itself. The earth is the gleam of the abyss.

The earth as superficial and withdrawn is burdensome. The calculation of a stone's weight on a scale misses just this "press" or "burden" of it. But this burden is not limited to stones. Calculation misses what is earthen of the earth, its burden; but this is as much to be found in a color as it is in a stone. The burden is not of a specific weight but of the earth—color, too, is thus a burden, as are "the pull of the weight of the stone . . . the dumb hardness of the wood . . . the dark glow of the colors" (*GA* 5: 52/38). The burden here names the relationship that the earth bears to us, the way it reaches out to us. The pull of the earth, its drawing power, and its burdensome shining, all this we might think in terms of the earth's gravity. The earth names the gravity and weight of existence.

Heidegger had explored such notions of gravity a few year prior to his formulation of the fourfold in his 1946 essay on the poet Rilke, "What Are Poets For?" For Rilke, finite existence is something "risked" (*gewagt;* GA 5: 280–81/210) and Heidegger understands gravity as the field of relations that keeps such risked beings hanging in the balance. What hangs in the balance, weighs (*wiegt*) upon the scales. What weighs in this manner is of a certain weight (*das Gewicht*), not solely a physical weight, but also the weight of a weighty issue or heavy topic, a matter of grave concern, importance (*Wichtigkeit*), or difficulty (*Schwierigkeit*). Heidegger had drawn explicit attention to this a few years earlier in his 1941–42 lecture course on Hölderlin's hymn "Remembrance" (*Andenken*), where he writes: "What is heavy weighs down and is a burden. What is burdened becomes heavy through the burden and even sluggish [*träge*]. But 'heavy' cannot be meant here in this way. The buoying airs, light, swaying, enchanting and playing, are not heavy in the sense of the sluggish [*des Trägen*], but rather of importance, fulfillment, and the auspicious" (*GA* 52: 106). What is neither secured, nor relinquished, but held in the balances as risked, does not stand there isolated and alone. It is subject to the force of gravity (*die Schwerkraft*). Heidegger follows Rilke in thinking this gravity as a relation of connection between things. "It is the ground as the 'with,' which mediately holds the one to the other and gathers everything in the play of risking" (*GA* 5: 282/211, tm). What exists is held by the attractive force of gravity; "it is borne [*getragen*]," Heidegger says (*GA* 5: 281/210, tm). The force of gravity provides a medium between things that allows for their co-presence and mutual connection. Gravity's pull (*der Zug*) brings everything into a relation (*der Bezug*) "with" others, and Heidegger takes pains to insure that "relation" not be understood as "the human 'I' relating an object to itself" (*GA* 5: 283/212). There are neither self-enclosed I's nor objects, when thought from the perspective of gravity, risk, and relation. Instead there is the radiance of what is, the withdrawal of the earth that enables the shining of things to reach us and appeal to us, to matter to us and weigh upon us.

For Jean-Luc Nancy, thinking gravity in this way leads directly to an undoing of the sensible/super-sensible distinction. Nancy's reflections in his essay "The Weight of a Thought" are particularly helpful for thinking this Heideggerian conception of the sensible (of the earth), though Heidegger is nowhere explicitly mentioned.[10] Nancy notes that while the intelligible has typically been considered the object of thinking and the material the object of weighing, he is inquiring after "what is proper to thinking *and* to weighing, to thinking *as much as* to weighing, thus being properly neither."[11] In other words, he seeks the sensible of the intelligible and the intelligible of the sensible, the co-belonging of the two in finite existence. Yet thinking can never grasp weighing, nor weighing thinking, Nancy will claim, and this even though the two are no longer thought as separate and opposed realms of the ideal and the material. Rather the collusion of the two in existence is what lends things and thoughts their weight. The thing, the thought, these are appropriable by neither a thinking nor a weighing as traditionally practiced. This density of existence, heavier than a thought and graver than a thing, precludes complete appropriation. Nancy names this "the absolute point of inappropriability: we have no more access to the weight of meaning than (consequently) to the meaning of weight."[12] And just this inappropriability is the weight, the burden of all earthly appearance. It is the reason Heidegger says that the press (*Lasten*) of the earth presses upon us (*entgegenlastet*). Existence is thoughtworthy, questionable, ponderous. If existence were weightless—and we should here note that the world can only have a weight, can only weigh on us, because there is no ground, that only the groundless has weight—there would be nothing to appropriate. All would already be appropriated without remainder. The facts of the world are impenetrable, precisely what Heidegger says of the earth. The gleam is inappropriable and never surrenders its particular resilient impenetrability. Nancy names it an opacity: "Meaning needs a thickness, a density, a mass, and thus an opacity, a darkness by means of which it leaves itself open and lets itself be touched as meaning right there where it becomes absent as discourse."[13] Meaning needs the earth, we might say, though in the following chapters I hope to show that meaning needs the sky, the divinities, and the mortals as well.

The earth as a bearing ground is set free to shine. To think this shining earth, then, means to no longer construe it along the hackneyed oppositions of metaphysics, as the sensible subordinated to the intelligible or as a matter dominated by form. Subordinating the earth to these oppositions is just as intrusive as weighing it on a scale. Calling earth the sensible deprives it of any meaning and takes away its weight. Calling earth material confines it within form and takes away its radiance. Heidegger's objections to both of these approaches should help further refine our conception of the earth's role in the fourfold.

When the earth is approached as the sensible, it is opposed to the super-sensible. But for Heidegger the senses are not devoid of an "intelligence" or "understanding." To be sure, one can already find such a "sensible understanding" in *Being and Time*. There, it is "only because the 'senses' belong ontologically to a being whose kind of being is an attuned being-in-the-world [*befindlichen In-der-Welt-sein*] can they be 'touched' and 'have a sense for' something so that what touches them shows itself in an affect" (*GA* 2: 183/*SZ* 137). This attunement (*Befindlichkeit*) is one of Dasein's existentials, one of the ways in which "the being of the 'there' maintains itself" (*GA* 2: 190/*SZ* 142, tm). But it is not the only one. Another existential, and one just as primordial to the being of the "there" is understanding (*das Verstehen*). "Attunement always has its understanding. . . . Understanding is always attuned" (*GA* 2: 190/*SZ* 142). Thus, the senses that are able to matter to Dasein because Dasein is mooded in a world are at the same time only able to matter to Dasein within a world that is likewise understood. One could thus get the impression that in *Being and Time* the senses play a subordinate role. Since the senses must wait for a prior opening of the world before they can be touched by anything in it, they could be seen as subordinate to being-in-the-world. And, since this world is one that is opened in understanding, the senses would again appear subordinate to understanding. One need not crane too far to see in this a duplication of the metaphysical subordination of the sensible to the intelligible, i.e., a ricorso of Platonic metaphysics.

But a glance ahead to *Kant and the Problem of Metaphysics* two years later serves to throw such a hasty reading in doubt. In this text Heidegger takes an opportunity to consider the question of sense and the sense organs more thoroughly and provocatively than in *Being and Time*. To put things simply, in *Being and Time* the sense organs were said to need Dasein if they were to sense anything at all. Now in the *Kant* book Dasein is said to need the sense organs, if there is to be any "there" at all. At least that is what one may gather from passages such as the following:

> Human intuition, then, is not 'sensible' because the affection takes place through 'sense organs,' but rather the reverse. *Because our Dasein is finite*—existing in the midst of beings that already are, beings to which it has been delivered over—therefore *it must necessarily* take this already-existing being in stride (*hinnehmen*), that is to say, *it must* offer it the possibility of announcing itself. *Organs are necessary* for the possible relaying of the announcement. (*GA* 3: 26/19, em)

Here the position of *Being and Time* is modified. The world does not precede sensation and its organs, rather *as the world of finite Dasein*—as mooded world, as understood world, as world "taken in stride"—that world must be opened sensibly in and through the sense organs. The priority of understanding that one could possibly find in *Being and Time* is lost, for the sensible is just as equiprimordial as the "intelligible."

It is only a few years after this that Heidegger addresses the role of the senses in the first elaboration of the artwork essay. There Heidegger writes that "the press of a stone, the dullness of a color, the sound and flow of a sequence of words are, to be sure, not experienced without the senses, but they are never and at no time authentically experienced through these alone either. The earth in its self-closing fullness is, if this characterization says anything at all, just as much sensible as insensible" (*UK1*: 13/13, tm). Appearance is not merely physical. It is always tied to meaning. Radiance does not happen in a vacuum, it streams through a medium, and this medium is one of sense. Whatever appears does so sensibly and sensually, not as a conglomeration of the "physical" and the "intellectual," but in the simplicity of sense. And the Freiburg lecture (second version), too, explicitly states that the earth cannot be thought in terms of the sensible when this presupposes an opposition to the super-sensible. In such a case, as Heidegger explains, art would be understood as "the presentation of something supersensible in a formed sensible material" (*UK2*: 52). Heidegger objects to this characterization on the grounds that "the artwork never presents anything, for the simple reason that it never has anything that can be presented, because the work first creates that which, through the work, for the first time steps out into the open" (*UK2*: 52). The earth cannot be subordinated to the presentation of a super-sensible content, symbolic, allegorical, or otherwise. By the time of the published essay, Heidegger sees the sensible as too closely tied to the idea of brute sensation (opposed to all that is super-sensible, intellectual, spiritual). But brute sensations such as these are precisely what we do not experience: "In immediate perception, we never really perceive a throng of sensations, e.g. tones and noises. Rather, we hear the storm whistling in the chimney, the three-motored plane, the Mercedes which is immediately different from the Adler. Much closer to us than any sensation are the things themselves" (*GA* 5: 10/8). Such an interpretation of the sensible as sensation, he says, brings the thing "too close" to the body, where body is understood as brute physicality (*GA* 5: 11/8).

Moving on, Heidegger's objection to thinking the earth as material is already found in the first elaboration of the artwork essay, where we learn that the matter/form opposition is indebted to Plato and Aristotle who understand form as what completes or finishes a thing. The resulting entity is understood as fixed, something contained and confined by its form, present-at-hand in the language of *Being and Time*: "As a being, the being that is finished is always something present-at-hand" (*UK1*: 10/334, tm). Such a conception belies the concealing character of the earth, precisely by framing it within a form as something present and available. The published version of the essay goes further along these same lines, by attributing the source of the matter/form distinction not to the things around us as such—"Matter and form are in no way original determinations belonging to the thingness of the mere thing" (*GA* 5: 13/10)—but as arising within the specific horizon of craft production.

Within this horizon and as the epitome of such production, Heidegger considers the tool in order to show the way in which the earth appears (or does not appear) in this paradigmatic product of the matter/form distinction. In the tool, the earth is put into service and "used up" in the process: "The stone is employed and used up in the fabrication of a tool, an axe, for example. It disappears in serviceability [*Dienlichkeit*]. The less resistance the material puts up to being subsumed in the equipmental being of the equipment the more suitable and the better it is" (*GA* 5: 32/24, tm). The shine of the earth is restricted and the earth submerges into the goal-directed utility of the tool. If matter and form are thought from out of the tool, then there is no place in the distinction for the shine of the earth.

Nevertheless, as the artwork essay makes clear, the serviceability of tools always operates within a context of what Heidegger terms "reliability" (*Verläßlichkeit*). Reliability points to the fact that serviceability does not occur in a void, but within a horizon of cares and concerns. In the famous treatment of Van Gogh's painting of a pair of shoes, Heidegger evokes such a horizon in his description of the peasant woman's "uncomplaining worry as to the certainty of bread, wordless joy at having once more withstood want, trembling before the impending birth, and shivering at the surrounding menace of death" (*GA* 5: 19/14). The pervading uncertainty and instability is the key to the passage. Serviceability takes place in an unreliable world. More precisely, serviceability takes place in the midst of the struggle between earth and world. The earth prevents all from showing itself, appears only as withdrawing, and this destabilizes the presencing of the world. There is no certainty in this situation and hence the need for tools in the first place. To see the tool as serviceable is to lose the earth in equipmental concerns. To understand these concerns as founded upon a situation (a struggle of earth and world) that can never be stabilized is to recognize the earth once again, even in the midst of serviceability. Reliability reestablishes a connection with the earth, if only implicitly: "By force of this [reliability] and through the tool, the peasant woman is admitted into the silent call of the earth, by force of the reliability of the tool she is sure [*gewiß*] of her world" (*GA* 5: 19/14, tm). The earth that is consumed in serviceability announces itself in reliability and this reliability is all the certainty we can ever have.

The anxiety and joy of the peasant woman stands in stark contrast to the "boringly oppressive usualness [*Gewöhnlichkeit*]" (*GA* 5: 20/15) of our tool projects once reliability has dwindled away. The reliability of equipment dies in usualness. The surprise and insecurity is gone, "at the same time use itself is ground down and becomes usual" (*GA* 5: 20/15, tm). This is the "disappearance of its reliability" (*GA* 5: 20/15), a disappearance which abandons serviceability to its own devices while closing off its supervening cares and concerns. "Only blank usefulness now remains visible" (*GA* 5: 20/15, tm), and in this, the used up and abandoned tool "obtrudes itself as the sole mode of being, apparently proper to it exclusively" (*GA* 5: 20/15, tm). This is the world of *machination*, in the language of the *Beiträge*. In this common form, the tool appears as something made or completed, a formed matter, and all connection to the earth is lost.

Such an earthless and machinational paradigm becomes the usual. Heidegger sketches the attendant and far-reaching consequences of it: "If one correlates form with the rational and matter with the ir-rational, if, moreover, one takes the rational to be the logical and the irrational the illogical, and if, finally, one couples the conceptual duality between form and matter into the subject-object relation [the subject as bestower of meaning, i.e., form], then one has at one's disposal a conceptual mechanism that nothing can resist" (*GA* 5: 12/9). The forgetting of the earth sets in place a metaphysical trajectory that is yet to reach its culmination. The bearing earth comes to fruition in just such endangered sensible radiance.

§8. The Nature of the Earth

The earth is a bearing that brings to fruition a radiant phenomenality. Heidegger informs us that this manner of appearing radiates through waters, stones, plants, and animals. The earth is not only "spread out" in these, but is "tending" to them as well. What appears is neither grounded and stabilized as a fixed presence, nor ungrounded and relinquished without relations to all around it; instead it is held by the earth's gravity. The earth holds all appearances within its pull, keeping them close, drawing them into relations, and thus "tending" to them. The earth tends by bearing, as the remaining away of ground (*Ab-Grund*). In his account of the earth's place within the fourfold, Heidegger names water, stones, plants, and animals, i.e., what we customarily call "nature," inorganic and organic, non-living and living. Examining Heidegger's conception of these in the surrounding writings of the period will provide us with four examples of the earthly mode of appearing, the same way of appearing that is operative in the thing. These "natural" considerations of Heidegger's around the time of the fourfold could also be seen to dramatically break with his own earlier thinking of nature in the much discussed 1929–30 lecture course *The Fundamental Concepts of Metaphysics: World, Finitude, Solitude.*

While this lecture course is certainly Heidegger's most thoroughgoing discussion of these matters in all his work, even to the point of engaging with contemporary scientific findings, this does not warrant its adoption as Heidegger's final view on the organism or the animal, despite increasing tendencies to the contrary. The course is representative of a period that Heidegger will leave behind in the half century of creative work before him. To call to mind exactly how early this course is, let us merely note that at this time Heidegger is not yet critical of "metaphysics" as opposed to philosophy; much less has he given up philosophy in the name of "thinking." In fact, Heidegger even still considers himself a metaphysician (this is the year of the lecture "What Is Metaphysics?"). At the time of this course there is no thinking of the earth, no *Contributions to Philosophy* and its thought of withdrawal, no "On the Essence of Truth" with its reflections on untruth and errancy, no worry about planetary technology, no National Socialism or rectorship, and no glimmer of the importance of Hölderlin or poetry in general. While Heidegger's later remarks on stones, waters, plants, and animals are nowhere near as extensive as the earlier elaboration, they nonetheless mark decisive shifts away from the thought espoused in that course. Before turning to these particular later occurrences, however, a shift in position is already observable from just the description of the earth within the fourfold.

First, in his presentation of the earth's role in the fourfold (cited above) Heidegger names stones, waters, plants, and animals as part of the earth. What this means is that these all participate in the fourfold. Insofar as it is the fourfold that is gathered into the things around us, this means that stones and animals, waters and plants, all participate in the thinging of the thing. Insofar as the thinging of the thing is determinative for the worlding of the world, stones and animals, plants and waters, all participate in the worlding of the world. This is already a substantial break with the 1929–30 course's famed thesis (to be addressed in greater detail in what follows) that the stone would be "worldless," the animal "poor in world," and the human "world-forming" (*GA* 29/30: 272/184). That position is even more stridently reiterated in the 1936 "Origin of the Work of Art" where the claim is that "The stone is world-less. Similarly, plants and animals have no world; they belong rather to the hidden throng of an environment into which they have been put" (*GA* 5: 31/23). In the fourfold, plants and animals are on par with waters and stones; one is no less constitutive of world than the other. Otherwise put, world building is not a privilege of anyone, not even of the mortals. The mortals are participants in the gathering of the fourfold that things in the thing, that worlds in the world, just the same as the earth and its cast of waters, stones, plants, and animals. No one has privileged access to world here. The prior privilege of Dasein atop a hierarchy is undone by this thought. World is no longer restricted to Dasein, nor is it the antagonist of earth. World is the property or possession of no one. What we witness with the fourfold, then, in this simple listing of stones, waters, plants, and animals in considering the earth, is nothing less than a reconfiguration of Heidegger's conception of world, moving beyond his earlier treatments found in the period of fundamental ontology as well as in his middle works. The consequences of this should not be underestimated.

Second, it is worth noting that Heidegger's German identifies each of these groups—stones, waters, plants, and animals—in words that begin with a *"Ge-"* prefix: *"Gewässer und Gestein, Gewächs und Getier"* (*GA* 79: 17/16, cf. *GA* 7: 151). This is noteworthy because it is in the very same lecture cycle in which these are named, *Insight Into That Which Is*, that Heidegger first discusses both the fourfold (*das Geviert*) and positionality (*das Ge-Stell*) and explicitly reflects on the import of this *"Ge-"* prefix. The force of the *Ge-* is that of a gathering together between singular beings: "We name the collection of mountains that are already gathered together, united of themselves and never belatedly, the mountain range [*das Gebirge*]. We name the collection of ways we are inclined to such and such and can feel ourselves so, the disposition [*das Gemüt*]" (*GA* 79: 32/30–31). The prefix then indicates what belongs together originally, i.e., that which exists "with others," we might say. The "range" of the mountains is not something added after the fact to them. They do not need to be joined together afterwards into a range, they exist from the outset as together with others and do so "of themselves" by their singular nature. This very relational existence is what the "Ge-" prefix tries to indicate in Heidegger's thinking.[14] The fourfold (*das Geviert*) is gathered together in this way, to be sure, but so is positionality (*das Ge-Stell*). Stones, waters, plants, and animals are all assigned this relational manner of existence through their designation as *Gestein, Gewässer, Gewächs,* and *Getier,* respectively. Thus, from the simple description of the earth within the fourfold, we gather that waters, stones, plants, and animals are all relationally existing and thereby participating in the worlding of the world.

a. Stones (*Gestein*)

In the *Fundamental Concepts of Metaphysics* course, "material" nature is considered under the rubric of the stone. From this perspective, the stone is ontologically the same as a river. Heidegger's thesis is that "the stone (material object) is worldless" (*GA* 29/30: 263/177). The worldlessness of the stone "is constitutive of the stone in the sense that the stone *cannot even be deprived* of something like world" (*GA* 29/30: 289/196). This deprivation or foregoing of world will be the purview of the animal. The stone on the contrary has no access to world and is worldless: "The worldlessness of a being can now be defined as its having no access to those beings (*as* beings) amongst which this particular being with this specific manner of being is. . . . [H]aving no access is precisely what makes possible its specific kind of being, i.e. the realm of being of physical and material nature and the laws governing it" (*GA* 29/30: 290–91/197). According to Heidegger, all of nature (material being) is without access to the rest of nature. The stone has no access to the river, the river no access to the stone. Ultimately, the being of nature is simple presence at hand, as Heidegger says regarding the stone: "It is—but is essentially without access to those beings amongst which it is in its own way (presence at hand), and this belongs to its being" (*GA* 29/30: 290/197). The stone is locked within itself.

The closure of the stone is such that it does not even touch anything, as this would require a moment of access. The fact of a stone lying on the ground is not taken to show that stones can touch, but instead a presumed inability of a stone to touch is used to interpret the stone that lies on the ground: "The stone is lying on the path, for example. We can say that the stone is exerting a certain pressure upon the surface of the earth. It is 'touching' the earth. But what we call 'touching' here is not a form of touching at all in the stronger sense of the word" (*GA* 29/30: 290/196). The stone does not even touch the earth, it does not have any access to the earth at all; "it lies upon the earth but does not touch it. The earth is not given for the stone as an underlying support which bears it, let alone given as earth" (*GA* 29/30: 290/197). The closure of the stone is complete: "In each case according to circumstance the stone crops up here or there, amongst and amidst a host of other things, but always in such a way that everything present around it remains essentially inaccessible to the stone itself" (*GA* 29/30: 290/197). The stone is thus paradigmatic of self-enclosed presence-at-hand.

Stone returns in one of the first discussions of the fourfold, the lecture "Language" of 1950, devoted to the work of the poet Georg Trakl, as well as in the 1953 Trakl interpretation "Language in the Poem." Here, the thought that stone would have no access to the world around it is completely abandoned. Instead, stone is now the figure of transition par excellence, the threshold. Heidegger will take this understanding of stone so far as to see in stone a mediation of one of the fundamental antagonisms of metaphysics, that of the sensible and super-sensible.

Heidegger's analysis in the 1950 text takes up the line "Pain has turned the threshold to stone" from Trakl's poem "Ein Winterabend," and the liminal position of the threshold is determinative for his new understanding.[15] The threshold in question is the limit between one thing and another, the space of differentiation (*Unter-Schied*) between them that is likewise the span of their connection. Heidegger speaks of it in language drawn from the analyses of the earth we have presented above: "The threshold is the ground-beam that bears [*trägt*] the doorway as a whole. It sustains the middle in which the two, the outside and the inside, penetrate each other. The threshold bears the between. What goes out and goes in, in the between, is joined in the between's reliability [*Verläßlichkeit*]. The reliability of the middle must never yield either way" (*GA* 12: 24/*PLT* 201, tm). For the threshold to function as threshold, for there to be the between, it must be endured and held open by something resilient enough to suffer its carrying out, i.e., by something turned to stone: "The carrying out [*Austrag*] of the between needs something that can endure, and in this sense is hard. The threshold, as the carrying out of the between, is hard because pain has turned it to stone." (*GA* 12: 24/ *PLT* 201, tm). Stone is the hardness that is able to endure the opening of the between, a tearing opening (a rift, *Riß*) that Heidegger finds to be the essence of pain.[16] This is not an insensitive hardening and numbed deadening at the threshold, as Heidegger makes clear: "the pain that became appropriated to stone did not harden into the threshold in order to congeal there. Pain presences enduringly in the threshold as pain" (*GA* 12: 24/*PLT* 201, tm). Stone cannot harden or stiffen completely if it is to be a bearer. It must still endure and sense the pain of separation that the threshold instantiates. The ideal of complete hardness that would function again as a kind of grounding must be given up. There must remain a softness or sensitivity in the very hardness of stone. Or rather, hardness is never so hard as to preclude the touch of what lies beyond it (pain). It is never so self-enclosed as to eradicate the world.

But it is not simply that a stone suffers pain; the stone is rather the embodiment of pain, or at the very least pain's shelter: "Pain conceals itself in the stone, the pain that, by turning to stone, preserves itself in the closedness of the stone" (*GA* 12: 59/*OWL* 182, tm). The hardness of the stone—which is not an abstract "hardness as such," but an earthly hardness—is itself a marker of pain, is hard on account of the prevailing pain. Stone becomes a testament to this pain. The seeming "closedness" of pain is itself a response to the painful exposure of world, to its place in the between. In fact, Heidegger will go so far as to claim, in regards to an old stone in Trakl's poetry, that "the old stone is pain itself, insofar as it looks earthily upon mortals" (*GA* 12: 59/*OWL* 182, tm). The hardness of enduring a painful exposure makes the stone a threshold whereby pain and stone themselves become indissociably linked in the between.

Insofar as the pain of the stone is the pain of exposure to the world beyond it, this pain is ineradicable. Trakl's "Heiterer Frühling" expresses this thought at the start of its last stanza: "So painfully good and true is that which lives"; something which would hold not only for the living, but for any existence whatsoever qua exposed.[17] Naturally, after this evocation of the painfully good, Trakl speaks of stone:

> And gently an old stone touches you:
> Verily! I shall be with you always.[18]

Not only is there a touch of stone here, pace the *Fundamental Concepts*, but, as Heidegger explains, "the colon after the word 'stone' at the end of the verse signifies that here *the stone* is speaking" (*GA* 12: 59/*OWL* 182, tm). Stone speaks to the wanderers, those who leave their abode to find themselves underway, between homes (it is a wanderer who arrives at the stone threshold in "Ein Winterabend"): "Silent since long ago, it now says to the wanderers who follow the stranger nothing less than its own reign and perseverance" (*GA* 12: 59/*OWL* 182, tm). The meaning of what stone says, the sense of stone, is that our existence as finite and exposed will always be one of hardness and pain.

The speech of stone, while perplexing, follows from the analyses in "Language" on the role or place of language for mortal existence. While we will address this more directly in our discussion of the mortals ("Language and Mortality" in chapter 5), a few brief remarks are nonetheless in order here. Heidegger is emphatic that language is not a possession of the mortal, nor that it expresses the thoughts of an "interior" (mortals have no "interior"). Indeed, it is a tenet of Heidegger's thinking of language that the human does not speak, but instead *"language speaks"* (*GA* 12: 10/*PLT* 188, among other places). Consequently, language (the *logos*) is no longer a property of the human, something it would possess, but is liberated from the human interior and set loose in the world. The *logos* comes to fill the world as the medium for what appears. Otherwise put, the medium of appearance is itself a medium of meaning. What appears there (in the world) appears meaningfully, or, better, it appears in terms of sense, where "sense" brings together the physicality of the sensual with the intellectuality of the sensible.[19] It names their jointure in the between. What appears in the world appears sensibly and sensually. The stone is able to speak to us because the stone is "in" sense. The materiality of stone loses its bruteness, as it were, in this exposure to sense. The stone that is the threshold endures the meaningful pain of this jointure between the sensible and super-sensible. This is what pain teaches and what the stone says.

b. Waters (*Gewässer*)

This view of material nature as a matter of mediation, transition, and sense is likewise found in Heidegger's treatment of water around the time of the fourfold, specifically his analyses of the rivers populating the poetry of Hölderlin, in interpretations from 1934 to 1948, a year before the first formulation of the fourfold as such.

In the 1934 course, Heidegger follows Hölderlin in thinking rivers as cutting paths across the earth, creatively delimiting areas of human dwelling and drawing lines of exposure to the lands beyond. "The river is not a body of water [*Gewässer*] that only flows past the place of humans, but rather its streaming, as land-forming, first produces the possibility of the grounding of the dwelling of humans" (*GA* 39: 264).[20] Insofar as this dwelling is always a historical one, of a particular people at a particular time, "the river is historical" (*GA* 39: 196). The river is not historical in the trivial sense that it would be historiologically documented. Rather, insofar as history (*Geschichte*) is thought in terms of an occurrence (*Geschehnis*), to be historical the river must be open to this event. The lecture courses of the early 1940s devote themselves to articulating the peculiar openness shared by both rivers and human dwelling.

In the lecture course devoted to Hölderlin's hymn "Andenken," rivers demonstrate that what is most one's own is always a relation beyond oneself to the foreign. The river is at each particular moment connected to both its source and mouth (where it meets the sea). So much so, in fact, that the source and the mouth are nothing other than the river itself. "Only the most distant distance corresponds to the nearness of what is most one's own. The source springs up and *is* the source as the river, which runs out as broad as the sea and so *is* the sea. The sea itself *is* the source at its most distant remove. The river is the source and is the sea" (*GA* 52: 186). The source and the sea are not terminal points bracketing the river, they are only found in the streaming of the river itself. The river is consequently always a departure from its source which nonetheless remains in connection with that source. Heidegger will likewise think this in terms of the activity of the thinker in the lecture course *What Is Called Thinking?* of 1951–52: "the thoughtful remembrance of what is to be thought [*das Andenken an das zu-Denkende*] is the ground source of poetizing. Poetizing is thus the water that at times flows backwards to the source, to thinking as thoughtful remembrance" (*GA* 8: 13/11, tm).

For this reason Heidegger asks "Can one ever be directly 'at' the source at all? How, when the source first points precisely away from itself in the direction of the river that arises from it?" (*GA* 52: 174). Instead of being "at" the source, "the most difficult thing is to draw near to the source" (*GA* 52: 174). One's own is not a possession, but a proximity. This source is understood as what is one's ownmost, one's historical destiny or fate, and according to the logic of the river, this fate is only one's own when it is understood in connection with the foreign (the mingling of rivers in the sea).

In the lecture course on Hölderlin's hymn "The Ister," the temporal dimension of the river is developed still further. The point is not that time flows by like a river; instead Heidegger follows Hölderlin in thinking the river as both intimating what is to come (as it heads to the sea) and passing away into what has been (in departing the source). "Both are, at the same time, in a concealed, unitary relation to what has been and what is of the future—thus to the temporal" (*GA* 53: 12/12). But they are more than just this relationship. "The rivers intimate and vanish into time and do so in such a way that they themselves are thus of time and are time itself" (*GA* 53: 12/12). Insofar as the river maintains a connection between its source and mouth, what has been and what is to come (or what is to come and what has been), then "remembering" what has been will be equally an intimation of what is to come. Heidegger can then state that "intimation does not simply relate to that which is coming, but at the same time relates to that which has been" and "inner recollection [*die Erinnerung*] would be altogether the *most profound* intimation when that which is to come, that with which intimation is otherwise concerned, comes out of what has been" (*GA* 53: 33–34/29, 34/29). The river thus enacts the bestowal of our historical fate as well as providing the guide for how to receive such a dispensation.

This transitional movement of the river is itself the condition for dwelling. The river is thus the location (*Ortschaft*) of human dwelling, not despite its wandering (*Wanderschaft*) but on account of it. "The river is the locality for dwelling. The river is the journeying of becoming homely. To put it more clearly: the river is that very locality that is attained in and through the journeying" (*GA* 53: 36/31). The river as a location is not a fixed place, but exhibits a kind of openness and invitation to what lies around it. (In the hymn it offers welcome to the visiting Hercules.) But the river is also the connection between what has been and what is to come. For Heidegger, this cannot be reduced to saying the river plays a spatio-temporal role. "The unity of locality and journeying cannot be conceived in terms of 'space' and 'time,' for the space with which we are familiar and the time to which we are accustomed are themselves offspring of a realm that first lets all openness spring forth from out of it, because it is that which clears and [is the clearing event of appropriation]" (*GA* 53: 203–4/166; Heidegger's brackets). This realm is the "place" of human dwelling, this connection between a place that is no longer considered contained, but understood relationally, and a history that is not understood as settled and determined but as arriving. Insofar as the river exhibits both of these traits, Heidegger can write that "The river itself dwells" (*GA* 53: 42/35).

The "Western Conversation," broken off in 1948, which is largely a commentary on "The Ister," further elaborates the role of the river in human dwelling. Commenting on Hölderlin's line that "Rivers make the land arable" (16–17), the conversation partners ponder the connection between the river and the bearing character of the earth:

> OLDER MAN: "Arable" is that which tends what grows and the thriving of the herbs and animals. The arable is what bears [*das Tragende*], what bears the gifts of food and drink and makes a gift of them as proceeds [*Erträgnis*].
>
> YOUNGER MAN: But not only this belongs to the arable, that it registers a profit and yields proceeds. The arable endures [*er-trägt*] in the more originary sense of bearing the human essence, carrying it *out* [*es* aus*trägt*], such that it is fulfilled in this bearing. "Rivers make the land arable." They awaken and protect what bears of the land [*das Tragsame des Landes*], which bears because it is proper to the earth. (*GA* 75: 74–75)

Rivers divide the land and delimit it into finite regions. The earth is not a homogeneous field, but a multitude of exposed places, with rivers taking part in the separation and connection of these. In this way it allows for a multiplicity of life, tending what grows and producing the variegated sustenance for such life. Yet there is more to the arable than productivity. The earth's bearing does not follow from a ground as its success. It bears more originarily, the younger man says, because it also furthers that which is beyond profit. This is the exposed character of human dwelling, to be sure, but it is also something true of all that lives, as we shall see in considering plants and animals, below.

In considering how the river makes the land arable and how the earth bears, the conversation partners are led to further consider the connection between the earth and the abyss:

> YOUNGER MAN: The human essence is delivered *over* to the bearing earth insofar as it bears the abyss.

> OLDER MAN: *This* bearing the rivers *call* forth out of the earth and they protect what bears [*das Tragsame*] when they make the land "arable." The rivers *bear* what bears and thereby what is borne, namely the abyss, *to* the humans, whereby they are able to dwell there where their essence is rooted.
>
> YOUNGER MAN: You mean that the humans dwell at the rivers not only when and not only because herbs grow there and animals go there. Rather, the rivers still properly invoke what bears of the earth [*das Tragsame der Erde*] as that which bears the essence of the human, something we have still scarcely considered.
>
> OLDER MAN: That is what I mean. (*GA* 75: 75–76)

Rivers make evident the non-foundational support beneath us, all around us even, as we are "to be borne by this [the river] as our element," says the older speaker, to which the younger interlocutor responds, "in the element of the river spirit a singular love wafts to our heart that blows away all willing through a releasement to the grace that liberates [*be-freyt*] everything" (*GA* 75: 64). The openness of the river meets our openness and this is likewise an openness to whatever grace may come, an openness that allows the things of the world their openness, and receives its grace in so doing. The consequences are drawn:

> YOUNGER MAN: You then think that grace would be the abyss?
>
> OLDER MAN: And the abyss grace. (*GA* 75: 76)

The earth bears what is beyond proceeds and profit by bearing that which is exposed to the coming of grace. Human dwelling and the thriving of life is always exposed to such grace.

What Heidegger's consideration of waters presents, then, is a thinking of connectedness and of the persistence of the origin in the midst of change and encounter. Rivers partition the earth creating borders that are at once zones of division and invitation. They remain connected with their source while embracing the foreign. In each case, they show that what is one's own is only such through its exposure to another, to what lies beyond it. The waters present this as what it means to dwell.

Heidegger's consideration of inanimate or material nature is ultimately a destabilization of the very "materiality" of it. The stone is not brute matter, the stone speaks. The stone is the materialization of pain, of crossing, it is the hardness of what holds open the world. Water for its part interrupts the landscape with division, stretching the origin forth into encounters, offering what is most its own as welcome to what comes. In both cases we are confronted with a thinking of transition and relationality, whereby what exists does so by extending itself toward another. This is Heidegger's response to those who would object that what he presents as true of stone or river is only applicable to the poetized stones of Trakl or the rivers of Hölderlin. Relationality is not a quality of objects. It is not something that can be observed by an otherwise untouched subject. It does not appear at a distance, it is closer than it appears. For there to be relationality, we must be relayed into it ourselves. The world appears relational to the poet who relates into it. In the 1934 course on Hölderlin this was expressed in terms of the historicality of a people: "River and poet both belong in their essence to the founding of the dwelling and Dasein of a historical people" (*GA* 39: 259–60). The 1942 "Ister" course is more direct: "When Hölderlin poetizes the essence of the poet, he poetizes *relations* that do not have their ground in the 'subjectivity' of human beings. These *relations* have their own prevailing, essencing, and flowing. The poet is the river. And the river is the poet" (*GA* 53: 203/165, tm, em). This is why the poet is not presenting symbols of an otherwise extant river or providing imaginative coloring for something otherwise actual. What the poet poetizes *is* that river, not a sign of it, as Heidegger never tires of repeating: "The rivers cannot be 'poeticized images' or 'signs of' something because they in themselves are 'the signs,' 'signs' that are no longer 'signs' of something else, nor symbols of something else, but are themselves this supposed 'something else'" (*GA* 53: 204/166).

The poetic presentation of material nature is thus not an embellishment of what otherwise already exists. The poetic presentation allows the thing in question to show itself as relational and this means at the same time that it shows itself as participating in a world of sense. The metaphysical separation of the sensible from the super-sensible—"only within metaphysics is there the physical and the sensual in distinction from the non-physical and non-sensual. Metaphysics is precisely the reign of this difference" (*GA* 75: 166)—no longer applies to the material nature of Heidegger's fourfold. We shall have opportunity to return to this line of thought in our discussion of the thing and world (chapter six).

c. Plants (*Gewächs*)

The earth is also spread out in plants and animals where its bearing-fructifying constitution is again visible. Around the time of the fourfold, Heidegger's considerations of plants revolve around a new understanding of growth and life, his considerations of the animal around exposure and death. Each of these is indebted to the bearing of the earth. Taken together they present a renewed conception of the organism that dramatically departs from Heidegger's treatment twenty years earlier in the

Fundamental Concepts of Metaphysics course (1929–30). Without repeating the entirety of this well-known, thoroughly discussed, and extensive analysis, a few points warrant restatement in light of the treatment of plants and animals that Heidegger will undertake twenty years later.[21] These concern what Heidegger calls the "disinhibiting ring" that surrounds each organism and the role of growth and death therein.

Heidegger's concern in the *Fundamental Concepts of Metaphysics* is with the issue of life, "the specific manner of being pertaining to animal and plant," there being no difference between them at the level of the organism (*GA* 29/30: 277/188). The thesis directing the investigation—though "hypothesis" is the better term given Heidegger's extreme reservations about the proceedings—is the famed claim that the living being, the animal, is *"poor in world"* (*GA* 29/30: 263/177).[22] This poverty is no absolute lack of world, since the animal does engage with what appears within its environment. But for Heidegger, this engagement is not wholly worldly because it still provides no access to beings as such. With no beings as such to comport itself toward, the animal is said to merely behave (*Benehmen*). This "behavedness" (*Benommenheit*—Heidegger is emphatic that we keep all sense of numbness or captivity away from this term) is "the inner possibility of behavior as such" (*GA* 29/30: 349/239), and means that the animal is a creature of drive and instinct. Behavedness, "the inner possibility of animal being itself," identifies animality as a matter of responsive behavior to solicitation (*GA* 29/30: 349/239, tm).[23]

The behavedness of the animal as collection of drives places the animal within what Heidegger terms a "ring" of behavior prompts: "drivenness as being driven from one drive to another holds and drives the animal within a *ring* which it cannot escape and within which something is open for the animal" (*GA* 29/30: 363/249). While the ring includes a kind of openness and the animal is said to relate to what is opened therein, the animal is nevertheless unable to "enter into" anything or "get involved" with anything [*sich einlassen auf*] available within the ring, "yet while it is certain that all instinctual behaviour is a relating to . . . , it is just as surely the case that in all its behaviour the animal can *never properly enter into something as such* [auf etwas als solches einlassen]. The animal is *encircled* by this ring constituted by the reciprocal drivenness of its drives" (*GA* 29/30: 363/249). Not being able to enter into something means not being able to relate to something as something that persists beyond the organism's immediate interest in it. Heidegger proposes that we understand this not being able to enter into anything positively as an "eliminative character [*des Beseitigens*] in respect of that to which it relates itself" (*GA* 29/30: 363/250). He finds "one of the most striking examples" of this in the behavior of insects like the praying mantis: "It is well known that after copulation many female insects devour the male of the species. After copulation the sexual character disappears, the male acquires the character of prey and is eliminated. The one animal is never there for the other simply as a living creature, but is only there for it either as sexual partner or as prey" (*GA* 29/30: 363–64/250). Nothing of the sexual partner persists once the sexual character disappears, the organism is not "involved with" the living being beyond the particular character in which it appears at the moment (not with it "as such"), but with a character that prompts certain drives. Thus Heidegger can write that "behavior as such is in itself each time an elimination [*Beseitigen*]" (*GA* 29/30: 364/250, tm).

This eliminative character is tied to the nature of organic, instinctual drive, which is understood by Heidegger in terms of a build up of charge. If we "reflect upon the instinctual drive intrinsically as such—rather than upon the instinctual activity into which it can be released—and consider the instinctual structure itself, then we can see that the instinctual drive precisely possesses an inner tension and charge, a containment and inhibitedness that essentially must be disinhibited before it can pass over into driven activity and thus be 'uninhibited' in the usual, ordinary sense of the word" (*GA* 29/30: 370/254). The driven response eliminates this build up of instinctual charge. The animal exists then within a "*disinhbiting ring*," responding to the prompts that it has access to according to its organic capacities (*GA* 29/30: 370–71/255). Heidegger is clear that the encirclement of the animal by this ring is not an "encapsulation," though he does say it is "like a tube" (*GA* 29/30: 370/255, 292/198, tm). There is still a kind of access operative here, but there is likewise a compulsion. This ring in all its ambiguity is ultimately "an essential character of life itself" (*GA* 29/30: 377/259).

Heidegger's analysis of the living being is admittedly incomplete. As he himself notes, it omits consideration of the movement proper to life. "All life is *not simply organism*, but is *just as essentially* process, thus formally speaking *motion* [Bewegung]" (*GA* 29/30: 385/265). This movement, what he names here motility (*Bewegtheit*), is the movement of the animal through the stages of its life. What the analysis lacks, in other words, is a treatment of growth: "in our everyday experience we are familiar with the birth, growth, maturing, aging, and death of animals. But all this reveals to us a *motility of a peculiar kind,* for here the organism as we now understand it does not simply happen to get caught up as it were in this motility. Rather, this motility determines the being of the animal as such" (*GA* 29/30: 385/265). Throughout its life, the animal is moved and responds to this motion with further movements of its own.

By omitting growth as motility, however, Heidegger has also omitted consideration of death, for "death is bound most intimately with the motility of life" (*GA* 29/30: 387/266, tm). Without a full account of the animal, nothing can be decided about its death, even whether this would properly be called a death as we understand it. Despite the most scientific of similarities, "it is questionable whether death and death are the same in the case of man and animal, even if we can identify a physico-chemical and physiological equivalence between the two" (*GA* 29/30: 388/267). The behavedness of the animal, its location within a disinhibiting ring, shapes not only how death might happen to it, but also how it might be toward death, or "come toward" its death. As Heidegger puts it, "From what has been said already it is easy to see that behavedness, as the fundamental structure of life, prefigures *quite determinate possibilities of death*, of *coming-towards-death* [Zum-Tode-kommens]. Is the death of the animal a *dying* or an *ending*? Because behavedness belongs to the essence of the animal, the animal cannot die, but rather only end, insofar as we ascribe dying to the human" (*GA* 29/30: 388/267, tm). At the time of fundamental ontology, the animal is denied its death.

All of these views on the organism undergo radical revision during the time of the fourfold. Even the fact that there are now separate analyses addressing plants and animals can be seen as a break with the perspective of the organism that guided the earlier lecture course.[24] The plant and animal are now thought in terms of an exposure to the world beyond them, a striking shift of register from the view that the organism would be locked within a disinhibiting ring. Heidegger's treatment of plants is likewise a rethinking of growth, his discussion of the animal a rethinking of both the animal's relation to death and the animal's difference from ourselves as well. These will be addressed in turn.

The term used in the presentation of the fourfold for plants and flora is *Gewächs*, the collective noun for all that grows and undergoes growth, *Wachstum*. In the privately printed "The Pathway" and the new "Introduction to 'What Is Metaphysics?,'" both dating from 1949, Heidegger takes the tree as the representative plant and develops his understanding of the growing being around it. In "The Pathway," the horizontal meandering of the path is complemented by the verticality of a tall oak tree, under which Heidegger would sit and puzzle over philosophy. The tree itself, however, teaches him about growth: "Meanwhile, the hardness and scent of the oakwood began to speak more clearly of the slowness and constancy with which the tree grew" (*GA* 13: 88/*HMT* 70). The measured growth of the tree brings together the hardness to endure with the delicacy of scent. Like the stone previously mentioned, the tree itself speaks: "The oaktree itself spoke: only in such growth is there grounded what lasts and fructifies; to grow means to open oneself up to the expanse of the sky and at the same time to sink roots into the darkness of earth; everything sound only thrives [*alles Gediegene nur gedeiht*] if it is, in right measure, both ready for the appeal of highest heaven and preserved in the protection of the bearing earth [*der tragenden Erde*]" (*GA* 13: 88/*HMT* 70, tm). Growth is the opening up of the dimension between the earth and the sky (we shall address this "between" and dimension in the next chapter). The hardness of the tree allows it to hold open this between while remaining rooted in the earth. What thrives (*gedeiht*) and grows sound (*gediegen*)—Grimms' dictionary attests to the etymological connection—does so through its exposure to the "between."[25] The plant testifies to this.

It is precisely this contact with the bearing earth that is forgotten in the history of metaphysics. Heidegger's 1949 introduction to his lecture of twenty years prior, "What Is Metaphysics?," makes this clear in a consideration of Descartes's image of the tree of philosophy. For Descartes, metaphysics is the root of the tree, physics the trunk, and all the other sciences are the branches. But this abstracts and extracts the tree from its nutritive and supportive context, the soil of the earth. Heidegger writes, "in what soil [*Boden*] do the roots of the tree of philosophy take hold? Out of what ground do the roots, and thereby the whole tree, receive their nourishing juices and strength? What element, concealed in the ground and soil, pervades the bearing and nourishing roots of the tree? What does the essence of metaphysics rest and move about in?" (*GA* 9: 365/277, tm). Metaphysics forgets the bearing of the earth and the nourishment it provides to the roots of the tree. And that is to say metaphysics forgets the other, if a note from the late 1930s is granted: "<Plants> *rooted* in an other—rootedness in the soil [*Boden-ständigkeit*]" (*GA* 73.1: 414).

The tree that is rooted in the earth, the life that is rooted in the earth, is not fused with that earth or "grounded" upon it in any foundational sense. To be rooted is to be interwoven and interlaced with the earth. What is rooted is in an embrace of the earth. The earth supports the tree by bearing it, by touching it and holding it. The roots do not "possess" the earth, they do not assimilate it in the drive to their own self-increase: "The ground and soil is the element in which the root of the tree essences, but the growth of the tree is never able to absorb this root-soil in such a way that it disappears in the tree as part of the tree. Instead, the roots, down to the subtlest tendrils, lose themselves in the soil" (*GA* 9: 366/278, tm). To be rooted is to forego possession and to lose oneself. The roots do so for the sake of the tree, Heidegger explains:

> the root of the tree . . . sends all nourishment and all strength [*Kräfte*] into the trunk and its branches. The root branches out into the ground and soil so that the tree, for the sake of its growth, can go forth out of the ground and thus can leave it. . . . The ground is the ground for the

roots, and in the ground the roots forget themselves in favor of the tree. The roots still belong to the tree even when, after a fashion, they abandon themselves to the element of the soil. They squander themselves and their element on the tree. (*GA* 9: 366/278, tm)

The very roots of the tree that would ground and stabilize the tree neither possess the earth nor preserve and steel themselves; instead they lose themselves in giving their strength to the trunk that they thereby support and nourish.

This entwining of roots in the soil is the only support they find. What grows is borne by the soil, but is nonetheless groundless. Heidegger's 1955–56 lecture series, *The Principle of Reason (Der Satz vom Grund)*, addresses a verse from Angelus Silesius on this very point. Silesius writes that "The rose is without why: it blooms because it blooms / It pays no attention to itself, asks not whether it is seen."[26] Heidegger reads Silesius's verse against the Leibnizian notion of a principle of sufficient reason, that everything has its reason or "ground" (*Grund*). The rose that blooms without why would bloom without a ground. Heidegger states,

Obviously the rose here stands as an example for all blooming things, for all plants and all growth. According to the words of the poet, the principle of reason does not hold in this field. On the contrary, botany will easily point out to us a chain of causes and conditions for the growth of plants. For proof of this we make use of the fact that, despite the saying of Angelus Silesius, the growth of plants has its why, that is, its necessary grounds without ever having had to bother with science. Everyday experience speaks for the necessity of the grounds of growth and blooming. (*GA* 10: 55/36)

There is no growth on a ground, only in a soil. Growth can only be groundless, without why, borne aloft into the opening of the sky. In the lectures, Heidegger wants to retain the term "ground," but with a transformation in its meaning. He wants to understand it precisely as we understand the bearing soil: "in a broader sense it [the word "ground," *Grund*] means the earth, the surface of the earth [*den Erdboden*]. And even today in the Allemanic-Swabian dialect *Grund* has the even more original meaning of 'humus,' which is loam [the "mature ground," *gewachsene Grund*], the heavy, fertile soil [fruitful, *fruchtbare Erdboden*]. For instance, a flower bed that has too little soil must be given more of it in order for there to be a favorable growth [*ein günstiges Wachstum*]. On the whole, *Grund* means the more deep lying and, at the same time, bearing realm [*tragenden Bereich*]" (*GA* 10: 143–44/96, tm).

What is rooted in the soil in this sheltering, bearing ground experiences a favorable (*günstiges*) growth because it grows into the open, exposed to the coming of grace [*Gunst*]. But it cannot do this on its own by asserting itself into the between, for if the between is to be a between, and not, for instance, a group of particular discrete beings, then it is a medium and, as such, is already touching that which would enter into it. The between has already issued its invitation, we might say. A few years earlier, in a 1954 speech at his nephew's ordination, Heidegger puts it in terms of gifts: the "earth and the sky above it bestow the majority of natural gifts. From them thrives [*gedeiht*] that which is strong enough to grow towards the gift of grace" (*GA* 16: 489). The earth and sky allow for the growth through them toward grace. They allow for a growth that is exposed to what comes.

What comes is nothing we would ourselves possess. Grace does not bring an increase in one's possessions. Rather, it brings an inclination to giving. In the 1950 interpretation of Trakl entitled "Language," Heidegger elaborates on the poet's image of a tree of graces. It begins depicting just the kind of rootedness and emergence that we have discussed: "The tree roots soundly [*gediegen*] in the earth. Thus it flourishes [*gedeiht*] into a blooming that opens itself to heaven's blessing" (*GA* 12: 21/*PLT* 198, tm). The tree occupies the between of earth and sky: "It spans both the intoxication of flowering and the soberness of the nourishing sap. The earth's abated growth and the bounty of the sky belong together" (*GA* 12: 21/*PLT* 198, tm). What Heidegger now adds to this picture of plant growth is grace: "The poem names the tree of graces. Its sound blossoming harbors the fruit that falls to us unearned [*die unverdient zufallende Frucht*]—the saving holy that is propitious toward mortals" (*GA* 12: 21/*PLT* 198–99, tm). The gift of grace that the tree receives from its exposed position between earth and sky is the gift of giving of itself. Just as its roots give their all to the trunk, so does the trunk give to the branches and the branches to the fruit that comes like an accident [*Zufall*] and falls unwarranted to mortals as grace. The gift of grace is of growth's fruition. Its fruit falls unwarranted when ripe.

In *Being and Time* (1927), Heidegger was reluctant to speak of Dasein in terms of its fruition or ripening. In that text Heidegger contrasted Dasein with a ripening fruit in regards to the relation they bear to their particular "not yet," the fruit that was not yet ripe and the Dasein that was not yet dead. For the fruit, its unripeness is not a simple absence or missing presence,

> the unripe fruit moves toward its ripeness. . . . The fruit ripens itself,
> and this ripening characterizes its being as fruit. Nothing we can think

> of which could be added on could remove the unripeness of the fruit, if this being did not ripen *of itself.* The not-yet of unripeness does not mean something other which is outstanding that could be objectively present. . . . It means the fruit itself in its specific kind of being. (*GA* 2: 324/*SZ* 243)

This brings the fruit quite close to Dasein, as Heidegger notes: "The ripening fruit, however . . . *is* the unripeness. The not-yet is already included in its own being, by no means as an arbitrary determination, but as a constituent. Correspondingly, Da-sein, too, *is always already its not-yet* as long as it is" (*GA* 2: 324/*SZ* 243–44). Heidegger finds the fruit to be "formally analogous to Dasein," though they differ in the ontological structure of their ends, ripeness and death (*GA* 2: 324/*SZ* 244). The fruit has a fixed terminus, ripeness, which fulfills it. Dasein has no such thing: "with ripeness, the fruit *fulfills* itself. But is the death at which Dasein arrives a fulfillment in this sense?" (*GA* 2: 325/*SZ* 244). The track along which the fruit develops (and we might see here already a prefiguration of the 1929–30 analysis of the organism) distinguishes it from Dasein whose end is not coincident with the fulfillment of a potential: "Even 'unfulfilled' Dasein ends. On the other hand, Dasein so little needs to ripen only with its death that it can already have gone beyond that ripeness before the end. For the most part, it ends in unfulfillment, or else disintegrated and used up" (*GA* 2: 325/*SZ* 244). Dasein is thus formally analogous to a fruit, but most distinct from it at the point of the fruit's culmination. Dasein is not subject to any necessity to ripen and end.

Heidegger's worry over distinguishing Dasein from the plant in *Being and Time* has abated in the later writings. Indeed, by the time of *The Principle of Reason* and its guiding example of the rose that blooms without why, Heidegger can write that "what is unsaid in the fragment— and everything depends on this—instead says that humans, in the concealed grounds of their essential being, first truly are when in their own way they are like the rose—without why" (*GA* 10: 57–58/38). This is more than a formal analogy to the rose—the rose now exists in a way toward which humans should aspire.

The connection between humans and plants is a close one in Heidegger's writings. In the 1959 lecture "Releasement," he wonders "does there not belong to every thriving of a sound work [*zu jedem Gedeihen eines gediegenen Werkes*] a rootedness in the soil of the homeland?," going on to cite Hebel's statement that "We are plants which—whether we like to admit it to ourselves or not—must with our roots rise out of the earth in order to bloom in the ether and to bear fruit."[27] Here the work is the gift that the human would bear as its fruit. But for this to be the case, the human must grow in a particular context or soil. Another 1959 speech, "Thanks to the Hometown of Meßkirch," cites Nietzsche in developing this point: "Nietzsche said 'The philosopher is a rare plant'; i.e. it needs its own soil . . . , whose secret growth- and preservative-forces are never detectable by chemical soil analysis. A rare plant needs a rare soil. And if there is anything to this, even just a little, then what is strange about our contemporary soil is characterized by the fact that this soil, the earth and the sky above it, has nothing exceptional [*Auffallendes*], nothing uncommon, nothing staggering" (*GA* 16: 560).[28] Were humans to live like the rose without why, they would find the new soil they need. The soil becomes the bearing ground by bearing the work that grounds the ground as abyss. In a sense this is what releasement entails: "If releasement towards things and openness to the secret awakens within us, then we can set out along a path that will lead to a new ground and soil. In that soil the creativity which produces lasting works could strike new roots" (*GA* 16: 529/*DT* 57–58, tm). Rootedness in the soil allows the plant to grow into the open bounty of the sky, to give its unwarranted fruit. This kind of growth into the open is no longer a matter of motility within a disinhibiting ring. The seemingly causal conveyance of the fruit to its ripeness (*Being and Time*) or the almost merely responsive behavedness of the organism (*Fundamental Concepts of Metaphysics*) are each surpassed in this thought of exposure and accidental (*zufällig*) fruition.

While Heidegger's writings of the period recognize the flourishing of what lives as a growing into the between, they also face up to the contemporary challenge that this growth faces by the will to planning and organization. In the early 1960s, Heidegger notes that contemporary humans face the threat "that they forfeit all powers of growth [*Wachstumskräfte*] through organization" (*GA* 16: 585). Growth requires exposure to the beyond, exactly what organization seeks to contain and control for the sake of security and certainty. The attempt to plan everything kills the very growth it would further. "Where only plans and what is planned are carried out, nothing grows. Growth, thriving, soundness [*Wachstum, Gedeihen, Gediegenes*] are only there where the play-space is spared for the unplannable" (*GA* 16: 614). For all its seeming control, however, the organizational drive is dependent upon these natural forces while unable to produce them from out of itself. They are irreplaceable; "indeed precisely these sources for the natural growth [*Wachstum*] of all sound [*gediegenen*] human beings are today so threatened as never before. The sources cannot be protected by artificial measures against an attack, either. No organization is capable of replacing those natural forces of growth [*Wachstumskräfte*]" (*GA* 16: 489).

The precarious position of these forces of growth, the delicacy of the between in which they grow, the sky through which they extend, and the earth in which they are rooted, all of this is in jeopardy. For Heidegger this means that what grows is in need of our care. "Building Dwelling Thinking" makes clear that this is the nature of our existence. "To be a human means: to be upon the earth as mortal, it means: to dwell. The old word 'building,' this says that the human would be insofar as he dwells, this word building signifies now at the same time: fostering and tending [*hegen und pflegen*], namely cultivating the fields, cultivating the vines. Such building only protects, namely what grows [*das Wachstum*], that which of itself maturates [*zeitigt*] its fruit. Building in the sense of fostering and tending is no producing" (*GA* 7: 149/145, tm).[29] Tending and cultivating what grows—"tending [*pflegen*], Latin *colere, cultura*" (*GA* 7: 149/*PLT* 145, tm)—is written into our existence. This does not mean that the plant world (or animal world) is dependent upon human intervention. What it means is that the nature of existence is exposed and affected by the world around it. What exists touches that world and is touched by it in turn. To be exposed is to suffer the ineluctable appeal of the world. It is impossible for us to leave the plants and animals alone, because they have already reached out to us and we to them. This is what it means to exist relationally, as exposed. It is a sentiment expressed by the phrase "I am human and nothing is foreign to me."[30] To ignore that appeal is still a response to it. There is nowhere untouched by us, no wilderness. There never was. For this reason, in his 1955 letter to Ernst Jünger, Heidegger will speak of "the garden of the wilderness [*der Garten der Wildnis*]" (*GA* 9: 423/320). The wilderness is nothing so wild as to be beyond the ken of human cultivation. The garden of the wilderness identifies this consequence of our existence, of being mortal upon this earth. It names the fact that "growth and tending [*Wachstum und Pflege*] are attuned to one another out of an incomprehensible intimacy" (*GA* 9: 423–24/320).[31]

The fruition of human growth upon this earth is dwelling. In a speech on the septicentennial of his hometown of Meßkirch, "Meßkirch's Seventh Centennial," Heidegger comments on the technological challenge to dwelling that even Meßkirch is now facing, noting "the television and radio antennas that we can make out serially on the roofs of the houses in the town. What do these signs show? They show that there where the humans 'dwell,' externally regarded, they are precisely no longer at home" (*GA* 16: 575/*MSC* 43, tm). But at the same time, against this technological intrusion, they also show themselves ready to dwell, and they do so through plants, flowers, "in the midst of the hometown, whose inhabitants have adorned their houses so richly and carefully with flowers—likewise a sign, namely that they are of a mind to tend [*pflegen*] to the right dwelling" (*GA* 16: 582/*MSC* 55, tm).

Heidegger's thinking of the plant, growth, soil, ripening, maturation, and cultivation (tending and fostering), reveal the plant to be something more than an organism trapped in an environment of disinhibiting prompts. It grows into the between of earth and sky, ungrounded, where it gives of itself in fruition. In fact, by the time of the fourfold, Heidegger will even draw out the etymological connections between the word for building and dwelling, *bauen* (via the Old High German *buan*), and that of *being* itself, in the German conjugations of "to be," namely *bin*, "I am," and *bist*, "you are" (see *GA* 7: 148–49/*PLT* 144–45). Given the role of *colere* intrinsic to *bauen*, it is not too much of a stretch to see this illustrating nothing less than an essential connection between being and the plants around us.

d. Animals (*Getier*)

Heidegger's location of animals within the fourfold under the aegis of the earth means that there should be an aspect of bearing to be found in animality as well. In the 1953 text "Language in the Poem," Heidegger rethinks animality in terms of its exposure to world. In so doing, what comes to the fore is a new relation between mortality and animality, blurring the distinction between the two. Obviously this marks a decisive break with the proposals of the *Fundamental Concepts of Metaphysics*, so it is surprising that this later text on Trakl is entirely overlooked in the wealth of literature devoted to Heidegger and animality, which largely presumes a clean distinction between the animal and the human in Heideggerian thought (the 1929–30 course is almost always taken as his final word on the matter).[32] This being so, after presenting Heidegger's later view of the animal, I will briefly address what it has to offer for questions of Heidegger's "ontotheological anthropocentrism."[33]

The consideration of the animal in the Trakl essay arises out of a thinking of departure and wandering. Trakl's poetry is full of wanderers who set out on dusky, twilight paths, away from the cottages of town and out toward the edge of the forest. Heidegger will read these wanderers as out between their homes and destinations, indeed, as figures of the between itself. They wander between traditional oppositions of metaphysics. The opposition that concerns us now is that between the sensible and the super-sensible, i.e., the opposition expressed in both the definition of the human as *zôon logon echon*, the animal having reason, and as the *animal rationale*, the rational animal. In both of these cases an antagonism between rationality and animality is written into the very definition of the human. Abandoning this antipodal construction not only releases the human from its pincers, it likewise releases the animal.

Heidegger begins from Trakl's line that "The soul is a stranger on this earth,"[34] explaining that "strange" (*fremd*) derives from the Old High German "*fram*," which means "on the way to . . ." (*GA* 12: 37/*OWL* 163, tm). The soul that is a stranger on earth is one that has set out on the way to somewhere else. It has left behind any domicile for paths on the way somewhere, without yet having reached any destination. The soul that is underway is thus "between" places. The soul is defined by this being underway, so much so that it is not even the source or "origin" of its own movement, but is "called" out along the paths it traverses. Heidegger asks, "to where is the stranger called?" and answers, in accordance with Trakl's poem, that the stranger is called "into the downfall [*Untergang*]" (*GA* 12: 47/*OWL* 171, tm). This *Untergang*, however, is not so much a downfall or even a "going under"; rather it is, translated just as literally, a "going among" or "going amidst" (*unter zu gehen*). The soul is called to be among the things of the world, which is to say, it is called into this between. If there is any downfall or demise to be had here, it is solely that of the self-centered and encapsulated subject that would imagine itself at home, master of the world, regarding it from on high.

Indeed, Heidegger describes this *Untergang* in just such terms of dissolution: "it is losing oneself in the spiritual twilight of blueness" (*GA* 12: 47/*OWL* 171, tm). To set out underway, to enter the between, is to enter this spiritual twilight of blueness. It is "spiritual" insofar as Heidegger follows Trakl in understanding spirit as a flame capable of offering inviting warmth at a hearth as well as burning everything to ashes in conflagration. Spirit as flame is never wholly one or the other of these, it is always in between. The loss of oneself by entry into the between occurs at "twilight" (*Dämmerung*), the crepuscular transition of the day. It is not simply the end of the day, but also the dawn of morning; "morning, too, has its twilight [*dämmert*]" (*GA* 12: 38/*OWL* 164). Twilight is always between the end and the beginning. Lastly, the between is a spiritual twilight of "blueness" insofar as blue is the color of twilight, of the time that is neither day nor night. Blue is the color of the trace, of what remains light in the dark and dark within light. As Heidegger puts it, "the brightness sheltered in the dark is blueness" (*GA* 12: 40/*OWL* 165, tm). In all of these aspects, the loss of self is revealed to be an entry into the between of relationality.

No longer at home and not yet at its destination, the wandering soul finds itself on the way somewhere. On these paths between enclosures, it wanders exposed. The essence of this soul as a stranger means that it is never at home, not even with itself. It is not defined by being in place, but by being underway, neither here nor there. Having left the closure of the home behind, it is exposed to what comes. This being underway is thus a condition for encounter, for seeing and being seen. Out among the blueness of twilight, the wanderer is caught sight of by a blue deer (*das blaue Wild*). Heidegger's rethinking of animality unfolds in his reading of this recurrent figure in Trakl's poetry.

Let us note at the outset that the animal in question is a deer, a game animal, a *Wild*. The etymological connection with the wilderness, *Wildnis*, should not be missed. But just as the wilderness is understood by Heidegger as a "garden of the wilderness" (*GA* 9: 423/320), indicating the ineluctable relationality of the human such that nothing of the wilderness is untouched, a similar understanding informs the thinking of the deer (*das Wild*). The deer will not be so wild as to remain completely foreign to us. There is a relation between wanderer and blue deer operative here. Trakl's deer is the "blue deer" (*das blaue Wild*), where blue once again names the slippage of the between, the blurring of just such oppositions as the wild and the civilized, for example, and the appeasement of the antagonisms that they establish. In fact, Heidegger follows Trakl in thinking of the *Wild* as the "shy deer," the "gentle animal."[35]

But the blue deer must enter the twilight, just as the wanderer must leave home. Heidegger follows Trakl in tracking this transformation of animal (*Tier*) into the deer (*Wild*). It begins with Trakl's depiction of ". . . An animal's face / transfixed before blueness, blue's holiness."[36] Heidegger elaborates the consequences of this exposure to blueness: "in sight of the blue and at the same time brought to self-restraint [*Ansichhalten*], the animal's face is transfixed and transforms into the countenance of the deer [*Antlitz des Wilds*] . . . In being transfixed, the face of the animal comes together. Its appearance gathers itself, composing itself, in order to look towards the holy" (*GA* 12: 40–41/ *OWL* 166, tm).[37] The transformation of the animal into the deer is coincident with the look out toward the holy, which we can provisionally sketch as the space of grace, or arrival (we will have opportunity to consider the holy more closely in chapter 4, "The Holy"). The animal is not some self-contained creature harboring an essence or species-being. The animal is instead what it is on account of a relation that carries the animal out past itself to situate it in the between, to transform it into the blue deer.

Exposed in the blueness, the deer is open for what comes, a witness to it. It observes what takes place along the twilit paths of the between:

> For a blue deer always follows
> these darker paths,
> an observer among the twilight trees.[38]

Trakl calls on the deer to assume this role of witness in regard to the stranger.

> the steps of the stranger
> rang through the silver night.
> Would that a blue deer were to remember his path.[39]

Heidegger asks, "who is the blue deer that the poet calls out to? An animal? Certainly. Only an animal? By no means. For it is supposed to remember [*gedenken*]" (*GA* 12: 41/*OWL* 166, tm). The remembrance of the deer is a looking past the present in two ways, first by remembering what it has seen, and second by seeing what is not simply present, but instead is likewise drawn out into the between along these twilight paths. This memory, this capacity for witnessing, makes the blue deer something other than an irrational animal. The deer is past the present in its recollection and this redefines its animality. "The blue deer is an animal, whose animality presumably does not rest in the animalistic, but in that observing recollection" (*GA* 12: 41/*OWL* 166, tm). The animal becomes the deer in looking beyond itself, certainly past any "disinhibiting ring" that would confine it.

To be sure, the transformation in question is a break with all manner of confinement for the animal. Heidegger's new understanding of the animal is on the basis of its exposure to blueness, i.e., in terms of the between.[40] This means breaking with the traditional abstractions and oppositions of metaphysical animality whereby it is set against the rational and intelligible. In the Trakl interpretation, this animal–rational diremption is thought of as a "curse" that has befallen us, though Heidegger is quick to explain that "not duality [*das Zwiefache*] as such, but rather discord [*die Zwietracht*] is the curse" (*GA* 12: 46/*OWL* 170, tm). Duality and difference are the gift of existence for us, modes of relating. Concomitant with that gift, however, is the curse of discord. The differences all too easily reify into antagonistic oppositions, not simply dividing the separated parties but urging them on to their utmost extremes. Animality becomes sheer wildness, with Heidegger observing that "due to this [to discord] each of the clans [*Geschlechter*, sexes, races, generations, tribes] is drawn into the unbridled uproar of the always isolated and sheer wildness of the wild game [*bloßen Wildheit des Wildes*]" (*GA* 12: 46/*OWL* 170, tm). Discord isolates each pole of the opposition that it institutes against the other—animality against rationality, for instance—such that the poles are deprived of all contact with each other. Animality is opposed to the rational and becomes sheer wildness and revolting brutality. "Out of the uproar of blind wildness it [discord] carries each clan into a diremption

[*Entzweiung*], and thereby casts it into unbridled isolation" (*GA* 12: 46/ *OWL* 170–71, tm). The segregation of the animal from the rational has led to the animal being understood as the brute wild beast.[41] It is isolated and quarantined within itself, trapped within its sameness to itself which drives it mad.

The transformation of animality likewise promises a transformation of humanity insofar as the antagonism between the animal and the rational has been written into the definition of the human as *animal rationale*. This dirempted being has not yet made its way into the indeterminacy of the blue. Heidegger cites Nietzsche that "this animal, namely the thinking one, the *animal rationale*, the human, according to a word of Nietzsche's, is not yet established" (*GA* 12: 41/ *OWL* 166–67, tm).[42] But for Heidegger this does not mean that the animal has not been sufficiently determined—indeed, he mentions that the contemporary human is all too decisively constituted and determined—rather that "the animality of this animal has not yet been made firm, i.e. 'brought home,' brought into what is native of its veiled essence" (*GA* 12: 41/ *OWL* 167, tm). The home for this human animal is out among the twilight paths. Its only home is on the way to . . . What is not yet established for it is no further determination, but the dissolution of these in the blue. The animality of this animal has not yet been allowed to remain veiled, indeterminate, so as to essence. The diremption and exacerbation of oppositions dissolves in the blue twilight. Heidegger writes that "the countenance of the deer in sight of the blue takes itself back into the gentle [*das Sanfte*]. For the gentle is, according to the word itself [Grimms' dictionary derives it from *sammeln*, to gather[43]], the peaceful gathering. It transforms the discord in that it converts [*verwindet*] what is injurious and scorching of the wild [*der Wildnis*] into an appeased pain" (*GA* 12: 41/166, tm). In the blue, the animal is no longer forced by its confinement to be ever only brute and wild animality. Rather than being endlessly goaded into ever purer forms of self-sameness, ever more extreme expressions of its irrationality, the animal in the blueness is able to be calmed and become gentle. The appeased and calmed pain remains a pain, but the discord of it is "brought to a turn" (*verwindet*). The discord is not forgotten as though it never happened; instead it is understood as dependent upon a prior field of relations from which it was an abstraction. The discord that arose from a drive to purity (of the animal, of the rational, of the space between them) is understood as dependent upon a preceding context of non-oppositional relations, a deformation of the between.

With the appeasement of discordant opposition, a new sense of animality can emerge. Heidegger refrains from trying to define it any further. Indeed, in some sense this would be impossible, insofar as the animal is now understood as essentially connected through its look with what it is not, and thus not simply present-at-hand for an assessment and evaluation. In Heidegger's words, "this animality is still far off and scarcely to be sighted. The animality of the animal here intended thus vacillates in the undefined" (*GA* 12: 41/*OWL* 166, tm). Let us note, however, that this animality is not unseen—there are traces. And if this new animality is as we have said, then it could never be fully present for the viewing anyway. It could only be sighted by a vision that likewise occurred within the between, one not constrained to the simply present, an observing recollection once again ("recollection" in that it does not see what is merely present).

What then does this tell us about the relationship between humans and animals? The stakes of this question are high, since Heidegger is often taken to be a "metaphysical humanist" who inserts a strict divide between the human and the animal, keeping each side in its purity free from contamination by the other. But in some remarks on childhood, we see that the child, immature Dasein, shares much with the animal. The 1928–29 lecture course *Introduction to Philosophy* devotes a few pages to the nature of childhood (more specifically to Dasein in both its early [*frühzeitliche*] and young [*frühmenschliche*] forms). Heidegger immediately specifies of young Dasein that "it is not essentially different without further ado [from mature Dasein], even if it is to be understood otherwise than as human" (*GA* 27: 123). Heidegger then worries over the methodological question of how to conceive of such a Dasein, deciding that it can only be pursued in something of a "privative manner, i.e. in departure from a positive foundational conception of Dasein" (*GA* 27: 123). The similarities with the treatment of the animal are striking. And just as the animal operated in a ring of behavedness (*Benommenheit*) which has connotations of a kind of captivated daze, so too is the child said to be in a "semi-conscious state [*Dämmerzustand*]" (*GA* 27: 125). Most importantly, however, the child does not simply comport to beings; rather "some being is already open to the child, although still no comportment to this being follows" (*GA* 27: 125). As Heidegger explains, "the semiconscious state which such a young Dasein is in, does not mean that there would be still no relation [*Verhältnis*] to beings, but rather only that this self-comporting to . . . [*Sichverhalten zu . . .*] still has no definite goal. The being-with the beings is to a certain extent still clouded over, not yet illuminated, such that this Dasein can still make no determinate use of beings" (*GA* 27: 126). So let us simply note that even at the time of fundamental ontology, there is recognition of a distinction between the adult and the child, that the human is not simply human. The category that is supposed to be preserved against contamination by an animal other, for example, is already compromised. Not all humans are alike.

Having said this, one of the grounds cited in support of Heidegger's purported metaphysical humanism is precisely the distinction between "dying" and "coming to an end" that we observed in the *Fundamental Concepts of Metaphysics,* but which is also to be found in *Being and Time* as well as in the Bremen lectures (see *GA* 29/30: 388/267, *GA* 2: 320/*SZ* 240–41, and *GA* 79: 17–18/17). It is worth a brief look at this now.

The transformation of the human in blueness would parallel that of the animal that is transformed into the blue deer. The human would become the mortal, a stranger to itself, defined by what lies most outside it, something that it can never possess and which keeps it open and disposed toward the world, its death. This is surely a shift from a thinking of the living being (*Lebewesen*) to that of the beings that can die (*die Sterblichen*), but it is a shift that is not automatically the privilege of the human. In "The Danger," the third of the Bremen lectures where Heidegger first develops the role of the mortals within the fourfold, he intones that "the human is not yet the mortal" (*GA* 79: 56/54). Mortality is not something simply pre-given as a distinction to the human against the rest of life. It marks a kind of transition out of the living being, out of humanity itself: "From the rational living being, the mortals must first come to be" (*GA* 79: 18/17, cf. *GA* 7: 180/*PLT* 176). Mortality is something that humanity does not possess.

A consequence of this is that it is not only the animal that does not die. It is the human, too. Heidegger makes this strikingly clear in notorious lines from the same lecture where he writes that "Hundreds of thousands die in mass. Do they die? They perish. They are put down. Do they die? They become pieces of inventory of a standing reserve for the fabrication of corpses. Do they die? They are unobtrusively liquidated in annihilation camps. And even apart from such as these—millions now in China abjectly end in starvation" (*GA* 79: 56/53). These are harrowing words, to be sure, but what they express is the fact that death is nothing pre-given. More, death is something that can be taken from another. No one may be able to die my death for me, but they are in the position to take that death from me, it would seem. Humans do not die, they come to an end. In this they are not distinct from animals. The idea that only humans would die and that this would mark an essential, even ontological, distinction from the animal must be surrendered.

Despite this, objectors might respond that Heidegger's conception of "mortals" is precisely what is at stake and that here, far from abolishing his anthropocentrism, he inscribes it all the more deeply. The idea of mortality by this account would be one more strategy of seclusion and quarantine to protect Heidegger's privileged version of "subjectivity" from contamination. Heidegger would be responding to the recognition of a disturbing similarity between animal and human. His response would take the form of a still more drastic flight away from this proximity into a shielded realm of purity. Now it would only be a cadre of human elite who achieve mortality and death, leaving the rest of humanity to end with the animals. Not every human is mortal, they might say, but only humans are.

And yet, what is mortality but a matter of exposure? Mortality is not a privilege of the human. In fact, mortality for the human is only possible through a liberation of animality, a rethinking of the animal, our relation to animals, and the animality of ourselves. Mortality is not at all a privilege of the human, and Heidegger notes this himself, and quite strikingly: "The name 'blue deer,'" Heidegger writes, "names the mortal" (*GA* 12: 42/*OWL* 167, tm). Obviously such a view calls into question the supposed anthropocentrism of Heidegger, a central tenet of the interpretations of animality in Heidegger. As one commentator, quite representative of these readings, claims: "The problem is rather that Heidegger uncritically accepts two basic tenets of ontotheological anthropocentrism: that human beings and animals can be clearly and cleanly distinguished in their essence; and that such a distinction between human beings and animals even needs to be drawn."[44] With the mortality of the blue deer, these no longer seem the case.

The animal, like the wanderer, like the poet, belongs to the between. The animal exists beyond itself and this means it requires that beyond to be what it is. This does not happen in a vacuum, it takes place on the earth, under the sky. What exposes itself on this earth and under this sky is marked by that exposure. It is a visible target that is unfailingly struck and fronted on all sides. But the exposed being is not simply the patient of exposure, it is the agent of it, too. All that appears (essences) marks the world around it, perhaps even finding it remarkable, memorable. What appears takes part in the reciprocal relation of exposure. Whatever appears beyond itself, in other words, whatever appears in the blue between, like the blue deer, offers the relations of support and witnessing that bear the world and make it bearable in turn.

Heidegger's thinking of the earth proposes an ungrounded mode of existence that sets the thing free to shine. On the groundless ground of the earth, on the abyss, there comes to fruition the shine of appearance. This destabilized sense of being reverberates through our understanding of nature as well. At the time of the fourfold, Heidegger rethinks the nature of stone, water, plants, and animals all in accordance with the ungrounded bearing of the earth. Stones bear and endure the pain of jointure and sense, waters make the land arable so as to bear proceeds and support dwelling, plants bear fruit in flourishing growth, and animals bear witness to and support the world of relations. The thing, too, will be constituted out of earth and will likewise exist in an ungrounded bearing. Thanks to the bearing of the earth, the thing is able to enter the between and remain connected with the earthly nature all around it. But the shine of the earth needs a space through which to shine, a medium for its appearance, and this is the sky. The sky partners with the earth in the constitution of the between.

3

Sky, Weathering Medium of Appearance

With the sky, Heidegger comes to think the wide expanse of appearance. Whereas the earth names an ungrounded bearing that suspends the thing in "mid air," we might say, the sky serves to name this space of suspension. What the earth bears is borne aloft into the sky. The sky thus enables the earth's ungrounded and superficial irruption into the realm of radiant appearance (of shining). The sky is the space (even the "spacing") of the earth's irruption. The earth could not be the earth without such a sky, there would be nowhere for it to appear much less conceal itself, nowhere for it to come to fruition. By making the sky a participant in the fourfold, Heidegger ascribes this expansive, mediated existence to every thing that is. The fourfold announces that earth and sky are inherent to things. If earthly existence is always a shining, radiant one, then earthly existence always takes place under the sky, for only the sky can distribute the peculiar radiance of the earth. To be ungrounded is to be distributed beyond oneself and the sky is what makes such distribution possible. But here, with this formulation, it sounds as though the sky would precede the earth and await its emergence. Such is not the case. The sky is opened along with that which emerges; what emerges traverses the sky in so doing. Which is to say there could be no sky without the earth, either.

Perhaps then, as the sky does not simply name a presence isolatable and locatable above us, we should hear a new sense to Heidegger's recurrent phrase *"unter dem Himmel"* ("under the sky"), that of being "amidst (*unter*) the sky." The earth does not name a solid ground beneath us and the sky does not name an empty space above us. The two would have to be thought together more intimately. Heidegger accomplishes this in considering what he terms the "dimension," the spacing *between* earth and sky (see *GA* 7: 198/*PLT* 218). Our first concern, then, will be with the nature of this dimension.

For its part, the sky is no empty space, but a field of alteration and transition, of shifting densities and depths. At its first formulation in "The Thing" we read:

> The sky is the path of the sun, the course of the moon, the gleam of
> the stars, the seasons of the year, the light and twilight of day, the dark
> and bright of the night, the favor and inclemency of the weather, drift-
> ing clouds, and blue depths of the aether. (*GA* 79: 17/16)

The sky is always a weathered sky. What appears in the light of day (or the
brightness of the night) does so within a particular climate or weather
pattern. Weather serves to name the non-homogeneous character of the
sky. What the earth enters in the dimension is nothing sheer and staid.
Instead, it emerges in a field of weather patterns, drifting clouds, and
ethereal flows. Our second concern in what follows will be to articulate
the weathered density of the sky, i.e., to understand the sky as a textured
and variegated medium of appearance.

Heidegger's characterization of the sky in "Building Dwelling Thinking" places additional emphasis on the movement of the sky, signaling
our third and final concern in considering the sky, the mobility of it,
more specifically, its temporal character:

> The sky is the *vaulting* path of the sun, the *shape-shifting* course of the
> moon, the *wandering* gleam of the stars, the seasons of the year *and their
> changes*, the light and twilight of day, the dark and bright of the night,
> the clemency and inclemency of the weather, drifting clouds and blue
> depths of the aether. (*GA* 7: 151/*PLT* 149, tm, em)

The sky is the domain of motion, i.e., of change of places across time.
What emerges into the dimension enters not only a heterogeneous field
of weather and resistance; it also enters the passing of time, of the day
and the year, of night and day, the hours and the seasons. The medium
of the sky is consequently a temporal medium, with temporality variegat-
ing the sky once again. To think the sky is thus to think the dimension
between earth and sky, the medium of earthly appearance, as well as the
domain of temporal alteration.

Before turning to this, however, it is worth considering how the sky
came to play such an important role in Heidegger's thinking. Indeed, of
all the elements of the fourfold, the sky is the one whose arrival seems
least prepared. During the early 1930s, there is evidently no place for
the sky. In the 1934 lecture course *Hölderlin's Hymns "Germania" and "The
Rhine,"* for example, Heidegger repeatedly names beings as a whole to
consist of "Gods, humans, earth," without mentioning sky.[1] Similarly, in a
diagram from the *Contributions to Philosophy* paradigmatic of Heidegger's
views at this time, we see these three players, Gods, the human, and the

earth, joined by a fourth, the world, with still no mention of sky (the "E" in the center would designate "Ereignis," the event of appropriation):

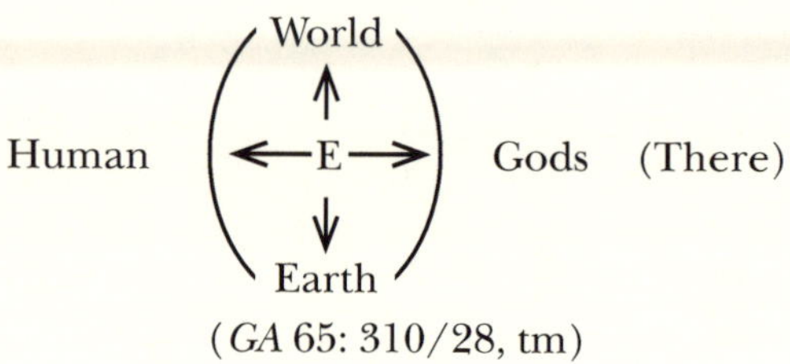

(*GA* 65: 310/28, tm)

In "The Origin of the Work of Art," however, a text that follows the schema given in the *Contributions to Philosophy*, Heidegger does indeed mention the sky. He writes of "the light of the day, the breadth of the sky, the darkness of night" (*GA* 5: 28/21), but he does so in a passage naming the earth ("we name this the *earth*"; *GA* 5: 28/21, tm). Light and dark, day and night, these are here aspects of the earth. In the work of the thirties, sky is earth.[2]

With the fourfold, the sky is disambiguated from the earth, pulled apart from it in order to bring the earth and sky into a still more intimate relation. But it would be wrong to think that the fourfold was just a slight modification of the schema from the 1930s, with sky replacing world. The entire relation is different. Even setting aside the important terminological distinctions that later emerge ("mortals" in place of the "human," "divinities" in place of "gods"), the fourfold is gathered around the thing, a thing that participates in the worlding of the world. Where the above schema would have the "E" of *Ereignis*, the event of appropriation, at its center, the fourfold places the reciprocal relation of thing and world. World is not something independent and separate from humans, gods, and earth, it is instead unfolded through their interactions. The fourfold intersects at the world, and each of the four are just as much a part of the world as any other; the earth retains no privilege in this, antagonistic or otherwise.

Even if we accept that during the 1930s, in "The Origin of the Work of Art," for example, the world played the role that we are now ascribing to the sky, i.e., that of a space for the emergence and radiance of the shining of the earth, the whole tenor of the situation is different by the time of the fourfold. The 1930s relation of earth and world was described in terms of a "conflict" or "strife" (*GA* 5: 35/26). With the fourfold, however, a new relation takes shape between the earth and the medium for its sensible gleam. Rather than a conflict, the earth and sky are joined in a "marriage" (*GA* 79: 11/10). Their antagonism is more explicitly a cooperation, and this a cooperation in the worlding of world, as we shall see. This marriage between earth and sky is what Heidegger terms the "dimension."

By including the sky within the fourfold, Heidegger situates all things in a heterogeneous and shifting medium of appearance. Such mediated appearing is indissociable from the thing. Indeed, it makes it what it is.

§9. The Dimension between Earth and Sky

Heidegger's thinking of the dimension does not come from out of the blue, but is already prepared for by his earlier thinking of the "between" in the 1930s. Indeed, the dimension is to be understood as precisely such a between, since "the essence of the dimension," as we are told, is "the between: the upward to the sky as well as the downward to earth" (*GA* 7: 199 / *PLT* 218). The thinking of the between is a key gesture in Heidegger's break with the traditional presuppositions of metaphysical philosophy. At the time of the *Contributions to Philosophy*, the between subverts the oppositional structure of metaphysical thought as such, including the oppositions between presence and absence as well as the sensible and the super-sensible. A consideration of the between will thus help to shed light on the sky's role in building the dimension between earth and sky.

a. The Between

In his formulation of the "between," Heidegger attempts to think the "there" of Da-sein apart from metaphysical notions of presence and absence. But now this between cannot be thought as such if one still holds that on the bounds of this between there would be found presence and absence, each in its own uncompromised integrity. The between *is* between presence and absence, but without there being presence and absence to bound it. In other words, the between *is not* between presence and absence. But this only because there is no total or integral presence and absence on the outskirts of the between to begin with; on the contrary, there is only the between. What presences in the between does so *between* the traditionally opposed poles of presence and absence. The between, however, is not dependent upon the prior existence of presence and absence, it is not a derivative of their relationship. Rather, it is the between that precedes, the between that is misrepresented and passed over in the thought of total presence and absence. The between names a thinking of what eludes the metaphysical notion of presence, while nonetheless touching right upon it.

The question of the relation between the between and its bounds is paramount here. For if the between is completely without relation to a bounding presence, then it no longer seems to be between anything. Rather it would be totally and completely the between, in precisely the same way that metaphysical presence is totally and completely present. In some sense, the between must be compromised by presence precisely in order to be between, otherwise it only goes to reinstate an order of purity, integrity, and homogeneity. But since now the between is in relation to presence, and presence itself is a misconfiguration of this between, there is only the between. This fundamental oscillation is the "essential sway" of the between, between presence and absence and *between their "between."*

Throughout the *Contributions to Philosophy*, Heidegger will refer to the between in terms that operate within a spatial and temporal register: it is the "land" for the "inventive thinking [*Er-denkens*] of beyng," for example (*GA* 65: 86/69), but also the site of historical appropriation: "History plays out only in the between of the encounter of gods and humans, with this between as the ground of the strife of world and earth; history is nothing other than the eventuation [*Ereignung*] of this between" (*GA* 65: 479/377, tm). This spatio-temporal consideration of the between is Heidegger's renewed attempt to think the "there" of Da-sein—a thirteen point list entitled "On the Essence of Truth" concludes with "Da-sein essencing as the 'between'" (*GA* 65: 354/280, tm). That the "there" of Da-sein would be the between—this requires a rethinking of the foundational oppositions inherent to metaphysical subjectivity. Signal among these once again is the sensible/super-sensible distinction.

In the *Contributions to Philosophy* this distinction is examined in terms of the body and soul distinction, more specifically in a consideration of the Platonic *chôrismos*, which names their "separation." In the *Phaedo*, Plato employs the term in presenting death as "the release and separation [*chôrismos*] of soul from body" (67 d). Platonic metaphysics, according to Heidegger, generates its notion of transcendence from out of this separation, treats this separation as a purity of its own, as something extant, a being—in Heidegger's terms, "the *chôrismos* is set up as a being, as it were; and this is the origin of 'transcendence' in its various configurations" (*GA* 65: 216/169, tm). The transcendent is an extant entity that is set apart by means of the extant separation of the Platonic *chôrismos*. The body/soul, sensible/super-sensible distinction is thus closely tied to this conception of *chôrismos*, and for Heidegger it is just this separation that is called into question by the between. "The 'between' of Da-sein overcomes the *chôrismos,* not, as it were, by throwing a bridge between beyng (beinghood) and beings—as if there were two present-at-hand riverbanks needing to be bridged—but by transforming beyng and beings at the same time into their simultaneity" (*GA* 65: 14/14, tm). There is no separation between beyng and beings, there is no *chôrismos,* and thus no transcendence in the Platonic sense. The between as space of inter-penetration and co-belonging allows the seemingly rigid oppositions of metaphysics to sink back into their groundless ground, exposing them as based upon a retreat before exposure itself, the sensible/super-sensible distinction included.

Relieved of the oppositional scaffolding of metaphysics, Dasein is no longer "separated" from the groundless ground. In discussing the earth, we were led to consider this groundless ground in terms of the abyss and such is the case here, for the "abyss" is the "site of the moment for the 'between,' and Da-sein must be grounded as this 'between'" (*GA* 65: 387/306). Dasein grounds itself upon this groundless ground, bears it, and in so doing, is itself the between. "Da-sein . . . essences as the *grounding* ground, as the 'between' and 'middle' of beings themselves" (*GA* 65: 223/174, tm). But more than this, Dasein is not only the between of beings, it is likewise "the between between *beyng and beings*" (*GA* 65: 343/271, tm). Once again, if we think we have got hold of the between by finding it between two presences, we have lost it. Thus it is still not enough to think Dasein as between beyng and beings—there must be a between between this as well, and Heidegger makes this clear, noting that "a between essences between us and beyng and that this between itself belongs to the essencing of beyng" (*GA* 65: 368/290, tm). In the *Contributions to Philosophy,* Da-Sein is released from the oppositions of metaphysics and ultimately forms the space of relation between beings, being, and beyng, a space of encounter and response (*Ent-gegnung, GA* 65: 454/358).

The between is thus the site of relations, not of presences. What stands here is not something integral and completed; it lies instead between "abandonment and hinting," the abandonment of beyng and the hint of its arrival (*GA* 65: 311/246, tm), between "call and belonging [*Zuruf und Zugehörigkeit*]," the call of beyng and its hearkening response (*GA* 65: 380/300). The between reveals the relational character of Dasein.

b. The Dimension

Heidegger considers the dimension in the context of Hölderlin's late poem, "In lovely blueness. . . ." The situation presented is one of a life that has become sheer toil. Hölderlin asks whether in such conditions it is still imaginable that a person would find their life worth living:

> When life is plaintive toil, is it possible
> for a person to look up and say: even in these conditions
> I still want to exist?[3]

Hölderlin's answer is an unreserved "yes" and this leads Heidegger to reflect on the role of this "looking up" (*Aufschauen*) in the general economy of life. Life might consist in an incessant toiling for earnings, "but the human is at the same time equipped," Heidegger writes, "to look up from within this region, and from here to look out of it, passing through it, to the heavenly [*zu den Himmlischen*]" (*GA* 7: 198/*PLT* 218, tm). Looking up draws the human out of the world of toil, a world of remuneration and equivalence, where everything has its price and toil is exchanged for the earnings to pay it. Indeed, "only in the domain of sheer toil does the human toil for the sake of 'earnings'" (*GA* 7: 198/*PLT* 218, tm). In our domain of sheer toil, the circulation of equivalences strives for a complete closure, the sameness of all circulating value. But even such a self-enclosing system as the domain of sheer toil has its outside. Looking up moves us up out of complete enclosure in a world of wages. It interrupts the sameness that is its stock in trade. Looking up brings us into contact with something different from the order of the replaceable and the constancy of presence toward which it strives. It brings us into a new spatial relation: "Looking up traverses [*durchgeht*] upwards to the sky while remaining down upon the earth. Looking up measures out [*durchmißt*] the between of the sky and earth" (*GA* 7: 198/*PLT* 218, tm). Looking up allows us to enter into this area between earth and sky, something which we do not attain as outside agents, but instead as those for whom or to whom the between has been fitted. As Heidegger explains, "this between is apportioned [*zugemessen*] to the dwelling of humans" (*GA* 7: 198/*PLT* 218, tm).

In looking up, the human traverses a dimension that is apportioned to it. Operative here is a reciprocal relation between the human and the dimension, between traversal and apportionment. The human is measured out to that which reaches toward it. This reciprocal relation of reaching and traversal—emphasized through the repeated use of terms prefixed by *durch-* ("through") and *zu-* ("to" or "toward")—is essential to the dimension. "We now name the apportioned measuring out [*die zugemessene . . . Durchmessung*], i.e. the measuring out that *reaches towards* [*zugereichte Durchmessung*], through which the between of sky and earth is opened, the dimension" (*GA* 7: 198/*PLT* 218, tm). The dimension is just such a texture of relation.

This reciprocity is so much the case that Heidegger inserts a marginal note in the text at the point where he first states that the human is "equipped" to look up out of toil. Since it might appear by this word "equipped" that the human simply asserted itself into this otherwise closed off field (the dimension), Heidegger places a note here asking "only this? more so: the human is referred, called, needed–" (*GA* 7: 198 n. f). The human does not enter into a dimension otherwise unprepared for it. Part of its being measured to the human is due to its reaching out to the human in advance, as referral, call, need. The human is already invited, in other words, to let itself into the dimension. The dimension's nature as a relational field requires this.

Heidegger makes clear that this reaching and apportioning dimension is not the result of a pre-given relation between earth and sky; "it does not arise from the fact that the sky and earth are turned toward each other," he says; instead, "this turning towards rests for its part in the dimension" (*GA* 7: 198/*PLT* 218, tm). The sky would not be there for the earth to turn toward it, nor the earth the sky, were it not for the dimension. There cannot be two independent parties that would then turn toward each other and in so doing create a dimension "between" them. No, for neither of these parties would be able to ever reach the other without the dimension enabling their achievement. The dimension is the medium for all traversal and reaching. The dimension makes possible the conduction of one thing to another. The dimension is not a void that would otherwise lock every being within a hard shell. Instead, the dimension is the permissive stretch of a suitable spacing: "The essence of the dimension is the lit up and thus measured out apportionment of the between: of the up to the sky as well as of the down to the earth" (*GA* 7: 199/*PLT* 218, tm). The dimension allows for a proliferation of relations between all that exists upon the earth and under the sky.

Another route to the thought of this dimension is found in the *Basic Principles of Thinking* lecture cycle of 1957. Starting from "the three-dimensional space familiar to us," Heidegger discusses the way that dimensions determine what lies within their scope (*GA* 79: 84/80). "As distinct from a line, a plane is another dimension. But the former is not merely stacked together into the latter"; that is, a plane is not something composed of a great many lines (*GA* 79: 84–85/80). The difference of a dimension is not something quantitatively reproducible from within a different dimension. But this does not mean that the plane has no relation to the lines, either. "Rather, in relation to the linear manifold, the plane takes this manifold up into itself" (*GA* 79: 84–85/80). By taking it up into itself (*in sich aufnehmen*), the planar dimension holds sway over the linear dimension. What distinguishes the planar dimension, however, is the way in which it treats the linear manifold so taken up. "In so doing," Heidegger says, "it [the planar dimension] is another domain for a rule [*Maßgabe*] in regard to this manifold" (*GA* 79: 84–85/80). To take something up is to take it under the domain of a rule, to bring it to appearance before the rule or standard of the domain. This relation between rule and domain is at the essence of a dimension. "The same holds for bodies in relation to the planar manifold. Bodies, planes, and lines each implicate a distinct rule. If we put aside the spatial restriction then a dimension shows itself as the domain of a rule" (*GA* 79: 84–85/80). A dimension consequently is the reach of a rule or stipulation (*Maßgabe*). But it is also more than this. A dimension has a particular way of taking up what belongs to it and this is what the rule is said to specify. Otherwise put, the "rule" in a dimension specifies how the dimension takes up its participants. We are dealing, in other words, with the interface between dimension and thing, the rule specifying the grip between them: "Thus rules and domains are not two distinct or separate things, but rather one and the same. The rule each time yields and opens a domain wherein the rule is at home and can be what it is" (*GA* 79: 85/80). Dimension and rule are inseparable because the rule is ever only the rule of engagement between dimension and thing, the rule for how that dimension embraces the thing, and the rule for how that thing spreads itself out across the reaching and apportioned between of the sky and the earth.

The dimension would be no "between," however, were it understood as something suspended between the earth and the sky. Rather, as a between, it is a field of relation. What lies within it, then, must likewise be relational. If the measure or rule is what establishes the way in which things appear in a dimension, then the measure of the dimension between sky and earth must be one that permits of relational participation within this dimension. Heidegger follows Hölderlin in taking the proper measure or rule for this dimension as no simple standard that would be at hand and awaiting application. Instead, the measure in this instance is god, as Hölderlin understands it, "God, as He who he is, is unknown for Hölderlin and precisely *as this unknown one* he is the measure [*das Maß*] for the poet" (*GA* 12: 201/*PLT* 220, tm). The unknown God is the measure, but not as something that first must become known and then applied, but rather directly as this unknown: "The measure consists in the way in which the God that remains unknown is revealed through the sky *as* this unknown" (*GA* 12: 201/*PLT* 220, tm). This is a strange measure, to say the least. It is one that is not "known" in the sense of something that could be comprehended, but neither is it completely "unknown" in the sense of something without any relation to us. Rather, the measure is one that announces itself as unknown without thereby becoming known. The measure, in other words, is a revelation of concealment: "The appearance of god through the sky consists in an unveiling that allows what it conceals to be seen, but lets it be seen not by seeking to rip what is concealed out of its concealment, but rather solely in that it shelters what is concealed in its self-concealment. Thus the unknown God appears as the unknown one through the sky's manifestness" (*GA* 12: 201/*PLT* 220–21, tm). Consequently, the standard for what appears in the dimension is nothing present at hand ("in no case a graspable stick or rod," Heidegger says; *GA* 12: 201/*PLT* 221, tm), but something that upsets the sheer opposition of presence and absence, a revelation of what does not show itself, a showing of non-showing. The measure, in other words, is a testament to the fact that all concealment must show itself if it is to be concealment. Without this appearing there is no concealing.

Since this measure grants an unconcealment to what appears, it runs counter to the standard role of measurement in the sciences. Heidegger had commented on this in the section of the *Contributions to Philosophy* entitled "Propositions about 'Science'" (§76, *GA* 65: 145–59/113–24). Here we read that "Every science, even a so-called 'descriptive' one, is *explanatory*: what is unknown [*das Unbekannte*] in the region is connected, by being led back in various modes and over various distances, to something known [*ein Bekanntes*] and already understood" (*GA* 65: 146/114, tm). Through the measurement of science, the unknown is made known. Nothing unknown should remain about it. It is to be entirely taken up into scientific knowledge and thereby explained. Explanation [*Erklärung*] makes clear, as the German term itself suggests, and it makes clear by eliminating the opacity of the unknown. In regards to the dimension that we are considering, however, the situation is quite otherwise. The measure is not used to assimilate the unknown into the purview of the known. It is not even used to assimilate the known to the unknown. Instead, it is not a matter of assimilating or transforming at all, but one of defamiliarization, we might say. It is in this lecture that Heidegger claims that to poetize is to measure. The measure of the poet is just this letting appear of concealment. "The poet calls into the familiar appearances something foreign [*das Fremde*] as that wherein the invisible joins itself [*sich schicket*] in order to remain what it is: unknown" (*GA* 7: 204/*PLT* 223, tm). The known is to be "made" unknown, or, better, the known is to be allowed to conceal itself as unknown. The difference is one between assimilation and relation. Scientific measurement contains the measured, poetic measurement releases it.

The dimension between sky and earth has its measure. This measure decides the interface of thing and world. Where the measure is a poetic one, a poetized (*verdichtet*) measure, the thing scintillates in concealing and revealing. The surface of the thing so understood is permeable to the world of relation. Through such a measure the things reach out to each other, reach out to us. Their reaching heads toward new relations, opening new paths of contact. The dimension is just this field of reaching. The 1962 lecture "Time and Being" says as much. "Dimension—it bears repeating—is here thought not only as the area of possible measurement, but rather as a passing through [*Hindurchlangen*], as a reaching that clears [*lichtende Reichen*]" (*GA* 14: 19/15, tm). A subsequent note to the manuscript likewise reads: "Dimension—the clearing reaching [*das lichtende Reichen*] / the reaching clearing [*das reichende Lichten*]" (*GA* 14: 21 n. 7). We might consider the relation a mutual one; the dimension is cleared insofar as there is a reaching through it and there can only be a reaching through where there is a clearing. The reaching brings its own clearing and the clearing its reaching. Heidegger describes such a situation in the concluding Bremen lecture "The Turn" in considering something else of the sky: the flash of lightning. "This sudden self-lighting is the lightning flash," Heidegger writes. "It brings itself into the brightness proper to it, a brightness it brought in with itself" (*GA* 79: 74/69). The reaching of the clearing (the clearing of the reaching) is just like that bolt, bringing its own illumination to the dimension between earth and sky.

We can see this in Heidegger's portrayal of the relationship between sky and earth in the lecture "The Thing," where he names their "reciprocal betrothal" or "mutual entrustment" a "wedding" or "marriage" (*Hochzeit; GA* 79: 11/10). Here, the wedding is enacted through both water and wine. Heidegger considers the water of a spring. There abides in water both the stones of the earth and the rain and dew of the sky, "in the water of the spring there abides the marriage of sky and earth" (*GA* 79: 11/10). Wine is the fruit of the grapevine "in which the nourishment of the earth and the sun of the sky are betrothed to each another" (*GA* 79: 11/10–11; cf. *GA* 7: 174/*PLT* 170, tm). The wine entrusts the sky and earth to each other.

The wedding of earth and sky is their entrustment and betrothal to one another, which takes place in the gathering of particular things in the world. A 1946–48 conversation on Hölderlin speaks of this as love,

> for heavenly love is in truth the love of the sky for the earth and, what says the same, the love of the earth for the sky. Not as though sky and earth were present beforehand and only reached one another in love, rather in love itself there first takes place, at the beginning of everything and in their singularity, the essence of the sky as the highest height of the joyful [*der Heitere*] and the essence of earth as the deepest depths of the abyss. (*GA* 75: 123–24)

Again we encounter the thought that the dimension or the between would not be consequent upon pre-existing poles of relation. Rather love is initiatory.[4] It is the relation that gives each to the other. In so doing, each of the partners needs the other and thus can only be itself from out of the relation. This love of earth and sky is likewise their marriage.

When Heidegger spoke at the wedding of one of his students in 1965, he elaborated on the nature of marriage, the *Hochzeit,* literally the high time, the time of the heights. He begins with reflections on what it means to celebrate (*feiern*), specifically in regard to celebrating the newlyweds. "Celebrating means here," Heidegger says, "holding oneself free for the uncommon, admitting oneself into this, recognizing it in its ownmost, honoring it" (*GA* 16: 611). Celebration is an honoring of the uncommon whereby what is honored is made high and elevated:

> therefore the time in which the elevated one is celebrated is called the elevated time [*die hohe Zeit*].—The *elevated* times [Hoch*zeiten*] are the church holidays, the festival days of the knights and the workmen; an *elevated* time is *also* the day of pairing [*Vermählung*]. We are familiar with *elevated* times now only as marriage [*Hochzeit*] and understand this word in the sense of pairing—one of the signs from the history of language by which we can discern how our saying power narrows, grinds down, and decays. (*GA* 16: 611)

A marriage, like that between the earth and sky, is an elevated time. Elevated times are those that honor something by raising it aloft. This elevation is a disengagement from the ordinary days of the laity, the working people. The strictures of the everyday are lifted, or rather, risen above. There is no longer the specification of a path or method as the most efficient or direct route as in everyday commerce. We are free to proliferate beyond these approved relations. These new, elevated, streaming relations likewise interweave us further into the world, joining and binding us to it, wedding us to that world, to the animals, plants, waters, and stones of it, to others, and to the things of the world as well.

Heidegger's advice to his student calls her to keep to this dimension and to adhere to this standard: "If in the future your common work is devoted to a field where number and weight provide the standard [*Maß*], then it is worth keeping in mind without presumption [*Vermessenheit*] that other, higher, yet ungraspable standard of the unmeasured and inmeasurable [*Unermeßlichen und Unermeßbaren*]" (*GA* 16: 615). To keep to this measure is to enter the dimension of the marriage of earth and sky, to wed oneself to that. The elevated time of the marriage celebration joining earth and sky is a disengagement from the world of work and toil. It shows that the total closure of the world is never possible. Toil can never be all. It shows that there is no closure that is not at once exposed. It shows that things can be otherwise, it ventilates the workplace. The evidence for Heidegger is everywhere; we are already in that dimension, it merely requires that one look up. Looking up, i.e., participation in the wedding celebration of earth and sky, warrants one's living on.

§10. The Sky as Medium of Appearance

Heidegger's depiction of the sky as a field that is weathered, literally, by the turbulence or placidity of the weather, as ethereal, blue, and cloud cast (we shall examine each of these in turn) all go toward disabusing us of the notion that the sky would be merely a homogeneous absence or void. Rather, what appears upon the earth does so under skies that vary in their distribution of the relations that emerge. The sky that provides for the eruption of earthly appearance is no absent expanse. Instead, it is populated and variegated, a medium.

a. Weather, Storms, and Lightning

Weather attends all that we do and leave undone. It also provides a basis for conviviality and conversation by the combined impact of its pervasiveness, cyclical regularity, and aberrant fluctuation. The sky *gives* us something to talk about: the weather. All that we do is done within an environment, as our lives take place immersed in a climate.[5] Whatever appears of the earth appears within a field of weather. Varying in intensity and assertiveness, weather denotes the *texture* of the sky as medium.

This texture is nothing at our disposal. Within Heidegger's depiction of the sky, weather is understood in terms of its "favor and inclemency [*die Gunst und das Unwirtliche*]" ("The Thing"), or its "clemency and inclemency [*das Wirtliche und Unwirtliche*]" ("Building Dwelling Thinking"). The weather allows us passage through it, but varies in the degree of its "clemency," with the term *das Wirtliche* stemming from the German word *Wirt*, a publican or a landlord, one who offers a welcome of sorts. This hospitality is thus how the weather will host us, how it will permit us entry, how it will support or sustain us, accommodate us, and cover us. Heidegger's presentation in "Building Dwelling Thinking" understands the weather as our temperamental host, at times admitting, at times barring our entry. Similarly, the presentation in "The Thing" connects the weather with a thinking of grace or favor (*die Gunst*).[6] This again emphasizes the fact that the weather is out of our hands, is something that comes to us and can do so in inclement and even threatening guises.

Heidegger's Hölderlin commentaries consistently explore these considerations of the grace and favor of the weather and do so in terms of a thinking of mediation. In the 1943 discussion of Hölderlin's hymn "Remembrance," Heidegger observes the struggle of sailors against the wind. They "battle with the contrariety of the winds and with the inclemency [*Ungunst*] of the weather. For the sea is open to all winds. The crossing is not always good nor univocal its direction. Much remains undecided" (*GA* 4: 135–36/157, tm; see also *GA* 52: 178). Unfavorable weather prevents a crossing, a delivery of what is sent along these waters. The storm is a threat to the transmissiveness of the medium. Storms similarly threaten the harvest that the countryman must tend in Hölderlin's ode "As When on a Holiday . . . ," leading Heidegger to note, "the countryman knows that his possessions stand under the constant menace of the weather, yet he finds that everything around him is at peace and delightful. He waits confidently for the future gift of the field and the grapevine. Fruit and man are protected in the favor [*Gunst*] that permeates earth and heaven and that grants something which will remain" (*GA* 4: 51/74). Everything is under the threat of these skies, but this weather grants the grace of survival, where this impossibility of annihilation, of pure absence, is nothing but another name for mediation. There will be no annihilation and this is ever always an invitation to endless destruction, the remainder always ever more threatened, as we have noted in our considerations of the atomic bomb (see "The Atomic Bomb" in chapter 1). And this is because here there is no object, integral and standing in place, that remains. Rather, that which remains is tied to what lies beyond it, and is only what it is in its exchange with this beyond. Such is the mediated existence of the remainder. The threat is a consequence of mediation, and simultaneously the precondition of grace.

For Heidegger the most intense and dense of weather patterns, the premier weather event, is the storm (*Sturm*), in particular the thunderstorm (*Gewitter*) accompanied by lightning (*Blitz*). This is true from the Alpine rhetoric and imagery of the 1930s notebooks, the poetic romanticism of the Hölderlin interpretations through the 1940s, and into the thinking of the fourfold in the late 1940s and 1950s. While a storm might seem the very definition of inclement weather, it is our exposure to the storm that determines our relation to what lies beyond us and thus determines our entry into the medium of the world.

First and foremost, the storm is a figure of exposure. The poet is exposed to this storm and the poetic task is to endure it. Poetry is thus not a matter of relating personal experience. "The poet does not work over the experiences of his soul, but rather stands 'under god's thunderstorm'—'with a bare head,' defenseless, abandoned and relinquished of his own accord" (*GA* 39: 30–31). Rather than recounting the experiences lived in a subjective interiority, the poet stands in "the most extreme exteriority of naked exposure to the thunder storm" (*GA* 39: 31). The poet must be naked, bare-headed, exposed to the onslaught of the medium. The poet thus evinces "the courage to endure the weather of the gods and to await the stroke of lightning" (*GA* 39: 148). In so doing, the poet is "exposed to the lightning of god" (*GA* 4: 44/61, tm).

Second, however, the storm is also a figure of communication. In the Hölderlin readings of the 1930s and 1940s, the poet's stance within the medium of the storm grants the poet a peculiar receptivity. Exposed to the storm, the poet is marked by this exposure. The lasting mark of this, the scar of communication (communication as exposure to a medium of sense), is the word. The storm is an event of communication. In a fragment to a poem, Hölderlin notes that "God speaks in the thunderstorm,"[7] a storm that Heidegger takes to name "the relation to god and his language" (*GA* 39: 63). In "As When on a Holiday . . ." the poet stands "with bare head" under "the thunderstorm of God."[8] The poet receives the communication and conveys it to an audience, amplifying and distributing it: "thunderstorm and lightning are the language of the gods, and the poet is he who has to endure this language without blanching, who has to take it up and place it in the Dasein of the people" (*GA* 39: 31). It is an affair of electrical transmission: "The poet compels the lightning bolts of the god into the word, capturing them, and places this lightning-charged word in the language of his people" (*GA* 39: 30). Whoever would receive the sending that is carried through this communicative storm must deal with these explosive words, must enter into this medium themselves. The exposure to the storm is thus not restricted to the experience of the poets. It must be endured by the poet's audience and readers as well. Since the poet enters the medium of the storm, the reader must do likewise. As Heidegger notes, we must be "prepared in the future to endure the weather of this [Hölderlin's] poetry" (*GA* 39: 23). Exposure to the storm likewise concerns the thinkers as well. In the short essay of 1933 entitled "Creative Landscape: Why Do We Stay in the Provinces?" Heidegger casts the labor of the thinker in terms of the resistance to a storm. He writes, "on a deep winter's night, when a wild, pounding snowstorm rages around the hut and veils and covers everything, that is the elevated time for philosophy. . . . The effort of linguistic articulation [*Prägung*] is like the resistance of the towering firs against the storm" (*GA* 13: 10/*HMT* 27–28, tm). The overcoming of resistance is the achievement of form. More precisely, in overcoming resistance and pushing beyond one's bounds, a communicative form is achieved.

To communicate is to enter a mediated existence and to bear such an existence is to remain, borne upon the groundless ground. Communicativity is a way of being (*beyng*). Already in the 1934–35 lecture course on *Hölderlin's Hymns "Germania" and "The Rhine"* Heidegger concluded of poetic experience that "Dasein *is* nothing other than *exposure to the overwhelming power of beyng*" (*GA* 39: 31). Exposure to the overwhelming power of beyng is exposure to the medium of communicativity. To be exposed to this is to be drawn into it, to have already entered it. We have always already entered the medium around us. We are seeping through it. To ask what it means to be human is to ask what it means to stand in a storm that grants us our existence. "The question who the human would be has only now broken open a path that at the same time leads off into the unprotected and thus allows the storm of beyng [*Sturm des Seyns*] to come over it" (*GA* 65: 300/237, tm). To abandon presuppositions and presumptions is to enter this storm bare headed, as it were. It is to enter the between, that "unprotected amidst [*Inmitten*] which unleashes the storm of ap-propriation [*Er-eignung*]" (*GA* 65: 243/192).

What does the onslaught of the storm reveal? According to the *Contributions to Philosophy*, nothing less than the singularity of beyng as such. From out of the storm there arises the "lightning flash [*Aufblitzen*] of the unique singularity of beyng [*einmaligen Einzigkeit des Seyns*]" (*GA* 65: 228/180, tm). The lightning flash is momentary—"the *moment* as the lightning-flashing of beyng [*Erblitzen des Seyns*]" (*GA* 65: 409/324, tm)— and as such it is one of the "rare events," one of the "events as such" (*GA* 65: 227/179, tm). The rare singularity at stake in the *Contributions* is thus not something that can be generally perceived.[9] While metaphysics begins with a storming assault encompassing beings as a whole—"from the immediate storming in [*Ansturm*] upon beings as such (*physis, idea, ousia*) only *presencing* was retained in the first beginning as graspable and paradigmatic for all interpretations of being" (*GA* 65: 260–61/205, tm)—any transformation out of metaphysics will be noted only by a few. "The error, of course, consists in thinking that an essential overturning [*Umschlag*]— one that lays hold of everything in a fundamental way—should at the same time and on the whole also be known by all and comprehended by all and play itself out in public. Only the few ever stand in the brightness of this lightning" (*GA* 65: 28/24, tm). The few are those who remain.

No account of the rhetoric of storms and exposure in the 1930s can avoid consideration of Heidegger's politics at the time. The exuberance of overcoming perceived or imagined resistance, the overt and heroic romanticism of surviving an onslaught of the storm comes to inform Heidegger's political writings while he is a party member of the National Socialists. The concluding line of his "Rectoral Address," for example, is a citation from Plato (*Rep.* 497d9) proclaiming, "all that is great stands in the storm" (cited at *GA* 16: 117/*HNS* 13). Endurance is a conquest of the elements and understood as a triumph. Standing firm in the storm is thus a cause for jubilation. Of Hölderlin's poetry, he writes, "the saying of this poetry is in itself the jubilation of beyng, the jubilating calm of beyng in the enduring of its storm" (*GA* 39: 255). In the *Contributions* this enduring brings a freedom: "the freedom of the belonging to the jubilation of beyng" (*GA* 65: 412/326). By the 1940s, however, we find a more nuanced view presented in the lecture course *Hölderlin's Hymn "The Ister"* (1942). Here we read that standing in the storm is not a matter of rigid resistance to its force. Instead, what survives the storm, what remains, is something pliant: "What truly stands steadfast must be able to sway within the counter-turning pressure of the open paths of the storms. What is merely rigid shatters on account of its own rigidity" (*GA* 53: 64/52).

By the time of the fourfold, these thoughts on the weather are recast with still greater emphasis on lightning and what its sudden flash brings into view. However, this now coincides with a move away from the triumphant tone of the 1930s. In the "Logos" essay of 1951, for example, the confrontation with the storm is no longer a jubilant conquest. Instead, it is the thoughtless contemporary world that clamors for the conquest and dispersal of all storms:

> at the beginning of western thinking, the essence of language flashed [*blitzte . . . auf*] in the light of being. But the lightning flash extinguished suddenly. No one held on to its streak [*Strahl*] or the nearness of what it illuminated.
>
> We only see the lightning when we place ourselves in the thunderstorm of being. Today the sole concern is with driving away the thunderstorm. We organize all available means for cloud seeding in order to have rest from the thunderstorm. But this rest is no rest. It is only a delusion, primarily the delusion of anxiety before thinking. (*GA* 7: 233–34/*EGT* 78, tm)

Whereas before there was a struggle against the storm, here there is almost a charge to preserve it in the name of thinking (recall the 1933 "Creative Landscape" essay). The flash of lightning can only strike from out of the midst of the storm. That is to say, the suddenness, or *immediacy*, of lightning only arises from out of the *medium* of a storm. Insofar as we participate in that storm, we prepare for the lightning bolt, for nothing sudden can appear without that preparatory work of preservation.

In the concluding pages of *Insight Into That Which Is*, at the end of the lecture "The Turn," we finally glean what the lightning brings: nothing less than a transformation out of metaphysics. This is presented in terms of a "turn" from the danger of technological positionality to a guarding of beyng. As Heidegger states, "the turn of the danger takes place suddenly. In the turn there suddenly lights up the illuminated clearing of the essence of beyng" (*GA* 79: 73/69). The suddenness of this turn leads Heidegger to think it in terms of the lightning flash: "This sudden self-lighting is the lightning flash [*das Blitzen*]. It brings itself into the brightness proper to it, a brightness it brought in with itself. In the turn of the danger, when the truth of beyng flashes [*blitzt*], the essence of beyng lights up; the truth of the essence of beyng enters" (*GA* 79: 74/69). The suddenness of the lightning here again should not be confused with a crude immediacy. When the lightning flashes, it brings with it an area of illumination. This area does not precede the lightning, but attends it. The lightning brings this illuminated expanse with it, so as to flash therein. Lightning cannot be separated from the arena of its flashing. Indeed, there would be no lightning were there not this illuminated space by which the bolt could reach us. The lightning that flashes here is thus no isolated independent entity, but a kind of momentary searing proliferation that spreads illumination across the sky. The bolt is thus always only found in a clearing. This fact, that whatever appears always appears in a relation to that which lies around it, something that holds for even the most instantaneous and singular of appearances, is the "truth" (medium) of beyng. The preservation of the storm is a preservation of the medial support of existence and this means a preservation of the truth of being.

In the flash of lightning a peculiar kind of vision is possible. Heidegger avers that "'to flash' [*blitzen*], according to the word and the issue at stake, is: to glance [*blicken*]" (*GA* 79: 74/70). This connection between flashing and glancing will be used to further articulate the relation between the viewer and what is seen. Heidegger continues, "in the glance [*im Blick*] and as the glance, essencing enters into its own illumination. Through the element of its illumination, the glance shelters back in the glancing whatever it catches sight of" (*GA* 79: 74/70). Glancing (*blicken*) is thus a way of regarding and comporting toward what essences. What essences is nothing self-contained, but that which is released into relations with all around it. Here, this means that what is essential "enters into its own illumination," which Heidegger explicitly refers to as an "element [*Element*]," i.e., a medium (*GA* 79: 74/70). Glancing is thus a way of regarding that does not objectify, but that releases. Instead of asserting itself, giving heed to its curiosity, and poking around in the world, glancing "shelters back" what it views. What is spotted by lightning light is caught sight of in a glance.

This relational character of glancing and its tie to mediation returns in the 1957 lecture cycle *Basic Principles of Thinking*. Here Heidegger elaborates this idea of glancing (*blicken*) in terms of a "catching sight" (*erblicken*) of something. "We only catch sight of that which has already sighted us," he writes, and understands by this a reciprocal relation between viewer and viewed (*GA* 79: 100/95). Such a connection challenges the notion of the human being as independent, encapsulated, and self-asserting subject, leading Heidegger to propose: "So that this relationship between sighting and catching sight can purely hold sway, we must abandon the position of the human as a subject, and thereby the subject-object-relation, and have found our way back into a more originary dimension of the human essence. We only catch sight of what has already sighted us, and indeed without our knowledge or effort" (*GA* 79: 100/95). Once again, glancing or catching sight is a matter of relating to what lies beyond oneself. For this reason, the idea of a subject must be abandoned just as much as that of an object; the encapsulation endemic to them obstructs the relation in question. Catching sight of the thing, we let it radiate beyond itself, radiate through its element. We let it shine, and we are able to bask in its beauty: "For only what we have caught sight of do we see, do we preserve as what has been seen (the beautiful)" (*GA* 79: 135/127).

One last modulation of this strange "glancing" (*blicken*) is found in the term "insight" (*Einblick*), which forms the title of the Bremen lectures as a whole, *Insight Into That Which Is*. We have said that the lightning flash that brings with it its own element allows us to catch sight of something that has already sighted us. Heidegger now terms this an insight: "Entrance [*Einkehr*] of the lightning flash of the truth of being is insight [*Einblick*]" (*GA* 79: 74/70). The lightning flash reveals our relatedness to what is and our role in the guarding (*bewahren*) of its truth (*Wahrheit*). Otherwise put, "insight [*Einblick*] into that which is—thus is named the lightning flash of the truth of beyng into truthless being" (*GA* 79: 75/71). What the lightning flash reveals at the time of the fourfold is now another kind of communication, the relatedness of all that is.

b. Aether

In thinking the sky as a medium of appearance we are not far from the much maligned thought of an aether. Indeed, the term itself concludes the depiction of the sky within the fourfold without further elaboration ("blue depths of the aether"). But the term "aether" plays prominently in the Hölderlin readings of the mid-1940s where it stands, not surprisingly, as a figure of mediation. Such figures abound at this time. Heidegger follows Hölderlin in thinking the holy (*das Heilige*) as a medium for both the appearance of the god (if only in traces) and for the hale (*das Heile*). Similarly, Heidegger reads Hölderlin's reflections on the joyous (*das Heitere*) as the medium in which the high and lofty can appear. We shall have opportunity to reflect on each of these in the pages that follow. But we should note in advance of these discussions that the holy and the joyous are synonymous for Heidegger: "The joyous originally heals. It is the holy. 'The highest' and 'the holy' are for the poet the same: the joyous" (*GA* 4: 18/37, tm). This same text of 1943 ("Homecoming/To the Kindred Ones") details a bit further the mediating character of the joyous: "at one and the same time, it [the joyous] is the clarity (*claritas*) in whose brightness everything clear rests, and the highness (*serenitas*) in whose strength everything lofty stands, and the merriment (*hilaritas*) in whose play everything liberated sways" (*GA* 4: 18/37, tm). Another name for the joyous (*das Heitere*) as the medium of the high and lofty would be the aether.

"'Aether' is the name of the father of light and of the all animating lightening air" (*GA* 4: 60/83, tm). This animating air is an air that enlivens all who come in contact with it. The aether is an air that has been "cheered up" (*aufgeheitert*) by its contact with other airs, other winds: "The northeast is the wind (Swabian, 'the air'), which in the poet's homeland cheers up [*aufheitert*] 'the air' (the aether) and makes the joyous expansively spacious" (*GA* 4: 84/109, tm). The joyous spreads through the medium of the aether. We thus come to stand in a new medium: "the northeast wind sweeps the sky clear. It gives a free, cool path to the rays and light of the sun (the heavenly fire). Along with the air, which all living beings and especially the sons of the earth breathe, *the sharp clarity of this wind brings the incorruptibility of the transparency of all things*. The northeast gives a flexible constancy to the atmosphere and brings to maturation the time of the undimmed mood" (*GA* 4: 84/109, tm, em). The medium is determinative of how things appear to us, and in this is similar to a mood.

The aether names the heights of the sky, the furthest reaches of the dimension. In this the aether is the counterpart to the abyssal character of the earth. Indeed, Heidegger will write of the poet that "that poet himself then stands in the open which is cleared 'from the aether on high, down to the abyss below'" (*GA* 4: 64/86, tm). While aether and abyss here designate the outer reaches of the open, their placement likewise opens the dimension, the between. No one gets to the bottom of the abyss, no one rises above the aether. There is no outside position to be had, and not because aether and abyss are the bounding termini of an enclosed earthly sphere, but because neither aether nor abyss are simply present for the surpassing. Aether and abyss guarantee that we are always in between.

Elsewhere Heidegger will use this same structural relation of aether and earth to trouble once again the distinction between the sensible and the super-sensible. His 1957 essay "Hebel—The Friend of the House" comes to its close with reflections on this distinction, cast now in terms of earth and sky. They form a brief commentary on a sentence of Hebel's that we have encountered before: "We are plants which—whether we care to admit it to ourselves or not—must ascend with our roots in the earth, in order to bloom in the ether and bear fruit."[10] Heidegger says of this:

> The earth—this word in Hebel's sentence names everything visible, audible, tangible, that bears us and is around us, inspires us and appeases us: *the sensual* [*das Sinnliche*]. The aether (the sky)—this word in Hebel's sentence names all that which we perceive, but not with the sense organs: the non-sensual, *the sense* [*den Sinn*], the spirit. (*GA* 13: 150/*HFH* 100, tm, em)

Just as mortal existence transpires between earth and sky, so too must it endeavor to think between the sensual and the sensible in a consideration of sense. The poet gathers these senses of sense together into what Heidegger now calls "sensible sense [*der sinnliche Sinn*]" (*GA* 13: 150/*HFH* 101, tm). This "sensible sense" would no longer deprive the corporeal of meaning nor isolate the spiritual in an abstraction. Instead, sensible sense presents us with a "thickened" (*verdichtet*) sense of what it means to appear, no longer beholden to segregating opposition. In the Hebel essay, the word of the poet "traverses [*durchmißt*] as the sensible sense the breadth of the play space between earth and sky. Language holds open the realm in which the human, upon the earth and under the sky, inhabits the house of the world" (*GA* 13: 150/*HFH* 101, tm). Language too plays the role of a medium, between earth and sky, between sense and sense.

Heidegger's thinking of the aether need not strike us as a moment of regressive anti-science in his thinking; it might also be seen as a way of engaging with the tradition of philosophy, specifically with Aristotle, who also provides an account of mediation. The Philosopher is concerned with a medium that would let what appears shine through (*diaphainein*). Aristotle calls this medium the "transparent" (*to diaphanes*; *De Anima*, B. 7). This transparent can be in either of two states: it can be potentially or actually transparent. When it is actually transparent, it is the "transparent *qua* transparent" (*De Anima*, 418b10). The name for this actualized medium is "light." The same medium, when unactualized and in potential, is named "darkness." A major difference between the two states concerns vision; one cannot see in darkness. The proper object of vision is color and color can only set the transparent in motion when that transparent is actually transparent, i.e., when it is light. For this reason, Aristotle says that "Light is a sort of colour of the transparent" (418b11).

But what is it that has this color? What is the transparent such that light is its coloration? The word *to diaphanes* names that which allows something else to "show through" it. The word neither specifies nor requires that *to diaphanes* itself be invisible or imperceptible. It would likewise be wrong to speak of it as "translucent," since light does not move. This was Empedocles's mistake, according to Aristotle: "Empedocles . . . was wrong in saying that light travels and arrives at some time between [*metaxu*] the earth and that which surrounds it" (418b20–23).[11] Light doesn't move through the between—it is that between in its actual transparency. What the transparent does is allow this color to come to view. The actuality of transparency lies in the shining "through" of color. This color has the power to set the transparent in motion (it is the *kinêtikon*, 418a31–418b1). Vision occurs only when the eye is stimulated by the motion of the transparent. What is seen is always at a distance from the eye, and it is this distance that the transparent spans. Aristotle insists in *De Anima* that perception cannot occur without this distance. There is no perception when the object of sense is coincident with its organ. That is to say, "if one places that which has colour upon the eye itself, one will not see it" (419a12–13).[12] Sensation is always sensation *of something distant*, and thus it requires a medium. This is why Aristotle objects to a view he attributes to Democritus. The latter seems to imply that the medium of sensation is a deleterious hindrance to the act of perception: "For Democritus did not speak rightly, thinking that if the intervening space [*to metaxu*] were to become a void, then even if an ant were in the sky it would be seen accurately" (419a15–17). It is not that the intervening medium diminishes our capacity to see, it itself makes it possible. There is no "immediate" perception. We perceive what is in-between, and this is here Aristotle's word (*to metaxu*): "Now it is impossible to be affected by the actual color which is seen; it remains for it to be affected by what is intervening [*tou metaxu*], so that there must be something intervening [*anangkaion ti einai metaxu*]" (419a17–20).

Perception is always a palpation of distance, of the transparent, of the between. To be a sensing being is to always touch the between—all the senses are senses of touch. The tangibility of light is found in shades and tints. Light colors our world. Alexander of Aphrodisias called color for Aristotle "a sort of second light."[13] But actual light is color. The absence of light is the potential transparency of a colorless darkness. Light is always in color, coloring the distances. For Heidegger, this color is blue.

c. Blue

> Air seen close at hand appears to have no colour, for it is so rare that it yields and gives passage to the denser rays of light, which thus shine through it; but when seen in a deep mass it looks practically dark blue. This again is the result of its rarity, for where light fails the air lets darkness through and looks dark blue. When densified, air is, like water, the whitest of things.
> —*On Colours*, 794a8–15

The Aristotelian author of a work in the school's corpus, *On Colors*, explains why the sky is blue. The white molecules of air are sparse and widely dispersed across the black of darkness. But the sky is so vast and deep as to allow for viewing large masses of these air molecules at once. When enough of these white molecules are visible so as to impede partway the encroaching darkness, the sky turns dark blue. The molecules themselves are not blue, they are white, and neither is the darkness, it is black. Blue is the product of their combination. It is the color of the white molecules standing out before the dark and obstructing it, concealing it, but also apparently blurring with it in our perception of the sky.

Blue is thus something of a depth-effect for the anonymous author. It is neither black nor white, but something arising between the two when viewed from a distance. The Heideggerian thought of blue is likewise tied to a thinking of depth. Indeed, the depiction of the sky in the first formulations of the fourfold agree in remarking "the bluing [*blauende*] depths of the aether" (*GA* 79: 17/16, tm, *GA* 7: 151/*PLT* 147, tm). Here the blue sky is presented as *blauend*, as actively "bluing." As bluing, the sky shifts through its blues, extending into the depths. The 1950 lecture ". . . poetically man dwells . . ." is even more direct: "the blue of the sky's lovely blueness [*Bläue*] is the color of the depths" (*GA* 7: 205/*PLT* 226, tm). This term "blueness," *die Bläue*, stems from Hölderlin's late prose-poem that bears no title but begins: *"In lieblicher Bläue blühet mit dem metallenen Dache der Kirchenturm"* ("In lovely blueness with its metal roof the steeple blossoms").[14] Blueness—this word already sounds like a form, a general term, or even an essence, while here such a sense is to be avoided. What Heidegger terms *die Bläue* is not a commonality among all shades of blue. Such a common blue could only level the differences between the various shades into a merely flat blue, while blue is the shifting color of depth itself.[15]

The depth in question is that of the dimension. As we have seen, depth is not a measure from one point to another, it is "between" these. Depth is the traversal and measuring out of that space. Heidegger's second commentary on Trakl, "Language in the Poem," presents us with the figure of a wandering stranger who is out along the paths of the forest. Heidegger traces the etymology of "stranger" (*der Fremder*) to the Old High German "*fram*," meaning "onwards to elsewhere, on the way to . . ." (*GA* 12: 37/*OWL* 163, tm). The wanderer has left home behind, but is also yet to reach a destination. Just as the dimension is between earth and sky, so too is the stranger between the home and the destination. The wanderer is "on the way," in the middle of the journey, we might say, in the midst of things. To be underway like this is to enter the blue: "The departed one looks ahead into the bluing of the spiritual night" (*GA* 12: 51/*OWL* 175, tm). The wanderer is underway as "Bluing [*Bläue*] twilights [*dämmert*] spiritually over the rough hewn forest."[16]

Twilight is the time of transition, blue is its deep color. Being underway is an entry into these depths and the acceptance of their ambiguity. The twilight *Dämmerung* could be either dawn or dusk, it could be an uprising or a downfall. The blue of twilight is neither the pitch black of night, nor the bright white of day. Twilight blue lies between these oppositions. Indeed, if we are to follow Heidegger, then we would have to say that a thinking of twilight precludes a thinking of black and white. Twilight makes evident that all is blue. Blue is the color between presence and absence, between day and night. There is no darkness simply opposed to light. Instead, darkness is the shelter of light. This sheltered trace of a light in the dark is blue. "The brightness [*Helle*] that is sheltered in the darkness is blueness [*die Bläue*]" (*GA* 12: 40/*OWL* 165, tm). Blue indicates the depths, the sheltering of apparent oppositions within one another; better, blue shines as the ineluctable remainder of light in the midst of the night, the remainder of dark in the midst of day. Blue is the color of the trace.

This twilight trace comes to organize the role of the poet. Heidegger's Trakl reading, ultimately an analysis of departure and being underway, is tied to his thinking of Hölderlin's poetization of departed gods (as elaborated in the opening pages of "What Are Poets For?"). The gods have flown, but they have left their traces. The night of their flight is not eternally black against an ever bright day, even if it is the night of the west, of the *Abendland*, the "evening-land" of the world. As the "world-night" nears its midnight, the traces of Godhood appear lost to the night, the very traces of these lost traces themselves "are nearly extinguished" (*GA* 5: 272/203, tm). But only "nearly," and it always "nears" midnight. Midnight would be black, what nears it is in blue. That there is blueness, and not the black, this is the hope of decline—the hope *of* the impossibility of midnight. It also means that these traces may be attended to, and it is here that the poet enters. The poet sings the traces of the flown gods. Because of this, because of these traces, and not because of these gods (though this is too quick, for we shall see that these gods *are* their traces), the world-night is "the holy night [*die heilige Nacht*]" (*GA* 5: 272/202, tm).

What Heidegger calls "the holy" is here tied to a thinking of the intermediacy, i.e., the blueness, of the dimension. Heidegger is even rather direct about this. "Blue [*Das Blau*] is no image for the sense of the Holy. Blueness [*Die Bläue*] itself is the holy, in virtue of its gathering depth which shines forth only as it veils itself" (*GA* 12: 40/*OWL* 166, tm). While we shall reserve a full discussion of Heidegger's thinking of the holy for our consideration of the divinities ("The Holy" in chapter 4), here we already find the holy connected with a simultaneous shining and veiling. The distance that emerges between revelation and concealment, the spacing of it, is depth, is blue, and now is holy. The holy (*das Heilige*) is the way in which all that is hale (*das Heile*) exists in lovely blueness, i.e., exists as revealed and concealed at once, as essencing. What appears in this holiness appears as hale. Or to put it another way, the hale is always attended by this halo of the holy, a fringe of relations. What appears in the blue twilight appears, relationally, holy. The holy names the medium of the blue night through which the hale and departed one wanders. On the way, the stranger is exposed to the twilight of blue and bears the pain of an existence so exposed, the pain of not being at home. But it is this very pain that admits him to the between. "Pain remains the pure correspondence to the holiness of blueness [*der Bläue*]" (*GA* 12: 61/*OWL* 183, tm).

Dark blue night is braced on each side by the crepuscular, and these keep it in touch with day. But day is simply another kind of blue. Day is not covered over by night, night does not suffer before day. The one does not underlie the other, they are the same. Heidegger thinks this sameness, the persistence of the trace, as blueness. The beginning taken in Hesiod is thus rightly corrected by Heraclitus: "The teacher of most is Hesiod. It is him they know as knowing most, who did not recognize day and night: they are one."[17] The blueness of the sky makes it the medium of traversal and departure. Blue is the color of mediated relations.

d. Clouds

The blue sky is a field of transition. But even here, we fail to think this through if we continue to think of the sky as equally blue or equally transitioning in all its places. Perhaps the term *die Bläue,* now heard as a plurality of shades of blue, is meant to keep us from such a thought. The sky is not a homogeneous field of manifestation. In the essay ". . . poetically dwells man . . ." (1951), Heidegger looks at a pair of lines from Hölderlin's poem "In lovely blueness [*Bläue*] . . . ," the poem from which the title of the essay is drawn, where Hölderlin wonders about the manifestness of god:

> Is he manifest like the sky? This
> I sooner believe.[18]

But if Hölderlin here voices a belief that god would be manifest like the sky, Heidegger adds a marginal note to the text at this point which simply reads "the clouds of the sky" (*GA* 7: 201 n. n). The clouds would thus stand here as a modification to the idea of god's manifestness, as a modulation of the sky's very "bluing." Where the blue of the sky led us to understand what exists as transitional and "on the way," thus precluding any notion of full presence, the emphasis on clouds keeps us from thinking even this transitional existence as something clearly present. Rather it is obscured by clouds. Clouds double the obfuscation of existence in the dimension.

Clouds are positioned in the between of the dimension where they provide a unique kind of coverage. The 1943 lecture "Homecoming/ To the Relations" discusses Hölderlin's eponymous poem which begins:

> Within the Alps it is still bright night, and the cloud,
> poetizing the merry [*Freudiges dichtend*], covers the yawning valley.[19]

Noting the intermedial position of this cloud, Heidegger explains the nature of its coverage: "The cloud sways between the peaks of the Alps and covers the ravines of the mountain ranges into whose lightless depths the cheering ray of light works its way down" (*GA* 4: 18/36, tm). We have already discussed how existence in the between is an existence that is not beholden to the integrity or purity of presence and absence, but instead is understood as drawn out into relations with what lies around it. This is no less the case for the cloud. In order to cover the ravine, the cloud must first uncover itself. In so doing, the cloud is brought into a relation with the sky. The cloud "uncovers itself before the towering brightness of the sky, while at the same time it 'covers' . . . 'the yawning valley'" (*GA* 4: 15/34, tm). The situation is again one of catching sight of something and being sighted, for "the cloud lets itself be sighted [*anblicken*] by the open brightness [of the sky]," though at the same time the cloud "looks into [*blickt*] that from where it itself is sighted [*angeblickt*]," i.e., the open brightness of the sky (*GA* 4: 15/34, tm). The coverage of the cloud is the appearance of the cloud in its own uncovered relation with the sky.

Through the cloud, what we are given to consider is thus a way of appearing that is *partly* covered. But this is not a case of one present object standing in front of another present object and thus blocking the view of an equally present spectator, nor of one present object overlapping another present object and thus "partly" covering it. By virtue of its existence in this between, the cloud is no present object at all. Accordingly, the operative sense of coverage is likewise distinct from these. The cloud that covers the ravines does not obstruct the passage of light into the crevasses. The cloud allows for the passage of a ray of light into the lightless depths. Let us state this the other way around: only due to the coverage of the cloud are the depths illuminated. The cloud that is spotted by the brightness of the sky covers the ravine precisely by virtue of allowing passage to the cheering ray of light. The coverage in question here is thus a manner of revealing. Cloud cover allows for a non-present appearing, for something to appear in its concealment. The ravine is not entirely lit up and at our disposal, it is just a ray of light that works its way down. The coverage of the cloud prevents the pitch black darkness of the ravine, but allows it to reach us nevertheless precisely as those dark depths. Insofar as clouds catch sight of and are sighted by the brightness of the sky, cloud coverage is a way of revealing.

This leads to Heidegger's claim, following Hölderlin, that "the cloud poetizes" (*GA* 4: 15/34, tm). Poetizing would be a way of letting things appear in their non-presence. Here the poet is not so much transmitting as allowing—allowing the ray of light into the depths, the depths are no longer utterly dark, they bear the trace of light (they shelter it, they are blue). To poetize would be to exceed oneself, to enter into a relational space. To poetize, "the cloud must go out beyond itself to that which is no longer itself" (*GA* 4: 15/34, tm). Thus Heidegger writes of poetizing not that it would be a generating of ideas on one's own, but rather "poetizing is a finding" (*GA* 4: 15/34, tm). What is poetized by the cloud does not fall out of the sky ("fall out of a cloud," as Heidegger says), but instead "comes over it as that for which the cloud abides [*entgegenweilt*]" (*GA* 4: 16/34, tm). The cloud abides, i.e., places itself in the blue between, and in so doing the cloud finds, i.e., receives, what is given (that "toward which" it abides, *entgegenweilt*). What is given is an invitation to joy and the cloud is thus said to poetize the joyous (*das Heitere*): "In that it poetizes, the cloud points up to the joyous" (*GA* 4: 18/37, tm).[20] In so doing, the cloud enters the medium of elevated appearance.

Abiding in the blue sky, the cloud is struck in turn by the brightness of that sky. This contact with an outside is nothing toward which the cloud is impassive. Instead, this contact upsets or animates the cloud, we might say. In Heidegger's terms, such contact "cheers" the cloud: "The open brightness in which the cloud abides cheers up [*heitert . . . auf*] this abiding" (*GA* 4: 16/34–35, tm). As so cheered, moved beyond itself, the cloud achieves the joyous: "The cloud is cheered up [*aufgeheitert*] into the joyous [*das Heitere*]" (*GA* 4: 16/34–35, tm). The brightness of the sky excites the cloud and brings it to pass just a sliver of light into the abyssal depths of the ravine. The excited buoyancy of the cloud is its movement to the joyous.

The spatiality of this should not be overlooked. What is cheered up is moved in a certain way, shifted as it were into the joyous, where this joyous comes to describe a kind of space. Heidegger says of the joyous, "we also name this the 'expansive' [*Aufgeräumte*]" (*GA* 4: 16/35, tm). The German term "*Aufgeräumte*" names both a cleared away space, a domain that has been brought into order, and the light-heartedness of joy; it names, we shall say, an "expansive" mood, endeavoring to hear both the spatial and the elevated in this single term. But the space that the joyous clears is a space wherein the percolating, expansive relations with others allow everything to be what it is. The joyous is a medium of relations which allows each thing to belong in place and be supported there by its relations to others. The joyous conducts these relations and provides the buoyancy for what is cheered up. It allows things to fit in: "The joyous [*das Heitere*], the expansive, is alone able to clear for another its fitting place. . . . In that this cheering up [*die Aufheiterung*] clears [*lichtet*] everything, the joyous thus preserves for each and every thing its essential space, that in which it belongs after its own manner" (*GA* 4: 16/35, tm). The joyous is this space of belonging where to belong is to situate oneself in relation to one's surroundings. The poetizing of the cloud is the reception of and the entrance into this space of belonging. The coverage of the cloud is a poetizing. It allows what it covers to bear a trace of difference. It protects what it covers so as to allow it the delicate entry into relations.

Heidegger's 1959 lecture "Hölderlin's Earth and Sky" returns to the role of clouds in Hölderlin and considers further the peculiarity of their coverage. Here Heidegger's concern is with what Hölderlin terms "the voices of destiny [*Stimmen des Geschiks*]."[21] These voices of destiny are voices to the extent that the voice is always carried by a medium, i.e., insofar as the voice is understood as resounding: "Voices? They resound [*tönen*]" (*GA* 4: 165/190, tm). What is sent voices itself as a resounding of destiny (reverberating between provenance and destination). Thus in regards to what is sent (*geschickt*) to us as destiny (*Geschick*), we need not speak solely and literally of "voices" of destiny, so much as understand here "reverberations of destiny." Following Hölderlin, the sky is one such resounding of destiny.[22] Since "what resounds is the sky," Heidegger observes that "its reverberation [*Stimme*] is the joyous mood [*die heitere Stimmung*] of the clouds" (*GA* 4: 166/190, tm). The sky is a space through which destiny resounds and cheers (upsets, animates, dislodges) the clouds into a joyous mood. As *Being and Time* had already shown, a mood is nothing at one's disposal, but a medium through which one encounters what appears. Insofar as the clouds are attuned, they are opened onto the medium that lies beyond them. The openness of the clouds means that clouds are not indifferent to the sky. Instead, the clouds are joyously attuned. As opened, they enter the medium of the joyous, *das Heitere*.

It is here that Heidegger returns to the covering, concealing character of the cloud. For it is what these clouds conceal that opens them up: "What attunes the clouds into an opening up [*ins Aufgeschlossene*] is precisely what they harbor in themselves: the 'loftiest appearance of the thunderstorm,' the lightning, the thunder, the storm, and the arrows of rain. The presence of the god is concealed therein" (*GA* 4: 166/190, tm). The clouds are unsettled not just by the brightness of the sky that comes from "outside"—the clouds are unsettled by what they harbor "inside" as well. There is something other to the cloud within the cloud—the most other other, in fact, and the one least present: the god. The clouds conceal the appearance of the god, where we have to understand that "the god only presences in that he conceals himself" (*GA* 4: 169–70/194, tm). The god is covered by clouds. But cloud coverage is nothing impassive. This was what warranted the designation of the clouds as "poetizing." And while Heidegger does not use this same term here, he does speak of "clouds of song [*Gesangeswolken*]" (*GA* 4: 168/193). The cloud coverage in this case allows the clouds to share in the animating, reverberating joy of the god—they sing of nothing else. What they conceal, they let shine: "Although the thunder clouds veil the sky, they belong to it and display the merriment [*Freude*] of god" (*GA* 4: 166/190, tm). Clouds evince the merriment—or rather, the *mediation*—of the god. Only when there is concealment can there be joy.

Clouds cover the sky without suffocating it. Their coverage allows for new dimensions in manifestation. The god appears. Light works its way into the depths. The cloud is afloat between the joyous heights of the aether and the abyssal depths of the earth. Its concealing reveals, poetizes, sings. Clouds poetize in concealing, whereby the revelation of concealment troubles the rigidity of the boundary that would keep the clouds pent up inside themselves. The clouds thereby bring distance and depth.[23] The word of the poet does the same, for the poet's language is the language of being: "Language is the language of being, just as the clouds are the clouds of the sky" (*GA* 9: 364/276).

§11. The Time of the Sky

What appears of the earth, appears under the sky. This means that it appears in a variegated medium of appearance, a weathered, ethereal, blue, cloud-cast space. Heidegger's depiction of sky within the fourfold, however, presents this medium not simply spatially, but temporally as well: "The sky is the vaulting path of the sun, the shape-shifting course of the moon, the wandering gleam of the stars, the seasons of the year and their changes, the light and twilight of day, the dark and bright of the night" (*GA* 7: 151/*PLT* 149, tm). What appears under the sky appears in time; or perhaps we would do better to say it appears temporally, in order to avoid the suggestion that this time would be an indifferent container. Heidegger's reflections on the time of the sky emphasize the changing of the hours of the day and the seasons of the year. These times vary in the quality of light and dark they present. In fact, the transition of light and dark betrays the non-homogeneous character of time, sheltering dark within light and light within dark. This prevents any simple closure of the periods of time upon themselves. Rather, they extend to us. It is just this kind of "natural time" that Heidegger views as befitting our dimensional existence. Upon the earth and beneath the sky, this time greets us in the temporal play of existence.[24]

a. "Natural" Time

> All the propositions of ontology are temporal propositions.
> Their truths unveil structures and possibilities of being *in the
> light of Temporality*.
> —*GA* 24: 460/323, em

The notion of a time of the sky, what we are here calling a "natural time"—a time of phenomenal appearance, rather than of abstract measurement—this is a notion explicitly ridiculed by Aristotle in the *Physics*: "as to those who declare the heavenly sphere itself to be time, their only reason was that all things are contained 'in the celestial sphere' and also occur 'in time,' which is too childish to be worth reducing to absurdities more obvious than itself" (*Phy.* 218 b 8–9). Despite the reservations of the philosopher, Heidegger increasingly concerns himself with the idea of natural time. It becomes a dominant concern with the fourfold.

Natural time, or a time that would be measured by the primitive givenness of day and night, was an interest of Heidegger's in the period leading up to and surrounding *Being and Time,* too. It is closely related to "clock time," as Heidegger makes clear in the 1924 lecture "The Concept of Time," where we read that "Dasein is there with the clock, even if only with the most proximate, everyday clock of day and night" (*GA* 64: 119/*CT* 15, tm). This measured clock time, of course, is a derivative way of dating time ("the *measurement of time* . . . is grounded *in the temporality* of Dasein"; *GA* 2: 548/*SZ* 415, tm), and thus unbecoming authentic Dasein. The very idea of a "natural" time is to be abandoned: "There is no nature-time, since all time essentially belongs to the Dasein" (*GA* 24: 370/262). Nevertheless, the time of the sky—the sun as "the 'natural' clock" (*GA* 2: 547/*SZ* 413)—this time is not so easily abolished—in fact, is never abolished, and especially not in *Being and Time.* In the closing sections of this text Heidegger is careful to show the necessary connection between the primordial temporality of Dasein and the time of the sky.

Now clock time, as a derivative mode of time (as a specific manner of dating time), is derivative in a double sense. First, as Heidegger goes to great lengths to show, it is founded upon the primordial ecstatic temporality of a Dasein who is thrown and futural. But secondly, it is derived from "natural" time. That is to say, natural time need not be clock time—or need not simply or solely be clock time. Heidegger's analysis of "The Time with which we Concern Ourselves, and Within-Timeness," paragraph 80 of *Being and Time,* has much to say about the sun and the sky and their necessary relation to Dasein. Heidegger leaves cracks in his analysis where the light of a day that would not be organized by a clock might still shine through.

As we know, Dasein does not exist in some authentic heaven detached from earthly affairs. Rather, as paragraph 79 of *Being and Time* made clear, "thrown and abandoned to the 'world,' it falls into it concernfully" (*GA* 2: 537/*SZ* 406, tm). This concern shows itself in the way that Dasein goes about in the world, in its circumspective understanding of things. The insight of paragraph 80 is that this sight requires light or brightness (*der Helle*): "Everyday circum*spective* being-in-the-world needs the possibility of sight, that is, brightness, if it is to deal concernfully with what is ready-to-hand within the present-to-hand" (*GA* 2: 545/*SZ* 412, tm). To be able to go about in the world, Dasein needs light. In the factically uncovered world to which Dasein has been fallingly abandoned, this light is provided by the sun. Let there be no mistake, Heidegger is not speaking analogously here. Immediately following the avowal of light's necessity he adds: "With the factical disclosedness of Dasein's world, Nature has been uncovered for Dasein. In its thrownness Dasein is delivered over to the changes of day and night. Day with its brightness gives it the possibility of sight, night takes it away" (*GA* 2: 545/*SZ* 412, tm).

Dasein is thrown, existentially so, and this throw is a throw into a world that will be understood circumspectively. For this it requires light.

The world into which—*the earth upon which*—Dasein is thrown is an earth beneath a sky that shines with a sun. Dasein is thrown upon the earth and under the sky. If there were no sun, then there would be no light, if there were no light, then there would be no possibility of sight, without sight no concern, without concern no factical instantiation of care (with concern a derivative mode of this), and without this instantiation, no instance of Dasein. If Dasein is to be fallen then it must be so under the sky. This is not an accidental condition, the earth is not an accidental place, the sky is not an accidental vault.[25]

The world wherein Dasein loses itself, the world which may concern Dasein to the point of absorption, is a world with a time all its own. In an earlier paragraph of *Being and Time*, Heidegger had already pointed out how for the Dasein absorbed in the world of its concern there is a "concernful understanding of oneself as they-self in terms of what one does" (*GA* 2: 446/*SZ* 337, tm). In paragraph 80, this is recast in a manner explicitly connecting Dasein with the day. Now Dasein "understanding itself in terms of its daily work" (*GA* 2: 545/*SZ* 412) is tied to that day. In this understanding, Heidegger explains, Dasein says to itself that "then, when the sun rises, it is *time for . . .*" (*GA* 2: 545/*SZ* 412). Concern therefore makes use of the sun in its being-ready-to-hand. "The sun dates the time which is interpreted in concern. From this dating arises the 'most natural' measure of time, the day" (*GA* 2: 545/*SZ* 412–13). The time of concern leads to the all too familiar and measured time, that of the natural clock, the sun.

Now clock time, for its part, is an inescapable side of Dasein's finite and ecstatic temporality. If we take Heidegger at his word, it is finitude itself that leads to Dasein's quantification of time, "since the temporality of Dasein that must take its time is finite, *its days are also already numbered*" (*GA* 2: 545/*SZ* 413, em). As finite, and thus as thrown, the ecstatic temporality of Dasein is always itself falling.[26] It can do no other, for as we shall see, this time is nothing pure or homogeneous in itself. Clock time names this falling. This is true no matter how much more "elemental" Heidegger may consider the ecstatic temporality of Dasein to be. In *The Basic Problems of Phenomenology*, the temporalizing (*Zeitigung*) of temporality is what "holds sway throughout the Dasein in a way even more elemental than the light of day as the basic condition of everyday circumspective seeing with our eyes, toward which we do not turn when engaged in everyday commerce with things" (*GA* 24: 437/307). Even though this temporalizing is more "elemental" than the time of day, this does not mean that it is able to exist without that day. Thus Heidegger can claim that the clock is a "factical necessity" (*GA* 2: 546/*SZ* 413). For Heidegger this Ur-clock is the sun. It is the course of the sun through the sky that makes up the natural clock that is *"always already discovered* with the factical thrownness of Dasein" (*GA* 2: 547/*SZ* 413, em). Being-thrown means that Dasein is delivered over to a clock that has (always) already been given in nature: "The disclosedness of the natural clock belongs to Dasein which exists as thrown and falling" (*GA* 2: 548/*SZ* 415, tm).

Since Dasein's understanding of itself in terms of its daily work relies upon a notion of day, and since the concern over that work requires light, mechanical clocks "must be 'adjusted' to the 'natural' one if they are to make the time primarily discovered in the natural clock accessible in its turn" (*GA* 2: 547/*SZ* 414). Even clocks that are not based upon astronomical observation (cesium clocks, for instance) end up ever more accurately measuring ever smaller parts of the day. This is the priority of day-time. Again, Heidegger traces this back to Dasein's temporality, "because the clock . . . must be regulated by the 'natural' clock, even the use of clocks is grounded in the temporality of Dasein that, with the disclosedness of the there, first makes possible a dating of the time with which we concern ourselves" (*GA* 2: 549/*SZ* 415, tm). There are two moments here. First, Heidegger claims that clocks must be regulated by the day; much earlier he had pointed out that "when we look at the clock, we tacitly use the 'position of the sun'" (*GA* 2: 95–96/*SZ* 71). Secondly, and as a consequence of the first moment, the use of clocks is based upon Dasein's temporality, because clocks must be regulated by the day. And what is this day? A factically necessary part of Dasein's *inescapably* fallen temporality. Dasein's own temporality is indissociably linked to this day. Heidegger was moving toward this thought as early as 1923, in the lecture course *Introduction to Phenomenological Research.* In the opening pages Heidegger discusses the etymological meaning of phenomenology, showing its root in the Greek φα (*pha*) and the connection of this with φῶς (*phôs*) "light," or, as Heidegger will understand it, "brightness" (*Helle*). Brightness is both the sun as present (*Gegenwart*) and the presence (*Anwesenheit*) of the sun, he says, in a brief interpretation of Aristotle's *De Anima* B. 7 (*GA* 17: 9/6). Brightness, then, is "the way of the authentic being of the sky, the letting-be-seen of things, the being of day [*Tagsein*]" (*GA* 17: 8/5, tm). Once again, however, in this 1923 course the sun likewise belongs to the being of Dasein: "To Dasein in the world there belongs the being-present-at-hand [*Vorhandensein*] of the sun, precisely *that* which we mean when we ascertain: *it is day*" (*GA* 17: 9/6, tm).

And corporeally so, since Heidegger points out that due to the presence of the sun, everyone brings a shadow with them: "In the shadow that constantly accompanies everyone, we encounter the sun with respect to its changing presence at different places" (*GA* 2: 549/*SZ* 416). Heidegger spends a whole paragraph with the intricacies of shadow measurement—

indeed, someone even supposedly says, "when the shadow is so many feet long, then we will meet each other over there" (*GA* 2: 549/*SZ* 416, tm)! But any entity will cast a shadow, thus providing a possible clocking of time. Regarding this sun-dial or shadow-clock, "Dasein does not even need to wear this clock, in a certain sense, *it is this clock itself*" (*GA* 2: 550/ *SZ* 416, em). *Dasein itself casts a shadow.* The falling of Dasein is a falling into natural time. Dasein is thrown into a clock.

Paragraph 80 of *Being and Time* closes with Heidegger asserting that world-time, i.e., the public time that is drawn from natural time, is a way of temporality's ecstatico-horizonal temporalization. This world-time must come to be understood "*as temporality [Zeitlichkeit]*," as a derived mode of this (*GA* 2: 555/*SZ* 420). This leads Heidegger to claim what Aristotle had dismissed as absurd, that time would be found in the sky: "Initially 'time' shows itself in the sky, that is, precisely where one finds it in the natural orientation *toward* it, so that 'time' is even identified with the sky" (*GA* 2: 554/*SZ* 419).[27] Simply put, the "there" of Dasein as a sunlit place upon the earth and beneath the sky is inherently temporal.

b. The Hours of the Day

The inkling of a natural time that we find in *Being and Time* comes to fruition with the thinking of the fourfold. It appears in the 1943 Heraclitus lectures on *The Origin of Western Thinking: Heraclitus,* the various Johann Peter Hebel interpretations of the 1950s, and, quite prominently, in the 1966–67 *Heraclitus Seminar* with Eugen Fink, as well as in other talks and lectures of this late period. What comes to the fore is the alteration of day and night, the changing of the seasons, and a concern for the sun, moon, and stars. The time of the sky, "natural time," is time as it is lived here upon the earth and under the sky, but it is lived only in response to the givenness of this time. This given time suits us, it is fitted to us (*zuge-messen*). Heidegger's consideration of natural time will thus concern itself with the ways in which this time comes to us. He considers the measure (*Maß*) of time and the periodicity of these measures, emphasizing the heterogeneity of the times that thus reach us, across the hours of the day and the seasons of the year. He will also understand them as rhythmic differentiations of light and dark. Such times come to us and draw us out. The time of the dimension between earth and sky, the time of this middle, is a time sent to us that we might grow into it.

Natural time is a time of the sun, of *Hêlios.* As Fink explains in the 1966 *Heraclitus* seminar, "*Hêlios* is the clock of the world, the world clock, not an instrument that shows times, but rather that which makes possible the hours that bring all" (*GA* 15: 62/*HS* 35, tm). Heidegger remarks that for the early Greeks this time is not one of concepts or theoretical explication, as "there is no theoretical conceptual determination of time as time with Homer and Hesiod. Rather, both speak of time only out of experience" (*GA* 15: 103/*HS* 61). Heraclitus, too, fits this list, since, as Heidegger adds, "he did not speak thematically about time" (*GA* 15: 105/*HS* 62). The time they experienced is that of day and night, which, as Fink explains, "are familiar to us as the changing conditions, as the basic rhythm of life, as presence and absence of the sun in her light in the domain of the open" (*GA* 15: 76/*HS* 44). Fink's remarks about presence and absence aside, the rhythms in question articulate the periods of time, time's measure. These measures are tied to the sun's movement across the sky and predate any calculative attempt to establish a mathematically determinate time. Fink explains them thus: "*Hêlios* does not tarry fixed at one single place, but travels along the vault of heaven; and in this passage on the vault of heaven it is light- and life-apportioning [*Zumessende*] and time measuring. The metric of the sun's course mentioned here lies before every calculative metric made by humans" (*GA* 15: 65/*HS* 37). The language of apportioning used here is the same language we have seen used in consideration of the reciprocal apportioning and traversal of the dimension. The times that reach us only do so through the dimension. Such times lie before human calculation because they are what first makes human life possible at all.

These measures are what is given to us. Following Heraclitus fragment 100, they are "the seasons [*hôras*] which bring all things."[28] These *Horae* (German, *Horen*, Greek, *hôrai*) are not to be understood solely as the seasons, but also as the hours. They serve to name the natural shares or measures of time with regard to both the year and the day. The *Horae* bring the time to us and it is this role of bringing that Heidegger stresses for a thinking of natural time: "The character of bringing belongs to time. In our language we also say: it comes with time, time will grant it. As long as we understand time as bare succession, bringing has no place" (*GA* 15: 63/*HS* 36, tm). These times are brought to us, given to us. As such, they are to be distinguished from time understood as a succession of formally identical nows. Fink expounds the point:

> the *hôrai*, the hours and seasons, are not to be taken as a stream of time or as a temporal relation that, subjected to metric leveling down, is measurable and calculable. Hours and seasons are also not to be taken as the empty form in contrast to the content of time, but as filled time which brings along and brings to completion [*erbringt und vollbringt*] each thing in its own time. The *hôrai* are not hollow forms, but rather the times of day and the seasons. These obviously stand in connection

> with a fire that does not, like lightning, suddenly tear open and stamp
> everything with the impress of its outline, but one that holds out like
> the heavenly fire and, in the duration, travels through the hours of the
> day and the seasons of the year. (*GA* 15: 65/*HS* 37, tm)

The bringing character of time is contrasted with a formal conception of time. Time is not an empty container of a content that is indifferent to it. Rather, time is filled. We might even say it overflows, in that time is precisely this movement toward us, not of sometime in general, but of this particular hour and this particular season. Time gives us these times and is nothing other than such a giving, though this giving is indissociable from what is given. There is not a form of neutral time persisting unperturbed behind the variations of the hours and seasons. There is just this diversity and plethora of the hours and seasons themselves. Time is the giving of something, of something capable of reaching us as given. Time showers us with hours and seasons. The times of the *Horae* are developmental times, as we shall see in considering the seasons of the year. What time brings is not something independent of time, something that could exist just as well on its own without having been brought to us. Instead, it is native to the hours that they be brought to us. What the hour is is this arriving of something, of this time.

Thus Fink claims that "we cannot understand the hours in the sense of fixed stretches of time or even as stretches of a homogeneous time, but rather as the times of the day and the year. These times of the year are not what abides, but what brings [*die Bringenden*]" (*GA* 15: 62/*HS* 35, tm). The emphasis on the hours and seasons is to disabuse us of the idea that time would be an empty, formal, homogeneous container. Indeed, the whole point of speaking in terms of hours is precisely to emphasize the differences among them and the bringing of change. Fink states it well: "If we look only toward the phenomenon of the sun's course, we see that *Hêlios* exhibits no even, homogeneous radiation, but rather timely differences in its way of being luminous" (*GA* 15: 66/*HS* 38, tm). It is these timely variations and differences that reach us.

In a 1954 essay entitled "On the Secret of the Bell Tower," Heidegger paints a portrait of his youth as one of the sexton boys (*Mesmerbuben*) in small town Meßkirch, describing the excitement of Christmas morning, and the thrill of attending the ringing of the bells in the bell tower. There are seven bells for the seven hours and Heidegger lovingly recounts them by name:

> the *Three*, which must be sounded every afternoon at three
> o'clock. . . . The *Three* was also the death bell with which "the signal"

was rung . . . When at four the "alarm-ringing" began (which "alarmed" the sleepers of the village from their sleep), there followed on the *Three* the darkly-sweet resounding of the *Alve*, then the *Child* (it rang for the teaching of children, religious instruction, and for the saying of the rosary), then the *Eleven*, that would also be rung daily, mostly by the sexton, because the boys were in school at this time, then the *Twelve*, which likewise took care of ringing at noon on a daily basis, then the *Klanei* which was set ringing with the hour hammer, and lastly the *Great*. With their full, weighty, wide-reaching resounding the matutinal ringing-in of the high feast days [*der hohen Festtage*] came to a close. (*GA* 13: 114–15)

These bells sound out the measures of time organizing village life. Each is distinct, associated with a particular task or playing a particular role in the course of the day. Heidegger's description of the situation leading up to the actual sounding of the bells gives us a hint as to how we should think the borders of these measures of time. They are not discrete:

The bells, especially the large ones, were to be sounded in the bel-fry itself. And unspeakably exciting was the preliminary "swinging" of the larger bells, whose clappers were fastened by the bell rope and would first be "set loose"—something that called for special handling techniques—when the bells were already in full swing. This occurred so that each bell, one after the other, could start in with its full ringing. Only an experienced ear could properly assess [*ermessen*] whether every time was "correctly" rung; for the ending of the ringing also occurred in the same manner only reversed. The clappers were 'taken up' in full swing of the great bells, and woe to a ringer unskilled at this who let the bell "travel." (*GA* 13: 114)

The bells that ring in the hours of the day do not start and stop all of a sudden—the instantaneity of their entrance into the ringing of the hours only emanates from a bell prepared for the task already set in full swing. The sudden peal of the bell sounding the hour only arises from the si-lence of this preparatory swinging.

These bells accompany both the hours of the day and the seasons of the year; they are fitted to the measures of a lived time. The bells join together the hours and the seasons and parish life plays itself out in ac-cordance with them:

The mysterious [*geheimnisvolle*] fugue in which the church celebra-tions, the days of vigil, the course of the seasons, and the morning,

> midday, and evening hours of each day fitted into each other so that
> always *one* ringing went through the young hearts, dreams, prayers,
> and games—it is surely this fugue that is sheltered *through* one of the
> most magical, most wholesome [*heilsten*], and most lasting [*während-
> sten*] secrets of the tower, so as to bestow it, in a constantly altered and
> unrepeatable way, leading to that final ringing into the refuge of beyng.
> (*GA* 13: 115–16)

The joining together of the hours and seasons is the secret of the tower.
This "fugue" is a secret insofar as the entirety of it is not given to us, but
instead the fugue "withholds" its secret so as to satisfy the conditions of
giving—and of giving that same withheld secret. The joining of the hours
and the seasons, the interweaving of the hours into the days, the days into
seasons, and the seasons into years, along with the harmony produced by
this is given to us and can only be so given on the basis of a withholding,
i.e., the secret of the bell tower. Viewed from this perspective, the secret
is not something unavailable to us, but precisely what is given in the jointure of the measures of time. The bells ring out the periods of natural
time in singular "unrepeatable" hours and seasons.

With this understanding of temporal measure, Heidegger thus understands time itself (natural time, the time of measures) to be fitted
to us. The "bringing" character of time does not name a static field or
container. The time that is brought is brought *to us*. This is a time that
we are capable of receiving, otherwise we would not remark it. This time
that is sent to us is thus fitted or apportioned to us. Fink explains that the
path of the sun is tied to the rhythms of life and growth, "if *Hêlios* holds
in his natural path, the growth that is illuminated by him has its blossoming and its proper times"; conversely, "for growing and living things, a
deviation from the measures that are sent would mean that the sun is too
hot, too close or too far away" (*GA* 15: 70/*HS* 40; *GA* 15: 69/*HS* 40, tm).
If growth is a striving and reaching, an unfurling of oneself into greater
openness, as we have seen, then it can only reach out through a time that
first extends itself to the growing being itself. Such a time then exists in
measures, as natural time.[29]

If, in accordance with the secret of the bell tower, we take the
bounds of these measures of time to be nothing self-enclosing, but rather,
apportioned—i.e., moving toward us, inclined into the world—then each
measure would itself already be opened onto another. No measure would
be self-contained or homogeneous. Each would pass through the others.
There would consequently be no rigid and fast distinction between day
and night. Indeed, insofar as the day is the day of the sun and the sun
itself is fire, the 1943 Heraclitus lecture course explains the way in which

fire contains its own extinction, and, analogously, the light of day the dark of night: "In 'fire' the relations of lighting, glowing, blazing, and the shaping of a broad expanse are essential, but so are those of consumption, of a clashing and collapse within itself, as well as a shutting down and fading out. Fire blazes and in this ignites the division between light and dark; igniting joins the light and the dark against one another *and into one another*" (*GA* 55: 161, em). The irruption of fire is the advent of the differentiation between light and dark. The irruption is momentary. Once again, it is only caught sight of in a glance: "In igniting there takes place that which the eye grasps in a glance [*Blick*], the momentary [*das Augenblickliche*], the singular, which dividingly, decidingly, separates the bright against the dark. The momentariness of ignition opens the play space of appearance against the region of disappearance" (*GA* 55: 161– 62). The glance lets us see something that might appear to be a coincidence of opposites, but nothing could be further from the truth. What the glance shows is that the seeming opposites do not stand opposed to each other from positions of purity at all, but instead that the light is already invested by the dark, that they are joined "against one another and into one another" (*GA* 55: 161). Heidegger explains:

> in its essence, the dark "is" the light and the light, in its essence, "is" the dark. At first we recognize this only in that there where the brightness is a pure brightness—and thus is a brightness beyond the measure that is fitting to us [*das uns gemäße Maß*], a brightness without regard to us—precisely in the face of such a sheer brightness we can no longer see. This cannot only lie on us, but rather must have its reason in that brightness and light in its essence is somehow a concealing. (*GA* 55: 33)

The glance sees this belonging-together of light and dark, of day and night. It sees the concealment in light and understands this as the light that is measured to fit us, natural light. Heidegger does not name it such, but the setting and rising of the sun itself would be due to this outbreak of darkness in light. Such a thought would be the Heideggerian complement to Milton's avowal that original sin set the world off its axis and brought about the seasons. Rather than sin, however, here we have the co-originary essencing of the dark, i.e., the setting of the sun, "this setting [*Untergehen*] as an entry [*Eingehen*] into concealment is equally and always already a rising [*Aufgehen*]. Only a sun that rises, that surrenders this rising, and that essences in such a rising can set" (*GA* 55: 154).

Such a "setting" of the sun, the key to thinking the nature of transition (and also to thinking a transitional nature), is lost on the ordinary understanding, which sees only oppositions. For such a mindset "'Setting' [*Untergehen*; downfall], that is to fall victim to decay or annihilation. 'Setting' is a transition into no longer being. Victory or downfall—being or non-being" (*GA* 55: 50). Such an oppositional form of thinking reaches its apotheosis in modern mathematical science. Here there is only the "being" of the sun's presence. This is against the transitional thought of a setting and rising. Indeed, for science, the sun never sets. As Heidegger explains, "the setting of the sun is surely not its 'annihilation' and by no means its non-being. Though admittedly, since Copernicus, the setting of the sun is indeed only an optical illusion. Modern science has the better answer for this. Sunsets are only for 'poets' and 'the lovestruck'" (*GA* 55: 50, cf. *GA* 15: 145/*HS* 87–88). The oppositional structure of scientific thought precludes a thinking of the mutual abiding of contraries (rising and setting).

The belonging-together of light and dark caught sight of in the ignition of flame is nothing restricted to light and dark; rather it reveals to us something about the nature of delimitation in general. Indeed, in the Heraclitus seminar Fink puts it thus: "day and night do not comprise any distinction you please, but rather the original form of all distinctions" (*GA* 15: 75/*HS* 43–44). This would include the distinctions between self and other, as well as between being and world. The light of the flaming sun is not a light that brings together light and dark solely within itself; rather the interpenetration of boundary that is thought in this belonging-together of light and dark is shared with all that appears in this light-dark light. "In this illuminating jointure beings as a whole appear and radiate [*erstrahlt*]" (*GA* 55: 163). What appears in this light radiates beyond itself into relations with the world.

c. The Night, Its Stars, the Moon

What radiates in this way can only do so because that light of day is measured to it and that light could only be so measured thanks to the darkness within, which drives it out of self-seclusion, disrupting the homogeneity of the merely bright. The relation of light and dark is played out across the hours of each day, and not solely the daylight ones. Night, too, participates in this cohabitation of dark and light just as much as day does. Already in the *Contributions to Philosophy*, Heidegger had defended the night against a false illumination, calling on us to "protect" the night: "How to find beyng? Do we have to light a fire to find a fire, or must we not instead first content ourselves with *protecting the night*? In so doing, the false day of everydayness may be resisted. What is most false in this are those who also know the night and believe to possess it when they light it up and abolish it with their borrowed light" (*GA* 65: 487/383, tm). In the

Heraclitus lecture course some six years later, this becomes emblematic of technological advance: "In the meantime, the modern metropolis, before the war and by means of a gigantic illumination technology made night into day, such that neither a heaven nor even its lights could be visible. As a result of this lighting technology, brightness itself became a produceable object and pressing concern. Brightness suffered a loss of its essence, i.e., of remaining what is inapparent in all appearing" (*GA* 55: 142). Technology threatens the dark with light, but to no avail. At least not to any final cancellation of the dark, since, as the 1957 lecture cycle *Basic Principles of Thinking* repeatedly makes clear, humans are ineradicably tied to the dark:

> darkness is perhaps in play for all thinking at all times. Humans cannot set it aside. Rather, they must learn to acknowledge the dark as something unavoidable and to keep at bay those prejudices that would destroy the lofty reign of the dark. Thus the dark remains distinct from the pitch-black as the mere and utter absence of light. The dark however is the secret of the light. The dark keeps the light to itself. The latter belongs to the former. Thus the dark has its own limpidity. (*GA* 79: 93/88)

This limpid dark is the night.

We are called on to protect and defend the night. The night is punctuated by stars that keep the night dark, rather than pitch-black. In the Heraclitus seminar of 1966–67, Fink makes the point explicit, observing that "the dark night is illuminated by the glimmering stars. In contrast to the closedness of the earth, the dark of night has by itself a fundamental illuminability" (*GA* 15: 75/43, tm). But Fink understands the relation of dark and light as the embedding of one within the other: "we see in the other stars the possibility of being lights in the darkness. Light shines in the darkness. That means that the circuit of lights is surrounded by the night. The stars and the moon indicate the possibility of the lights being imbedded in the dark of night" (*GA* 15: 90/53). Fink thinks the light as distinct from the dark, though related to it. By his account, light needs the dark in order to form the background for its emergence. Light and dark are related in this, to be sure, but they remain in pure opposition— light is light and dark is dark. Heidegger's understanding of the measured time of the sky gives us to think a light that would be inhabited by darkness and a darkness that would bear light, something utterly foreign to Fink's construal here.

Instead, we have to think the stars as moments of light that radiate through the night sky (which is nothing pitch-black), but can only do so due to the darkness harbored within each of them. This would be the secret of their twinkling, the disruption of any pure illumination. The stars are thus displaced within themselves, inclined into the night, as we might expect. This allows them to draw near each other, to constellate, if the term be allowed. The 1945 conversation between a scientist, scholar, and guide, entitled "Anchibasiê," takes up just this nearing of the stars through the night. It ends with the three pondering the night:

> SCIENTIST: a night which gleams forth ever more maginificently–
> SCHOLAR: more astonishing than the stars
> GUIDE: because it brings near the distances of the stars to one another.
>   (*GA* 77: 156/102, tm)

The night is here understood as the space through which the stars draw near. The dark light of the stars is opened onto the night. The night must be able to receive them and distribute their radiance, mediate between them, bring them together, and in bringing them near [*nähern*] stitch them together [*näht*] as well:

> GUIDE: For the child in the human, the night remains the seamstress
>   [*Näherin*] who brings near [*nähert*], so that one star next to the
>   other gleams in silent light.
> SCHOLAR: She joins the lights together without seam or hem or yarn.
> SCIENTIST: The night is the seamstress who in sewing brings near
>   [*nähernd näht*].

She works only with nearness, which makes distant what is remote [*die das Ferne fernt*] (*GA* 77: 156–57/102, tm). Night grants the stars their nearness to each other. She does so as the seamstress of the stars. Contra Fink, who claims in the *Heraclitus* seminar that the stars are "embedded" in the sky, Heidegger understands them instead as stitched. To stitch the stars into the sky is to join them to that sky, to connect them to it at their edges. The night does this by allowing the stars to stream into it. The night sky receives the stars and gives them their place so as to shine. Here we are no longer dealing with discrete entities with independent identities that abut one another, but instead with radiance within a medium, i.e., with stars that overflow into the night and a night that receives them and distributes their light. Only as medium can the night bring stars near.

As stitched together in this way, the stars streak out into constellations.[30] For Heidegger, "constellation" designates a relationship of nearness maintained by the most remote (one thinks of Nietzsche's "star friends"). In the 1953 lecture "The Question Concerning Technology," the most remote are the reign of positionality and the thinging of things, which Heidegger here discusses in terms of a "saving" (*das Rettende*, cf. *GA* 7: 29/*QCT* 28). The relationship between positionality and this saving he names a constellation:

> The inexorability of positionality and the restraint of what saves [*des Rettenden*] draw past one another, like the path of two stars in the movement of the starry skies [*Gestirne*]. Yet this going past is harbored in their nearness.
>
> If we glance into the ambiguous essence of technology, then we catch sight of the constellation, the stellar course of the secret.
>
> The question concerning technology is the question concerning the constellation in which disclosing and concealing take place, in which the essencing of truth takes place.
>
> But indeed what help to us is a glance into the constellation of truth? We glance into the danger and catch sight of the growth [*das Wachstum*] of what saves. (*GA* 7: 34/*QCT* 33, tm)

The stars are near in going past.[31] Their course is that of the secret, of something withheld, but not absent. This secret holds together the ambiguous essence of technology, i.e., technology as irresistible conversion to value and replaceability, on the one hand, and technology as harboring the trace of singularity, as sheltering it even in the midst of its pursuit, on the other. The constellation is the relation between these stars, growth within the danger, a trace of darkness in the light, even these lights, the stars, themselves in the darkness. They twinkle and that is all the salvation we require. (We need only look up.)

But if the night is not opaque, this cannot be credited solely to the presence of the stars. There is also the moon, a literal reflection of the sun in the midst of the night sky. Heidegger takes up the moon in his considerations of Hebel, the self-described "friend of the house" (*der Hausfreund*), in the decade following the formulation of the fourfold. For Heidegger, this "house" is ultimately the world, and the friend of this world is the poet. But this is not the only friend of the house; Heidegger calls attention to Hebel's own determination of the "authentic friend of the house" as the moon (*GA* 13: 140/*HFH* 94, tm). The ensuing discussion brings together the two friends of the house in a manner that not only elucidates the work of the poet, but also that of the moon.

Heidegger writes that "as the moon brings a light with its shining, so too does the earthly friend of the house, Hebel, through his saying, and indeed a mild light. The moon brings the light in our nights. But the light that it brings it did not ignite by itself. It is only the reflection which the moon has previously received—from its sun, whose gleam equally illuminates the earth" (*GA* 13: 140–41/*HFH* 94, tm). The moon is not the source of its light, but instead brings the light of day into the night. The presence of this brightness within the dark yields what Heidegger here calls a "mild" light. The moon keeps the night from achieving a tenebrous pitch-black opacity, it "remains awake in the night," and in so doing, it "admits all things into a mild, scarcely noticeable light" (*GA* 13: 141/*HFH* 94, 95). The mildness of the moonlight allows what appears to maintain an aspect of discretion and concealment.

For Heidegger this is the "naturality" of nature, the nature we have discussed under the auspices of "natural" time. In articulating this natural nature, Heidegger returns to the very terms used in his considerations of the day: "What is natural of nature is that rising and setting of the sun, the moon, and the stars, which immediately addresses the dwelling humans in avowing to them what is secretive of the world" (*GA* 13: 145/*HFH* 97, tm). The natural in nature is bound up with an understanding of sun, moon, and stars as capable of reaching and addressing us. This would not be possible if those heavenly bodies were not already inclined and radiating toward us. Otherwise put, this address and avowal would not be possible without the essential interplay of light and dark that we have addressed above in terms of the hours of the day. And insofar as whatever reaches us or addresses us can only do so on the basis of a concomitant withholding (the withholding that serves to stretch open the space of delivery), what is directly addressed to us is likewise something secretive. The sun, moon, and stars, in addressing us, withhold themselves from us, which is only to say that they radiate and shine in a sky capable of distributing them. Both day and night evince the character of "natural" time, a time that is sent to us in measures.

d. The Seasons of the Year

The time of the sky that is fitted to us is one in which we grow. This is its dimensional character, where the dimensional indicates a reciprocal apportioning and traversing. Given to us in measures, we grow into this time. The measures themselves are therefore determinable in terms of the stages of growth or maturation. These make up the seasons of the year (three for the Ancient Greeks). The 1966–67 Heraclitus seminar goes the farthest in thinking the seasons as stages of growth. Heidegger asks "what are the seasons [*Horen*]?," and in his answer explains each of them in terms of maturation: "*Thallô* is the springtime, which brings the shoot and blossom. *Auxô* means summer, ripening and maturing. *Karpô* means autumn, the picking of the ripe fruit. These three seasons are not like three time periods; rather, we must understand them as the whole maturation" (*GA* 15: 62/*HS* 35, tm). The opposition posed is between the time of maturation (*Zeitigung*), on the one hand, and a time of successive periods, on the other. Fink elaborates, "in order to win an understanding of the maturational character of the seasons, we must disregard homogeneous time, which one represents as a line and as bare succession and in which the time content is abstracted. Such an abstraction is impossible with the seasons" (*GA* 15: 63/*HS* 35–36, tm). Heidegger will not even allow Fink the claim that the movement of life in nature is a rising and falling: "Do you really understand fruition as a falling?" he asks (*GA* 15: 63/*HS* 35, tm). Instead, "age corresponds to fruition in the sense of a becoming ripe, which I understand not as a falling, but instead as a kind of self-fulfillment" (*GA* 15: 63/35, tm). The maturation in question then is a kind of temporalizing (*zeitigen*) that breaks with the notion of sequential, serial succession.

Instead, in maturation, each phase is already implicated in the others, something we overlook if we understand the periods of time as discrete spans. Heidegger explains, "spring, summer and autumn are not periods, but something constant [*Stetiges*]. Their maturation has the character of a constancy [*Stetigkeit*], in which an *alloiôsis* [qualitative alteration] is contained" (*GA* 15: 62–63/*HS* 35, tm). There is a steadiness to the seasons whereby spring is not divorced from autumn, but constant throughout it. They interpenetrate in the movement of fulfilling maturation, whereby fall is not opposed to spring or somehow independent of it. The situation is similar to what we have already encountered in the 1954 text "On the Secret of the Bell Tower." There Heidegger wrote that the hours of the day and the seasons of the year were joined together in a "mysterious fugue" whereby "the course of the seasons [*der Gang der Jahreszeiten*] and the morning, midday, and evening hours of each day fitted into each other, so that always *one* ringing went through the young hearts, dreams, prayers, and games" (*GA* 13: 115). The one ringing that Heidegger emphasizes is what he later calls the "whole maturation."[32] The bells syncopate the hours of the day with the seasons of the year across this doubly measured time of maturation.

Heidegger explains that "if time comes into play with the seasons [*Horen*], then we must let go of calculated time. . . . Also, we may not separate the content of time from the form of time" (*GA* 15: 63/*HS* 35–36, tm). Calculated time relies on an empty form of time to structure its compartmentalized contents. (Heidegger mocks the idea of thinking the parts of the day in terms of sequentially opening "chests" or "trunks" in the Heraclitus lecture course; *GA* 55: 134.) The time of the seasons cannot be thought in terms of form and content because the seasons are *hôrai.* Time does not exist abstractly outside of these seasonal conditions to subsequently fall into them from elsewhere. Time is temporal through and through; it does not precede its own instantiation and differentiation into the hours and seasons. Instead, it exists as on the way to us and in arriving. Its way of being is a being toward us, an inclination, a going.

The 1953 Trakl essay "Language in the Poem" even supplies an etymological connection for thinking the year in terms of a passage or going: "'To go' [*Gehen*], *ienai,* means in Indo-Germanic: *ier-,* the year" (*GA* 12: 43/*OWL* 168, tm). The rising (*Aufgehen*) and setting (*Untergehen*) of the sun are just as much connected to this "going" of the year as is its course (*Gang*) through the seasons. And just as we discussed the blue twilight in regards to the day, the same ambiguity and movement holds for the seasons of the year as well, since "the twilight is the declension of the sun's course [*die Neige des Sonnenganges*]. This entails: the twilight is just as much the declension of the day as also the declension of the year" (*GA* 12: 38–39/*OWL* 164, tm). The year is modulated into periods just as much as the day is. For the day these periods are its hours; for the year, its seasons. Both are due to the "declension" or—shading the term *Neige* in the direction of the German *Neigung,* "tendency" or even "tilt"—due to the "inclination" of the sun, i.e., that it is never present in place, but always on the go.

The going of the year, the movement of the seasons, is once again a relation of bringing that reaches out to us. The 1943 essay "Homecoming/ To the Relations" discusses the reach of time as the greeting of an angel. There is the "angel of the house," who greets us as the earth, and there is also the "angel of the year," who greets us in the play of light. The greeting of this angel is our contact with time, the bringing of the year:

> "The year" makes room for the times that we call the seasons. In the "mixed" play of fiery brightness and frosty darkness that the seasons [*Zeiten*] grant, things blossom and close once again. The seasons "of the year" in a reciprocation of the joyous make a gift to the human of a while [*das Weile*] that is apportioned to the human's historical residence in the "house." "The year" offers its greetings in the play of lights. The joymaking light is the first "angel of the year." (*GA* 4: 17/36, tm)

As the offering of light, time reaches us. It invites us into the joyous, playfully soliciting us, though only for a brief while. (We will revisit this while in considering the thing's relation to world in "The Thing Abides," chapter 6.)

Humans reply to the givenness of time by themselves participating in the marking of its measures. They do this through their holy days and holidays of festival and celebration. This is externally evident from the examination of a calendar: "The calendar is actually a festival-calendar. The festivals are regularly repeating occurrences, established in their sequence, within the historiologically characterizable sequence of weeks, months, and seasons" (*GA* 52: 67). But for Hölderlin and Heidegger alike, the festival is "not an occurrence in the frame of and on the basis of history, but rather *'the festival is itself the ground and the essence of history'*" (*GA* 52: 68). It is such because it is given to us, apportioned to us, greets us: "What is festive of the festival, that which each time lets the festival take place, is the inceptual greeting *of* what greets" (*GA* 52: 70). Humans share in the syncopation of time by their festivals, which reply to the givenness, or greeting, of time with a responsive greeting of their own. It should be clear by now that the greeting of time is the soliciting touch of the medium, teasing us out to grow further into time. Our festivals are our acceptance of that mediated, temporal, heavenly condition.

The sky allows for all appearing upon the earth. It provides a field for its emergence, one that is never homogeneous, but diversified through weather, dense with aether, covered with clouds, ever shifting through blues, and measured by time. The sky as a medium lets what appears radiate through it. The sky modulates, mediates, and distributes appearances. Whatever appears is weathered by the sky, not just by the abrasion of its aethereal texture, but also by its temporalizing. We are weathered by time, thanks to the sky. What appears does so through the spatiotemporal mediation of the sky. The sky and earth thus form a dimension that allows for reciprocal communication and mutual contact. The dimensional character of the sky is visible in its very lighting, in which the light and the dark repeatedly and rhythmically unsettle each other. This unsettled medium of dark light reaches us and greets us, allows us to look up through it and be reached by the arrival of joy. To be a thing is to radiate through this sky meaningfully, as we shall see.

4

Divinities, Hinting Messengers of Godhood

Heidegger's presentation of the divinities (*die Göttlichen*) within the four-fold is not something that arrives without notice. Heidegger had occupied himself with questions religious and divine from early on. The year of publication for *Being and Time*, 1927, found Heidegger lecturing on "Phenomenology and Theology." Prior to this, the 1921 lecture courses on the phenomenology of religion crystallized concerns operative from the very beginning of Heidegger's lecturing career. Retrospectively, in the "Conversation on Language" (1953), Heidegger points out that his interest in hermeneutics began during the theological study of his youth, noting that "without this theological background I should never have come upon the path of thinking" (*GA* 12: 91/*OWL* 10). Texts from this student period are extant, too, in contributions to the journal *Der Akademiker* dating from 1910–1913 and addressing issues such as "Psychology of Religion and the Subconscious."[1] Despite all these forays, none of this could prepare his reader for the full onslaught of things divine in the decades to come. Heidegger's later presentation of God, the gods, the last God, the dead God, the God of metaphysics, godhood, the flown gods, the arriving gods, the divinities, the holy, the unholy, the hale, and the unhale all arrive as matters for thinking after his 1934 encounter with Hölderlin. In Hölderlin, Heidegger found a poetic thinking of divinity's abandonment, a thinking that he could hold over and against the death of God announced by Nietzsche.[2] While Nietzsche could be read as still thinking in absolutes, or at the very least, in terms of reversals—the God who lived now has died—Heidegger could employ this newly found Hölderlinian thinking precisely in order to interrupt such metaphysical conceptions of a pure presence or absence of divinity. In this light, Heidegger's thinking of divinity concerns itself not with a simple life, death, or rebirth of divinity, but with hints and traces that announce a world between presence and absence.

So positioned, these hints are fragile, delicate, and easily missed. They could not exist at all were it not for the buoyancy of the medium that supports them. For Heidegger, this medium is "the holy" (*das Hei-*

lige). Any conception of God, the gods, or godhood can only appear within the medium of the holy. The divinities are the "messengers" of this, that hints and godhood are all tied to the medium of the holy that supports them.

The identification of the divinities in both "The Thing" and "Building Dwelling Thinking" is rather brief. Only two sentences are offered. The first of these is the same in each identification, the second is altered. In "The Thing" we read:

> The divinities are the hinting messengers of godhood. From the concealed reign of these there appears the God in his essence, withdrawing him from every comparison with what is present. (*GA* 79: 17/15)

and in "Building Dwelling Thinking":

> The divinities are the hinting messengers of godhood. From the holy reign of these there appears the God in the present [*Gegenwart*] or he withdraws into his veiling. (*GA* 7: 151/*PLT* 147–48, tm)

In what follows, we take up each of these determining aspects of the divinities in turn: that they hint, that they are messengers, and that their message concerns godhood. For now it is worth emphasizing that the central determination of the divinities is that they are messengers.

And this is why divinities are involved in the thinging of the thing. Things are inherently messengerial. They are connected to something beyond themselves. By writing the divinities into the very nature of things, Heidegger is constituting things as intrinsically bearing a message. Otherwise put, things are inherently *meaningful*. It is of their nature to be communicative, to bear a message/meaning. Their messengerial constitution makes them meaningful by tying them to a beyond that they do not possess. As relational, things are meaningful. As such, the divinities not only allow for communication with the divine, but for the communication of meaning as such. The divinities insure that meaning can reach us and this fact is ontologically transformative, calling for a rethinking of what Heidegger earlier understood as hermeneutics.

In what follows we will track the twinkling of hints, the hermeneutics of messaging, and the mediation of the holy in order to ultimately address the meaning of the divine and its role in the thinging of the thing.

§12. The Hint

> . . . For the one who yearned
> the hint was enough, and hints are,
> since long ago, the language of the gods.
> —Hölderlin[3]

The divinities are said to be messengers of godhood that "hint" or "wink" (*winken*). The hint (*der Wink*) emerges as a term of art in Heidegger's thinking around the time of his first writings on Hölderlin (1934–36) where he follows the poet in deeming such hints to be "the language of the gods" (*GA* 39: 32). These early moments soon culminate in the *Contributions to Philosophy* (1936–38), which elaborates the hint in relation to the enigmatic figure of the "last God." From the outset, then, the hint is connected with the divine. The hint remains active in Heidegger's thought into the forties and fifties, where it serves as the title for a poetry collection from 1941 (*Winke, GA* 13: 23–33), identifies the divinities within the fourfold, and receives a second in-depth treatment in the 1953 "Conversation on Language" between a researcher (Heidegger) and a Japanese interlocutor. This latter context, arising out of and informed by these earlier concerns, will play a predominant role in our understanding of the divinities. Here, by means of the hint, Heidegger articulates a relationship to withdrawal and language that will orient his hermeneutic approach to the divinities in the fourfold.

a. Etymology

Within the family of West Germanic languages, the noun *der Wink* (derived from the verb *winken*) is found in both Old High German (before 1100) and Anglo-Saxon (450–1150), finally reaching the English language as "to wink." According to the Grimms, the verb at its earliest originally named a movement of the eyelids without gestural significance (a nictitation or involuntary blinking).[4] Innocently enough, it could also mean to go to sleep. Subsequently, however, the movement of *winken* came to participate in the "language of gestures" (*Gebärdesprache*) where it donned a variety of meanings according to context. It came to mean among other things: a giving of signs, to do or observe something primarily through the eyes, and the expression of a will or of intellectual content through gestures. It meant above all to give signs of concession (*gewährung*) and agreement. But the Grimms also find a few other meanings of some importance to the topic at hand. *Winken* has meant to let come, to intimate and stand in expectation, to near, and to call something here, bring it forth, and/or awaken it. The term can also mean "to wave," where the gesture of waving can beckon, greet, or invite.

By and large these meanings are preserved in the closely related English word "wink" as well. The English word has a history stretching over a thousand years (the *OED* lists 897 as the earliest occurrence and 1937 as the latest where, not surprisingly, a wink is equal to one two-thousandth of a minute), and many, if not the majority, of its meanings are associated with the eyes. To begin with, wink can mean a short spell of sleep ("forty winks" as a phrase comes with the nineteenth century), a blink of the eye, a glance of the eye, or a twinkling (first of stars, then of the eyes). Such optical meanings predominate in the period of 1300–1600. Between 1600 and 1900, however, the leading use of the term emphasizes the signifying power of the wink. Wink now can rather banally mean to make a sign or to signal with flags or flashlights, but the significance presented by the wink is more usually that of intrigue and clandestine cooperation. Further, to wink is to shut one's eyes to an offense or fault that one has noticed as such (to intentionally disregard and overlook it). And it can also mean the momentary closing of the eye in order to convey intimate information. Perhaps most importantly, the wink shows that one is in league with another, it means to be complaisant with an offending or contumacious person or to connive at the doings of such. The eye and belonging-together themselves come together in the English word "wink" and reverberate through Heidegger's implementations of *der Wink* (one need only recall the derivation of *Ereignis* which reaches back to *Eräugnen*[5]). What then of this winking?

b. The Hints of the Last God: From Representation to Belonging

The hint first comes to light in Heidegger's lecture course on *Hölderlin's Hymns "Germania" and "The Rhine"* of 1934–35. The guiding text for our purposes is Hölderlin's hymn "Rousseau," where we read: "hints are, / since long ago, the language of the gods."[6] The connection evinced here between the hint and the divine will stay with Heidegger throughout his career. Heidegger explains that "even in our everyday dealings, the hint is something other than a sign, hinting something other than the pointing out of something, something other than the mere calling attention to something" (*GA* 39: 32). Instead, the hint should be viewed in terms of a relationship. As we have seen, the same German word for hint, *der Wink*, can also be translated as "to wave." Heidegger first explicates the hint in just these terms: "at a departure, for example, waving [*Winken*] is a retaining of nearness despite an increasing distance and is, conversely, at an arrival, the making manifest of the distance still reigning in a pleasing nearness" (*GA* 39: 32). Determinative here is that the hint is a bridging of distances, the creation of a proximity in severance. The hint brings together the "here" and the "there."

This same ambiguity of the hint is remarked a few years later in Heidegger's first published text on Hölderlin, "Hölderlin and the Essence of Poetry" (1936). Here Heidegger comments on these same lines of Hölderlin, noting that "the saying of the poet is the grasping of these hints, in order to hint them further along to the people. This grasping of the hints is a reception and indeed at the same time a new giving" (*GA* 4: 46/63, tm). To grasp the hint is both to receive and to give. The hint brings us into a relationship with that which is hinted and, by drawing us out in this manner, it likewise inclines us to a further giving of the hint to others. In the Hölderlin readings, this hinting is predominantly a matter of the gods. Indeed, in the first lecture course Heidegger will go so far as to consider the hint not simply as the "language" of the gods (where this would be understood as an utterance originating with the gods), but instead as these gods themselves: "The gods, however, hint simply in that they *are*" (*GA* 39: 32). It is the nature of the gods to hint. Their very being is a hinting. The "essence of hinting" (*Wesen des Winkens*) is thus no referring, but precisely a way of being (*GA* 39: 32). The *Contributions to Philosophy* unfolds this way of being of the hint.

We might typically think of a hint as pointing to something beyond itself, as *hinting at* something, but *der Wink* does not do this, at least not in the way that a cipher or symbol points to a meaning elsewhere. Ciphers and symbols operate metaphysically, trading on a sensible/super-sensible divide whereby the sensible symbol points beyond itself to its super-sensible significance. In the *Contributions* the use of ciphers and symbols is called "the last consequence of 'ontology' and 'logic,' which have not been overcome, but are precisely presupposed" (*GA* 65: 280/220), where such use "presupposes the previous metaphysics" (*GA* 65: 79/63). Heidegger's later views do not differ here. The "Dialogue on Language" (1953) agrees with this estimation, finding that "in terms of their reference, hints and gestures are different from signs and ciphers, which are all native to metaphysics" (*GA* 12: 111/*OWL* 26, tm). For this reason, symbols, signs, and ciphers can all be filed under the rubric of "metaphor," where, as *The Principle of Reason* (1955–56) states, "metaphor is based upon the distinguishing, if not complete separation, of the sensible and the nonsensible as two realms that subsist on their own. The setting up of this partition between the sensible and nonsensible, between the physical and nonphysical is a basic trait of what is called metaphysics and which normatively determines Western thinking" (*GA* 10: 72/48). Simply put: "The metaphorical exists only within metaphysics" (*GA* 10: 72/48). Metaphors, ciphers, symbols, etc., have guided the understanding of language throughout the metaphysical tradition and Heidegger sees this as concomitant with the determination of the human being as the *zôon logon echon*, the *animal rationale*. The human so conceived is "that living being whose essence lies precisely in that by which it is symbolized, i.e., precisely in the possession of this symbol (*logon echon*)" (*GA* 65: 502/395). Ciphers, symbols, and metaphors attend a conception of language grounded in the metaphysical understanding of the human and operating through representation. But *der Wink* does not represent.

But if they do not represent, then what do hints do? Heidegger provides a clue in a section of the *Contributions* entitled "The Continuance of the Abandonment by Being in the Hidden Mode of the Forgottenness of Being" (§56), where he itemizes ways in which the abandonment of being announces itself. One of these ways reads, "the self-certainty of no longer letting oneself be called; the hardening against all hints; the *incapacity* for awaiting" (*GA* 65: 118/94, tm). Hints call to those not hardened against them. To perceive the hint is to find oneself called from out of the midst of the abandonment of being. The call that ultimately comes to us (*der Zuruf*) must be understood as sent, i.e., as both arriving and withholding itself at once: "The *call* is a befalling *and* a staying-away [*Anfall* und *Ausbleib*] in the secret of appropriation [*Ereignung*]" (*GA* 65: 408/323, tm). The call reaches us, falls upon us like an attack, but at the same time it remains, at least in part, outside our reach. Such a call provides us with a first approximation of the workings of the hint, where Heidegger speaks of "*this call* of the most extreme hinting" (*GA* 65: 408/324, tm). Hints do not represent, they call.

From within the machinational landscape of the abandonment of being, these hints call to us while withholding themselves from us. To befall and yet to stay away is another way of naming withholding, or what Heidegger also terms "hesitating refusal" (*die zögernde Versagung*), where "hesitating refusal is the hint" (*GA* 65: 380/300, tm).[7] To see the hint is to see this hesitant refusal and to do so from within the purview of the abandonment of being. To perceive the hint is thus to be brought to the limits of abandonment, where abandonment can no longer be understood as a discarding or dereliction. Instead, perceiving the hint allows us to see the relationship that abides in the abandonment of beyng between those abandoned and beyng itself, precisely in the form of this refusal and its hesitation. Just as in the early Hölderlin lecture course, hinting (waving) was a bridging of distance, so too is it here, now taken to the extreme. The distance to be brokered is the greatest imaginable: "In the essence of hinting lies the secret of the unity of the most intimate nearing with the most extreme distance, the measuring out of the broadest time-play-space of beyng. This greatest extremity of the essence of beyng requires the greatest intimacy of the distress of the abandonment of being" (*GA* 65: 408/323, tm). The distance measured out here is that stretching from abandonment to belonging. Hints transform abandonment from disposal to belonging. Thus it should come as no surprise that the unworld of machination itself is what hints: "Machination as the essencing of beinghood gives a first hint into the truth of beyng itself" (*GA* 65: 127/100, tm). The first hint is found in the beinglessness (i.e., beinghood) of the machinational landscape.

Hints then calls us out of abandonment and in so doing they show that abandonment is not yet complete, but at the very same time, in the twinkling of an eye, they likewise show that beyng is no longer present. Hints reveal that abandonment is endless. We can always be abandoned further, there is still a hint that can be squelched, overlooked, or simply reified into a sign or symbol of something merely absent. But this likewise means abandonment can never be so complete as to sever our belonging to beyng. We can even hazard a step further: abandonment makes possible that belonging in the first place. Were beyng simply present, were we not abandoned, but in a mandated adherence to beyng (now beinghood), there would be no belonging, there could be no intimacy across distance. *Beyng needs its abandonment to be (seyn).* Hints hint at nothing other than this. This is why Heidegger can speak of machination as a gift or donation of being, why the withdrawal of being is always a refusal: "*refusal is the foremost and utmost giving* [Schenkungs] *of beyng, indeed it is its inceptual essencing itself*" (*GA* 65: 241/190, tm).[8] Hesitation hints.

But if the unworld of machination twinkles with the hints of a hesitant beyng, and if these hints call to us, whither do they call? An answer is provided by Heidegger when he speaks of the coming ones (*Die Zukünftigen*). The coming ones "take over and preserve the belonging (which is awoken by the call) to the event and to its turning, and thus they come to stand before the hints of the *last God*" (*GA* 65: 82/66, tm). Before addressing the role of the last God in relation to the hint, let us first note that it is precisely in standing before the hints, acknowledging them, that the coming ones preserve a belonging. Hints call for a belonging. Heidegger speaks of the "appropriation [*Eignung*] of the belonging, grounding, sheltering Dasein to the hint" (*GA* 65: 262/206, tm) and the achievement of this appropriation is the task of Dasein, the task of encountering the hints that call to us and tell of being's abandonment. To discern these hints is no longer to view the world in terms of sheer presence and absence, but to see in all presence a withholding and in all absence a trace of departure.

The coming ones "get the hint," though their search does not seek something present. Heidegger rightly diagnoses this situation, noting that "if someone seeks and does not find and therefore is compelled into forced machinations, [then there is] no freedom for reserved waiting and the ability to await upon an encounter and a hint" (*GA* 65: 400/317, tm). To seek something present, whether one finds it or not, is already to swing oneself into the unworld of machination. The coming ones do not seek at all—rather they wait. The inability to wait is itself the hardening against all hints mentioned above. Waiting does not leap to conclusions, but keeps itself in a reserved bearing, where one must "be able to wait in this clearing until the hints arrive" (*GA* 65: 242/191, tm).[9] The reserve (*Verhaltenheit*) necessary for this enduring waiting is "modesty" (*die Scheu*), "modesty is the way of drawing near and remaining near to what is most remote as such (cf. the last God), that in its hinting—when held in modesty—nevertheless becomes the nearest and gathers in itself all relations of beyng" (*GA* 65: 16/15, tm).[10] Modesty brings the coming ones near to the last God and thus to the event of appropriation itself, for "in his hinting, being itself—the event of appropriation as such—becomes visible for the first time" (*GA* 65: 70/56, tm). *Der Wink* thus occupies the extremes, is both the last and the first, the hint of both the last God and the first lighting up of *Ereignis*.

If hints call us to what is outstanding, then for the Heidegger of the *Contributions* this can only be a call to this last God, who, as Heidegger explains, "has its *essencing* in the hint" (*GA* 65: 409/324, tm). Here we hearken back to the first Hölderlin course, where Heidegger pronounced the gods to exist as hints. The hints of the last God would seem the condition for any divine being whatsoever: "the hints of the last God are in play as a befalling and a staying-away of the arrival and flight of the gods and their sovereign sites" (*GA* 65: 408/323, tm). If there are to be these gods, this outside to the machinational abandonment of being, then they will exist as hints, not present or absent entities. For this reason there can be no proof for either the existence (presence) or non-existence (absence) of a God.[11]

The last God, essencing in and as hints, is the most outstanding of the outstanding. The lastness of this last God, its finality, does not refer to its position within a chronological sequence of gods (as if one could lay them out in a terminal series: Zeus . . . Christ . . . the last God). The ultimacy here is of a different sort altogether. The last God is nothing that can ever arrive, where this is equated with a coming-to-stand-in-complete-presence-before-a-subject. Arrival is the affair of things present-at-hand (airplanes, for example, arrive sooner or later or do not arrive at all). The winking essencing of the last God excludes it from comparison with what can have arrived. Instead, the last God is constantly arriving. The hint is a hint of the last God's arriving. As such, the last God can be named "the most coming of the coming [*den Kommendsten des Kommenden*]" (*GA* 69: 211; cf. 208). Hence, the last God *does arrive*, but only in the mode of *not yet arriving*, or rather, of *only ever arriving*; in other words, his "lastness is his coming" (*GA* 69: 211).[12] For this reason the last God will *out-last* all other gods. By dint of its nature, all the other gods that have arrived will precede it. The last God will never have done with its coming. Thinking the hint in conjunction with the last God allows us to see the pivotal role hints play in the overcoming, or rather conversion (*Verwindung*) of metaphysics. Any belonging that emerges from withdrawal can only do so as hint.

c. The Extra-Linguistic: Hint and Gesture

In Heidegger's later thinking, the hint is no longer cast in terms of the tension between machination and the coming of the last God, at least not explicitly so, but instead with regard to language. The focus on abandonment and belonging in the *Contributions* shifts to a concern with finding a proper language for thought in its engagement with the thoughtworthy. Ultimately this is nothing linguistic at all, insofar as the linguistic would indicate something spoken. Instead, Heidegger emphasizes what we might term the "extra-linguistic" aspects of language, that which is said without speech (the unsaid, we might say). For this reason, the "Conversation on Language" (1953) takes up the hint in terms of gesture. This "Conversation" between a researcher (who stands in for Heidegger, though is never so named; he has, however, written the same books as Heidegger, delivered the same lectures at the same universities as him, and worked with the same people upon the same problems and at the same time as Heidegger) and a Japanese interlocutor is of unparalleled importance for Heidegger's later thinking of both hints and the messengerial, as we shall see.

The conversation itself proceeds slowly, at times reticently, with the interlocutor cautioning us not to be misled into "refining the conception of the hint into a guiding concept in which we would pack everything" (*GA* 12: 109/*OWL* 25, tm). The researcher agrees with this, claiming that "even the talk of a hint already risks too much" (*GA* 12: 111/*OWL* 26, tm). The concern is in part to avoid treating the hint as something present-at-hand that could be identified in terms of a single referential function. To treat the hint as such would be to understand it as a sign or cipher of something else, and thus resign it to the purview of metaphysics, for reasons we have seen. In fact the hint is not something present at all.

The Japanese interlocutor (J) and the researcher (R) propose thinking the ambiguity of the hint in terms of withholding, bearing, and gesture, as in the following exchange:

> J: We understand all too well that a thinker might prefer to hold back the word that is to be said, not so as to keep it for himself, but instead to bear it towards [*entgegentragen*] what is thoughtworthy.
> R: This is in keeping with hints. They are riddlesome. They hint *to* us. They hint *away*. They hint us *toward* that from where they are unnoticeably conveying us [*uns zutragen*].
> J: You think hints in their belonging-together with what you have elucidated by the word "gesture" [*Gebärde*].
> R: So it is. (*GA* 12: 111/*OWL* 26, tm)

A certain reticence is in keeping with hints, a kind of not speaking. The word is held back. But in being held back, it is likewise borne ahead toward what is to be thought. If naming is the application of names to objects, then this is not a naming. If anything it is a letting be named. The word is held back in order that it might receive its essential marking from the thoughtworthy. If instead the word that is held back here were to attempt to name the thoughtworthy, it could only produce an artifact. Rather, the word is held back so as to allow the thoughtworthy to show itself. The way it shows itself is understood in terms of gesture.

Gesture (*Gebärde*), hearing the German *Ge-* prefix of the word, names "the gathering of a bearing [*Versammlung eines Tragens*]," a concentrated bearing (*GA* 12: 102/*OWL* 18).[13] When the interlocutor observes that this definition pointedly avoids describing bearing as the possession or action of a subject, the subsequent exchange unfolds what we might term a hermeneutic thinking of the gesture. Bearing is not named our possession, the researcher responds:

> R: Because what authentically bears, first bears itself *to* us [*uns sich erst zu-trägt*].
> J: We, however, only bear our share towards it [*entgegentragen*].
> R: Whereby that which conveys itself to us [*uns sich zuträgt*] has already registered our counter-bearing in what it conveys to us [*unser Entgegentragen schon in den Zutrag eingetragen hat*].
> J: Consequently you name gesture: the gathering which originally unites within itself a counter-bearing and a conveying [*Entgegentragen und Zutrag*]. (*GA* 12: 102/*OWL* 18–19, tm)

There is a mutual implication involved in all gesture. As a "gathering" of bearings, gesture unites what is borne to us with what we bear toward it. Gesture arises at the interface of the two. There is a priority operative however, in that what "authentically bears" must first be borne to us. Our counter-bearing is a response. This would not be possible, however, if what is originally borne to us were not already suited to us. We must be able to receive it insofar as it is fitted to us. If we were not, it would go unremarked. What impinges upon us, then, is suited to us in advance and hence able to reach us. In responding to this, we give birth to a gesture. Gesture names the interface between bearings; it is the "condensation" [*Versammlung*] of these bearings.

Gesture is thus a response that first makes evident the address to which the response is offered.[14] In this, gesture hits upon what Heidegger calls the essence of language. This is not a matter of speaking (*sprechen*) but of saying (*sagen*), the latter not dependent upon vocalization or utterance, as Heidegger explains in the 1957 *Basic Principles of Thinking:*

> Even the speechless gesture, precisely this, resonates in saying, not because there is a language of gestures and forms, but because the essence of language lies in saying. Gestures are not at first mere gestures that subsequently express something and then become a language, rather gestures are in themselves what they are through saying, wherein their bearing, enduring, and conveying [*Tragen, Ertragen und Zutragen*] each time remain already gathered. Gestural bearing is determined by saying and is thereby constantly the resonance of restraint [*Ver-haltens*]. The gestural first attunes all movements. The nonessence of the gesture is the gesticulation. Pure gestures are speechless, but they are not word-less. They are so little this that they constantly are achieved in terms of a saying and through such a saying. The nonspeaking essence of language resonates in saying. (*GA* 79: 169–70/159–60)

Hints are like gestures in displaying the reciprocity of a bearing. They thereby resonate with the essence of language. They show that language occurs without speech, indeed, that saying and meaning are sent to us, that the unsaid announces itself, and this whether explicitly spoken or not.

Given this understanding of gesture, when we are told that a thinker might keep back a word in order to "bear it toward" what is thought-worthy, what we find is the thinker in question responding to an address pre-given. The word held toward the thoughtworthy receives its radiance and is marked by that. It now hints of it. It would then seem that the thoughtworthy could merely be read off of the word. The word in this case would bear something of a fingerprint or footprint of the thought-worthy on the basis of which we could work back to that thoughtworthy thing itself. Nothing could be further from the truth, for what is thoughtworthy is not something that gives itself entirely, immediately. Were this the case, there would be no call for hinting. Rather, the thoughtworthy itself is withdrawn. Two years earlier, in *What Is Called Thinking?* (1951–52), Heidegger had already explained, "the reason thought remains outstanding is not only, and not primarily, that the human has cultivated thought too little, but because what is to be thought about, that which properly provides for thought, has long been withdrawing. . . . This withdrawal which properly provides for thought is the most thought-provoking" (*GA* 8: 28/25, tm). The withheld word is borne toward this withdrawal of what is to be thought. Between the withdrawals there emerges a hint. Hints announce this withholding.

But at the same time, the hint would make evident a certain limitation of our thinking, that the "fitting" way of thinking the thought-provoking still eludes us. In "The Essence of Language" (1957–58) Heidegger makes this explicit:

> Hints hint in multiple ways. A hint can hint at that towards which it hints in so simple and fulfilled a manner that we let ourselves loose there utterly univocally. But a hint can also hint in such a way that it refers us in advance and persistently to the thought-provoking, from where it hints away. In regards to this, what the hint hints toward it only lets us surmise as the thoughtworthy, for which the fitting way of thinking is still lacking. (*GA* 12: 191/ *OWL* 96, tm)

While this might sound a limitation to the hint, it is really the way in which we come to comport ourselves to the matter of thought. The fitting way of thinking is always lacking. As the refrain of *What Is Called Thinking?* makes clear, *"most thought-provoking is that we are not yet thinking"* (*GA* 8: 6/4). But this does not mean we are devoid of the thought provoking and thoughtworthy. Rather, the hint is what "saves" us from this divorce.[15] The hint lets us surmise despite withdrawal. Surmising is the fitting way for bearing the withdrawal of thought.

The hint, the wink, is consequently a strange form of communication. According to the researcher, "the hint would be the basic character of the word" (*GA* 12: 109/24, tm). The interlocutors also agree that a word might "hint of" (*erwinkt*) the "essence of language" (*GA* 12: 109/24, tm). As we have seen, the hint does this in its role as gesture. What the hint ultimately hints at is nothing that could be said. Instead it hints at the "extra-linguistic" essence of language. It does not speak, but nevertheless says. When the interlocutor asks "What does 'to say' mean?" the researcher replies with an identification that will stay with Heidegger throughout his career: "Presumably the same thing as 'to show' in the sense of: letting-appear and letting-shine, this however in the manner of hints" (*GA* 12: 137/*OWL* 47, tm). The hint is not simply a referent to something else, it itself is what shows itself. The hint is the word of withholding itself. To say the hint is to show it. The hint shows the non-presence of the world, the impossibility of thought, and the limits of language. In this it surpasses metaphysics, as the researcher says: "with a glance into the essence of saying, thinking first sets out along that path which takes us back out of the merely metaphysical representation, into the attentiveness to the hints of that message, whose messengers we would properly like to be" (*GA* 12: 137/*OWL* 47–48, tm). If we are to understand the office that the divinities carry out through hinting, then it is to this messengerial role that we now must turn.

§13. Messengers

The divinities are messengers and in this they are like angels, *hoi angeloi*, who are also messengers and envoys, the ones who announce (*angelein*).[16] A 1944 passage entitled "The Angel" in one of Heidegger's sketches toward a commentary on Hölderlin's "Dichterberuf" ("The Poet's Vocation")[17] lists the following terms, each of which shall acquire importance in the discussion that follows:

> Messengers. Bringing hints. Hinting. (Appropriating [*Er-eignen*].)
> *hermêneus hermêneuôn*—Poet.
> (Hermeneutics.) (*GA* 75: 299)

The sketch shows the announcement of the angels to be a matter of hinting, as is the case with the divinities in the fourfold. This messengerial role for angels is adumbrated slightly more in the 1943 lecture devoted to Hölderlin's hymn "Homecoming/To the Relations." Here we read of the medium of the heights, the joyous (*das Heitere*), which is extended to us. Heidegger understands this in terms of a greeting, saying "those, however, who offer [*entbieten*] the greeting of the joyous are the messengers [*Boten*], *angeloi*, the 'angels'" (*GA* 4: 16/35, tm). The angels, as those who greet, require the medium of the joyous for this greeting to be able to reach across a distance. The reach of greeting is so tied to its medium (the joyous), in fact, as to bring this along with it: "as the ones who greet, they [the angels] bring the joyous to shine, in the clarity of which the 'nature' of things and humans is preserved as hale [*heil*]" (*GA* 4: 17/36, tm). The following section (Godhood) will develop this sense of the hale in terms of a health and wholeness found only in exposure to a beyond. The joyous medium allows things and humans to appear in "clarity," to be preserved as hale. The joyous, as medium of angelic greeting, allows the gods to reach us, if only in traces. Ultimately, what greets us is that medium of the joyous itself: "The joyous is the essential ground of the greeting, i.e. of the angelic, wherein what is ownmost of the gods consists" (*GA* 4: 20/39, tm). Angels as messengers bring the medium of the joyous to humans. If we are now to think of the divinities of the fourfold as messengers, then this messengerial aspect must be included in the thinging of the thing.

To this end, the "Conversation on Language" could be said to develop a hermeneutics of the message. The thought at stake here, however, is one that explicitly departs from Heidegger's earlier hermeneutic endeavors, including that of *Being and Time.* The differences are instructive for a thinking of the thing.

a. Hermeneutics from Facticity to Understanding

The "Conversation" provides something of a history of Heidegger's engagement with hermeneutics, from his initial forays in the lecture courses of the early 1920s, to the project of a hermeneutic-phenomenology in *Being and Time,* and up to his abandonment of the term in his later work in favor of a thinking of "message." The reasons for this shift are to be garnered from this path of thought, beginning with the 1920 lecture course *Phenomenology of Intuition and Expression: Theory of Philosophical Concept Formation.* The interlocutor's teacher, Count Kuki, purportedly attended this course in Freiburg and a transcript of the course made the rounds in Japanese phenomenology circles, we are told. Despite his fascination with the course, Count Kuki could never communicate its importance to his student. Instead, Kuki could only repeat the phrase "hermeneutical phenomenology" without further elaboration (cf. *GA* 12: 90/*OWL* 9).

The hermeneutic importance of this lecture course derives from its critical "destruction" of two contemporary (1920) attempts to ground philosophy in life or lived experience: *Weltanschauung* philosophy of the sort practiced by Spengler and the transcendental psychology of Natorp. The course provides the first full elaboration of "destruction" as a phenomenological technique, where it functions as a clearing of the ground for a phenomenological retrieval of life. What the destruction seeks is life in its facticity, and this term, too, first comes to prominence here.[18] The achievement of facticity is the aim of philosophy itself, with Heidegger proclaiming at the course's conclusion: "Philosophy has the task of preserving the facticity of life and strengthening the facticity of Dasein" (*GA* 59: 174/133). Heidegger's attention to "philosophical concept formation," then, is an investigation of the phenomenological source in life of conceptual philosophy itself. Philosophy, as a particular way of factical life, seeks to grasp the life of which it is a part. This can be understood neither in terms of an "a priori" valuation or an arch-subjective "constitution" of the world (pace Spengler and Natorp).

Heidegger's recounting of the course locates it as an early attempt to escape subject–object dualism. The researcher says of it that "it was my concern to make visible something entirely other, something which I first intimated only obscurely, if not confusedly. With such youthful leaps, one is easily unjust" (*GA* 12: 121/*OWL* 34–35, tm). The "entirely other" in this case is a mode of existence other than that of objective presence standing in opposition to a subject. Rather, here it is a matter of grasping things in terms of their relational significance and of attending to the directions-of-meaning and contexts-of-significance that situate the phenomenon in question, a method that Heidegger identifies with phenomenology: "The reduction to the genuine sense-complexes and the articulation of the genuine sense-directions comprised in them is the ultimate phenomenological task" (*GA* 59: 74/56, tm).

Unfortunately, a fuller elaboration of this other way of being is lacking in the course, which focuses more on the destruction of contemporary *Erlebnis* philosophies. Retrospectively, the researcher is able to cast the course as an attempt to reach what "has been" (*das Gewesene*):

> in the lecture course just named much had to remain unclear. No one is able to place themselves outside the dominant circle of conceptions with a single leap, and above all not when it is a matter of the well-worn tracks of thinking hitherto, tracks that run off into the inconspicuous. Besides, such a setting of oneself against the hitherto is only ever fitting in that what seems to be a revolutionary will attempts before all else to win back what has been [*das Gewesene*] more originally. (*GA* 12: 123/*OWL* 36, tm)

While the course never explicitly discusses hermeneutics per se, these are nevertheless the ideas that would have attracted Count Kuki's attention and led to his fascination with the "hermeneutical."

The Heideggerian thought of hermeneutics has always been a matter of winning back a non-objective, relational mode of being, as Heidegger makes clear in his 1923 course, *Ontology: The Hermeneutics of Facticity*. The researcher recalls that it was here he first employed the term "hermeneutics" explicitly.[19] Here, hermeneutics is understood as a method that will provide access to a particular kind of being, that of facticity, which is nothing other than the being of Dasein. Indeed, Dasein seems to be the only being to exist in this factical manner for Heidegger at the time: "*facticity* is the designation for the being-character of 'our' 'own' Dasein" (*GA* 63: 7/5). Hermeneutics serves the self-understanding of factical Dasein: "Hermeneutics has the task of making the Dasein which is in each case our own accessible to this Dasein itself with regard to the character of its being, communicating Dasein to itself in this regard . . . In hermeneutics what is developed for Dasein is a possibility of its becoming and being for itself in the manner of an understanding of itself" (*GA* 63: 15/11). But we would be mistaken if we understood this as the application of a particular method (hermeneutics) to a particular object (facticity). Rather, hermeneutics is the proper method for philosophizing precisely because it does not grasp facticity as its object: "The relationship here between hermeneutics and facticity is not a relationship between the grasping of an object and the object grasped, in relation to which the former would simply have to measure itself. Rather, interpreting is itself a possible and distinctive how of the character of being of facticity. Interpreting is a being which belongs to the being of factical life itself" (*GA* 63: 15/12).

As with the *Phenomenology of Intuition and Expression*, the goal is to uncover the relational context of things, and destruction again forms a necessary part of the procedure. "The tradition must be dismantled," Heidegger writes, "only in this way is a primordial position on the subject matter possible. This regress places philosophy once again before the decisive contexts" (*GA* 63: 75/59). These contexts are typically lost to us through the objectification and severance of beings as present-at-hand. The contexts revealed are those of meaning, contexts that comprise the significance of the world for Dasein. For Heidegger of the time, this means that beings are still thought in terms of their utility for Dasein, the one for whom they are useful or significant: "The beings-which-are-there in everydayness are not beings which already *are* in an authentic sense *prior to* and *apart from* their 'in order to do something' and their 'for someone,' but rather their being-*there* lies precisely in this 'in order to' and 'for'" (*GA* 63: 95/73). They are for Dasein. The course concludes with reflections on "care" as a way of comporting to these relational contexts: "what it [care] is concerned about and attends to is the context of references itself" (*GA* 63: 101/78). The course thus presents hermeneutics as a way of being that is capable of grasping its own factical being as Dasein. A phenomenological "destruction" is again necessary to free up the relational context of things. At this time, these relational contexts are always understood on the model of use, something that is in complete agreement with *Being and Time* four years later.

In his later writings, however, Heidegger abandons the term "hermeneutics" and the reasons for this are best seen in contrast to the rationale motivating the use of the term in *Being and Time*, the text where Heidegger's hermeneutic concerns find their most forceful and cogent expression. These have to do with the role of understanding in hermeneutics and with its attendant notion of circularity. When the Japanese interlocutor asks why the term "hermeneutics" was chosen at all, the researcher responds, "the answer to your question lies in the introduction (§7 C) of *Being and Time*," and it is to these pages that we now must turn (*GA* 12: 91/*OWL* 9, tm). Entitled "The Phenomenological Method of the Investigation," this section investigates the notion of phenomena in its first part (7 A), discussing how a "phenomenon" is a direct self-showing and thus is to be distinguished from an "appearance," which functions more like a symptom of something that does not show itself but which the appearance indirectly reveals. It takes up the role of *logos* in its second part (7 B), arguing that it is not so much a matter of speech as of letting something be seen and allowing it to come into view. Finally, in the third part of the section, "The Preliminary Concept of Phenomenology" (7 C), these senses of phenomenon and *logos* are brought together in the idea of phenomenology, where the goal is "to let what shows itself be seen from itself, just as it shows itself from itself" (*GA* 2: 46/*SZ* 34).

And yet, what shows itself does so in various states of concealment, thereby calling for a procedure like the "destruction" of the 1920 course. The phenomenal ground—which was earlier understood in terms of "experience" or contexts of meaning—must now be "wrested" from the objects of phenomenology.[20] Mere looking on is not enough for phenomenology: "The idea of an 'originary' and 'intuitive' grasp and explication of phenomena must be opposed to the naïveté of an accidental, 'immediate' and unreflective 'beholding'" (*GA* 2: 49/*SZ* 36–37). That being said, the concealed self-showing of phenomena is itself a way in which they show themselves, even if a partly concealed or even deceptive one. Nevertheless, as Heidegger famously claims, "however much semblance, so much being" (*GA* 2: 48/*SZ* 36, tm). Being is found in this showing. Being shows itself as phenomenal. And for this reason, Heidegger can state, in another famous claim, that "*ontology is possible only as phenomenology*" (*GA* 2: 48/*SZ* 35).

Insofar as this phenomenological ontology requires us to work through the concealment of the beings that appear to us in order to see them in their being, insofar as we are always already involved with these beings, in however "everyday" or superficial a manner, and insofar as it is we who ask the question of the meaning of being in the first place, and, indeed, from out of our position as beings in being, then this phenomenological ontology is "hermeneutical." Dasein inquires into something (being) with which it is already involved. In section 7 C of *Being and Time,* referred to in the "Conversation on Language," Heidegger explains his choice of the term "hermeneutics" in the following way:

> The *logos* of the phenomenology of Dasein has the character of *her-mêneuein,* through which the proper meaning of being and the basic structures of the very being of Dasein are *announced* [*kundgegeben*] to the understanding of being that belongs to Dasein itself. Phenomenology of Dasein is *hermeneutics* in the original signification of that word, which designates [in a first sense of the term] the business of interpretation [defined earlier as phenomenological description]. But since the discovery of the meaning of being and of the basic structures of Dasein in general exhibits the horizon for any subsequent ontological research into beings unlike Dasein, the present hermeneutic is at the same time "hermeneutics" in the [second] sense that it works out the conditions of possibility for any ontological investigation. Finally, insofar as Dasein has ontological priority over all other beings—as a being in the possibility of existence—hermeneutics, as the interpretation of the being of Dasein, receives the third specific and, philosophically understood, primary meaning of an analysis of the existentiality of existence. To the extent that this hermeneutic elaborates the historicity of Dasein onto-logically as the ontic condition of the possibility of the discipline of history, it contains the roots of what can be called "hermeneutics" only in a derivative [fourth] sense: the methodology of the historical humanistic disciplines. (*GA* 2: 50/*SZ* 37, tm)

The reason that Heidegger understands phenomenology as inherently hermeneutical is because phenomenology involves the *understanding* of the very being (*Sein*) that is constitutive of Da-*sein* itself. In this, it is like the "business of interpretation," which is never presuppositionless, but always operates from out of the shared prejudices and presuppositions of a historical position. In other words, Dasein does not exist "outside" of being and then come to grasp this as an object of investigation—Dasein is already involved with being from the outset (indeed, each time it has its being to be). And this is the case however implicit, latent, informal, lazy, average, everyday, and/or pre-conceptual the understanding of being operative here may be. Indeed, the presuppositions that guide Dasein's interpretation of being (what Heidegger will term "its fore-having, its fore-sight, and its fore-conception") make up what he calls "the *herme-neutical situation*" (*GA* 2: 308/*SZ* 232).

But this is where the break between his earlier and later views occurs. In *Being and Time,* this "hermeneutical situation" is understood in terms of a circle. "Every interpretation which is to contribute some understand-ing must already have understood what is to be interpreted," Heidegger informs us, before asking "if interpretation always already has to oper-ate within what is understood and nurture itself from this, how should it then produce scientific results without going in a circle?" (*GA* 2: 202/*SZ* 152). The circularity follows from construing the hermeneutic relation here as a making explicit, whereby a latent or implicitly held position is confirmed or clarified in the explicitness of an interpretation. The "fore-structure" operative here is tripartite, beginning with the "fore-having" of a background understanding of a totality of relevance (the ability to isolate a particular tool only ever follows on a prior understanding of the totality for Heidegger), a "fore-sight" that approaches this totality of rele-vance with a particular interpretation in view, and a "fore-conception" that decides how to conceptualize the interpretation. For this reason, "this circle of understanding is not a circle in which any random kind of knowledge operates, but it is rather the expression of the existential *fore-structure* of Dasein itself" (*GA* 2: 203/*SZ* 153). This same fore-structure is at play in Dasein's understanding of being; indeed, Heidegger's own em-phasis on "preparation" and the preliminaries necessary even for asking the question of being can be seen as attesting to this same fore-structure. It is a fact of being *in* the world. Hermeneutic circularity is tied to the understanding of Dasein.

When we say this, however, we must recall that in *Being and Time* not all beings are "in" the "world" for Heidegger. The things do not *exist* if we take this term in its strictest sense. Only Dasein exists as circular in any hermeneutical sense: "The 'circle' in understanding belongs to the structure of meaning, and this phenomenon is rooted in the exis-tential constitution of Dasein, that is, in interpretive understanding. Be-ings which, as being-in-the-world, are concerned about their being itself have an ontological structure of the circle" (*GA* 2: 204/*SZ* 153). Indeed, if circularity were anything that belonged to beings other than Dasein, we would have to drop the use of the term at once: "However, if we note that the 'circle' belongs ontologically to a kind of being of presence-at-hand (subsistence), we shall in general have to avoid characterizing something like Dasein ontologically with this phenomenon" (*GA* 2: 204/*SZ* 153, tm).

This rift between the circularity of Dasein and the non-circularity of all other beings is replete with consequences for our understanding of the meaning of beings. Since it is this circularity which establishes the contexts of meaning for Dasein, all other beings are without meaning:

> Insofar as understanding and interpretation constitute the existential
> constitution of the being of the there, meaning must be conceived

> as the formal, existential framework of the disclosedness belonging
> to understanding. Meaning is an existential of Dasein, not a property
> that is attached to beings . . . Only Dasein "has" meaning in that the
> disclosedness of being-in-the-world can be "fulfilled" through the be-
> ings discoverable in it. *Thus only Dasein can be meaningful or meaningless.*
> (*GA* 2: 201/ *SZ* 151)

This means that beings are not meaningful on their own, as it were, but
only for Dasein. They are meaningful qua understood, which is to say
that meaning is not something that these beings participate in without
further ado. Simply put, "all beings whose mode of being is unlike Dasein must be understood as *unmeaningful,* as essentially bare of meaning
as such" (*GA* 2: 201–2/ *SZ* 152). Beings are only ever meaningful thanks to
the understanding of Dasein. This understanding is something done to
beings—they are *understood.* Beings are either present-at-hand or ready-
to-hand and each time thanks to the understanding of Dasein, *with no help
from the beings themselves.* They might as well not even be there. Indeed,
they cannot be-there (*da-sein*).

With the introduction of the thing into Heidegger's thinking in the
Bremen lectures, this hermeneutical situation dramatically changes. We
find a first sense of this shift in the "Conversation on Language," where
the question of the hermeneutic circle explicitly arises. In this context,
the Japanese interlocutor wonders how we can ever enter into a dialogue
of language when this is a matter of being addressed by language itself
and we have no idea of how to listen for this. The researcher remarks
that "I once called this strange relation the hermeneutic circle" (*GA* 12:
142/ *OWL* 51). The interlocutor reminds the researcher that *Being and
Time* makes the hermeneutic circle something unavoidable, to which he
responds:

> R: . . . this necessary acceptance of the hermeneutic circle does not
> mean that the notion of the accepted circle gives us an originary
> experience of the hermeneutic relation.
> J: Then you would abandon your earlier conception.
> R: Quite—and indeed to the extent that the talk of a circle always re-
> mains superficial. (*GA* 12: 142/ *OWL* 51, tm)[21]

In the following, we shall see that the superficiality of the circle is precisely due to its exclusion of beings from the determination of meaning.
This compromises any hermeneutics that would ground itself in circularity. As the researcher remarks, "it would scarcely have escaped you that
in my later writings the names 'hermeneutics' and 'hermeneutical' are

no longer employed" (*GA* 12: 94/*OWL* 12, tm). Heidegger's later thinking of the messengerial redresses this omission and in so doing revivifies hermeneutics as well, if now under a different name.

b. A Messengerial Ontology

The 1949 appearance of the divinities names them messengers (*Boten*). The divinities' role in the thing will be to convey meaning. In so doing, the divinities allow Heidegger to propose a model of meaning that cannot be reconciled with the guaranteed return of the circle. Since the messengerial is construed in terms of sending, there will be an ineradicable withdrawal that runs through every exchange of the sequence, a withdrawal concomitant with the proffering of the message itself. Insofar as the divinities are located within the fourfold, they are essentially involved in the thinging of the thing. This means that the messengerial sending of meaning cannot be dismissed as an epistemological or hermeneutical concern over against more pressing ontological concerns. Instead, what the presence of the divinities within the fourfold means is that meaning itself is ontological. Simply put, and thanks to the divinities, beings participate in a way of being that is meaningful.[22]

In 1953, Heidegger again returns to the Greek sense of the term *hermêneuein*, though now with a different sense in view.[23] The researcher explains:

> The expression "hermeneutic" derives from the Greek verb *hermêneuein*. That verb is related to the noun *hermêneus*, which can be brought together with the name of the God *Hermês* by a playful thinking that is more compelling than the rigor of science. Hermes is the messenger of the gods [*Götterbote*]. He brings the message of destiny [*die Botschaft des Geschickes*]; *hermêneuein* is that putting-forth [*Darlegen*] which brings tidings [*Kunde*] insofar as it is able to listen to a message [*Botschaft*]. Such putting-forth develops into the interpreting [*Auslegen*] of what the poets have already said, for the poets, according to the saying of Socrates in Plato's dialogue *Ion* (534e), *hermênês eisin tôn theôn*, "are messengers of the gods." (*GA* 12: 115/*OWL* 29, tm)

The hermeneutic is like Hermes in that it bears a message. In Hermes's case, that is the message of destiny. In saying this, we must here understand destiny (*Geschick*) in terms of a sending (*schicken*). The *Geschick* is "destiny" insofar as this is understood as something sent to us, the *Schicksal* ("fate") that comes to us. Thus we might render *Geschick* as "dispensation" rather than "destiny." Hermes brings the message of dispensation.

But a messenger is only a messenger insofar as he or she bears a message. The messenger is a recipient of the message that is given. This means that the message will participate in the logic of giving we have considered above (see "The Time of the Sky" in chapter 3). To be given, there must be something withheld of the message. The message must maintain a connection with its sender in order to remain a message. If Hermes were to simply appropriate the message as his own, there would be no more message and he would not be a messenger. Instead, Hermes must be able to take up the message without making it his own and deliver it to someone else who must do the same. They must receive the message *as delivered by Hermes.* They receive what has been received by another from another.

The message that Hermes delivers is a message that has been heard. The message we receive is dependent upon the hearing of the messenger and then upon our own hearing as well. In 1951 when Heidegger lectured on the meaning of *logos* for Heraclitus, he proclaimed that "we have heard [*gehört*] when we belong [*gehören*] to what is avowed" (*GA* 7: 220/ *EGT* 66, tm). We only hear what has already claimed us as that to which we belong. But how do we belong? We belong by standing in a relation with something, belonging is a relation. Only what we are related to already can address us. Only what we are able to relate to can address us, and it does so in that very relation. We hear the claim of a relation (belonging). We belong to it in that it is fitted to us, i.e., it is "perceptible" by us. But to belong to something is not to assimilate it. I always belong to another, something other than me, and this means I always may not belong, may be abandoned by that to which I belong. The message, in other words, is nothing fixed and in place, nothing that could ever be given entirely in any event. To have heard the message is to insist on a distance from it and, paradoxically enough, this space is that of non-belonging and non-receipt.

This original sense of hermeneutics as a putting-forth (*Darlegen*) or exhibition subsequently achieves the sense of an interpretation (*Auslegung*), when what is put-forth is unpacked and laid out (*ausgelegt*). Interpretation is thus dependent upon this original givenness of the message: "All this makes clear that the hermeneutical does not first mean interpreting, but instead, already before this, the bringing of the message and tidings" (*GA* 12: 115/ *OWL* 29, tm). What is hermeneutical is the conveying of a message.

All this talk of sending, destiny, and messaging orbits around a rethinking of being on the part of Heidegger. Being itself is now construed in terms of a rift that brings relation. The name for this is the "twofold." When pressed on why he emphasizes the original sense of hermeneutics, the researcher responds that not only did this thought of the hermeneutical open up the path of *Being and Time,* but "what mattered then and still does is to bring the being of beings to appearance; admittedly no longer after the manner of metaphysics, but rather in such a way that being itself comes to shine" (*GA* 12: 116/*OWL* 30, tm). Hermeneutics is a matter of bringing the being of beings to appearance. Following the original sense of hermeneutics, then, and breaking with both the idea of hermeneutic circularity and the tradition of metaphysics (which may well include *Being and Time* at this point), the being of beings should be thought of in terms of the sending of a message. It is in this sense that being can be treated as a claim that makes its way to us (an *Anspruch*) or an avowal that reaches us (a *Zuspruch*). To think of such an approach of being itself, however, requires disabusing ourselves of the thought that being would be isolated and contained. The thought of being that Heidegger broaches in the "Conversation" is that of the "twofold" (*Zwiefalt*; we should again refrain from confusing the "fold" in place here with the German *Geviert,* unfortunately translated as "fourfold"). Instead, as the researcher concludes: "Being itself—this says: the presencing of what is present, i.e. the twofold [*Zwiefalt*] of the two from out of their single fold [*Einfalt*]. It is this that claims [*Anspruch*] the humans for its essence" (*GA* 12: 116/*OWL* 30, tm). To hear the message will be to correspond to this claim.

The "two" of the twofold consists of the particular beings that are present along with presencing as such. If we hew a little closer to the text, however, we see that this twofold is itself "being itself" for Heidegger. The relation between the two is thought of in terms of a "fold" (*Falt*).[24] The fold is a bend in an otherwise sheer field. By virtue of the hinge or crease of the fold, this field is brought into greater proximity with itself. The field is folded upon itself as though it were two, the whole time maintaining a space between the folded sheets or limbs. With Heidegger's emphasis upon a "two" fold, then, we are meant to hear the two "limbs" of the fold, the beings and being, as belonging together, to be sure, but as nevertheless spaced apart from each other. The language of folding gives us to think this relation in terms of surfaces that *touch* one another, that *are* each other, though now separate and spaced. In short, the twofold names the interface between being and beings, their separation from each other endemic to their belonging together. The term "twofold" emphasizes the dehiscence of being. Being is nothing self-separate from beings, it is nothing "on its own" or "in itself." Instead, it always ever only names a relation, neither one thing nor the other, but the medium through which beings stream and shine (being in its "truth"). Without the differential established by beings, this medium would ossify. To be being, there must be beings. And the converse also holds: beings need being for the spacing through which they unfurl their relations. The "radiance" of being is the shimmering movement of its mediation, the paths of relation darting through it, the paths of relation that being itself "is." This is why Heidegger can say that "being itself comes to shine" as the twofold (*GA* 12: 116/*OWL* 30, tm). The twofold names the self-spacing of being whereby the being of beings conducts the radiance of beings. This is why the researcher can distinguish between "'being' as the 'being of beings,'" i.e., the beinghood of metaphysical construals, and "'being' as 'being' in respect of its proper sense, that is, in respect of its truth (the clearing)" (*GA* 12: 104/*OWL* 20). By the guarded space of truth, i.e., the clearing, being is understood as spatial (topographical, to use a later term). Being radiates.

The figure of the "message" accords with this. The message is both given and delivered. It is open on both ends, as it were. It cannot be given without maintaining a relation to the donor, it cannot be received without establishing one with the recipient. Neither can fully "own" the message as sent. Neither the donor nor the recipient is the author of it. Instead, each must "disown" it, in part so as to allow it its reach. The message extends between donor and recipient, it runs through them, dragging them out of themselves and exposing them each to the other. The *Spruch* of the *Anspruch/Zuspruch* names the hook by which the message catches us in contacting us and draws us out of ourselves to receive it. The message is radiance itself.

The split of the twofold allows it to resonate beyond its bounds and lay a claim upon us. The twofold thus relates to us. This idea of relation breaks with the conception of an independent, isolated subject and object. It is the mature expression and consummation of Heidegger's earlier hermeneutical thinking. As the interlocutor states, "you abandoned this region of subjectivity and the expression belonging to it through entering into the hermeneutical relation to the twofold" (*GA* 12: 123/ *OWL* 36, tm). And yet, this relation cannot be considered as a simple interaction between two independent parties. Instead, a thorough thinking of sending requires that we abandon the idea of independent parties altogether. For this reason, Heidegger objects to terming this relation a "relation" (*Bezug*), favoring instead the expression of "need." When we use the word "relation," then, we must bear this in mind:

> R: Thus we are not allowed to say any longer: relation to the twofold, since this is no object of representation, rather, the reign of a need [*das Walten des Brauches*].
>
> J: Which we never immediately experience, however, so long as we represent the twofold only as the difference which becomes visible by a comparison that attempts to hold what presences and its presencing apart from one another. (*GA* 12: 119–20/*OWL* 33, tm)

As we have seen, the twofold is no mere separation of presencing from what presences; to think so is to remain within the frame of representational thought. We might also hear in this a rejection of the "ontological difference" that dominated Heidegger's earlier thinking of fundamental ontology (we shall thematize this in the conclusion). This reciprocal "relation" of need, the reign of need, is what Heidegger now thinks as the guiding idea for hermeneutics:

> R: . . . the word "relation" means to say that the human would be needed in his essence, would belong, as the essencing one that he is, in a need [*Brauch*] which claims him [*ihn beansprucht*].
>
> J: In what sense?
>
> R: Hermeneutically, i.e. in regards to the bringing of tidings [*Kunde*], in regards to the preservation of a message [*Verwahrens einer Botschaft*]. (*GA* 12: 119/*OWL* 32, tm)

Need allows Heidegger to think a reciprocity that he sees foreclosed in the metaphysical thought of "relation." Need names a belonging in separation. There are no independent parties here, since each requires the other to be what it is. The twofold needs the human. Indeed, when we think of the twofold as sending its "tidings" (*Kunde*) to humans, then "the human essences as the human insofar as he corresponds to the claim of the twofold and attests [*bekundet*] to this in its message" (*GA* 12: 116/ *OWL* 30, tm). There are no tidings without this attestation on the part of the human. There must be reception if something is to be given. The tidings are again not an independent party that could exist unperturbed outside of this reception. The attestation is the attestation of the tidings, is these tidings themselves, which do not precede in any way their attestation. This is the "preservation of the message" for which humans are needed. This is why Hermes is the "messenger of the gods": he brings the gods themselves who are nothing but this messaging of them. The thought of sending culminates in this. The sent does not precede its reception. Far from cancelling or ending the sending, reception allows it to be what it is, i.e., the message sent.

Participating in this reciprocal need, the human likewise needs the twofold if the human is to exist as mortal, finite, and limited. Mortal existence is exposed essentially to what lies beyond it. But to be mortal is not to be the creator of this exterior, it is to be "thrown" into it, arriving "late." To be mortal is to come after the world in such a way that the world comes to you. We are late to the world's arriving, are only who we are *after* it reaches us, not "prior" to that reaching. Like the lightning that cannot arrive without bringing its own brightness with it, whatever arrives enters into the clearing it brings with it, never before this. For this reason,

Heidegger can term the twofold the "originarily familiar" (*anfänglich Ver-traute*), that which "before all else has been entrusted [*zugetraut*] to our essence" (*GA* 12: 120/*OWL* 33, tm). This is the appeal of the twofold, its sending and message. Heidegger exploits the etymological derivation of *der Bote* (messenger, herald, envoy) from the verb *bieten* (to bid, offer, provide) in making this point in the "Conversation":

> J: Although veiled as such, the twofold has each time already offered [*angeboten*] itself to the human.
>
> R: The human, insofar as he is human, listens to this message [*Botschaft*]. (*GA* 12: 128/*OWL* 40, tm)

Because mortality is subject to the appeal of the world, the human is the one to whom the message is addressed and likewise the one whose exposure makes it addressable.[25] The human is so essentially related to the message of the twofold that the human can be named in regards to this: "The human is the herald [*Botengänger*] of the message that avows [*zuspricht*] to him the disclosure of the twofold" (*GA* 12: 128/*OWL* 40, tm). The herald is intimately tied to the message, is needed, but we now know this need to be a reciprocal one. The need (*Brauch*) is not simply the "usage" (*Brauch*) of the human by the twofold, as though the latter were an indifferent tool or implement for the taking. Instead the human participates, as we have seen: "The herald [*Botengänger*] must come from the message. But he must also already have gone toward it" (*GA* 12: 142/*OWL* 51, tm). The human goes to the world that comes to the human. The message is received at the limit where human meets world, a limit that is ultimately no point-wide line, but is permeated and interfacial, a space of breadth (*Weite*, an expanse, an important term in the "Conversation"), a clearing, the enjambment of world. The message is met at this limit: "As the herald of the message [*der Botengänger der Botschaft*] of the disclosure of the twofold, then, the human would be at the same time the one who goes to the limit of the limitless [*der Grenzgänger des Grenzlosen*]" (*GA* 12: 129/*OWL* 41, tm).

The thought of the message is meant to amend our way of understanding and crack open its presumed self-enclosure. The message reaches us, while never assimilating itself to us. It remains connected to a sender who lies beyond us (we will develop this idea in the following section). The failure of Heidegger's earlier hermeneutical efforts was to focus too intently on the role of understanding on the part of Dasein and to mistakenly attempt an overcoming of subject–object duality through the figure of the circle. With the emergence of the fourfold in Heidegger's thought, with the entrance of the thing as itself ecstatic, these conceptions must fall aside. The thinking of the "message" is ontological through and through. By engaging with it, "there then takes place the departure from all 'it is'" (*GA* 12: 146/*OWL* 54, tm). This departure consummates the earlier hermeneutical attempts of Heidegger. As we have seen, in the "Conversation," Heidegger recasts the intent of the 1920 lecture course *Phenomenology of Intuition and Expression: Theory of Philosophical Concept Formation* as one of attempting "before all else to win back what has-been [*das Gewesene*] more originally" (*GA* 12: 123/*OWL* 36, tm). What has been names the departure from all "it is." The researcher does not consider this departure a negation, but rather "as the arriving of what has-been" (*GA* 12: 146/*OWL* 54, tm). The conversation concludes by explicitly bringing together this thinking of what has-been with that of the message. The interlocutor wonders about the coming of what has-been:

> J: How are we to think this?
>
> R: As the gathering of what endures [*die Versammlung des Währenden*] . . .
>
> J: which, as you recently said,[26] endures as a granting [*das Gewährende*] . . .
>
> R: and remains the same as the message . . .
>
> J: which *needs* us as heralds. (*GA* 12: 146/*OWL* 54, tm)

We are needed by the granting of what has been. The arriving of what has been is its sending. It reaches us in departing from all "it is." In this way, what has been *is* the message, and it needs us to attest to it and to herald its arrival.

Returning to the fourfold and the role of the divinities therein, to be a messenger is to be implicated in the act of sending. The messenger hears, receives, and delivers the message. In so doing, the messenger first attests to a peculiar way of being, one that could not exist apart from this attestation. It is a being of traces, of withdrawal, and nonetheless of appearing. The messenger delivers a message that has no first source or final destination. But in thinking of the divinities we cannot rest with this conception of the messenger, for we have yet to consider a crucial component of their divinity itself: godhood. If divinities are hinting messengers of godhood, then we must consider their messengerial role in conjunction with the godhood to which they attest.

§14. Godhood

The divinities are the winking messengers of godhood (*Gottheit*). But what is godhood? The word would seem to name a *form*, that in which all gods participate. Godhood would then identify fundamental characteristics that all gods bear in common. But a God is not something present-at-hand to be found in common. As per the first depiction of the divinities in "The Thing," Heidegger states that the essence of God is such that it withdraws him "from every comparison with what is present" (*GA* 79: 17/16). Since there are no gods present nor any possibility of comparison, the thought of godhood as a form must be abandoned. Instead, Heidegger would have us think it as a medium. It is not a quality the gods would possess, but something they would be *in*.

Heidegger deals directly with godhood in the 1946 essay on Rilke, "What Are Poets For?" Here godhood is associated with the aether, something we have already discussed in terms of mediation (see "The Sky as Medium of Appearance" in chapter 3). Heidegger writes that "the aether wherein alone the gods are gods, is their godhood" (*GA* 5: 272/202, tm). As this aether, godhood is again something that the gods are "in." To explain this, Heidegger speaks of the "element" of godhood, taking element in the sense of the proper environment for something (gamblers are in their element at the card table, for instance): "The element of this aether, that wherein godhood itself still essences, is the holy" (*GA* 5: 272/202, tm). Godhood would indicate a particular region within the medium of the holy. We hear as much in the 1939 lecture "As When on a Holiday," where Heidegger explains that "the holy is not holy because it is godly [*göttlich*], rather the godly is godly because, in its way, it is 'holy'" (*GA* 4: 59/82, tm). If godhood is the medium of the God (is something "godly"), then godhood itself can only appear within the holy. The holy is its element. Another text from 1946, the "Letter on 'Humanism,'" expands on this notion of element: "The element is what authentically enables: the enabling [*das Vermögen*]" (*GA* 9: 316/241, tm). While we shall consider this sense of enabling more fully in the next chapter ("The Ability, the Capacity, to Die," chapter 5), we can already note here that the element is what allows a thing to be what it is in its ownmost (a gambler apart from a card table is something less than a gambler; completely severed from it, there is no gambler). The element, as medium, is permissive, it allows, it grants. For Heidegger, then, to enable something means "to preserve it in its essence [*in seinem Wesen wahren*], to maintain it in its element" (*GA* 9: 317/242). Its element *is* its essence, its essencing is unthinkable without it. For its part, the medium (element) is not indifferent to what appears within it; rather it embraces it, preserves it, allows it to be what it is essentially (allows it to essence). The element of something enables what it harbors. The element (medium) allows it to essence. Now the element of godhood is "the holy" (*das Heilige*). Consequently, the holy preserves the godhood of the gods, sustaining them and allowing them to essence in this.

If the divinities are to be the hinting messengers of godhood, then an understanding of their role entails that we work through the multi-layered relations that Heidegger proposes between godhood and the holy, the holy and the hale, and, ultimately, godhood and the very God(s) that would appear therein.

a. The Holy

The holy first comes to the fore in Heidegger's readings of Hölderlin and from the outset it indicates a particular medium for appearances. In the case of the 1934–35 lecture course on *Hölderlin's Hymns: "Germania" and "The Rhine,"* that medium is a fundamental mood (a *Grundstimmung*), one that Heidegger follows Hölderlin in designating as "holy mourning" (see *GA* 39: 87).[27] Here the holy is considered the *Uneigennützige*, the "altruistic" or "personally useless." The holy names a kind of altruism, one that "no longer stands at all in the realm of utility and thus not in that of the useless either, which is also still evaluated in terms of utility" (*GA* 39: 84). In this regard, the holy marks a liberation from the presuppositions of utility, which include availability for the assessment of an object's worth as a means to an end. Eluding these kinds of evaluative assessments (as to what counts as a means, which ends are to be pursued, etc.), what is holy is no longer replaceable by equally valuable means to the same end. Withdrawing from utility, the altruism of the holy renders what lies within it singular. For Heidegger, that this fundamental mood of mourning would be holy means that this mourning brings no personal advantage to whoever it claims, but instead is a "self-opening affliction [*Bedrängnis*], which places itself before the flown gods, guarding their flight and enduring what comes [*die Kommenden*]" (*GA* 39: 223). In the holy, we suffer the affliction of not-having (Heidegger and Hölderlin will elsewhere emphasize the importance of "poverty" in this regard).[28] We are not confronted by completed "objects" to be had. Instead, the holy mood allows us to encounter the non-objective, what is neither useful nor useless. The holy allows us to encounter "what comes." That the holy would be connected with the flight and arriving of the gods, with traces we might say, and, most importantly, with a thinking of "coming," this all remains with Heidegger's conceptions of the holy across his readings of Hölderlin. What changes, however, is the focus. In this early course, Heidegger understands the holy (*das Heilige*) in terms of a mood through which things appear (we have previously examined the "joyous" as both a mood and a medium; the same analysis applies here). In the later writings, the emphasis shifts more to a particular way of being that the holy allows, a way of being that Heidegger terms the "hale" (*das Heile*). The holy is the medium for the appearance of the hale. Over the next decade, the holy increases in importance for Heidegger, as evidenced in the 1939 lecture devoted to Hölderlin's poem "As When on a Holiday . . . ," and the two 1946 texts, "The Letter on 'Humanism'" and "What Are Poets For?" Each of these furthers our understanding of godhood, the holy, and the hale in Heidegger's later thought.

In the "Letter on 'Humanism,'" Heidegger programmatically sketches the relations obtaining between godhood, the holy, and being: "the holy, which is first only the essential space of godhood, which itself again first bestows [*gewährt*] the dimension for the gods and the God, alone comes to shine when previously and with long preparation being illuminates itself and is experienced in its truth" (*GA* 9: 338–39/258, tm). So while the godly and godhood are dependent on the holy, we now see that the holy is dependent on being, or more precisely, the *truth* of being and the lighted *clearing* it brings about. Consequently we are faced with (at least) three moments of the relationship. The truth of being allows for, or (following the notion of element sketched above) "enables," the holy, which allows for (enables) godhood, which in turn allows for (enables) the God(s). Heidegger repeats this triple relation a little later in the text: "The essence of the holy can only be thought in terms of the truth of being. The essence of godhood is to be thought only in terms of the essence of the holy. Only in the light of the essence of godhood can there be thought and said what the word 'God' is supposed to name" (*GA* 9: 351/267, tm). It is important to note in both of these claims that Heidegger does not simply speak of "being" but the "truth of being." With this he points to the spacing of being, i.e., the understanding of being as no common trait among beings, but instead as the receptive space essentially co-implicated in their shining. Only when we understand what exists to require this medium of being (this clearing, *Lichtung*, this particular "lighting") for its radiant appearing will we be in a position to understand the peculiar mediated relations of the holy and godhood. The holy ultimately articulates the mutual need (the interface) between medium and mediated.[29]

The mediating role of the holy is most fully explored in the "Holiday" essay, where Heidegger follows Hölderlin in thinking the holy as riven with tension. It is both nature—"The holy is the essence of nature" (*GA* 4: 59/82)—and chaos—"chaos is the holy itself" (*GA* 4: 63/85). "Nature" insofar as this is thought in relation to (though not identical with) the Greek sense of *physis*, which Heidegger glosses here as "the emergence into the open, the illuminating of that clearing [*das Lichten jener Lichtung*] in which anything appears at all, presents itself in its outline, shows itself in its 'appearance' (*eidos, idea*), and thus is able to be presencing each time as this or that" (*GA* 4: 56/79, tm). The holy is nature insofar as this names the emergence of the clearing wherein something each time appears. But the holy is also "chaos" where this is understood as "that gaping from out of which the open opens itself, thereby granting to everything distinct its delimited presencing" (*GA* 4: 63/85, tm). The holy is consequently understood as this strife between nature and chaos that provides an open arena for appearing. Such a tensed opening is a site of mediation:

> The open mediates the relations between everything actual. The actual consists only of such mediation and is therefore something mediated. What is mediated in this way *only is by virtue of mediacy*. Thus mediacy *must be present in everything*. The open, however, which first provides a realm in which belong all relations toward and with one another, itself arises from no mediation. The open is itself the immediate [*Unmittel-bare*]. Nothing mediated, be it a God or a human, is therefore ever able to reach the immediate immediately. (*GA* 4: 61/83, tm, em)

What exists (referred to here as the "actual" for exegetical reasons) does so only because of the mediating force of the medium of the holy. What exists is relational and does not precede these relations. For this reason, the medium, the holy, is elsewhere called the "constantly former [*stets Einstige*]" (*GA* 4: 63/85, tm). What exists does not "precede" the medium in which it is found (we shall see that despite this appellation of the "former," the medium does not simply "precede" what is found within it, either): "Nothing that is real precedes this opening, but rather always only enters into it. All that appears is already surpassed each time by it" (*GA* 4: 63/85). What exists as relational is each time attended by a medium that surpasses it, providing it with a "beyond" through which its relations can stream. This field of relations supports the thing in its appearing in the open.

Mediation enables relation and thus intimacy. Hölderlin begins a draft entitled "Figure and Spirit" with the words *"Alles ist innig,"* "everything is inner" or "all is internal."[30] Heidegger glosses this in the "Holiday" lecture as saying "Everything only is, in that it shines forth from out of the intimacy [*Innigkeit*] of the all-present. The holy is intimacy itself" (*GA* 4: 73/95). The German word *Innigkeit* means both interiority and intimacy. Heidegger is able to understand the two senses at once through his thinking of mediation. *Alles ist innig* means everything is within the medium. All is immersed. To be within the medium is to be permitted the extension and reception of relations to others, it is to be *intimate*. Within the medium all is related. This intimate interiority is the holy. We are immersed (*eingetaucht*) in it, baptized (*getauft*) by it.

The open itself, we are told, is no mediate particular thing and is thus immediate. But this "immediate" is nothing unqualifiedly outside of mediation. In fact, we might think of the immediate as the im-mediate, as "in-the-mediate," naming now an immersion in mediation, for the immediate is nothing less than mediation itself:

> That which is present beforehand in everything gathers everything individuated into the one presence and mediates to each its appearing. The immediately all-present is the mediatrix [*Mittlerin*] for everything mediated and this means for the mediate. The immediate is itself never something mediate, to the contrary the immediate is, strictly speaking, mediation, i.e. the mediacy of the mediate, because it makes these possible [*ermöglicht*] in their essence. (*GA* 4: 62/84, tm)

As medium, the immediate is nothing "immediate." To be sure, the immediate is no particular thing within the medium (nothing mediated in this way). Instead, as not this, it is the im-mediate, that is, the medium itself. The medium is a necessary accompaniment to all that is mediate. It is always tied to the mediated as the "mediacy *of the mediate*." Mediation and the mediate do not stand over against each other as independent parties. For this reason, the holy is not something that can be located and achieved. It remains "unapproachable" in this regard. What appears in the holy does so "altruistically," we might say, or relationally.

This relational existence is unsettled. It is out of the ordinary in breaking with the habitual confinement in which beings find themselves. Indeed, in the same language that we have seen Heidegger use ten years later regarding the atomic bomb (see "The Atomic Bomb" in chapter 1), Heidegger designates the holy as the horrifying:

> The holy as the un-approachable [*Un-nahbare*] renders every attempted immediate intrusion of the mediate in vain. The holy transposes all experience out of habituation and thus deprives [*entzieht*] experience of its place. Setting-apart [*ent-setzend*] in this manner, the holy is the horrifying itself [*das Entsetzliche selbst*]. But its horror [*Entsetzlichkeit*] remains concealed in the mildness of its light embrace. (*GA* 4: 63/85, tm)

The holy dislodges things from their customary stance (i.e., as objectively present), but does so in order to open them to the field of relations that sustains them. The same unsettled state is both the horrifying (existence as threat) as well as the embracing (what is able to reach us in intimacy). The inseparable combination of these is nothing less than the possibility of belonging.

What is able to belong to this mediated immediate is nothing stable or independent. At the time of the "Holiday" lecture, Heidegger is likewise compiling the notebook entitled *The History of Beyng* (1938–40). Thus it is no surprise that the motif of a "coming" (*das Kommen*), which is of central importance to the notebook, would likewise appear in the elaboration of the holy.[31] To be sure, for the holy, "the manner of its presence is a coming [*das Kommen*]. . . . The holy is quietly present as what comes [*als Kommendes*]. For this reason it can also never be represented or grasped as an object" (*GA* 4: 67/89, tm). That the holy is what comes should again keep us from imagining it as something self-present. To be coming is to be underway, to be neither here nor there, neither present nor absent, but something in-between or "in the middle" of these. For its mediacy, the medium can only ever be coming. Only this grants it the viscosity it needs to shuttle relations to and fro without trapping them in a reified position.

The thinking of the holy is a thinking of how the medium needs the mediated. The medium and the mediated require each other, are essentially connected to each other. This means that in order for one to essence and to be what it is—Heidegger will say that in the medium of the holy "each only performs that which it is" (*GA* 4: 65/87, tm)—there must be the other. The mediated only exists by virtue of the medium, and vice-versa. Each can only be understood relationally. What this means is that neither is independent of the other. The mediated are not present-at-hand objects that are subsequently deposited in an otherwise indifferent medium that can take them or leave them with no effect upon its existence (essence). Correspondingly, the medium cannot be thought of as a "possibility condition" for the mediated, either, as this would presume the very independence that prohibits all mediation.[32]

Heidegger's reading of Hölderlin's hymn "As When on Holiday . . ." locates this belonging-together of the mediated and the medium in the poetic word. The poet's song gives voice to the holy. The holy is named by the poet, a thought in keeping with the famed lines of the "Afterword to 'What Is Metaphysics?'" of 1943: "The thinker says being. The poet names the holy" (*GA* 9: 312/237). In naming the holy, the poetic word is understood to be a "mediated" word. The poet speaks in a way that allows the words their widest reach. Poetic language is understood here to reverberate with ambiguities and variant meanings, to form connections with other words, other thoughts, and other things through the relations it unfolds and the relations it allows. The poetic word is born from a sacrifice of linguistic utility along with the relations that utility privileges and prescribes (clarity, univocity). As such, the word is allowed to resonate freely. The poetic word is released into its sounding. This sounding can only resonate through a medium and for Heidegger's reading of Hölderlin, this medium is the holy. The poet evokes the holy. By virtue of this evocation, "what is coming [i.e., the holy] is said in its coming" (*GA* 4: 76/98). The poetic word stands as what is mediated in the medium of the holy. In considering the sky, we addressed Heidegger's conception of the self-lighting of the lightning flash that "brings itself into the brightness proper to it, a brightness it brought in with itself" (*GA* 79: 74/69; see the remarks at "Weather, Storms, and Lightning" in chapter 3). What appears needs the medium wherein it appears precisely in order to appear. The same is here said of the holy: "The holy makes a gift of the word and itself comes in this word. The word is the appropriative event [*Ereignis*] of the holy. Hölderlin's poetry is now an inceptual calling, that is itself called by what comes, saying this and only this as the holy" (*GA* 4: 76–77/98, tm). The holy comes in the word.

And yet this co-belonging contains in itself already the demise of the holy. The relational existence of mediation—of the essential belonging-together of medium and mediated—threatens to devolve into objectification or commodification: "Yet precisely because of this, that the holy is assigned to a mediation by the God and the poet and is sheltered in song, the essence of the holy threatens to turn into its opposite. The immediate would thereby become something mediated" (*GA* 4: 72/94, tm). The medium (the immediate, what is not mediate but medium) is threatened with construal as just another objective being. This threat of reification is not something avoidable, but constitutive. The between, the middle ground of mediation here, is not an independent order of existence somewhere apart from the realm of metaphysics. Nothing could be further from the truth. Instead, as relational, the medium must always sustain relations with metaphysics as well. The threat comes from the holy itself: "this lastingness [*Bleiben*] of the holy, however, is threatened by the mediation of the word of the song, a mediation that stems from the holy itself and is required by its coming" (*GA* 4: 73/95, tm). The holy needs the very mediated party that presages its downfall. That *physis* would require *technê* (*GA* 45), that beyng would pursue itself with its own forgetting (*GA* 79), that being is in itself conflictual (*GA* 4), and now that the holy contains its own demise, all these ideas are so many ways of avoiding a breezy dualism that would establish two distinct orders of being, the one the simple "overcoming" of the other. To think the holy, to think relation, is to leave "overcoming" behind. The threat of the holy is not without consequence for what appears within it. When Heidegger returns to a thinking of the holy after the war (1946) it is this threatened nature of existence that comes to the fore under the rubric of the "hale."

b. The Hale

Heidegger's 1939 reading of "As When on a Holiday . . ." articulates the mediating role of the holy, but as to what appears in that holy, it only offers the poetic word. While this is already a break with his earlier conception of the poet, as mediator between gods and people, it nonetheless omits an important piece of the puzzle that his post-war thinking provides, a conception of "the hale" (*das Heile*). The sense of the hale in the 1946 essay "What Are Poets For?" is that of an existence ever threatened with extinction.

The depiction of our situation at the outset of "What Are Poets For?" is seemingly bleak. The day of the gods has passed, we are told, and an ever spreading darkness draws over the age. The time is needy. In fact, "the world-age is defined by the remaining away [*Wegbleiben*] of God, by the 'default [*Fehl*] of God'" (*GA* 5: 269/200, tm). That the gods are outstanding, that they fail us, should not be mistaken for their absence. This is part of the threat that they bring, that we would think them absent. The situation is otherwise, worse we might say, for it is not simply that the gods are missing, godhood itself is directly affected: "Not only the gods and the God have flown, but the gleam of godhood is extinguished in world history" (*GA* 5: 269/200, tm). The gleam of godhood names the radiance of the God that suffuses the medium of godhood; without gods no godhood. With darkness falling and spreading, the situation is already so dire "that it is no longer able to mark the default [*Fehl*] of God as default" (*GA* 5: 269/200, tm). The default is ignored or simply construed as absence. The age nears its midnight.

As it nears midnight, the neediness increases. The gods are flown and their medium evaporates with them. Such a medium would be where we might find traces of their flight. Indeed, Heidegger even equates the trace with mediation (the element): "The element of the aether for the arrival of the flown gods, the holy, is the trace of the flown gods" (*GA* 5: 272/202, tm). It is their trace insofar as gods do not exist trapped in themselves, but already exude beyond such bounds. These transgressive relations, as traces, are no small part of their godhood (element). Indeed, they could be said to constitute it. The element, the medium, is their trace. Nevertheless, Heidegger emphasizes that not only are the gods gone and godhood gone, but even the medium of godhood, the holy, is gone. More, even the trace of this holy is fast fading: "Not only is the holy as the trace of godhood fading away, rather even the trace of this fading trace is nearly extinguished. The more the traces are extinguished, the less can mortals attend to hints" (*GA* 5: 272/203, tm). Trace and hint are thus to be thought similarly, both indicating a non-presence that points past itself to what lies beyond it, as we have seen. Now we are threatened with the loss of the trace of the trace: "In the meantime even the trace of the holy has become unrecognizable. It remains undecided whether we experience the holy still as the trace of the godhood of the divine [*Gottheit des Göttlichen*], or if we still even encounter a trace of the holy. It remains unclear what the trace of the trace could be. It remains in question how such a trace would care to show itself to us" (*GA* 5: 275/205, tm). In the world-night we fail to even encounter the holy, much less understand it in regards to godhood. We lack even the trace of the holy to lead to godhood to lead to the withdrawal of the gods.

This abyssally abandoned trace of the holy is precisely what Heidegger terms the "hale" (*das Heile*). The outlook is just as grim for the hale, since "not only does the holy as the trace of godhood remain concealed, rather even the trace of the holy, the hale, appears to be extinguished" (*GA* 5: 295/221, tm). *Das Heile*, the "hale," has the sense of something that is safe, undamaged, or intact. The integrity it denotes can be understood in terms of robust health as in the phrase "hale and hearty," or in terms of fulfillment and of being a "whole." But *das Heile* is a paradoxical whole for things, a whole which is not "wholly" present. Heidegger uses the term adjectivally to modify *Ganze*, "entire, whole," in precisely this sense. He also employs the term *das Heile* in relation to *das Unversehrte*, the "unharmed, unhurt, undamaged," a term which can also be heard literally as "that which is not brought to an increase," i.e., that which remains within its own limits and is not forced to come totally to presence according to a foreign measure. Such total presencing is at odds with presencing as whole or hale. In this regard, *das Heile*, the trace of the holy, names a manner of presencing that can be viewed in contrast to that of the standing reserve. The hale is the thought of an essencing freed from the technological demand of total revelation for assessment and requisitioning. Whereas technological challenging-forth demands a presencing that can be appropriated totally and without resistance by the willing subject, the essencing of the hale retains a preserve of concealment. Such a concealment, in opposition to the standing reserve, prohibits replacement by maintaining a difference between things, by placing a difference within things themselves—or better, placing things within a differentiating medium essential to their essencing as such. The hale is more than itself because "what it is" is essentially related to the holy. It requires the holy for its relational existence, it needs this medium through which to stream.

Given the somber proceedings, Heidegger's claim is that the trace of these gods, the glimmer of their godhood, has been extinguished in world history. Since the hale is said to be the trace of this extinguished trace of departure, and since this extinguished holy is said to be that which enables the hale, it would seem to follow that the hale, too, must be extinguished. But Heidegger cannot go this far. While he does state that "the gleam of godhood [i.e., the holy] is extinguished in world history," such a statement is made only as a positive result following upon the immediately preceding sentence that "in the default of God something still more troubling announces itself" (*GA* 5: 269/200, tm).[33] The announcement of this troubling matter preserves it for thought. Heidegger's position here is thus in accordance with his reading of Hölderlin's hymn "The Ister." Where Hölderlin writes, "but what the river does, / no one knows,"[34] Heidegger points out in the eponymous lecture course that it is only in Hölderlin's naming of this concealed doing of the river that it is preserved precisely as concealed: "The poetic word unveils this concealment of the river's activity, and indeed unveils it as such an activity [i.e., as a concealed one]. This unveiling is poetic" (*GA* 53: 21/19).[35] Further, each time Heidegger seems to make such gloomy proclamations concerning our present plight we must attend to the hesitations and provisos he employs: "the trace of the holy, the hale, *appears* to be extinguished," or "not only does the holy as the trace of godhood become lost, but even the trace of this lost trace is *nearly* extinguished" (*GA* 5: 295/221, tm, em, 272/203, tm, em). The hale, therefore, is not to be regarded as simply extinguished, but rather as essentially endangered. The threat threatens the extinction of the hale, the closure of the holy, the evaporation of godhood, and the demise of the gods themselves. The threat would be complete surrender to the commoditized workings of contemporary technology.

The hale that would balance all of this upon its shoulders is itself fading: "the hale withdraws. The world becomes hale-less" (*GA* 5: 295/221, tm). The withdrawal of the hale is the withdrawal of the mediated, relational essencing of things. What presences now apes objecthood and would seem to close off anything like the hale: "Perhaps what characterizes this world-age consists in the closure of the dimension of the hale. Perhaps this is the sole unhale" (*GA* 9: 352/267, tm). The "dimension of the hale" is the dimension wherein the hale is found, i.e., the holy.[36] The holy is the dimension of the hale. The sole unhale, then, would be the closure of that holy wherein alone the hale can appear. This is so because whatever appears in the holy does so as hale—for otherwise it could not appear. Appearance itself is hale. Consequently, the unhale would be the absence of appearance, or its full presence. Heidegger writes that "still a few mortals are able to see the the haleless [*das Heillose*] threaten *as* the haleless" (*GA* 5: 295/221, tm). The threat of the haleless would be the threat of the closure of the holy and the concomitant eradication of the hale. The two are intertwined, since it is not only that the hale is solely found in the holy, but, reciprocally, that also "only in the broadest scope of the hale is the holy able to appear" (*GA* 5: 319/240, tm). Instead of this haleless situation of the closure of the holy, we are under the threat of it. At root, it is the same threat as the threat of the atomic bomb, only the inverse. Instead of annihilation it is the threat of consummation. Within this reign of the haleless (*das Heillose*), there is still found the unhale (*das Unheile*), which names the consummation of presence advanced by metaphysics. But every closure is always an exposure. There is nothing enclosed. The unhale must be hale. Even metaphysical objectivity at its deepest self-enclosure maintains a surface in suffusion. To see this is to be like the poets Heidegger speaks of, who "are on the way to the trace of the holy because they experience the haleless as such. Their song makes the land holy" (*GA* 5: 319/240, tm). Experiencing the haleless as such they witness the exposure of the unhale. They see it now as trace, where "unhale as unhale traces for us the hale. The hale callingly hints at the holy. The holy binds the divine [*das Göttliche*]. The divine brings God near" (*GA* 5: 319/240, tm). Let us note that this (abyssal) list does not conclude in presence, but deferral and default. The gods are near, but not yet here.

The 1945 text "Evening Conversation in a Prisoner of War Camp in Russia Between a Younger Man and an Older Man" proposes that the healing (*heilen*) of our unhale condition takes place through exposure. The conversation opens with the younger man remarking how in the midst of the camp "something salvific [*etwas Heilsames*] suddenly overtook me from out of the rustling of the wide forest," wondering "wherein indeed this healing [*Heilende*] could lie" (*GA* 77: 205/132, tm). We have a provisional answer already from our considerations of the dimension—it is in the ability to look up. From out of the work camp—"between the walls of these barracks, behind barbed wire" (*GA* 77: 206/132)—looking up offers us an exposure to the beyond, or, as it is here termed, an exposure to the breadth of the expanse (*Weite*). The older man proposes that "perhaps it [the salvific] is what is inexhaustible of the self-veiling expanse that abides in these forests of Russia" (*GA* 77: 205/132). But the forest lies within this surrounding expanse, not the other way around. The older man notes that this expanse, properly understood, "leads us out and away" (*GA* 77: 205/132, tm). In that we are "in" this expanse, we are likewise led out through it away from ourselves. We permeate it. As the younger man remarks, "the expanse carries us to what is objectless [*Gegenstandlosen*], and yet also keeps us from dissolving into it" (*GA* 77: 205/132).

Healing is found in exposure, but exposure is hindered by reification and the reflexive retreat of the self deeper into itself. Refraining from this objectifying and commoditizing tendency of the human leads to what Heidegger terms "waiting." Waiting is a non-reifying approach to the world. It is the relationship of the human not to what is present, but to what is peculiarly not present, to what is relational, to what comes: "waiting is letting come" (*GA* 77: 217/142). The salvific is found in this, or rather, arrives as this, "because in the experience of coming—and it is this for which we wait, and in such waiting our essence first becomes free—because in the simple experience of all this, the salvific that grows toward us draws near" (*GA* 77: 218–19/142, tm). As the younger man asks, "what else could that which heals [*das Heilende*] be, other than that which lets our essence wait" (*GA* 77: 226/147).

In waiting we make space for an arriving without demanding complete arrival. Waiting lets things be hale (*heil*). Waiting lets the holy (*Heilige*) come. In so doing, waiting heals (*heilt*). But this healing is not the entry into a different order of being or the achievement of a world completely apart from the commoditized unworld of technology. The salvific lies in exposure, what is healed is exposed to what comes, for instance, to the coming of grace: "Being first grants to healing the ascent into grace" (*GA* 9: 360/273, tm).[37] The salvific exposure to the expanse "heals by soothing, but never removing, the pain" (*GA* 77: 230/150). Pain is not simply "overcome" (*überwindet*), but is "converted" (*verwindet*). Healing maintains a relation to pain and this means to metaphysics, to the object and the standing reserve. Only in this tension can there be the hale. Healing is accepting that we are not yet healed.

c. The God(s)

Given this connection between the hale, the holy, and godhood, what then of the God itself? The depictions of the divinities within the fourfold both make mention of God. After proclaiming the divinities the hinting messengers of godhood, we read in "The Thing" that "from the concealed reign of these there appears the God in his essence, withdrawing him from every comparison with what is present [*dem Anwesenden*]," and in "Building Dwelling Thinking" that "from the holy reign of these there appears the God in the present [*Gegenwart*] or he withdraws into his veiling" (*GA* 79: 17/16, *GA* 7: 151/*PLT* 147–48, tm). We should note in both instances that the God appears or withdraws only via the holy and concealed (non-present) reign of the divinities, where again the latter cannot be understood as the "condition of possibility" for God. The 1943 elucidation of Hölderlin's hymn "Homecoming/To the Relations" makes this clear in a manner quite in keeping with what has gone before. Here, Heidegger comments on a seeming slip in terminology on the part of Hölderlin in this poem where entities that are first termed angels are subsequently referred to as gods. Heidegger rhetorically asks whether the gods have been demoted to mere angels or whether these gods now are to be thought in addition to the angels. The answer in each case is no, for "with the name 'angels,' the being of those who were otherwise called gods is said more purely. For the gods are the cheerful ones [*die Aufheiternden*] who, in cheering up [*Aufheiterung*], offer the greeting that sends the joyous [*die Heitere*]. The joyous is the essential ground of the greeting, i.e., of the angelic, wherein what is ownmost of the gods consists" (*GA* 4: 20/39, tm). The gods are indissociable from their angelic mediation.

Returning to our guiding depictions of the divinities, both statements also assert a certain ambiguity or uncertainty to God. In the first case, the appearance of God is such that it withdraws the God from comparison with the present-at-hand. We have already noted the role of singularity in the thinking of the holy. The God's mediated essencing renders the God unavailable for complete assessment and subsequent implementation in a means-end relationship. In the second case, there seems to be an option proposed of either the God becoming present or withdrawing. But if we are to be true to the nature of godhood and mediation, then we would have to proclaim this a false dilemma. God in godhood is both present and withdrawn, presences *as* withdrawn. This is how the God appears "in his essence."

In ". . . poetically dwells man . . . ," a lecture from 1951 delivered two months after "Building Dwelling Thinking" and important for the thinking of the fourfold, the status of this essencing God is pursued the furthest. Here, God is supposed to provide the measure or standard for the poetic dimension. But God is not present for the taking, nor is God something that could even be considered "known." In the experience of the default of the gods, the God remains unknown. But it is precisely this that allows him to be the measure: "As that which He is, God is unknown for Hölderlin and as this unknown he is precisely the measure for the poet" (*GA* 7: 201/*PLT* 220, tm). God as unknown becomes the measure, not in order to become known, but precisely as that which elides the very distinction between the known and unknown. To take God as the standard is consequently to take another kind of presencing (essencing) as the standard, one that is neither known nor unknown. As Heidegger notes, "the *manifestness* of God [*Offenbarkeit Gottes*], not merely He himself, is secretive" (*GA* 7: 201/*PLT* 220, tm). The manifesting of God, his essencing, is secretive. It is neither a presence nor an absence. There is a concealment that is essential to it. The God appears as concealed: "The appearing of God in the sky consists in an unveiling which lets that be seen which conceals itself, but does not let it be seen by seeking to wrest it out of its concealment, but rather solely in that it protects what is concealed in its self-concealing" (*GA* 7: 201/*PLT* 220–21, tm). Protecting concealment rather than driving it out into the open becomes the standard for the dimension between earth and sky. Such a way is indeed the only way that a God might arrive, though the gods are yet to arrive.

The strange essencing of God is irresolvable. What is one to make of gods no longer here, who have departed, who leave traces, who have not yet arrived? The answer depends on our understanding of the "not yet," no accidental figure of speech in Heidegger's work, but a pivotal notion. It already surfaces in the 1936 essay "Hölderlin and the Essence of Poetry," where it serves to name the neediness permeating our age, the precondition of our own responsibility: "This [i.e., *now*] is the time of *need*, because it stands in a doubled lack and not: in the no-longer of the gods that have fled and the not-yet of what comes [*des Kommenden*]" (*GA* 4: 47/64, tm). The point shows up in the Rilke interpretation as well: "Perhaps the world-time will now completely become the needy time. Perhaps but also not, not yet, always not yet [*noch nicht, immer noch nicht*], despite the unmeasurable distress, despite all suffering, despite the nameless sorrow, despite the peacelessness growing forward, despite the escalating confusion" (*GA* 5: 271/201, tm). Always not yet, always no longer, without end, without origin, or such but only in these traces, traces no longer thought as dependent upon another world for their truth; there is no world other than this world, which is precisely *not yet* a world. Heidegger excoriates Jünger, Rilke, and Nietzsche, too, on this very point, as we shall see ("The Metaphysical Completion of the *Animal Rationale*," chapter 5), as metaphysical representatives of an other world—of *any* world—even if for these three it is *this* world that is to be that other world, a conversion brought about by the subsumption of a transformed humanity into the world (a humanity consummated—and not to be mistaken for *no longer* human—in the Worker, the Angel, the *Übermensch*). When Heidegger wonders "whether and how in the emergence of the holy an appearing of God and gods can begin anew," he is contemplating alternatives to this situation of metaphysical completion (*GA* 9: 338/258, tm). An answer lies in our relation to things.

The unknown God will not be made evident and still remain God. The God is foreign to the world that is familiar to us. Nevertheless, only with this strangeness as the measure do we sketch out a dimension in which things might retain a foreignness, where things might "alienate" themselves in their radiance through the world. The unknown God enters the world at the level of things:

> What remains foreign for the God, the view of the sky, is the familiar for humans. And what is this? Everything that shines and blossoms in the sky and thus under the sky and thus upon the earth, all that sounds and is fragrant, rises and comes, but also everything that passes and falls, that also laments and goes silent, that also blanches and darkens. Into this, which is familiar to man but foreign to the God, the unknown imparts itself [*schicket sich*], in order to remain protected within it as the unknown. (*GA* 7: 204/*PLT* 223, tm)

The radiance of things shelters the unknowability of God. This radiance is the gleam of things. In "What Are Poets For?" Heidegger asks, "how could there ever be a residence appropriate for the God, if *a gleam of godhood in all that is* had not beforehand begun to shine?" (*GA* 5: 270/201, tm, em). Our relation to things, their releasement into shining, is a preparation of the residence for God. But this residence will not be anything other than the cultivation of a medium capable of bearing and remarking the trace of the gods' departure. We must prepare a space for the trace, for the non-present, for radiance. The divinities offer us the chance of retaining this world. They are called the "preservers" (*Erhaltenden*) by Hölderlin because "as the ones who greet they bring the joyous to shine, in whose clarity the 'nature' of things and humans is *preserved as hale* [*heil*]. What remains guarded as hale, is 'homely' in its essence. The messengers greet from out of the joyous that allows everything to be homely" (*GA* 4: 17/36, tm, em). The hale things allow a residence for the God and likewise for the mortals. The divinities who message to us only ever offer us the invitation of this world. To receive the message is already to have entered it, thanks to the grace of the God(s).

§15. The Meaning of the Divine

As hinting messengers of godhood, the divinities bring meaning to the thing. More precisely, as there is no thing preceding its meaning, the divinities do not bestow meaning or impose it (this is not a *Sinngebung*); rather, they extend the invitation of meaning. In thinking the divinities, Heidegger thinks the reach of things. In treating of the earth and sky, we considered the ungrounded essencing of the thing, its earthen quality, as well as the textured medium that receives it, the sky. The divinities could be seen as specifying the rules of engagement between thing and world, as the ambassadors of a kind of structural law, as it were. This law would prescribe that the foreign must appear in order to be foreign. Failure to abide this would entail oblivion. The divinities bring the foreign *as* the foreign, allowing for what one might term an appropriation of the inappropriable. This is nothing less than the condition of meaning as such. The divinities enact meaning.

Meaning for its part is ever only an affair of the mortal. Meaning is finitude; finitude *means* . . . . The finite as delimited is exposed. Meaning is found nowhere other than here, at this limit or surface of exposure, for it is only here that we can be reached, addressed, called out by what comes to us, what arrives, what concerns us, what strikes us as meaningful. We are addressed at our limit and this address is the impact of meaning. Finitude implicates its own beyond and is struck by that beyond in return. Whatever is delimited simultaneously sketches its own beyond. The finite does this so essentially that it is inextricable from that beyond. What appears to us does so precisely as something that reaches us. It comes to us from where it is. What appears is (the) given. To be given is to be sent. The given radiates in reaching us. And we are already out ahead of ourselves in reaching it in its concernful approach. What concerns us (*geht uns an*) approaches us (*geht uns an*). The given "issues" forth to us. What is given arrives as an issue for us. It comes to us as meaningful. This arriving of the meaningful is not due to any bestowal of meaning on our part. We do not bestow so much as receive the meaning that we are prepared for, the meaning we are enabled to receive. This is the truth of the claim that "I am human and nothing is foreign to me."[38] Meaning emerges from the interface, not the understanding, of a particular being.

In our examination of messengership, we noted the way in which delivery of the message was always the extension of a withdrawal, the bringing of a trace. This establishes the communicative texture of the world. The medium is not pixilated so much as gestural, reaching beyond itself to pass along the withdrawal that sets it in motion, making it worldly. This is why Heidegger proposes such elaborately repercussive structures in his thinking of the divine—the hale is the trace of the holy is the element of godhood is the trace of the gods who have flown. Such reverberations are the only way to properly think mediation. Mediation cannot be thought on the basis of intervention and the intermediary. To do so is to presume the very self-identity that hinting, messaging, and mediation undermine from the outset. There is not a donor-pole and a recipient-pole with a single mediator arbitrating between them. The model presumes not only self-identity on the part of the poles and the mediator, but alienation of the poles from the medium. Finite existence is not extricable from its surroundings, from its immersion in mediation. Otherwise put, mediation is not a matter for three. It is four or more, but never and nowhere is it three. We see a flash of this in a passing moment from the "Conversation on Language." When the conversation turns to Plato's *Ion*, the researcher explains that "Hermes is the messenger of the gods [*der Götterbote*]. He brings the message of destiny [*des Geschickes*]; *hermêneuein* is that putting-forth which brings tidings insofar as it is able to listen to a message" (*GA* 12: 115/*OWL* 29, tm). The messenger of the gods, be this Hermes or a poet, is the one who brings the gods in his messaging. Hermes listens to the gods, picks up their hints in their withdrawal, and gives these hints to the people who hear them as sent. Hermes is not intervening between a present at hand people and gods. The gods withdraw (the message itself is presented as an effect of the two-fold, i.e., the non–self identity of beyng), their hints are heard, these hints are then spoken, and are there to be heard again. The putting-forth (*Darlegen*) must become an interpretation (*Auslegen*), as we have seen. In response to this the interlocutor says, "I love this little dialogue of Plato's that you have named. At the passage that you intend, Socrates conducts the relationship still further, in that he supposes the rhapsodes as those who bring tidings of the word of the poet" (*GA* 12: 115/*OWL* 29, tm). The interlocutor wishes to add yet another layer of mediation to the puzzle. The researcher seems to ignore the remark: "From all this it becomes clear that the hermeneutical is not foremost interpretation, but rather, before this means the bringing of the message and tidings" (*GA* 12: 115/*OWL* 29, tm). The researcher passes over this further layering of mediation because it adds nothing to the situation already underway. Once mediation is set in place in a manner not subordinated to the logic of the three, no additional layering will increase the abyss of meaning we have entered into. There are not degrees of mediation such that the addition of rhapsodes to the series will alter anything in the least. Once there is the (doubled) doubling of relations, once the poles themselves are split and implicated in a beyond that mediates them and delivers their relationships, thereby delivering they themselves to themselves, we have already entered the ungrounded abyssal viscosity of meaning. Meaning is four or more but never three.

If finitude is always tied to its beyond and this beyond is always messaging itself to us, why is this context of meaning construed in terms of the divine? The question answers itself insofar as the divine—or, more simply, "God"—has always served to populate this beyond. God is the figure of surpassing as this has been understood across the history of metaphysics. For Heidegger, this means the beyond has been construed on the basis of a particular being, the most powerful one and highest one, but a particular being nonetheless. Without thinking mediation and the communicativity of the medium, this God is as good as dead, if not worse, while oblivious to us and us to it. Heidegger is not interested in God as agency, so much as God as surface of exposure. God is the figure of surpassing. What the divinities of the fourfold make evident is that *even this God must appear.* What surpasses us must appear to us if it is to be an issue for us. God testifies to the law of mediation, that all that is must appear. The divinities allow the medium to show "surpassing." What is beyond us is not beyond us, but is now appearing to us as beyond. This is what the divinities bring, the invitation to participate in this beyond. The significance of God lies in demonstrating that what surpasses the mortal must appear to the mortal nonetheless. The divinities testify to the tensile strength of the medium, so to speak, that it is able to bring the most beyond right to us and even shelter it here in the simple things around us. The messengerial structure of meaning means that the divine can appear to us even in unholy times, that the gleam of godhood is still to be found in things.

Put another way, we have seen that Heidegger's break with the binarism of subject-object dualism in favor of a thinking of the between results in a situation of danger and threat where the thinging of the thing is endangered by technological replaceability. But utter replacement never comes. We are never annihilated, always only not yet and on the way to this. But this is to approach the matter from its "negative side," if such language be allowed—from the side of the total absence we can never achieve. For the same relation holds positively, too, on the part of presence. If God figures as the pinnacle of presence's self-presentation, then this too must enter the messengerial field of mediated appearing. Absence cannot be found, it is always remarked, and the same holds for the sheer presence of God. This too is remarked. Absence as well as presence, the ultimate tension of metaphysics, both make themselves known in mediated announcement. The divinities illustrate not only the way in which the divine appears to us, i.e., as a message sent (*Götterbote*), but also that the divine must appear as well by virtue of our finite condition. Finitude implicates the beyond, is tied to it. Metaphysics thinks this as God. The finite cannot dispose of metaphysics, it is tied to this as well. The beyond is never *terra nova* or untrodden. Thus, finitude implicates the divine and must do so in order to be finite, understood now not as a derivation from the infinite but as the site that sustains that infinite in existence in the first place. Neither is independent, each has need of the other. In fact, need names nothing other than this mutually enabling relation. The finite needs the infinite, the infinite, the finite.

And yet there is a troubling aspect to this need. It surfaces from the very outset, in the lecture "The Thing." Even before the divinities are introduced within the depiction of the fourfold, they appear in a discussion of sacrifice. Here, the outpouring of a jug is under consideration. The pour of the jug can go to quench a thirst or it can be spilled out as a sacrificial oblation. Heidegger states, "in the gift of the pour that is an oblation, the divinities abide in their way, divinities who *receive back* the gift of the giving as the gift of a donation [*das Geschenk des Schenkens als das Geschenk der Spende zurückempfangen*]" (*GA* 79: 12/11, em). The divinities are there to *zurückempfangen*, to receive or welcome back what is sacrificed and lost. But this receiving back would seem to cancel any chance of such sacrifice. The divinities (and with them the logic of the trace and of meaning that we have sketched throughout this chapter) would offer a kind of assurance or guarantee against loss, annulling its very possibility. The most extreme act of waste would find its way back into the waiting arms of divinity; received back, welcomed back even.

The divinities would then perform something of a unifying function, ensuring that everything finds its way back into the divine union. This is what the mortals would need from them, the assurance that their sacrifices would be received, gathered back to the divinities. To be sure, Heidegger will think the divine explicitly in terms of the One, the *hen*. As Fink explains in the 1966–67 *Heraclitus* seminar: "The relatedness of *hen* and *panta* mirrors itself in the relation of gods and humans. Since *hen* is no factual unity but rather the unity of *logos*, gods and humans are those struck by the lightning of *logos*. They belong together in the *logos*-happening" (*GA* 15: 190/*HS* 117). This emphasis on receiving back and divine unity would seem to undermine all of Heidegger's efforts to think the divine in terms of hinting, messaging, and mediation. Ultimately, one might claim, the divine is the One and Heidegger remains a metaphysician in his obeisance to this figure of divine reconciliation.

One could look to the 1945 "Evening Conversation" to show that Heidegger's very thinking of mortality is inherently tied to this divine One. Here, the prisoners consider two ancient definitions of human being: that of the *zôon logon echon*, the animal having reason, and that of *ho thnêtos*, the mortal. The older man sees the definition of mortal as providing an exit from the strictures of the animal with reason and as offering us an opening onto relationality and a connection with the gods:

> Whenever we previously spoke about the essence of the human—and that means about the occidental determination of the essence of the human—each time you focused only on the characterization of the human as the living being that thinks. To be sure, this definition was already common in the ancient Greek world. But in the most ancient Greek world, the human was thought otherwise—namely, as *ho thnêtos*,

as the mortal in distinction to the immortals, the gods. This characterization of the human seems to me to be incomparably deeper than the
one first mentioned, which is gained by means of holding in view the
human by himself, isolated and detached from the great relationships
in which he properly stands. And among these relationships, the one he
has to the gods has priority above all others. (*GA* 77: 221–22/143–44)

The younger man objects to the idea that the more recent definition
would somehow lack in profundity in comparison with the older one. In
making his point, he takes recourse to the One. As the younger prisoner
explains: "Only the common interpretation of the definition of the essence of the human as the *zôon logon echon* seems to me to be shallow. Yet
if we finally learn to think that *logos* originally means gathering, then the
definition of the human with regard to *logos* says that his essence consists
in being in the gathering, namely, the gathering toward the originally
all-unifying One" (*GA* 77: 223/145). With this, we see the sameness of the
definition of the human as mortal and as *zôon logon echon*; both understand the human in relation to the immortal and thus the One: "If the
human as the mortal is experienced in distinction to the immortals, he
is obviously thought with regard to the gods and the divine. And if *logos*
means the gathering toward the originally all-unifying One, whereby the
One is the divine itself, then the two essential definitions—which initially
appear as almost incompatible, or at least as foreign to one another—
basically think the selfsame" (*GA* 77: 224/145).

Before rushing to conclude that Heidegger would be a thinker of
reconciled union, we must pay heed to the role of *logos* in the gathering
of this One. For, as Heidegger explains in the essay "Logos" of 1951, "the
essence of *logos* would provide a hint [*Wink*] into the godhood of God"
(*GA* 7: 227/*EGT* 72, tm). If we think godhood in terms of this gathering,
then the relation of the One to the many changes. In the 1967 *Heraclitus*
seminar, Heidegger proposes that thinking the relation of the *hen* and
panta properly will do away with the idea of these as two independent
parties or relata:

> When we speak of the "relation between *hen* and *panta*," then it seems
> as if we were thinking about a relation between the two which we
> have localized objectively and for which we then sought a bow which
> spanned them. In the end, however, the matter stands in such a way
> that *hen* is the relation, and that it relates to *ta panta* in that it lets them
> be what they are. So understood, the relation is, in my opinion, the
> decisive point that our determination must reach and that whereby the
> idea of two relata is eliminated. (*GA* 15: 175–76/*HS* 108, tm)

The one is not the polar opposite of the many, but the relation of the many to each other and what lies around them. The One does not supervene over the many, but lets them be.

What then does this tell us of the divinities who "welcome back" loss and would seem to recuperate all sacrifices? What this thinking of the One allows us to see is that this is not the cancellation of loss, but its effulgence. *To be loss there cannot be anything utterly lost,* this is the peculiar logic of it. There must be that which suffers loss and this can be nothing other than the One. The One is the fact of infinite, endless loss. Otherwise all would already be lost and there would be no loss to endure. If the divinities ensure anything, it is that no loss will ever be completed. The divine One serves to distribute the reverberation of that loss to us. If the lost were simply lost, we would not suffer or mourn. Mourning grants access to the no longer present, makes us attentive to the traces not yet extinguished of what has-been. As the 1934–35 Hölderlin course proclaims, such mourning is holy.

The divinities give us the meaning of the thing, though nowhere is this grounded in a stable presence. The divinities hint, they do not speak univocally. They are messengers or mediators who bring what they message to presence as sent. And what they hint at in their messaging is godhood, the ever retreating abyssal layering of media for the appearing of what can no longer be objectively present, the hale thing. The divine preserves such things by subjecting them to endless destruction; this is the "horror" of the divine (it "transposes" things out of objective presence). But the divine is also the site of all that is meaningful to us, all that we are capable of losing.

By thinking divinities as messengers and placing these messengers within all things, Heidegger gives us a new way to consider meaning itself. Things are now inherently meaningful because things are intrinsically tied to a beyond outside them. That beyond always leaves its mark on things. These marks are the marks of meaning. Meaning names how we are marked by what lies beyond ourselves. By casting the messengers of thingly meaning as divinities, Heidegger allows us to see that even the most foreign to us, even the God itself, must be remarked to be meaningful. Even the withdrawal or flight of such god/gods must be marked to be meaningful. Even the gods themselves cannot overcome this condition of meaning, that there be a marking, that there be a message, that there be divinities. The divinities name the meaning of the thing.

5

Mortals, Being-in-Death

The mortals are sequentially the last member of the fourfold to be named in the presentations of 1949–50. Henceforth, the name of "the mortals" (*die Sterblichen*) will largely, though not exclusively, replace that of Dasein in Heidegger's thought. And yet it should not be forgotten that the name "Dasein" was itself, too, a replacement or displacement of what had previously stood to name the essence of the human. "Dasein" was a break with the idea of a self-enclosed subject. Against the interiority of such a subject, against "consciousness" (*Bewußtsein*), Heidegger proposed the exteriority of *Dasein*: "In *Being and Time* the term 'Dasein' is used in place of 'consciousness'" (*GA* 9: 373/283). Heidegger's commitment to the thought of existence as exposure, his insistence on exteriority, is also the ground of his objection to thinking the human in terms of animality, as the *animal rationale*. The animal is the name for an existence that is thought on the basis of life and thereby trapped within an environment catering to life's needs. Life does not allow access to an outside—it is instead cravenly concerned with insulating itself in a suffocating satiety.

Why then rechristen existence as mortal? Provisionally we might list a few reasons. To rename Dasein as (one of) the mortals is to shift the terms of propriety from being (Da-*sein*) to dying (*die Sterblichen*). We might see in this something of an "anthropological concretion" of existence; the name would no longer indicate a relation to being in general, but instead a particular and determinate way of being, indeed the most particular, that of dying. "Mortals" would thus lack the supposed formalism of Dasein.

Let us further note that what lies at the heart of the traditional names of the human—the Greek conception of a *zôon logon echon*, a "living being possessing the logos," as well as the Roman *animal rationale*, the rational animal—is in each case life (*zôon, animal*), a living being at the foundation of a logico-rationality. These most traditional conceptions of "human" essence think the human as an animal, an animate and living being (*Lebewesen*), to whom there has been added the property of logical-rational thought, a specific difference peculiar to humans alone within the animal kingdom. Such thinking determines the essence of the "human" to be nothing more than that of a monkey with a thinking-cap.

Against such thinking of the *living* being, Heidegger now more directly opposes that of the mortals: *das Lebewesen* vs. *die Sterblichen.*

Lastly, the name "mortals" breaks with that of Dasein in another way as well, for "mortals" is always plural, a point one cannot claim literally in regards to "Dasein." "The mortals" is always plural, even when, on the rare occasion, Heidegger uses it in the singular.[1] A community of mortals is thus written into the very name. The name mortals could thus be seen to respond more sharply to concerns Heidegger already evinced in *Being and Time*, that Dasein must die, that it is distinct from the animal, and that it is always with-others. The name mortals would simply organize these concerns and bring them more to the fore. And while one might object that these concerns were already operative in *Being and Time*, it is by no means self-evident that Heidegger's later construal of the mortals still rests upon the earlier death-bound thought of *Being and Time*. The exact relation between these we shall have opportunity to explore in the analyses ahead.

Both depictions of the mortals in "The Thing" and "Building Dwelling Thinking" emphasize the mortals' ability to die, but from there the accounts diverge considerably (and more so than with any other element in the fourfold). In "The Thing" these remarks lead to a rather cryptic consideration of death as the "shrine" of the nothing and conclude with a consideration of the difference between the mortal and the animal:

> The mortals are the humans. They are called the mortals because they are able to die [*sterben können*]. Dying means: to be capable of death as death [*den Tod als Tod vermögen*]. Only the human dies. The animal comes to an end. It has death as death neither before it nor after it. Death is the shrine of the nothing, namely of that which in all respects is never some mere being, but nonetheless essences, namely as being itself [in the published version this last phrase is amended to read "even as the secret of being itself"; *GA* 7: 180/*PLT* 176, tm]. Death, as the shrine of nothingness, harbors in itself what essences of being. As the shrine of nothingness, death is the refuge of being. The mortals we now name the mortals—not because their earthly life ends, but rather because they are capable [*vermögen*] of death as death. The mortals are who they are as mortals by essencing in the refuge of being. They are the essencing relationship to being as being.
>
> Metaphysics, on the contrary, represents the human as an animal, as a living being. Even when the *ratio* reigns over the *animalitas*, the human being remains determined by living and lived experience. From rational living beings, the mortals must first come to be. (*GA* 79: 17–18/17)

In "Building Dwelling Thinking" the remarks on dying lead to a consideration of mortal dwelling in its relation to earth, sky, and divinities:

> The mortals are the humans. They are called the mortals because they are able to die [*sterben können*]. To die means, to be capable of death *as* death [*den Tod* als *Tod vermögen*]. Only the human dies and indeed continually, as long as he remains upon the earth, under the sky, before the divinities. (*GA* 7: 152/*PLT* 148, tm)

In what follows the issues raised in both of these depictions shall be addressed. First is the relationship between the mortal and the *animal rationale* whereby a mortal way of belonging to the world might begin to be articulated. We will then turn our attention to two ways in which these later depictions diverge from the analysis of death in *Being and Time,* first in regards to mortality understood as an "ability" to die, and second in regards to the presentation of death as the shrine of the nothing and the refuge of being. Having accomplished this we will briefly consider the relation between mortality and language. Finally we will return to the characterization of a mortal belonging to the world and cast this in terms of a mortal dwelling per the elaboration of "Building Dwelling Thinking."

By placing the mortals within the fourfold, Heidegger completes his relational constitution of the thing. Things are not objects apart from us qua subjects. We are not only addressed by them, we are integral to their very essencing as such. Without us there would be no things. But this should not be taken to mean that things are dependent upon us for their existence. We do not create these things. Instead, that we are integral to things means that no thing that exists relationally can do so without laying a claim upon us. To say that we are integral to things is simply to say once again that we do not exist apart from things. We do not create them, they claim us. The fourfold constructs a relational thing, it renders things relational. Relationality cannot be relationality without involving us as well.

§16. The Metaphysical Completion of the *Animal Rationale*

> Praise the quality in him which cannot be given or snatched away, that which is the peculiar property of the man. Do you ask what this is? It is soul, and reason brought to perfection in the soul. For man is a reasoning animal [*Rationale enim animal est*

homo]. Therefore, man's highest good is attained, if he has fulfilled the good for which nature designed him at birth.
—Seneca, *Epistle* XLI: 8

Seneca's letter to Lucilius, in keeping with the Stoic doctrines of his school, asserts the human to be the rational animal, a translation of the Greek *zôon logon echon*. Rational in possessing the eternal element of reason, the "peculiar property" constitutive of the human, and animal in being born into a role decided by nature. The highest good for the Stoics lay in bringing the freedom of reason into accord with nature through the wholehearted playing of one's role. In regard to the Greek definition, Heidegger writes in *Being and Time* that its subsequent interpretation "in the sense of *animal rationale*, 'rational living being,' is not 'false', but it covers over the phenomenal basis from which this definition of Dasein is taken" (*GA* 2: 219/*SZ* 165). This phenomenal basis is the openness of world, the world-forming of *Dasein*. Through the Stoic thought of an "accordance" between the rational animal and nature as a whole, the ground is laid for the modern, worldless subject's assimilation into its environs at metaphysics' end. Heidegger's critique in the decades following can thus take as its target the contemporary avatars of the *animal rationale*: the worker (Jünger), the angel (Rilke), and the overman (Nietzsche). In each of these cases, and in place of Stoic accordance, we find the ideal of a seamless merger between self and world. Such an ideal of total belonging, however, is simultaneously the end of the world in the eradication of the difference constitutive of it. And in each case, this disastrous belonging is tied to a transformation of animal life.

In the "Letter on Humanism" Heidegger understands the *animal rationale* to be nothing less than the progenitor of humanism as such. Roman humanism, and "every kind that has emerged from that time to the present," Heidegger adds, "has presupposed the most universal 'essence' of the human being to be obvious" (*GA* 9: 322/245). This presumption precludes any further thinking into the essence of the human so construed and falls back upon the traditional interpretation of the human as *zôon logon echon*, now understood in its Latin translation as *animal rationale*: "The human being is considered to be an *animal rationale*. This definition is not simply the Latin translation of the Greek *zôon logon echon*, but rather a metaphysical interpretation of it" (*GA* 9: 322/245–46). As a metaphysical interpretation, the conception of the human as *animal rationale* is unable to think the exteriority and exposure determinative of human existence (and in this letter Heidegger rethinks the ecstatic, a standing-*out*, as now a standing-*in*: "Such *standing in* the clearing of being I call the ek-sistence of human beings"; *GA* 9: 323–24/247, em).

Nevertheless, and as in *Being and Time*, Heidegger writes in the "Letter" that "this essential definition of the human being is not false. But it is conditioned by metaphysics" (*GA* 9: 322/246).

Now the definition of the human as *animal rationale* is not false in the sense that it would have nothing to do with the human at all. Rather, the fact that it has been the operative definition of the human for millennia is more than an accident of history. The human is defined by metaphysics, to be sure, but this relation to metaphysics is itself essential to existence. Heidegger's broad sketch of the human qua rational animal in "The Overcoming of Metaphysics" (1936–46) makes this explicit. Here we read that "metaphysics belongs to the nature of man" (*GA* 7: 71/*EP*87), a claim that Heidegger emends after a colon by "*animal* (sensuousness [*Sinnlichkeit*]) and *rationale* (non-sensuous [*Nicht-sinnliches*])" (*GA* 7: 71/*EP*87), a two-fold qualification with respect to both form (the genus/species classification) and content (the sensuous/nonsensuous opposition). The *animal rationale* thus roams through the territory staked out by Plato and Nietzsche, the co-termini of metaphysics, encountering all the snares of the opposition and all the pitfalls of the classification. So besieged, the human remains "arrested by the unexperienced difference [*Unterschied*] of beings and Being" native to this terrain (*GA* 7: 71/*EP*87). Why unexperienced? Because this determination of the human is actually a "definition" of humanity, logically formed as the specification (*rationale*) of the genus *animal*. The exteriority (or in-standing) of *humanitas* that Heidegger seeks is excluded from the outset when one begins by carving out portions of *animalitas*. From here one can only arrive at the human as a modified and outfitted animal, as a beast equipped with reason. Dasein's way of being each time mine is not captured in its difference to the present-at-hand. Even the opposition of sensuous/nonsensuous is a separation from within this sameness of presence-at-hand, but not a difference.

The culmination of this inheritance from the *animal rationale* is found in the collapse of the distinction between animal instinct and human reason: "Until now, 'instinct' was accepted as a characteristic of the animal which makes out and pursues what is useful and harmful to it in its sphere of life and strives for nothing beyond that" (*GA* 7: 93/*EP* 106, tm). This "now" is the end of metaphysics, where technology reigns over not a "world" but over what Heidegger repeatedly terms an "unworld" (*GA* 7: 91/*EP* 104, 94/107, 96/109) brought ever closer through technology, ever nearer to a single point of self-enclosure. This process of technification is not without a corresponding transformation in thought, as reason becomes a calculative reckoning after utility and securing before loss. The very animality of the rational animal itself is regarded so, becoming "thoroughly subjugated in each of its forms to calculation and planning (health plans, breeding)" (*GA* 7: 93/*EP* 106, tm). Utilitarian instinct active within the animal's sphere of life is more than analogous to the utility based technology shrinking the distance (and difference) of the world: "The drive of animality and the *ratio* of humanity become identical" (*GA* 7: 93/*EP* 106, tm). Insofar as reason distinguished the human from the instinctual animal, the human is no longer so distinguished.

The *animal rationale* is not a time-worn, antiquated, or out-moded notion. To be sure, Friedrich-Wilhelm von Herrmann finds it at the base of our understanding of imagination and poetry, of language and thinking, at the foundation of metaphysics, at the bottom of our onto-theological relationship to God, and at the root of biological racism, National Socialist or otherwise.[2] The *animal rationale* names a contemporary event, one locatable in the works of Jünger, Rilke, and Nietzsche.

a. The Worker (Jünger)

In Heidegger's 1934–40 notebooks on Jünger he declares Jünger's "fundamental position" to be that of "*homo—natura faber militans*. Ernst Jünger" and explicitly sees this as an outgrowth of the ancient determination of "*homo: animal rationale*" (*GA* 90: 43). Jünger's "naturalization" of the human, his determination of him as "worker," and his understanding of this as "militarized" all work toward an ideal of perfect belonging. This ideal motivates Jünger's key works of the 1930s, particularly *Der Arbeiter* (The Worker), "Die totale Mobilmachung" ("Total Mobilization") and "*Über den Schmerz*" ("On Pain"), where a two-fold transformation into what Jünger terms the *Gestalt* of the worker is set before the reader. Provisionally we could say that this transformation takes place in both the subject and object sphere alike, though if it does so, it does so only to the detriment of this distinction, in favor of total belonging.

From Jünger's perspective, the "objective" existence of the world is being shaped by the technological will toward its mobilization. "Mobilization" is here understood as a way of existence definable only in terms of use toward a greater goal, its mobility found in a continual circulation through economies of replacement. This "total mobilization" is "total" in at least two ways. It is not only the mobilization of the totality of everything, i.e., all particular entities, but the mobilization of everything in a totalized manner, i.e., toward no goal other than itself. The goal is thus useless, sovereign, aesthetic. The only goal that can satisfy this condition for Jünger is war, a totally mobilized war for its own sake, whereby victory and defeat are meaningless. By Jünger's reasoning, Germany lost the

World War I precisely on account of its failure to mobilize completely. Had it done so, the very idea of loss would have been nonsensical.[3]

As for the "subject," the worker is the one who corresponds to this world, indeed even drives for its completion. For Heidegger, it is in Jünger's "On Pain" that "the position of *Der Arbeiter* is driven furthest forward" (*GA* 9: 403/305, tm) because in this essay Jünger treats of the transformations necessary to bring about this new "type of life," the "third sex" of the worker.[4] What is required is a transformation of the animal dimension of existence. More specifically, the body is to be treated as an object and disciplined, regarded from the "command height" of the mind as an expendable "outpost" in battle.[5] Jünger points to the discipline and self-objectification of athletes, models, and soldiers as avatars of this worker. The key to the transformation is the achievement of a hardness that no longer feels any pain: "The transformation which completes itself in the individual we indicated in another place as the transformation of the individuum into the type or worker. Observed against the standard of pain, this transformation presents itself as an operation through which the zone of sensitivity [*Empfindsamkeit*] is cut out of life, and in this context it appears at first as an injury."[6] Heidegger notes of passages like these in Jünger's work that "Jünger opposes hardness and stoniness against 'sensitivity' [*Empfindsamkeit*] and thus remains, even if in the form of a reaction, on the whole 'sentimental.' The essence of 'sentimentality' does not rest in a muddle of feelings, but rather in that the feelings are regarded only as feelings, and that means as appearances of subjectivity, and as something 'lived' [*erlebt*]" (*GA* 90: 265).

The completed transformation of the worker, relieved of sensitivity in body, brings about an unprecedented "melting away of the difference between the organic and mechanical world."[7] The worker fits into the technologically transformed world around it. In fact, with no longer a difference between the human and its environs, "world" is no longer the appropriate term; Jünger's own designation of "workshop landscape" (*Werkstättelandschaft*) is by far the more fitting.[8] This new stoicism, wherein the worker is in accord with the new nature of technology, is projected as the new way of life, and the aesthetically justified spectacle of war is regarded as that life's creative force. Precisely this understanding of life as persisting beyond the difference between human and world culminates the *animalitas* of the *animal rationale*. It appears again in Rilke.

b. The Angel (Rilke)

Heidegger's contortive reading of Rilke is organized around a number of "basic words" that he locates in the poet's work. Pursuing four of these words here—nature, open, departure, and angel—will gain us access to Rilke's role in thinking the *animal rationale* in its metaphysical completion.

For Rilke, nature as a force is the ground of existence (the "volle Natur" of the *Sonnets to Orpheus*), and in the improvised verse that Heidegger chooses to interpret the force of this ground of existence is depicted as a risking, venturing, or wagering: "es wagt uns."[9] For Rilke, we are no dearer to this primal ground of existence than are plants or animals—all of these alike have been risked. In the poem, Rilke names this condition and the nature that so risks us "life" (line 9) and in so doing, according to Heidegger, he hearkens back to the ancient Greek determination of being as both *physis* and *zôê*.[10] Otherwise put, Rilke names the relation of beings to their being as that of the wagered to the wagering itself.

But to be wagered or ventured is not to be surrendered and forgotten—there would equally be no risk in that. What is wagered has neither been lost nor recuperated. The wagered is suspended between these options, momentarily poised between their collapse. To be ventured is to maintain an endangered relation, but one that holds everything together. Wagering is a connecting for Rilke, and the recurrent imagery of gravity, force, center, and sphere in his poetry attests to the importance of this. The whole of these relations, the unbounded space within and through which they occur, is what Rilke terms "the open." In a seemingly violent moment of the interpretation, Heidegger is careful to distinguish the sense of open in Rilke from his own use of the term. "If one attempted to interpret what Rilke has in mind as the open in the sense of unconcealment and what is unconcealed, one would have to say: what Rilke experiences as the open is precisely what is closed up, unlit, something that continues into a boundlessness such that it is incapable of encountering anything unusual, or indeed anything at all" (*GA* 5: 284/213, tm).[11]

Heidegger's use of the term "open" is intimately related to his notion of world as it is the world that is opened by Dasein; his charge that Rilke's open is truly the closed assumes its importance when thought in relation to world, for Rilke's open will be precisely the metaphysical equivalent of the non-world encountered in Jünger. Rilke in a letter to a reader: "You must understand the concept of the 'open,' which I have tried to propose in the elegy, in such a way that the animal's degree of consciousness sets it into the world without the animal's placing the world over against itself at every moment (as we do); the animal is in the world; we stand before it by virtue of that peculiar turn and intensification which our consciousness has taken."[12] The elegy to which Rilke refers is the eighth of his *Duino Elegies*, which has much to say about the place of humanity *before* the world:

> That is what fate means: to be opposite,
> to be opposite and nothing else, forever.
>
> . . . .
>
> And we: spectators, always, everywhere,
> turned toward the world of objects, never outward.[13]

This *gegenüberstehen* of the human is the posture of representation, *Vorstellung*, and in opposition to the animal "in" the world, this pose relegates the human to a constant "departure" from the world, another of Rilke's basic words. This departure likewise installs the human as a creature of will and technological process, which effects yet another additional layer of separation between human and the sheer belonging to world of the animal.

Humans actively further this alienation through technology. In these pages, Heidegger presents a particularly Rilkean view of technology (we have quoted from this before) characterized in terms of a "calculating production," one that still operates representationally:

> This representing knows nothing of the intuitable. What is intuited in the look of things, the image [*Bild*] they offer to direct sensible intuition, falls away. The calculating production of technology is an "action without image" (*Ninth Elegy*). Facing the intuitable image [*Bild*], deliberate self-assertion [i.e., the will allied with technology], in its projects, places a scheme based only on calculated constructions [*Gebilde*]. When the world enters into the objectiveness of contrived constructions, it is placed in the insensible [*Unsinnliche*], the invisible. (*GA* 5: 305/228–29, tm)

Technology here caters to the modern subject in transforming the externality of the sensible world into an invisible, non-sensible, internal possession. Heidegger adds that for Rilke, "the sphere of the objectivity of objects remains within consciousness" (*GA* 5: 305/229).

Heidegger follows Rilke in understanding this contemporary human, alienated from the world, to be a businessman, a salesman, a *Kaufmann*. The transformation that Rilke proposes in a late poetic fragment is one whereby "the risk passes over / from the salesman's hand to the angel," with "angel" as another basic word of Rilke's.[14] This is a move that Heidegger understands as "the reversal of departure" (*GA* 5: 315/236, tm). It is likewise a move that effects a modification of the sensible, for "in accordance with its [the angel's] bodily nature, it has transformed the possible confusion of the visibly sensible into the invisible" (*GA* 5: 313/235, tm). The angel effects a reversal of the separation that removed the human from the world, thus providing a consummated reintegration with the world. The angel thus evinces "an essence that is already secure in beings as a whole" (*GA* 5: 312/234, tm), a situation of renewed animal belonging. Heidegger postpones an explanation of how "within the completion of modern metaphysics, there belongs to the being of beings a relation to such a being [as the angel]" (*GA* 5: 312/234, tm), but the answer is clear from within the present context: subjectivity has been thought from out of *animalitas* and as a modification of it. Just as Heidegger's notion of finitude cannot be grasped as derived from an infinite, so too is the human not to be derived from the animal. Because metaphysics begins so, it requires such an "infinite" figure. For Rilke, the angel stands as a moment of reintegration with the open, but for this it must pay the price of the world.

c. The *Übermensch* (Nietzsche)

Certainly much of Heidegger's concern regarding Jünger and Rilke was proposed to him by his confrontation with Nietzsche, the philosophical basis of the two. Supporting their thought of worker and angel is the Nietzschean figure of the *Übermensch*, the one who overcomes a bygone humanity and is the new master of the earth.[15]

In Nietzsche one finds a compelling nexus of being, life, and will to power. Life, like will to power, is that which seeks to go beyond itself, and the values that the will to power posits stand in the service of life. As Zarathustra succinctly states, "where I found the living, there I found will to power."[16] This life of will to power is all there is. The same equation of life with being that is found in Rilke is also found in Nietzsche: "Being—we have no idea of it apart from the idea of 'living.'—How can anything dead 'be'?"[17] Will to power names life, and life names being. Thus Nietzsche can claim in all boldness, "*this world is the will to power—and nothing besides!*"[18] What is is alive and what lives is will to power.

Heidegger finds this three part equation of life, being, and will to power to be "the sole question; *the* question" in regards to Nietzsche (*GA* 47: 85). The question in the equation of life, will to power, and being is nothing other than the question of animality. What is at stake is the status of a life that would exceed or evade any mere biologism. Such a life would have to depart from the metaphysical opposition of the sensible/ super-sensible, would have to break with the Platonic division of these realms. The question of life is thus at the same time the question of Nietzsche's Platonism, whether to be read as a simple *Umdrehung* (inversion) or as subtle *Herausdrehung* (twisting-free).[19] It is a question, in short, of whether Nietzsche is capable of thinking life beyond metaphysics, the question that will decide whether we can attribute a new understanding of the body, a "new sensuousness," to Nietzsche (*GA* 6.1: 213–24/ *N1*: 211–20).

Zarathustra, attended by animals of his own and preaching loyalty to the earth, is a central site for the posing of this question. Zarathustra teaches the *Übermensch* and this figure proffers a negation of the essence of humanity as it has been understood hitherto, i.e., as *animal rationale*.[20] But according to Heidegger, the *Übermensch* "negates it nihilistically," which is to say metaphysically (*GA* 6.2: 264/ *N3*: 217), and this in two ways: 1) The negation in question is simply directed at the traditional human privilege of rationality and the ascetic virtue system of which it is part. The life-denying, rational, ethical, Christian subject, the *"sublime miscarriage,"*[21] is to be replaced by the life-affirming *Übermensch*, the former's sterile reasoning replaced by a reckoning, calculating, and evaluating in the service of life. 2) The nihilistic negation is not a transformation of the opposition animal/rational, but merely the collapse of it. The negation does not do away with thought, but "takes it back into the service of animality (*animalitas*)" (*GA* 6.2: 264/ *N3*: 218, tm).

With this, animality, too, is changed and no longer the "mere sensuality [*Sinnlichkeit*]" (*GA* 6.2: 264/ *N3*: 218) opposed to reason, but rather what Heidegger will term "body" (*Leib*): "The name *body* identifies the distinctive unity in the constructs of domination in all drives, urges, and passions that will life itself" (*GA* 6.2: 264/ *N3*: 218).[22] The *Übermensch* occupies this body, rejecting anything outside of itself other than will to power (the empowering for overpowering), and (in an insidious return of the worldless *cogito*) attempting to decide its own essence purely from out of itself alone (see *GA* 6.2: 272/ *N3*: 226; *GA* 6.2: 235/ *N3*: 191). As Heidegger explains, "the *Übermensch* lives because the new humanity wills the being of beings as will to power. It wills such being because it is itself willed by that being, i.e., as humanity unconditionally left to itself" (*GA* 6.2: 273/ *N3*: 227, tm).[23] In this light, when Zarathustra rises and asks, "verily, do I still live?,"[24] Heidegger can sharpen this question to "does my will correspond to the will which, as will to power, pervades the whole of beings?" (*GA* 7: 104/ *N2*: 214, tm).

The *Übermensch* is stitched into the fabric of reality as will to power expands and preserves its power technologically. Technology shelters everything in the security of the standing reserve (*Bestand*), while constantly expanding its scope across the earth. The *Übermensch* as correspondent figure to the world from which being has withdrawn is thereby the new master of the earth (though, as we have seen, "desert" would be the more appropriate term here).[25] But in reigning over the abandonment of being and driving this process forward, the *Übermensch* likewise preserves and safeguards the trace of abandonment, keeping it from slipping into annihilation: "The truth of beings as such and as a whole is defined by will to power and eternal recurrence of the same. That truth is safeguarded [*verwahrt*] by the overman" (*GA* 6.2: 282/*N3*: 234). Heidegger's Nietzsche hinges on this single fold.

Our uniting of Nietzsche, Rilke, and Jünger as inheritors of the *animal rationale* was nothing arbitrary. Heidegger himself notes that Rilke's Angel "despite all difference in content, is *metaphysically the same* as the figure of Nietzsche's Zarathustra" (*GA* 5: 312/234, tm), and we are in a position to immediately add to this equivalence the figure of Jünger's worker, who assumes the form or *Gestalt* of hardness so as to seamlessly belong. Heidegger's notebooks at the time likewise unite these figures as well. From the Jünger notebooks (of whom Heidegger also writes, "Ernst Jünger is the sole genuine heir to Nietzsche"; *GA* 90: 227) we read: "'*Gestalt*'— Zarathustra / Angel" (*GA* 90: 293) and from the 1938–39 notebook *Die Überwindung der Metaphysik* (The Overcoming of Metaphysics):

> Contemporary positions within the completed metaphysics, without being more of a match for the essence of this:
> 1. the political "world-view." "World-view" as rubbish; the will to power vulgarly as "vitality" and "biological."
> 2. the adventurer in the elementary and the return into the indestructible (E. Jünger).
> 3. the transformation into the "inner" (interior of the world) and the recognition of the "earth" (R. M. Rilke). (*GA* 67: 113–14)

The metaphysical completion of the thought of the *animal rationale* has shown itself at work in Rilke, Jünger, and Nietzsche. The original difference that this determination posits is collapsed but not thought. The collapse occurs in the merger of a complete subject with the world. The figure of the animal stands for native belonging to the world—or rather to the "workshop landscape" or to the "Open" or to the "*will to power— and nothing besides!*"—to these identical unworlds of the desert. Beginning from *animalitas* in order to think humanity only yields a human ready to be disciplined, taught, bred, or educated into its *new* animalistic role of completed subjectivity, the inheritance of *paideia*. Coextensive with this ultimate transformation of the *animal rationale* is a reconstrual of the relation between the elements *animal* and *rationale*, now grasped as the sensible (*das Sinnliche*) and the technological, whether this reconstruction take the form of an excision of the sensible for assimilation to the technological (Jünger), the obstruction of the sensible by the technological (Rilke), or the transformation of the sensible in the mastery of the technological (Nietzsche).

But completion is nothing so unequivocal, completion not as mere switch of emphasis, body now over spirit, but as the more seductive release felt from the collapse of a distinction irritating and solicitous all along. Removing the binarisms of traditional thought, "overcoming" them in short, is not to be mistaken for thinking through the belonging together in difference of being and the human. Metaphysical completion is purely negative, though *in the guise* of a new positivity . . . nihilistic negation. And this is the danger in all "twisting free" (*Herausdrehung*). If twisting free is the three-fold "[1] twisting free of the Platonic opposition [2] into a disclosedness [3] beyond Being as presence,"[26] then the middle term is the most ambiguous, the moment of "twisting free into *alêtheia*, into disclosedness (*Erschlossenheit*)."[27] For here, rather than twist free, one may instead become wrapped up and strangled, suffocated in an unworld of total immanence. Strange, however, that here the Platonic opposition is in some sense gotten free of as well; strange, too, that being here is no longer presence, but standing reserve (*Bestand*), and strangest of all, that this closed off world is never so hermetic as when its openness is preserved as trace.

For their part, the mortals will always evade this seamless integration of a subject with environment. To be mortal is to "belong" to the world without "being" the world, we might provisionally say. Belonging is a relation of difference, one that the mortal accedes to through its ability to die.

§17. The Ability, the Capacity, to Die

Heidegger's discussion of the mortals within the fourfold emphasizes their "ability" or "capacity" to die. And while *Being and Time* presents Dasein as an "ability" or "potentiality of being" (*seinkönnen*), there is no explicit mention of an "ability" to die.[28] Even if there were, around the time of the fourfold Heidegger undertakes a major rethinking of ability and capacity (*Vermögen*) in ways directly informing his conception of the mortals. The consequence is that where *Being and Time* emphasizes a "being-towards-death," the later thought can be construed as proffering a "being-in-death" as the source of our ability to die.

a. Being-toward-Death

"Death is nothing to us," or so had Epicurus claimed in his letter to Menoeceus.[29] And with this claim, Epicurus broke with the idea that death was something we could experience at all, "since when we exist, death is not yet present, and when death is present, then we do not exist."[30] Epicurus thus effectively negates the idea that death is something we might positively experience or possess. Instead, and this is the only alternative for Epicurus, it is nothing to us. Death is not something, but nothing. Here, the oppositional logic that dictates the choice of terms is in full display. More than two millennia later, Heidegger takes up the motivation of the thought that death would not be a possession, but instead of embracing the contrary, Heidegger instead allows death to disrupt this oppositional structure itself. Death will thus be neither something we have nor do not have, for it is neither something nor nothing. Instead, death is that to which we are "toward."

As Françoise Dastur points out, Heidegger's notion of *Sein zum Tode* "is usually translated 'being for death' or 'being towards death', but what it signifies is simply a being in relation to death."[31] This relation is distinct from other relations, however, as it is the very opening of relationality as such. Heidegger writes that, "when Dasein exists, it is already *thrown* into this possibility [of death]" insofar as existence itself is always defined by this possibility (*GA* 2: 333/*SZ* 251). Death is both what is most my own, that which no one else can "take" from me or "do" for me, and that which I may never possess (when it is present, I am gone). What is most my own is thus not a possession, but instead something "outside" of me—or rather, it is not "something" at all, but instead a relation to what lies beyond me. When what is most my own is nothing I possess, then a relation is named between myself and a death beyond my sphere of control or possession, a relation, in short, between death and world, as Heidegger explains: "Initially and for the most part, Dasein does not have any explicit or even theoretical knowledge of the fact that it is delivered over to its death, *and that death thus belongs to being-in-the-world*" (*GA* 2: 333–34/*SZ* 251, em). Death belongs to being-in-the-world and is likewise what is most our own. Death inclines us into the world, slants us "toward" the world. Being-toward-death is being-in/toward-the-world.

Heidegger names this being-toward-death "dying" (*sterben*) and the whole famed first chapter of division two of *Being and Time* could be said to revolve about thinking what has passed for the "presence" of death as the "nearness" of death in dying. The metaphysical thought of a pure presence, and with it a pure absence, is disrupted by death. Death is no pure presence in Dasein, the presence of which entails a pure absence of being. Rather, "as the end of Dasein, *death is* in the being of this being *toward* its end" (*GA* 2: 343/*SZ* 259). What has passed for being (that which "is") is really the "toward." What is is toward. Dying names a way of being in which Dasein is toward its death (*GA* 2: 328–29/*SZ* 247). A marginal note to Heidegger's copy of *Being and Time* reiterates the point: "The relation of Dasein to death; death itself = its arrival—entrance, dying" (*GA* 2: 319 n. a/*SZ* 240 fn.). Death is in an arriving that will never have done with it. The point hearkens back to Epicurus: there is no death beyond the dying. Thinking death in terms of this "toward" means re-thinking the very "possibility" of death, and breaking with the idea that it would be something that has "not yet" occurred or would even be some-thing in the least realizable.

Nevertheless, a "not yet" is said to belong to Dasein insofar as it exists as a potentiality of being (*GA* 2: 310/*SZ* 233). Dasein is not yet dead. Yet this not yet is nothing lacking from or outstanding to Dasein. It can-not be thought of like the last quarter of a three-quarter's full moon, for example. The not yet of this quarter moon is a problem of our percep-tion, not of its being; that outstanding quarter of the moon is really there. The situation is otherwise with Dasein. The not-yet in this case "'is' not yet 'real' [*wirklich*] at all" (*GA* 2: 324/*SZ* 243). The quotation marks tell the story here. Our not yet cannot be said to "be" anything, when being is only thought of as "reality." The not-yet is not real in a reality that has been thought as actuality. And insofar as actuality is taken to be a realm of *activity* (specifically of causal activity) that likewise includes in its func-tioning its counter-concept of *passivity*, the death of Dasein will not be ascertainable in terms of a passivity either. We can see this in Heidegger's remarks on "suffering." It is those who remain behind the dead person who suffer the loss of the death. The dying person does not suffer, i.e., does not *passively* undergo, any loss of being, and this is so much the case that Heidegger must again resort to quotation marks when discussing our presumed access to this loss, "the loss of being as such, which the dying person 'suffers,' does not become accessible" (*GA* 2: 318/*SZ* 239). Neither an activity nor a passivity, the not yet of Dasein names our way of being, neither active agent nor passive recipient of the world, but rather an inclination "toward" it. This is being-toward-death.

Consequently, the temptation must be resisted of thinking being-toward-death as a way of being that is running toward death or has death as its goal. And even when Heidegger expressly speaks of a *Vorlaufen*, literally a "running ahead," to death (less literally, an "anticipation" of death), this should not be construed as an advance upon a goal. There is no end to the death we run to. We can neither escape it nor catch it. It is just this "endlessness" that calls for a rethinking of "end." Death is not an "end" that we might reach in running ahead like this. The sense of "end" here has changed. The not-yet of Dasein names a relation to an end, to a limit, "just as Dasein constantly already *is* its not-yet as long as it is, it also always already *is* its end" (*GA* 2: 326/*SZ* 245). We should then hesitate before proclaiming Dasein to be *at* its end, where this end would be conceived of as an unyielding wall into which Dasein crashes back upon itself. Rather, Dasein is "at" its end only insofar as it is "towards" its end: "The 'ending' which we have in view when we speak of death, does not signify a being-at-an-end [*Zu-Ende-sein*] of Dasein, but rather a being-toward-the-end [*Sein zum Ende*] of this being" (*GA* 2: 326/*SZ* 245). Indeed, there is no other way for Dasein to be in a relation to its end and still be understood as existing. If Dasein did not construe ends in this way, it would actually be dead. Dasein can never be at its end, but can only be exposed to that end. Otherwise put, the only "end" of Dasein is found "at" its exposure. In being-toward-death being is everywhere exposed to death ("toward" as "exposed").

It is common to think this death as a possibility for existence. To be sure, Heidegger names death "the sheer impossibility of existence" (*GA* 2: 339/*SZ* 255, tm), i.e., "the possibility of sheer impossibility-of-Dasein" (*GA* 2: 333/*SZ* 250, tm). But possibility itself is commonly taken to be directed at—if not always arriving at—actuality, and this thought must be derailed. It is the they that is always out to actualize its possibilities, to get them at its disposal, to have them present-at-hand. But this possibility of death is an impossibility—it is useless and cannot be directed toward any goal. With italics of his own, Heidegger can claim "*As a possibility, the nearest nearness of being towards death is as far as possible from an actuality*" (*GA* 2: 348/*SZ* 262). This possibility of impossibility is *extremely* far from actuality. It itself is the *most extreme* (*äußerste*) possibility. It is so extreme, in fact, that it cannot be actualized: "As possibility, death gives Dasein nothing to 'be actualized' [*Verwirklichendes*] and nothing which it itself could *be* as something actual [*als Wirkliches*]" (*GA* 2: 348/*SZ* 262, tm). We have seen above that death escapes the distinction of active and passive, traits we identified with the "reality" of the real. Without this tether in "actuality" death seems to likewise elude the distinction of the actual and the possible. For really, what sense does it make to speak of possibility when this has been severed from actuality, when the possibility itself is an impossibility?

It is the they who claims that death *is possible* for anyone at any moment, and to think that one has countered this strategy of willed ignorance by pointing out that death *is possible* for me and *is possible* now at this very moment, is to simply reinstate the weak sense of possibility to which they cling. That death is possible at any moment could not be further from the truth—death is present at every moment, though present in a mode of presence that is not-yet present. Thus one could hazard the shocking claim that there is no death, or, even more perversely, that I am as dead as I will ever be, in order to name this Valdemarian presence.[32]

A most extreme possibility which is itself an impossible possibility and not to be actualized—a strange "possibility" indeed. It keeps Dasein from ever merging completely with reality (actuality).[33] It keeps it ever "towards" the world, towards its death, and towards the end, the three terms now synonymous.

b. Being-in-Death

In the considered view of Werner Marx the relation to death in Heidegger's thinking of the mortals is the "inverse" of that in *Being and Time:*

> Already in *Being and Time,* death accrued to Dasein as one of its "possibilities." We recalled that Dasein, as potentiality-for-Being, could anticipate death as an insurpassable possibility. In so doing, Dasein could "conclude" this potentiality as a whole. Now man's relationship to death is thought of "inversely," as that of death to man. Humans "are" or "have their essence" *in* death as the "gathering sheltering," the "refuge" [*Ge-birge*]. They no longer stand over against death so as to be able to anticipate it as that which comes toward them, but rather they find their place *in* it.[34]

The "inversion" that Marx diagnoses is a shift from a running ahead toward death to a joining oneself into death, from an anticipation to a kind of nestling or finding of one's place, from a "toward" to an "in." Dastur echoes Marx in her determination of this shift in Heidegger's views: "If in *Being and Time* authenticity is defined in a still quite Hegelian way as *Dasein's* capacity to stand and face the gaze of death, in later writings, when 'mortal' becomes the proper name of man, it is a question of man's gaining access to and entering death."[35] Dastur, too, speaks of an entering into death. In both cases, then, it is a shift from "being-toward-death" to what we might call "being-in-death" and for Heidegger this shift is made possible by his new designation of death as a *Vermögen* of the mortals, an "ability" for, a "capacity" for, or even an "enabling" of death.

In a claim he is wont to repeat, Heidegger writes: "The mortals are the humans. They are named the mortals, because they are able to die [*sterben können*]. Dying means, to be capable of [or: to enable] death as death [*den Tod als Tod vermögen*]" (*GA* 79: 17/17).[36] But we should not rush to understand this capacity as leading to a certain performance or achievement. We cannot understand it in the everyday sense of a potential that accomplishes itself in actualizing a change. The capacity of the mortals is not oriented towards realization, in other words. Realization presumes a fully formed field of reality wherein all realization will take place and the occupants of this field, the *realia*, are understood as real, i.e., discrete and self-contained. Instead, with the shift to being-in-death put in play by this mortal capacity, death becomes *the medium of mortality*.

Rather than a matter of realization, capacity is inextricably bound up with being in an element. Death is the element of mortal existence and mortals are capable of entering it. The 1946 "Letter on 'Humanism'" expounds the interrelation of capacity and element in its opening discussion of thinking, where we are told that to judge thinking in terms of logic would be "equivalent to a procedure which attempts to evaluate the essence and ability [*Vermögen*] of a fish in terms of the extent to which it is able to live on dry land" (*GA* 9: 315/240, tm). Doubtless, the ability of the fish is best evaluated in the water, its element, and the same holds for thinking: "the element is that from out of which thinking is capable [*vermag*] of being a thinking" (*GA* 9: 316/241, tm).[37] Capacity or ability is always tied to its element or medium. In fact, Heidegger goes a step further, seeming to identify them: "The element is what properly enables: it is the enabling [*das Vermögende: das Vermögen*]. It embraces [*sich annehmen*] thinking and so brings it into its essence" (*GA* 9: 316/241). The element "embraces" what is within it. This *sich annehmen* is an embracing, but not in an indifferent manner. It is an embracing only insofar as it is a tending to . . . and a taking upon oneself of something. The verb *annehmen*, without the reflexive, simply means to accept, to adopt, to assume. In reflexive formulations, however, this "taking" acquires the sense of a seeing to, looking after, or tending to. It can be literally heard as a taking upon oneself, a taking into account, and even, without too great a stretch, a taking responsibility for. The element takes responsibility for what is within it, takes it up, takes it up into itself, takes into account what is essential for it, and in so doing enables it.

Death would thus be the element within which the mortal essences.[38] The relation between the element and what it enables, between death and mortals, is not one of indifference. Insofar as the capacity (*Vermögen*) is a "tending to," it can be understood in terms of a liking or affiliation (*Mögen*): "To tend to a 'matter' or a 'person' in its essence [to take this upon oneself, to take responsibility for this], this means: to love them: to like them [*sie mögen*; to affiliate with them]. Thought more originarily, this affiliation [*Mögen*] means: to make a gift of essence [*das Wesen schenken*]" (*GA* 9: 316/241, tm).[39] The element loves what it enables. Death loves the mortals. In "The Danger," Heidegger uses precisely this language to describe our relation to death: "To die, however, means to carry out death in its essence. To be able to die means to be capable of carrying this out. We are only capable of it, however, when our essence is endeared to the essence of death" (*GA* 79: 56/53). The element and what it enables are affiliated and endeared to each other at an essential level. The element "tends to" what it enables and "brings it into" or "makes a gift of" its essence. The element surrounds what it enables—like water around a fish, death around the mortal—and thus allows it its essence, which means that it allows it the room to expand itself, to go beyond itself, to relate to what lies around it. Death allows there to be something around the mortal, something through which it can stream. Streaming through the element, the thing is "enabled" to be what it is, it is allowed "to essence." What is enabled is thus a relationship.

The medium cannot be indifferent to the thing, but must allow it passage, not simply allow it, but even encourage it. This is why enabling is an affiliating, where "such affiliating is the authentic essence of capacity [*Vermögens*], which not only performs this or that, but rather can let something 'essence'—which means 'be'—in its place of origin [*Her-kunft*]. It is the capacity of affiliating [*Das Vermögen des Mögens*] by 'force' of which something actually is able [*vermag*] to be" (*GA* 9: 316/241–42, tm). The mortal is allowed to be in its origin, literally the place where it "comes from." The mortal comes from death insofar as only in relating past itself is the mortal the mortal. This is simply another way for Heidegger to say that the limit is where something begins (something "coming" here). It begins from its relations beyond itself, it begins in its origin. And the mortal can only do so through death. Its "origin" is precisely the medium around it through which it is allowed to be what it is. Death allows for mortality.

When Heidegger designates the mortals as the ones who are capable of death, he names death as the element in which they thrive, or die, for there is no difference. Death is the element of mortality, that through which the mortals move. Death is nothing we harbor within us, rather, we are soaking in it. Death is not even some possibility off beyond us or one that we opportunely face at moments of authenticity. Instead, the truth of death is that it is everywhere around us. Thus, in another repeated claim, "only the human dies, and, to be sure, continually" (*GA* 7: 152/*PLT* 150; cf. *GA* 7: 200/*PLT* 222), for we are continually within our element. We are in it. We live amidst death. We asphyxiate without it, like fish on dry land. Death is nothing apart from us, it is our best and closest friend. More than this, we are related, affiliated, and endeared to each other (it introduces us to all its other friends, we might say). We need not go looking for death, since as our element, it is everywhere around us. To seek for signs of death, one need look no further than the world around us. The world is death. This world is our death. We die always *in* the world and *of* the world. Death is nothing we harbor within us; instead, it shelters us, enabling us to be what we may be. Death enables us, where "to enable something [*etwas vermögen*] here means: to guard it in its essence, to retain [*einbehalten*] it in its element" (*GA* 9: 317/242, tm). We need no longer guard against death, for death itself stands guard for us.

Since it is this death that lets us be what we may be, mortal death can still be construed in terms of "possibility," but now thought in conjunction with capability and affiliation. As he explains, "this capability [*Vermögen*] is the genuine 'possible' ['*Mögliche*'], that whose essence rests in affiliating [*Mögen*]" (*GA* 9: 316/242, tm). The possible is nothing beyond us that awaits realization, it is a possible relationship that has already taken hold of us; i.e., it is already supporting us in the world, in the midst of death.[40] Possibility is another way of affiliating us with death, endearing us to it and it to us. Possibility is the *danse macabre* of mortal existence. And to be sure, Heidegger is careful to keep at bay the thought of possibility as something to be actualized: "Admittedly, under the dominance of 'logic' and 'metaphysics,' our words 'possible' and 'possibility' are only thought in distinction from 'actuality,' which means in terms of a determinate—metaphysical—interpretation of being as *actus* and *potentia*, a distinction which is identified with that of *existentia* and *essentia*" (*GA* 9: 316–17/242, tm).

Mortality is our affiliation to, even love of, the element of death. But as every lover knows, liking, loving, and affiliating are worlds apart from sheer identification (more precisely, they are "the" world away from such seamless belonging, as we have noted). Thus to be "in" our element means being opened up to that "inning" (to contort a term to our purposes) without entirely occupying it. As a relationship, we must relate to it and belong to it, and not in some collapsed belonging or complete merger. To draw the drastic consequences of this, this means that we cannot simply "be" the mortals, if to be mortal is to be "in" death. Instead, we have to both be and not be the mortals. Mortality is the condition of mediation and as such it entails that we be "not yet" the mortals, otherwise we could not be *in* anything at all, much less death. To be in a medium is to be always arriving, otherwise one would be trapped in a container, a marble in a sack. Thus Heidegger will at times claim that "the mortals are the humans" (*GA* 7: 180/*PLT* 176, tm; *GA* 7: 152/*PLT* 148, tm), or that "the human essences as the mortal" (*GA* 7: 200/*PLT* 219, tm), but such claims only serve to emphasize that "the rational animals [i.e., the humans] must first *become* the mortals" (*GA* 7: 180/*PLT* 176) or, in short, that "the human is *not yet* the mortal" (*GA* 79: 56/54, em).[41]

What is at issue in the talk of the mortals, what is at issue in the talk of enablement, is, simply put, a reconception of existence. The "becoming" mentioned in "The Thing," where we "must first *become* the mortals," is not to be understood as indicating a movement from one state into another. Rather this "movement" of becoming is no movement at all—it is instead a way of being, a being "not yet" mortal and "no longer" human, a way of being the between (*das Zwischen*). In this sense, no one dies in the sense of *sterben*, for no one is among the mortals. But this is again to deny the not-yet its full force. The only "presence" of the mortal, the only "achievement" of mortality that is possible is that of not-yet being the mortal. Consequently, in regard to the grizzly, oft-quoted passages from "The Danger," the internees of the camps and those starving from the blockades do not *die* in the camps or in China, *and we do not either*. We are all not yet the mortals. And this is not because the National Socialists somehow stripped us of our proper death (to say this would be to say that one could take another's death from them, a statement that would make death utterly exchangeable, that would likewise allow one to die in place of another). Rather, this is our way of being, we "are" not-yet in the midst of death.

Both *Being and Time* and the thought of the mortals agree in finding a non-metaphysical aspect of presence within the notion of dying. And yet their disagreement is at where they appear most similar, in the conception of the not-yet. What enablement comes to indicate in the thought of the mortals is a belonging in non-belonging as well as the impossibility of any "complete" belonging beyond non-belonging. Enablement means that humans are not-yet the mortals and can never *be* the mortals. Dasein, for its part in *Being and Time*, can be its not-yet, can be authentically. Not-yet and not-yet are not the same.

§18. The Shrine of the Nothing, the Refuge of Being

Surely the most evident change between the death of *Being and Time* and that being died by the mortals rests in Heidegger's strange designations of death as the "shrine of the nothing" and the "refuge of being" (*GA* 79: 18/17). Thoughts such as these are nowhere to be found in the earlier work. Death is no longer restricted to the concerns of a particular being's being. Death is ontologically promoted into an interest of being and nothingness alike.

a. The Shrine of the Nothing

Etymologically, the German "*Schrein*" is similar to the English word "shrine," naming a box or coffer that would typically contain the relics of a saint, as with a reliquary chest.[42] "Shrine" also names a case for a dead body, i.e., a coffin or even a tomb. The corpse within such a coffin is not available for the viewing. And the relic, too (often simply the body part of an extraordinary corpse), is likewise hidden within its case, for even when encased in glass the *power* of this reliquated finger or tooth is encased somewhere still further within, inaccessible to sight.

In Phillipe Ariès's history of death in the west, *The Hour of Our Death* (*L'Homme devant la mort*), he writes of the practice of concealing the body after death, emphasizing the power of what is so concealed: "the dead body, formerly a familiar object and an image of repose, came to possess such power that the sight of it became unbearable. Now [the 13th century], and for centuries to come, it was removed from view, hidden in a box, under a monument, where it was no longer visible."[43] For him this move to concealment is a "major cultural event" and a "major development in the rituals of death."[44] By concealing the unbearable body, an attempt is made to paradoxically ward off the death that had already befallen the person. In Ariès' words, "the refusal to see the corpse was not a denial of physical individuality but a denial of physical death."[45] Understood in a Heideggerian manner, the "denial" of death that Ariès sees is a denial of the death that would be unqualifiedly opposed to life. Concomitant with this "denial" is a preservation as well, and thus a break with the very opposition of life and death, even of being and nothing. Sallis notes this in commenting on Heidegger's invocation of the shrine: "A shrine is also, especially as the German *Schrein*, a case or casket in which, most notably, the dead one would be enclosed, sealed off, and in a sense preserved as one who would *be dead*, who would—if it were only possible—both be and not be, producing a coincidence of being and nothing."[46] The point of the coffin is not to secrete away the body, or, rather, this was not the point of what the coffin arose from, not the point of the *Totenbaum* or "tree of death" that Heidegger envisions as part of a peasant household.

Burial in hollowed trees dates back to the Bronze Age. The use of "treetrunk coffins" or death-trees, *Totenbäume*, was a practice continued through the middle ages.[47] Peasant life as construed by Heidegger places the "death-tree" within the house. Far from trying to hide the body, the death-tree was incorporated into the design of the home, as Heidegger describes in "Building Dwelling Thinking" (1951) where the construction of the peasant home or farm house "does not forget the altar corner [*Herrgottswinkel*] behind the community table; it made room in its chamber for the hallowed places of childbed and the tree of the dead [*Totenbaum*], for that is what they call a coffin [*Sarg*] there, and in this way it sketched for the different generations under one roof the character of their journey through time" (*GA* 7: 162/*PLT* 158, tm).[48] The tree of death lets the dead one be part of our lives. It is a matter of bringing the departed into the home. To do so is to introduce the dead into a new grouping of relations as well as a new topographic arrangement involving the house and the neighborhood. Commenting on changes in coffin production, Heidegger states:

> The carpenter in the village does not complete a box for a corpse. The coffin is from the outset placed in a privileged spot of the farmhouse where the dead peasant still lingers. There, a coffin [*Sarg*] is still called a death-tree [*Totenbaum*]. The death of the deceased flourishes in it. This flourishing determines the house and farmstead, the ones who dwell there, their kin, and the neighborhood.
>
> Everything is otherwise in the motorized burial industry of the big city. Here no death-trees are produced. (*GA* 79: 26/25)

The death tree is already in the house before the dead peasant has died. The peasant's death grows in the death tree. It flourishes in it, Heidegger says. Taking up themes from our floristic consideration of the earth, we might expect that this death comes to ripeness and fruition with the entry of the peasant into the tree. The privileged spot is the place for the growth of death. Death grows for the peasant, but it also spreads itself out, pervading the home, a constant reminder of "life's journey," and also extending beyond it into the community (where it is noticed, where it obliges, where the rites of mourning socialize the death).

When Heidegger speaks at a homeland festival in Todtnauberg in 1966, he recalls the building of his hut by the recently deceased Pius Schweitzer (who planned and built it) and the joiner (*Schriner* or *Schreiner*) Oswald Kaiser: "The other master [alongside Pius Schweitzer] who worked on the construction of the hut was the joiner Oswald Kaiser. The front window in the hut built by him still fits today down to the millimeter after nearly 45 years" (*GA* 16: 643).[49] The *Schreiner* does more than build houses, however, "the joiner was a well-meaning, quiet man. For many Todtnaubergians, he made the 'death-tree,' that is, the coffin [*Sarg*]" (*GA* 16: 643). The death tree is made by a *Schreiner*, a joiner, one who builds

Schreine. If death is the shrine of the nothing, then it is the death-tree of the nothing as well, for this is the shrine par excellence.

What then is the work of a shrine? The 1949 lecture version of "The Thing" introduces the idea after proclaiming that the mortals are those who are able to die. "Death is the shrine of the nothing," Heidegger writes, "namely of that which in all respects is never some mere being, but nonetheless essences, namely as being itself. Death, as the shrine of nothing, harbors in itself what essences of being [*das Wesende des Seins*]" (*GA* 79: 18/17). The nothing in question, the nothing enshrined by death, is no particular being, and this is something that it shares with being as such. Death is the shrine of no particular being, but nonetheless there is something that essences there. The nothing of the shrine is not a being, but it nonetheless essences. For the same reason, the enshrined nothing is likewise no simple negation of beings, i.e., is not unqualifiedly nothing. This "nothing" nevertheless essences in the shrine. It is that which is essencing, *das Wesende,* of being, *des Seins.* This essencing is thus a convergence of being and nothing. Death is the shrine of this. Death enshrines the essencing of what is "between" being and nothing. In enshrining this, death "harbors in itself" (*birgt in sich*) this essencing and protects it.

The shrine thus performs a preservative function. It keeps the dead one from dying, or, more appropriately, it keeps the dying one from their death. There is neither pure negation nor annihilation here thanks to the shrine. What is enshrined is not nothing, though this is indeed the shrine of the nothing. It is maintained in a state "between" being and nothing. What is enshrined is not dead and the shrine does not spirit the body away. Instead it grants it a pervasive presence in the home and environs. Visiting the shrine, commemorating the departed, thinking on him or her, all of this keeps the dead in our hearts and thoughts, as we say. In so doing the dead one has not passed away, but remains with us, preserved.[50] Enshrinement is the adoption of a relational existence that all-pervasive death makes possible.

Death is the shrine of the nothing, but of a nothing that nonetheless essences. But what is it that is within the shrine? What does death protect and preserve? Nothing less than the mortals themselves. It is the mortals who are being-in-death, they are the ones enshrined by death and able to enter that death as medium of their existence. Death itself preserves this in-between (or mediated) condition for the mortal. The shrine, which is death, preserves a state which escapes the metaphysical dualism of presence/absence. Death enshrines, i.e., enables, what lies within it. Thanks to the protection, or rather *mediation,* of death, the mortals are able to essence. The mortals are those who repair to the death-trees, enshrined in death, bringing together being and nothing in their essencing.

b. The Refuge of Being

Through this protection, death is called a "refuge" (*Gebirg*) for being: "As the shrine of nothingness, death is the refuge of being [*Gebirg des Seins*]. . . . The mortals are who they are as mortals by essencing in the refuge of being. They are the essencing relationship to being as being" (*GA* 79: 18/17). The mortals, who essence in death, essence in the refuge of being. Refuge, *Ge-Birg*, as Heidegger sometimes writes it, can be thought in terms of a concentrating and gathering together of all the ways of *Bergung*, of sheltering and harboring, protecting and concealing. These are gathered at their most concentrated in death.[51] Death is the refuge of being because it relieves it of the obligation to unqualifiedly be, to be present. Death grants being concealment. It brings a protection to being just as much as to the nothing. Death gives weight to the nothing and alleviates being.

The third Bremen lecture of 1949, "The Danger," provides a lengthy, and in part perplexing, discussion of death that elaborates just this point of "The Thing." We have cited part of this already, but the passage warrants quoting at length:

> Indeed in the midst of these innumerable dead, the essence of death remains disguised. Death is neither the empty nothing, nor is it merely the transition from one existence to another. *Death belongs in the Dasein of the human as appropriated from the essence of beyng.* Thus death harbors [*birgt*] the essence of beyng. Death is the highest refuge [*Gebirg*] of the truth of beyng itself, the refuge that in itself shelters [*birgt*] the concealment [*Verborgenheit*] of the essence of beyng and gathers together the sheltering [*Bergung*] of its essence. Thus the human is first and only capable [*vermag*] of death when beyng itself from the truth of its essence brings the essence of the human into the ownership of the essence of beyng [*in das Wesen des Seyns vereignet*]. . . . To be capable [*vermögen*] of death in its essence means: to be able to die [*sterben können*]. Those that are able to die are first of all the mortals in the weighty [*tragenden*] sense of this word. Massive distresses innumerable, horrific undying death all about—and nevertheless the essence of death is disguised from the human. The human is not yet the mortal. (*GA* 79: 56/53–54)

If the human is to be in a relation to the essence of being, to any essence whatsoever, then the human has to enter into a medium of relation. For a relationship to being as such, to the essencing of being—or rather to the essencing of beyng, since its withdrawal character is precisely of concern here—that medium is death. Death harbors the essence of beyng. The refuge gathers together all manner of sheltering the essence of beyng. When Heidegger writes that death is the refuge of the "truth" of beyng, this only confirms our conception of essencing as medial (since truth is the medium of that which is guarded). To be capable of death, to become the mortal—the human cannot do this alone. As the passage from "The Danger" cited above explains, beyng itself must bring the human into its custody, the custody of the essence of beyng. The human must be delivered over to beyng and this by beyng. But beyng cannot do this alone. It can only offer the invitation. A marginal note to the 1949 text "Introduction to 'What Is Metaphysics?'" gives us a way to think this invitation. Where the text speaks of "enduring what is most extreme (being towards death)" (*GA* 9: 374/284, tm), Heidegger adds the note: "Letting death come toward and upon oneself, holding oneself in the arriving of death as the refuge [*Ge-Birg*] of ~~Being~~" (*GA* 9: 374 n. a/284 n. a, tm). What we glean here is an indication of how the mortals who essence in the refuge of being are "in" that death. They are not in it without further ado; rather, that death is arriving at them. The invitation of death is always arriving. Arriving here names the way a medium permeates what it comes in contact with; in this case, the permeation of mortal existence by death.

Death provides being with its refuge. The refuge of being is the reprieve of being, that it need not be itself alone. Death removes the demand from being that it stolidly be and allows it a show of weakness. The weakness of being in this sense would be its incessant arriving, that it is "not yet" present. Being takes refuge in its arriving. Understood as arriving, being is allowed to remain withheld from us in the very arriving that gives it to us. By allowing being a refuge, death lets us see the "absence" of being simply as a retreat to its refuge. This retreat is a withdrawal, however, and one generous enough to leave us its trace. The refuge of being is the giving of its trace. Death is the trace of being.

The passage from "The Danger," above warns us that the essence of death is disguised. Death is all about but it does not permeate, it does not touch us. To accept the invitation is to approach the refuge. But insofar as death is always arriving, we can never be said to simply "be" "in" death. Instead, we are always only ever entering. We are "not yet" the mortals for this reason. But we should likewise understand by this that such a condition is as mortal as we ever can be. To be mortal is to not yet be; it is to still be receiving the arriving of death. Were this over and done with, there would be no mortal as there would simultaneously be no death.

The refuge of being *is* the shrine of the nothing. By enshrining nothingness, death gives it a way of essencing. By providing a refuge for being, death gives it a way of essencing, too. It allows being to conceal itself (to essence) and still to be. It allows the nothing to show itself and still not be. Being and nothingness essence in death. Mortality allows them a non-oppositional relation. The mortals are those who essence in the refuge of being, those who essence in the shrine of nothingness.

Thus, on the basis of such argumentation, we can agree with Werner Marx when he says that "not only is the 'ontological' problem of the relationship between Nothing (the Not) and Being determined in another manner than before, but a meaning is also ascribed to death that has not been recognized until now."[52] For Marx this means that "we thus think Heidegger's determination of death further, so that death both grants Nothing and Being the possibility of disclosure, manifestness, as well as lending them the character of a 'secret.'"[53] It is to this secret that we now must turn.

c. The Secret of Being

In the lecture version of "The Thing," Heidegger speaks of death as the shrine of the nothing: "Death is the shrine of the nothing, namely of that which in all respects is never some mere being, but nonetheless essences, namely as being itself" (*GA* 79: 18/17). The same lines are repeated when this text is first published in the proceedings of a 1950 conference at the Bavarian Academy of Fine Arts.[54] When "The Thing" is reprinted in the anthology *Vorträge und Aufsätze* in 1954, however, a single alteration is made. Now we read the following: "Death is the shrine of the nothing, namely of that which in all respects is never some mere being, but nonetheless essences, *even as the secret of being itself*" (*GA* 7: 180/*PLT* 176, tm, em). What we find in the shrine is not being itself, but instead its secret.[55]

But alongside this claim that death enshrines the secret of being, let us recall what we have already shown–that it is the mortals who are enshrined in death insofar as death is their element. Thus the secret in question is intimately tied to the secret of the mortals. The mortals would even live out this secret through their dying. For Heidegger it is another way of speaking about their affiliation with the world around them—the things of the world, to be sure, but also their relations with others. The secret of being, in other words, is why the name mortals is always plural.

Heidegger's conception of the secret here grows out of his work of the early- to mid-1930s.[56] The idea is introduced in "On the Essence of Truth" (1930, first lectured in Bremen), where it is linked to the preserving power of concealment. Concealment, or what Heidegger calls here "un-disclosedness" (*Un-entborgenheit*; *GA* 9: 193/148), affects beings as a whole. This concealment is "older" than the openness of any particular being, to be sure, but it is also "older even than letting-be itself" (*GA* 9: 194/148). Heidegger wonders why letting-be, which itself bears a relationship to concealing, is not itself covered over by this concealing, asking "what conserves [*verwahrt*] letting-be in this relatedness to concealing?" (*GA* 9: 194/148). Strangely enough, the answer is concealment itself: "Nothing less than the concealing of what is concealed as a whole, of beings as such, i.e., the secret; not a particular secret regarding this or that, but rather just this one thing—that everywhere the secret (the concealing of what is concealed) as such pervades the Da-sein of the human" (*GA* 9: 194/148, tm). As paradoxical as it sounds, it is the secret itself that keeps letting-be from being concealed, or, rather, keeps it from falling into oblivion. The secret of being is that concealing (un-disclosedness) needs revealing (disclosure). Concealment keeps disclosure from being concealed! Concealment cannot do away with the revelation of letting-be without abolishing itself at the same time. The secret of being is the announcement of concealment, an announcement that keeps concealing from falling into oblivion. Such a concealment is ineradicable from being. "On the Essence of Truth" thus effects a move away from the understanding of being presented in *Being and Time* (where the question of being is to be disinterred from the history of its concealments) toward that of the *Contributions to Philosophy* (where concealment is necessitated by the withdrawal of beyng).

The idea of the secret as a revelation of concealment is pursued in the 1934 Hölderlin interpretation, *Hölderlin's Hymns: "Germania" and "The Rhine."* We again see here that if the secret be thought of as completely concealed, then no access to it would be possible. But in this case there would be no secret: "the secret is not a trunk [*Schranke*, a case without the commemorative context of the shrine] lying beyond truth, rather it is itself the highest form of truth; for in order to let the secret truly be what it is—the concealing preservation of authentic beyng—the secret must be revealed as such. A secret not known in its unveiling power is no secret" (*GA* 39: 119). The secret names a concealment that is announced. It marks a kind of non-presence and non-absence that must be protected and sheltered in order to show itself. As the 1943 essay on Hölderlin's hymn "Homecoming" puts it: "Surely we never know a secret by unveiling it and dissecting it, but rather solely in that we protect [*hüten*] the secret *as* secret" (*GA* 4: 24/43, tm). A secret that was somehow unannounced could only reiterate the metaphysical idea of an inner essence, in the most substantial sense possible. It would be an in itself, a noumenon. Whatever would be so constituted would be an encapsulation of itself. How would it get outside of its casing? It could never do so.

The secret is essential to any relation to the other at all. Without the secret, there would be no other, for, as Derrida explains, "if the other were to share his reasons with us by explaining them to us, if he were to speak to us all the time without any secrets, he wouldn't be the other, we would share a type of homogeneity."[57] The secret differentiates me from the other and thus *singularizes.* Without singularization, the other is replaceable by any other other, as am I. But this other's other, without singularization, would itself be the same, and this in a manner not to be understood dialectically. Thus we should amend Derrida's claim that without any secrets we would *share* a type of homogeneity with the other, for this homogeneity would be nothing shared at all. Sharing presupposes and requires the same singularization accomplished by the secret. Without this there is perhaps assimilation and amalgamation, but certainly no sharing. To borrow a distinction from Jean-Luc Nancy, the sharing of the secret is a question of sharing our "being in common" and not the matter of a homogeneous "common-being."[58]

Yet death is the shrine of nothing, there is nothing in the crypt. I have nothing in secret and nothing differentiates me from the other. Each of us has nothing to differentiate us, we would *share* this nothingness of difference. But how does one share nothing? We could ask with Derrida (who might as well be speaking about the precise passage from "The Thing" with which we have been concerned): "What is a secret that is a secret about nothing and a sharing that doesn't share anything?"[59] We would at once share and not share what differentiates us. We would be like each other, wholly other—or, in Derrida's peculiar locution, "*every other (one) is every (bit) other* [*tout autre est tout autre*]."[60] For our secret to be a secret it must be shared, there must be the other.

Death, the shrine of the secret; the secret, that nothing differentiates me from the other; the other, wholly other. The secret in its concealment must be revealed to the other, otherwise there will not have been a secret. Yet this revelation is the hardest thing, and not while so many people are said to have trouble "opening up." Each partner is wholly exposed to the other. Paradoxically, this is where the secret shows. To expose oneself is to expose one's secrets. This exposure to the other is so fundamental that no thought of an encapsulated presence is open to it, it shatters the "solipsism for two" (*GA* 24: 394/278, tm) that bases "identity" in the ego, the ego as self, the self as self-same. It is the secret that distinguishes me and this secret is only revealed as such in an exposure to the exposed other. The self as self-other. Even in total revelation there is something withheld. But this is not to say that the self is not wholly exposed, nor that what is withheld could be more exposed, nor even that what is withheld simply cannot be exposed; rather, what is "withheld" *is* exposed, and this is the presencing that "withholding" names. What reveals itself as concealed is the secret. And contrary to popular belief, one can never trade secrets; the secret singularizes and one never even knows it to begin with.[61] I reveal myself wholly when I keep the secret—without this there would be no self to reveal! Openness depends upon (loves) such hiding.

Death is the nothing we share without sharing, a secret nothing accompanying our existence. The singularization of death lets us be able to be with others. Again in the first Hölderlin lecture course, *Hölderlin's Hymns "Germania" and "The Rhine"* (1934–35), Heidegger distinguishes community (*Gemeinschaft*; note the "*mein*") from society (*Gesellschaft*) solely on the basis of death. Heidegger is speaking of Hölderlin's utterance that we are a conversation.[62] This does not first create the relations of each of us to the other, Heidegger says; it does not first create "community," but rather presupposes it. "The original community does not first emerge through the taking up of reciprocal relations—in this manner there only arises society—rather community *is* through the current ties *of each individual* [*Einzelnen*] to that which binds and determines each individual by exceeding them" (*GA* 39: 72). Community thus enjoys a founding position over and against society, the latter having to wait upon community to open the relations that it would subsequently take up and codify. This originary opening of relations, however, is singularizing; it concerns the human as a singularity, i.e., as a mortal, and this in relation to something excessive [*überhöhend*]. Heidegger goes on to explain the bond of this community in terms of the camaraderie in the face of death experienced by soldiers at the front:

> The camaraderie of the front soldiers has its ground neither in that one would have to meet new people because other people from whom one was distant were missing, nor as well in that one first agrees about a common enthusiasm. But rather, solely and at its deepest, in that the nearness of death places each one beforehand into the same nullity [*Nichtigkeit*] as a sacrifice [*Opfer*] such that this would be the source of the unconditioned belonging to one another. Precisely death, which every single human must die for itself, which singularizes to the extreme every individual upon itself, precisely death and the readiness for its sacrifice [*Opfer*] produces before all else the space of community from out of which camaraderie can arise. (*GA* 39: 72–73)

The secret of being allows for a community of death. This is the reason why the name "mortals" is always only a plural name. There is no mortal alone; thanks to the secret, there are only the mortals. Or rather, and this too should be thought in terms of the secret, there are only not yet mortals.

Enshrined and out of sight, can a secret even be read? In a section of *Being and Time* from which we have amply quoted, section forty-nine, entitled, "The Delimitation of the Existential Analysis of Death against Other Possible Interpretations of the Phenomenon," Heidegger claims a certain unreadability about the "structure" of death: "Since Dasein never becomes accessible at all as something present-at-hand, because being possible belongs in its own way to its kind of being, even less may we expect to simply read off [*ablesen*] the ontological structure of death, if indeed death is a distinctive possibility of Dasein" (*GA* 2: 330/*SZ* 248, tm).

The ontological structure of death is not available to be read off from a superficial view of Dasein. The structure of death can't be read off because it is encrypted. And here one should observe that both the German "*Schrein*" and the English "shrine" share a Latin origin. Both come from *scrinium*, a scroll case or book chest. The shrine preserves and keeps that which is to be read, the secret in death's cryptic structure, all the while preventing its reading. And just as one can say that the death proper to Dasein can't be read off it [*ablesen*]—the text is encrypted—so too could one say that the life proper to Dasein can't be lived off it [*ableben*, a word translated by "demise"]—that life is encrypted, too.

§19. Language and Mortality

If death cannot be "read off" of Dasein, this is not because death has nothing at all to do with language. Rather, with the introduction of the mortals into Heidegger's thinking, death and language intertwine. In considering the *zôon logon echon* we emphasized the role of the *zôon*, the animal of the *animal rationale*, and the transformations of this at the end of metaphysics. Now, however, we must look to the *echon*, the "having," of this animal. This small word is often overlooked in considerations of this early definition of human being. The *echon* of the *zôon logon echon* ultimately outfits the human with a space of interiority, writing it into the very definition of what it means to exist. By breaking with this definition of humanity in favor of mortality, Heidegger gives up this inner space of subjectivity as well. There is nothing internal to the mortal, no interiority, no inwardizing. The mortal is unqualifiedly exposed (*schlechthin*).

But the prime possession of this animal was *logos*. More, this possession distinguished the human from all the other animals that precisely did not possess *logos*. Now with the advent of mortality, there is no longer an interior wherein to keep such things. Thinking existence as defined by death—or rather, by dying, by a death it can never "have"—means liberating *logos* from the prison house of consciousness. There is no "there" wherein the *logos* could stand as an acquisition. This does not compromise the meaningfulness of experience. Far from it and to the contrary, only here does the meaning of experience emerge. *Logos* has left the mind to saturate the earth. The *logos* is no longer in us—instead we are in the *logos*. Thinking mortality entails just such a rethinking of *logos* and language.

This is at the root of Heidegger's criticisms of notions of *Sinngebung* or "meaning bestowal," the idea that the human would project a meaning or value onto an otherwise inert, meaningless, valueless object. Meaning is nothing that can be simply given. (We will see presently that Heidegger understands "naming" in a manner utterly distinct from the appending of appellations as well.) Meaning is not subsequently applied to the world, it is there from the outset. This is the critique of Rickert in the 1910s and 1920s as well as of Ernst Jünger from the 1930s through the 1950s. Meaning is the being we encounter.[63] For Heidegger, the mortal does not possess the *logos* so much as bathe in it.

This understanding of *logos* as a medium also informs Heidegger's claim that "the human acts as though *he* would be the shaper and master of language, while indeed *language* remains the master of the human" (*GA* 7: 148/*PLT* 144, tm; cf. *GA* 7: 193/*PLT* 213). Indeed, "*language speaks*" (*GA* 12: 10/*PLT* 188). Language cannot be comprehended, objectified, and stored away, reliquated, in a word. This is how one treats a "dead" language. But what if language required our dying? We would not be master of it, it would no longer be at our disposal. Instead, it would show us our death. It does this in part by showing us the world. We die nowhere other than here and from nothing other than that here. But language also allows us to "represent" death. Language lets the death we cannot have appear to us. Language lets us mark this non-having, or, rather, language lets itself be marked by this non-having, attesting to it, making a place for what cannot be possessed and can never be present.

Heidegger himself later comments upon this perplexing relation between death and language in an oft-quoted passage from "The Essence of Language" (1957–58). In it, he speaks of the relation between them in terms of a reaching:

> The mortals are those who are able to experience death as death. The animal is not capable of this. But the animal cannot speak, either. *The essential relationship between death and language flashes up, but is still unthought.* But this can nevertheless provide us with a hint [*Wink*] as to the way in which the essence of language draws us into it [*uns zu sich*

be-langt] and in so doing relates us to itself, assuming that death belongs together with that which reaches us [*was uns be-langt*]. (*GA* 12: 203/*OWL* 107–8, tm, em)[64]

Commentators have wrestled with this "unthought" of Heidegger's and have interpreted it in various ways. Werner Marx, for example, finds death and language to share a general aletheic structure that he sees in the event of appropriation (*Ereignis*): "death belongs together with the event of appropriation, to which . . . saying also belongs."[65] Françoise Dastur sees in language "the phenomenal attestation of the hold death has over us."[66] John Sallis wonders "whether mortality is not only the proper name of man but also the very condition of possibility of names as such, that is, whether the relation to death is not always already in play in the very opening of language."[67] Lastly, we might also name Giorgio Agamben, whose *Language and Death* explicitly understands itself to "thematically investigate this relation," observing that "to experience death as death signifies, in fact, to experience the removal of the voice [the animal voice] and the appearance, in its place, of another Voice [the event of language itself] . . . which constitutes the originary *negative* foundation of the human word. To experience Voice signifies, on the other hand, to become capable of another death. . . . To consent to the taking place of language, to listen to the Voice, signifies, thus, to consent also to death, to be capable of dying (*sterben*) rather than simply deceasing (*ableben*)."[68]

For our part, we will try to read this relationship and the "reaching" included within it in light of the foregoing analyses of the "elemental" or medial character of death. In this way we will follow Heidegger in construing language as a realm of reaching, a space of invitation, a space of listening, and, indeed, as the house of being itself. Hopefully this will provide us with insight into both language and mortality, a glimpse into the meaning of the world.

The passage cited above wonders about a connection between language and death that would be located in the "reaching" of each of these. They share the motion of drawing us into them. Death and language are media we are "in." The passage turns on the term *belangen* (to prosecute; to arraign), which Heidegger takes in its originally Middle High German sense of to reach out (*ausreichen*) or to extend oneself (*sich erstrecken*). What *belangt uns*, what comes to us in a *belangen* is likewise something that concerns us. Earlier in the same lecture, Heidegger had explained *belangen* in terms of a reciprocity:

We admittedly understand the verb "*belangen*" only in its customary sense, which means: to arraign someone for questioning, for a hearing. But we are also able to think *Be-langen* in a higher sense: to reach for [*be-langen*], to appoint [*be-rufen*], to safeguard [*be-hüten*], to retain [*be-halten*]. The reach [*Be-lang*]: that which in reaching out after our essence lays claim to it and thereby lets it arrive in that where it belongs. (*GA* 12: 186/ *OWL* 91, tm)[69]

What death and language share, then, according to Heidegger's statement of this unthought relationship, is this reciprocal reaching-retaining whereby what reaches us (death and language) invites us into it and lets us belong there. Death and language share in the mediation of the mortal.

This reaching character of language had concerned Heidegger some five months prior, in the 1957 lecture cycle *Basic Principles of Thinking*. In fact, the lecture cycle culminates in a wide-ranging consideration of the nature of language. Here Heidegger proclaims the essencing of language to be a "realm" (*Be-reich*), with the understanding that "this word is here claimed as a *singulare tantum*" (*GA* 79: 168/158). The peculiar sense that Heidegger wishes to be heard in the word concerns a manifold reaching. Realm, he says, "names something singular, that wherein all things and beings extend to one another [*zu-gereicht*], reach over [*über-reicht*], and thus reach [*erreichen*] one another, and redound [*gereichen*] to the benefit and detriment of each other, fulfill [*ausreichen*] and satisfy one another" (*GA* 79: 168/158). The "realm" is thus the field of connections and relations that compose the texture of the world. The realm is the medium for the reaching of things whereby they establish themselves in the world and maintain their residence there through innumerable relations, both sustaining and sustained. This medium is loose enough to let the things reach us, yet viscous enough to keep things from impacting us all at once. The tension or viscosity of the medium allows things to arrive and come to light. These are the things that reach us and attain (*erreichen*) importance. We connect with them, they impact our lives, through language. Indeed, this is so much the case that language is even the medium whereby we can proclaim there is nothing unattainable or unreachable to us, since even the unattainable must announce itself as such: "This realm alone is likewise home to the unattainable [*das Unerreichbare*]" (*GA* 79: 168/158). The unattainable is found nowhere other than here, in relation with us. Language ensures the persistence of relation.

Taking language in this way, as medium of relations, means rethinking our role in it. Speaking can no longer be construed as an exteriorization that appends names to things. Language is not expulsive like this, so much as impulsive—it draws us in. Speaking is an in-vitation. The lecture "Language" (1951), itself one of the first namings of the fourfold as a whole (falling between the 1949 Bremen lectures and the 1951 "Building Dwelling Thinking"), stresses this invitational character of language. The analysis begins with naming. Naming is not the distribution of titles or the applying of monikers; instead, "naming calls," it "calls into the word" (*GA* 12: 18/*PLT* 196, tm). In naming, something is called into the words of language. Heidegger thus turns the discussion to what we might term the logic of "calling" (*rufen*). In calling, we bring what is called closer to ourselves—"it brings the presencing of what was previously uncalled into a nearness" (*GA* 12: 18/*PLT* 196, tm). Calling calls out to something that it might come to this nearness. But in so doing, Heidegger explains, calling does not strip what it calls of its distance. Calling brings closer without cancelling distance. Instead, calling introduces a middle ground, so to speak, neither present-at-hand before us, nor utterly absent and apart from us. Calling extends across this middle ground, calling out that something might come in: "Calling itself calls and thereby constantly thither and hither [*hin und her*]; hither: into presencing, thither: into absencing" (*GA* 12: 18/*PLT* 196, tm). The call thus stretches between the present and absent. Its calling calls what is called precisely into this between space. As Heidegger puts it, "in the call, the place of arrival that is called along with the call is a presencing that is sheltered in absencing" (*GA* 12: 19/*PLT* 197, tm). Calling provides this space for the thing. Such a place is nothing that one could simply occupy. It is a place of arriving, not of completed arrival. As such, the call can be heard as an invitation and understood as a beckoning (*heißen*): "the naming call beckons to enter into such an arriving. Beckoning is inviting" (*GA* 12: 19/*PLT* 197, tm). As one can only be invited into such a place, the naming call constitutes a beckoning.

What is invited into this cannot be anything merely present, but something that extends to us while being distant from us. What is invited is already arriving. What is beckoned to enter is no isolated thing, but just such a coming. As such, the invitation is not to a discrete party, but to a relation. The invitation extends to a coming thing that brings with it its relation to world. As coming, what is invited is opened and exposed to a world around it and so essentially so that it brings this world with it. Thus Heidegger will speak of a "thing-world" or "world-thing" in regards to this (*GA* 12: 26/*PLT* 203). The invitation extends to the very relationship between thing and world. What will appear in this place of arriving will be a thing that exudes beyond itself into world, a world that pinions itself around things. The medium of language allows for the unfurling of this relation.

If speaking is an invitation to enter language, then listening is its acceptance. Such hearing enjoys a certain primacy for Heidegger. "Before all else, mortal speech must have heard the behest [*Geheiß*]," he writes, the behest that "calls world and things" (*GA* 12: 29/*PLT* 206, tm). Such hearing cannot be construed as simply a precondition for speaking; rather this hearing occupies the same space as speaking—they are the head and tail of this relationship to language. Listening is speaking: "every word of mortal speech speaks out of such a listening and as such a listening" (*GA* 12: 29/*PLT* 206). Simply put, "mortals speak insofar as they listen" (*GA* 12: 29/*PLT* 206).

In "Logos" (also from 1951), Heidegger makes just this point in commenting on Heraclitus. What is to be heard is not the voicing of a speaker: "As long as we only listen to the wording as the expression of a speaker, we are not at all listening" (*GA* 7: 220/*EGT* 66, tm). Such voicing remains human, not mortal: "you hear not at all authentically as long as you only hang your ears on the sound and flow of a human voice in order to snatch up its way of speaking for yourselves" (*GA* 7: 221/*EGT* 67, tm). Instead, mortal hearing is distinguished from human hearing on just this point: "mortal hearing must be directed at something else" (*GA* 7: 221/*EGT* 67, tm). Immersed in death, mortals are able to hear past the discrete words of human speech. Instead, mortals hear "something else," they hear the radiance of words, we might say. Heidegger will often address this surplus and relational reach of words in terms of the silence or stillness of language.

To have heard the address, behest, claim, avowal, or promise of language is not to take possession of it. The ear is not an organ of apprehension, but of opening. When Heidegger wishes to address the way that we poetically receive the measure or standard for the dimension, in regards to such measures (*Maßnahmen*) he speaks of "a taking [*Nehmen*] that never snatches the measure to itself, but instead takes it in a gathered perceiving [*Vernehmen*] that remains a hearing" (*GA* 7: 202/*PLT* 221, tm). Hearing does not snatch a thing away into isolation, but instead comes to it with a "gathered" hearing, a hearing that is in tune with the dispersal of the words themselves through the relations they articulate. A gathered hearing is in accordance with a radiant wording. What this means is that what enters the ear is equally outside the ear. To hear is to let things reach oneself and this means to let things radiate, to let them be *so that* they might reach one.

In hearing things relationally, the mortals cannot exclude themselves from these relations. Once relationality is unfurled, there is nowhere free of its claim. To think relationally, to hear in this way, is to find oneself implicated in the very worlding of the world. Mortals hear what they hear now as a claim. Mortals belong to what they hear and hearing itself is nothing other than this: "We have heard [*gehört*] when we *belong* [gehören] to what has been addressed" (*GA* 7: 220/*EGT* 66, tm). To hear is to participate in your appropriation. To hear is to accept this and invite this: "To belong to speech—this is nothing else than in each case letting whatever a letting-lie-before [i.e., the *logos*] lays down before us lie gathered in its entirety" (*GA* 7: 220/*EGT* 66). In taking us up, language "grants a residence for the essence of the mortals" (*GA* 12: 11/*PLT* 190, tm).

Speaking of language as granting us a residence brings us to what is certainly Heidegger's most famed formulation regarding language and another instance of its spatial or rather medial construal: that language is the "house of being" (*GA* 9: 313/239). Heidegger is clear in the "Letter on 'Humanism'" (where this statement is found) that it is not meant in any metaphorical sense: "The talk about the house of being is not the transfer of the image 'house' onto being. But one day we will, by thinking the essence of being in a way appropriate to its matter, more readily be able to think what 'house' and 'dwelling' are" (*GA* 9: 358/272). The house is a space of protection: "Protection [*Hut*]," as Heidegger informs us in "Building Dwelling Thinking" is "as the same word says: a *Huis*, a house [*Haus*]" (*GA* 7: 160/*PLT* 156, tm). The house of being offers protection to being.

The nature of this protection is best seen by considering its absence in the technological challenge to things put in place by positionality. In "The Danger" Heidegger states that:

> Positionality's essence lets the thing go without guard. In our language, where it still originarily speaks, the word "guard" [*die Wahr*] means protection [*Hut*]. In our Swabian dialect this word "guard" [English, "ward"] means: a child entrusted to maternal protection. Positionality in its positioning lets the thing go without protection—without the guard of its essence as thing. (*GA* 79: 46/44–45)

The protection offered to the thing is a sheltering guarding of it. This guarding (*wahren*) is a letting the thing be in its truth (*Wahrheit*). The protection of the house that language affords to being is a protection through the guardianship of truth.

In the 1957 lecture cycle, *Basic Principles of Thinking*, Heidegger explicitly states what he means in saying language is the house of being: "'House' here means precisely what the word says: protection [*Hut*], guardianship [*Wahrnis*], container [*Be-hältnis*], relationship [*Ver-hältnis*]. . . . In the phrase just cited, 'language' is not conceived as a speaking and thus not as a mere activity of the human, but rather as house, i.e. as protection [*Hut*], as relationship [*Ver-hältnis*]" (*GA* 79: 168/158).[70] It is not accidental that so many of the terms used here are forms of *halten*, "to hold," for as the "Letter" explains, "'hold' in our language means 'protection' [*Hut*]. Being is the protection [*Hut*] that, through its truth, protects [*behütet*] the human being in his ek-sistent essence in such a way that it houses ek-sistence in language. Thus language is at once the house of being and the housing of the human essence" (*GA* 9: 361/274, tm). The implication of the human in language likewise extends to the role of guarding and protecting being. Language is no possession of the human; "rather, language is the house of being in which the human being ek-sists by dwelling, in that he belongs to the truth of being, protecting [*hütend*] it" (*GA* 9: 333/254, tm). To dwell in the house of being, under its protection, is to belong to the truth of being by protecting it.

Language as the house of being provides protection for being, a protection that spreads across the space of truth. Language "protects" being in that it lets it arrive. In this arriving into protection, what arrives has already opened itself to relations. This openness of the thing in its truth is the vulnerability that needs protection. Only with the protection of truth do things show themselves relationally, a way of being that, as we have seen, implicates us in the relations and can make of us guardians of the truth of being. Protection allows the thing to radiate. Language would be the radiance of beings.

But this also means that the protection of things would be their radiant, relational fringe. This complex of relations allowed for by language would act as a kind of buffer to the thing. What arrives relationally does not do so all at once. As we have noted, it is a coming. In coming, things do not appear all at once, they precede themselves through their relations. Their coming gives itself to intimation. What comes can be prepared for, it can adapt itself and comply (*sich fügen*) with that which is. In sheltering and protecting being, language lets it arrive and be prepared for, rather than (like the object of metaphysics) irrupt suddenly and all at once with no announcement. The object always forces its entry and cannot be welcomed (though, strictly speaking, all appearing—our own included—is already invitation and welcome, willy-nilly). Language invites beings into the space of their protection (to be hale).[71]

Another way to put this, touching on what was said in the previous chapter regarding a "messengerial ontology," would be to say that in protection, beings appear *as* beings. But this does not mean that beings appear "as" something other than what they are.[72] It does not mean that something else would underlie what appears and that we would be denied access to this only to be left with the husk that this something else appears "as." No, this "as" cannot be understood in so grammatical a manner. It does not move us away from that which is appearing to something else, but instead names the way of being of that thing itself. To appear "as" is to appear in a coming. "As" names the way of being of streaming. With things cut open through relations, the "as" names the bleed of things, their surpassing of their bounds as they soak into their surroundings, complying with these.

Returning to the mortals, as capable of a death that they will never possess, the mortals are given over to language as a way of marking that never absent non-presence. The world that death delivers the mortal to is a world of language. To be mortal is to be already beyond oneself, to be ineluctably tied to what you cannot have: death, world. We die in the world of the world. Earlier, when we cited the lengthy passage from "The Danger" proclaiming that death would be the "highest refuge of beyng," we omitted one sentence from the passage as reproduced since at that time it would have distracted from the focus of our inquiry. Now, however, we are in a position to take up that sentence and consider it. It runs: *"Death is the refuge of beyng in the poem of the world"* (*GA* 79: 56/53). Here the mysterious connection between death and language is stated as clearly as Heidegger is able. The world is understood as thickened into a poem, i.e., as inherently meaningful. Within this world of language, beyng is able to shelter itself. It marks its non-presence here as death. The world could not be meaningful, could not be the poem that it is, without this sheltering protection of death. Death passes being into language.

The hint provided into the unthought relation between death and language is that there will always be the unthought. We will never have thought enough. We cannot escape this thoughtlessness in the least. What remains unthought is the thinking of mediation and relation, of relationality and *Ereignis*. But how could it be otherwise when what we are trying to think is a reaching and all reaching is likewise a withholding, per the logic of giving we have already discussed. It is impossible to think this completely, because it is not there for the thinking. Mortals are those who can name (invite into language) the unthought of language.

§20. Dwelling in Death, Residing amidst Things

Mortality is inseparable from dwelling. The mortal life is a delimited life, one of surfaces, tensions, enthrallments, and ecstasies. It is a life of immersive exposure. This is so much the case that we err to think the mortal as interiorizing, as even possessing an interior. Heidegger's critique of *Erlebnis*, lived-experience, could be viewed in such terms. The mortal possesses no interior wherein to store these experiences. The *Erlebnis* critique is in part a critique of the objectification of experience made available to a hungry public for their consumption, but the mode of this consumption is interiorization. *Erlebnis* always plays itself out in an interior. But the mortal is outside itself, ever entering, arriving, coming into the medium around it, ever distributed away from itself in sustaining relations.

This exteriority of the mortal can almost be said to be the very opposite of the interiority of *Erlebnis*. The mortal turns the *zôon logon echon* inside out. Mortality is sheer exteriority, or, rather, as much an exteriority as Heidegger will allow. We know that what surpasses us must mark its passing and that these traces are the gift of that withdrawing. Even in regard to mortal exteriority, there is nothing so completely outside as to not be referable to an "inside." Which is only to say there is no absolute exteriority. The most that Heidegger can allow himself is a movement outside, a becoming external, an infinite externalizing, but one that always must be understood as an arriving "in" the world.

Such an arriving is intrinsically vulnerable. The same movement that lets it arrive in the world likewise reveals it as assailable. If it were self-enclosed, it could not come, could not even appear, but it would also not be assailable. Any attack upon this object could only ever be an accidental one, from without. With mortal arriving, the attack is essential, intrinsic to what the mortal is as a being-in-the-world. The opening that allows for arriving likewise allows one to be targeted by the forces and relations of the world. We enter a world that has us in its sights. The relations we let loose in the world also lay claim to us. If not for these supports, we could not surface here. Our being-in-the-world is always a being-impinged and an impinging. Otherwise put, mortality is inextricably worldly. How we comport to this world, receive these claims, and amplify these relations is constitutive of how we are in this world, how we *dwell*. Mortality is always a dwelling.

This dwelling is thus utterly distinct from the seamless belonging we encountered in Rilke, Nietzsche, and Jünger. There it was a concern for the transformation of the sensible so as to ensure the security of a perfected belonging; here mortal vulnerability is on full display. Against senseless closure we find here an inviting exposure. The belonging of metaphysics is a cessation, the end of insecurity. Such belonging is an encompassing and incorporating, an absorption of difference. The dwelling of the mortal finds no such closure or ending. In this regard, it could be said to be "infinite," where the finite would designate the closed-off and encapsulated. (In the next chapter we shall see that Heidegger understands the infinitude of relationality in just these terms.) To be finite would then be to be "infinite," to be always arriving and never ending, never consummating in a "belonging" (quotation marks here because belonging itself is only possible through the thrown open relations of this endless arriving; belonging only ever occurs across distances and differences, not homogeneity). Consequently, to be mortal would be to never finish dying, to never finish anything—to be immortal, properly understood. Heidegger says as much in one of his late Hölderlin interpretations, "Hölderlin's Earth and Sky" (1959), claiming that "the mortals die their death in life. In death the mortals become *im*-mortal [un-*sterblich*]" (*GA* 4: 165/190, tm).[73]

The mortals never finish dying, which is to say that they never finish dwelling. To dwell is to die, as "Building Dwelling Thinking" makes clear: "only the human dies and indeed continually, as long as he remains upon the earth, under the sky, before the divinities" (*GA* 7: 152/ *PLT* 148, tm). Two months later, in ". . . poetically dwells man . . . ," the point is made again: "only the human dies—and indeed continually as long as he abides upon the earth, as long as he dwells" (*GA* 7: 200/*PLT* 219, tm). As long as the mortal dwells, it dies, it can never die enough. Its dying is its exposure to world, again not as something over and done with, but as an arriving into world. The same dying that is enabled by the non-coincidence of my existence and my death (the absence of death) keeps me spilling past myself into world. The world is constantly radiating, streaming, and even, in language, appealing to us, addressing us. It issues to us. To be mortal is to be continuously impinged, continuously hailed. Or continuously killed, since this is one of the terms we use for the reception of death from another. Mortality is continual engagement with this mass appeal. Dwelling is the way one lives the response to this infinite appeal of the world. Dwelling is how one dies.

Dwelling is thus exposure. But just as one is never exposed alone, one is never exposed to objects either. If the vulnerability of exposure lies in its coming (if coming is an abrading that strips us of any encapsulating containment) then one is ever only exposed to coming itself. In coming to world, in exposure, one is likewise exposed to what comes. Only what comes could reach us in our exposure. Dwelling must be a letting come. To let something come is to let it be at once both more than it is and less than this. It is more in that it surpasses its bounds in the unfurling of relations that reach out to us and claim us. It is less in that it thereby never arrives in full. Dwelling lets there be this more and less that claims us. Dwelling means to leave open the appeal of the world, to participate in one's own assailing, to be complicit in one's own dying. Simply put, dwelling is how you receive radiance.

Dwelling is the allowing of radiance. Radiance is material, medial, meaningful, and multiple. Each of these facets is harbored in the fourfold. Dwelling is thus a comportment towards the fourfold and it is presented as such in "Building Dwelling Thinking":

> The mortals dwell insofar as they save [*retten*] the earth—taking the word in the old sense still familiar to Lessing. Saving does not simply tear away from a danger, saving means authentically: to let something free into its own essence. To save the earth is more than to use it up or even to work it. Saving the earth does not master the earth, does not subordinate the earth to itself, from which point it is only a small step to unrestricted exploitation. (*GA* 7: 152/*PLT* 148, tm)

Dwelling saves the earth. This notion of saving is something that Heidegger explains throughout the 1950s and 19060s. In the last lecture of the Bremen lecture cycle, "The Turn," Heidegger asks "what does 'to save' [*retten*] mean? It says: to let loose, to disengage, to free [*freyen*], to spare [*schonen*], to shelter, to take under protection [*in die Hut nehmen*], to guard. Lessing still uses the word 'salvation' [*Rettung*] in an emphatic manner with the sense of justification: to restore something to its right, the essential, and to guard it therein. What genuinely saves is what guards, guardianship" (*GA* 79: 72/68). Lessing titled a series of short essays in defense of forgotten or condemned figures in the history of ideas "Rettungen" or "Vindications."[74] To save the earth is to protect it and in so doing to vindicate it, by letting it be essentially what it is. The essencing of something is an opening of relations. Consequently this essencing can only take place under certain conditions, i.e., in certain media, particularly those of guardianship and protection. In a sense, to save is to allow something to be as vulnerable as it can be, utterly exposed and opened onto the world, and to protect it in this. It also entails the foregoing of mastery. To let something shine and radiate is to relinquish control over it. To let shine is to release from servitude and the harness of utility. Mortal dwelling lets there be this *material* (earthly) radiance of things. It is more than a mere keeping from danger: "Saving, thought in the originary sense, says: to justify something in its essence, to ground [*begründen*] it constantly anew—to found [*stiften*]. To save in the authentic sense is something more than just managing to tear something away from a danger" (*GA* 16: 585). Saving is not something over and done with, but something to be always taken up again, an infinite task.

> The mortals dwell insofar as they receive [*empfangen*] the sky as the sky. They allow the sun and the moon their course, the stars their path, the seasons of the year their boon and their hardships, they do not turn the night into day and day into a harried restlessness. (*GA* 7: 152/ *PLT* 148, tm)

Dwelling receives or welcomes the sky. Again the role of dwelling is in part a relinquishing of mastery. Here there is an acceptance not only of receptivity, but of varying conditions for reception. This seasonal and even daily variance is not simply tolerated, it is welcomed. Such alteration keeps any one state from predominating and reifying itself. Recall that already in the *Contributions*, Heidegger had urged us to "content ourselves with *protecting the night* [die Nacht zu behüten]" (*GA* 65: 487/383, tm). In so doing, he tells us, "the false days of everydayness" can be warded off (*GA* 65: 487/383). The concern is similar here: to let the natural measures hold sway, to not eliminate the difference between night and day in the quest for a homogeneity of unending productivity, which Heidegger elsewhere in the *Contributions* terms "that 'and so forth' which is neither day nor night" (*GA* 65: 263/207). The welcoming of the sky is the relief that there is something beyond the sheer toil of our harried existence, that there is something into which we might "look up" (*aufschauen*).

Without this intrinsic self-differentiation of the sky through these periodic alterations, there would be no "slippage" in the sky. The sky would not be receptive and commutative. We have already seen that the way in which night and day belong together, with each preventing the other from achieving complete ascendancy, allows for the transmissibility of the sky itself qua medium. The sky is not consolidated and fixed in one state. Instead, it allows for an uncontrollable distribution of relations. The sky allows something to be held back and for what appears to come to light. The radiance of what appears is *medial*, conducted across a diversified field. Radiance requires such a medium so as to shine.

> The mortals dwell insofar as they await [*erwarten*] the divinities as the divinities. In hoping, the mortals hold the unhoped for up to them. They wait for the hints of their arrival and do not fail to recognize the signs of their default. They do not make gods for themselves and do not pursue service to idols. In the unhale they still await the withdrawn hale. (*GA* 7: 152/*PLT* 148, tm)

Dwelling is a waiting and a hoping. As such, it fosters the conditions for a new arriving. We have already noted that "waiting is letting come" (*GA* 77: 217/142). Here, instead of hoping for something that would subsequently become present, hoping is the opening of a relation that allows the unhoped for to show itself. To hope is to let there be this unhoped for. Hoping is thus not tied to a particular object one would wish to make present. It is similar to waiting in this, which does not expect or demand something come. Hoping is opening a relation to the beyond, where the unhoped for might appear. Hope always includes this unhoped-for aspect by virtue of its uncontrolled opening. A trace of the unhoped-for appears in all hoping, we might say. Indeed, in regards to the divinities, dwelling would appear to be a welcoming of traces. Mortals wait for hints, find signs of arrival even in default, and do not despair in the face of the pervading unhale. Instead, mortals know the unhale to be a modulation of the hale, even the "withdrawn hale." Thanks to the divinities there is no absence that is not marked, everything is marked. The world is a palimpsest. Marking means differentiation and differentiation means codified systems and languages conducive to meaning. Mortal dwelling lets there be the fragile communicativity of the hale. Its radiance becomes *meaningful* for us, not despite of, but on account of the prevalence of the unhale.

For this to be so, these hinting messengers of godhood cannot be reified into static figures. Mortal dwelling does not ossify the divinities into either gods or idols (there being no difference between these as each is a present being). The goal is not to give up mastery in order to stand in service to another. Mastery is not transferred to the gods, but relinquished on the whole. In the lecture "The Turn" Heidegger claims that only when the human "disavows human stubbornness," which we can understand as the drive for mastery, is he/she capable of responding to a claim, i.e., understanding it as meaningful, "in that he looks toward the divinities as one of the mortals" (*GA* 79: 76/71).

> The mortals dwell insofar as they accompany [*geleiten*] those of their own essence, namely that they enable [*Vermögen*] death as death, in the use of this ability [*Vermögens*], so that there may be a good death. To accompany the mortals into the essencing of death in no way means to make death into one's goal as an empty nothingness, nor does it mean to overshadow one's dwelling through a blank staring at the end. (*GA* 7: 152–53/*PLT* 148–49, tm)

To dwell is to be exposed to others. This is not simply a numerical point, that dwelling is never the activity of one alone, but rather a point about the nature of mortality itself. The mortals need each other. Heidegger names this mortal belonging to one another an "accompanying" (*geleiten*: accompanying, escorting, conducting, initiating), a term that emphasizes both that we are underway in existence and that throughout our existence we lead and are led by the other. Mortals must be led or initiated into what is most their own by another. Their essence is to be capable of death as death, but for this they are not themselves sufficient. They must be guided into this. Heidegger says in 1951 that "we mortals *encourage* [ermuntern] one another" (*GA* 16: 471). This encouraging accompaniment is mortal dwelling, a bearing witness to the world and others.

Heidegger orients this accompanying around the notion of a "good death." While he does not specify exactly what he means, we can consider this death in light of its historical predecessors. Phillipe Ariès, for example, finds a shift in conceptions of the "good death." In the first instance, a good death is decided by how one undergoes the moment of death. Ariès elaborates that death in the late Middle Ages was ritualized around the deathbed with the dying person playing the central role in the proceedings, as both victim and master of ceremonies. With death coming to be viewed as the site of a battle between good and evil, how one weathers this last trial becomes all important. As Ariès writes, "the salvation of man is determined at his death."[75] The idea soon informs "the popular belief that it was not necessary to take such pains to live virtuously, since a good death redeemed everything."[76] By the end of the fourteenth century, the hour of death is devalued and a "model of the good death" emerges as that of "the death of the righteous man who thinks little about his own physical death when it comes, but who has thought about it all his life."[77] When Heidegger writes that mortals introduce each other to the use of their ability to die so that there might be a good death, it would seem to be to this latter sense that he is referring. This would also accord with the period of peasant life that he seems to favor. For death is no instant within life for Heidegger (contra the earlier focus of the "good death"), but instead that wherein we move and live from the outset.

Mortal dwelling would thus find a good death where death is no longer understood as befalling an individual from the outside, but as a medium into which we must be ushered by another. Again, dwelling entails a renunciation of mastery, even over one's own death, and a willingness to receive the help and assistance of another. No one is enough—there is always another essential to who we are but lying beyond us. Mortality, too, radiates. Radiance itself is always *multiple*, sharable. And as we have spoken of preparation as a buffer for arrival, we should bear in mind that "no transformation occurs without an anticipatory escort [*Geleit*]" (*GA* 7: 98/*EP* 110).

Radiance is material, medial, meaningful, and multiple. Dwelling is the allowance of this. This allowance Heidegger now understands as a "sparing" (*schonen*): "Sparing means: to protect [*hüten*] the fourfold in its essencing" (*GA* 7: 153/*PLT* 149, tm). Sparing is the protection of radiance, a letting essence. What we spare (*schonen*) is let shine (*scheinen*) and comes to radiate in beauty (*schönen*). There can only be this radiance where there is *essencing*, the way of being for that which holds itself back in order to come forth in radiance. What essences is not challenged forth into availability. To allow for this, protecting does not simply do nothing, but must stand vigilant over the fragility of this shining: "Protecting itself does not consists only in that we do nothing to what is protected. Authentic protecting is something *positive* and occurs there where we let something into its essence in advance, when we properly shelter some-thing back into its essence, it corresponds to the word 'to free' [*freien*]: to shelter in peace [*einfrieden*]" (*GA* 7: 151/*PLT* 147, tm). To protect is to let something essence in a space of freedom. It is to create that guarded space of freedom for what essences. Dwelling creates the conditions for things to appear at peace: "Dwelling, being brought to peace [*zum Frieden*, the space of Freedom], means: remaining at peace in the free-space [*ein-gefriedet bleiben in das Frye*], i.e. in the space of freedom [*das Freie*], which spares each thing in its essence" (*GA* 7: 151/*PLT* 147, tm). Sparing is thus an invitation to exposition. What is spared is allowed into a space of free-dom (a breadth or expanse) where it exposes itself as radiant. "*The fun-damental character of dwelling is this sparing*" (*GA* 7: 151/*PLT* 147).

And yet this radiance cannot exist independently and alone. It must be "housed" somewhere. What is it that the mortals are called on to spare or protect? Heidegger asks, "how do mortals accomplish dwelling as this sparing? Mortals would never be able to do this, if dwelling were only a residence upon the earth, under the sky, before the divinities, and with the mortals. Dwelling is far rather *always already a residence with the things*. Dwelling as sparing preserves [*verwahrt*] the fourfold in that with which the mortals reside: *in the things*" (*GA* 7: 153/*PLT* 149, tm, em). Dwelling is the taking up of a residence among things. Thus it is only possible as a "building" (*bauen*), a maintenance and construction of things. To pro-tect radiance is to dwell amidst things.

Heidegger terms this comportment towards things "releasement" (*Gelassenheit*), in the 1955 lecture of that name. This releasement is a twofold bearing, both a "*releasement toward things*" and an "*openness for the secret*" (*GA* 16: 527/*DT* 54; *GA* 16: 528/*DT* 55, tm). In the essay, re-leasement is construed as a counterforce to the prevailing technological domination. Part of this domination lies in our bondage to technologi-cal objects. Heidegger proposes "saying 'yes' and 'no' simultaneously" to these objects (*GA* 16: 527/*DT* 54, tm). In so doing, we do not entirely refuse technology (say "no" to it), something that would be impossible to accomplish anyway (even the forester is positioned by the cellulose industry, we should recall), but we do not entirely accept technology as it is either (say "yes" to it). Nor do we accept some devices and not others or say yes to all technology but only up to a certain point. Instead, saying both yes and no means seeing what is non-present in technology. Heidegger explains this as "we allow the technological objects into our daily world and at the same time leave them outside, that is, resting on their own as things, things that are nothing absolute, but rather remain referred to something higher than themselves" (*GA* 16: 527/*DT* 54, tm). The ambiguous relation to technological objects is itself a recognition of the fact that the sheer standing reserve (or "commodity") is impossible. For this comportment to be the "releasement towards things" that Heidegger advocates, we must see the thingly in even the standing reserve: "In this comportment we view the things no longer as merely technological" (*GA* 16: 527/*DT* 54, tm). We must see that even what appears in the most fixed of technological pathways of recirculation and replacement is nonetheless exposed. And we must say yes to that exposure while saying no to its purported self-enclosure. The ambiguity of our releasement is precisely the ambiguity of the limit that both confines and exposes. Releasement to things is a comportment to limit.

The released relation to things is also understood in terms of the secret. As we know, technology is another name for being. Technology dominates our current epoch, but this was not always so, at least not in this manner. The technological is something that has come to us over history (*Geschichte*). It is sent (*geschickt*) as dispensation (*Geschick*) to us. This means that there is something likewise held back in it. This inherent incompletion of the technological, its essencing (that it comes to us coincident with a withdrawal), is what the technological world seeks to cover over in presenting itself as completed perfection and self-enclosure. As Heidegger states, *"the sense of the technological world conceals itself"* (*GA* 16: 527/*DT* 55, tm). Releasement is the acknowledgement that even the most technological of devices is given, i.e., bears the marks of withdrawal. Through such an acknowledgement, we understand ourselves now in contact with that which withdraws: "If we now attend properly and constantly to the fact that everywhere in the technological world a concealed sense touches us then we stand at the same time in the realm of that which conceals itself from us and indeed conceals itself in that it comes to us" (*GA* 16: 527–28/*DT* 55, tm). This is the same ambiguous, yes/no comportment to what is not present and available for unilateral assessment (only the completely present could be entirely affirmed, only the utterly absent could be fully denied). Perceiving the traces of this withdrawal lets there be what Heidegger terms the secret: "What shows itself and at the same time withdraws itself in this manner is the basic trait of that which we name the secret. I name the bearing by force of which we hold ourselves open in the technological world for its concealed sense: *openness for the secret*" (*GA* 16: 528/*DT* 55, tm).

Dwelling lets things remain secretive. It protects them in this. Dwelling even allows the things to display their secrets radiantly. Their material, medial, meaningful, and multiple radiance is itself their secret, the shining mark of its withdrawal. To dwell with things in this way is to let them not show themselves. In so doing, the things are not given to us entirely. Instead, they relate to us and implicate us in their essencing.

They are not indifferent to us. They give themselves as not self-evident. They come to us, in other words, as intrinsically interpretable. They make room for us in this. Such things let us dwell: "Releasement to the things and the openness for the secret belong together. They offer us the possibility of residing in the world in an entirely different manner" (*GA* 16: 528/*DT* 55, tm). This different manner is that of relationality. We come to dwell and reside in a world of relations. At the conclusion of the 1957 lecture cycle, *Basic Principles of Thinking*, Heidegger states this directly and emphatically: "*We remain settled upon this earth in relationality* [im Verhältnismäßigen]" (*GA* 79: 175/165).

Such is mortal dwelling in its radiance, our admission to the fourfold—"the mortals *are* in the fourfold, in that they *dwell*" (*GA* 7: 152/*PLT* 148, tm). But such dwelling is not an innate quality. We are "not yet" the mortals. Indeed, mortals themselves are dependent on others who introduce them or teach them. Otherwise put, to be mortal we "*must first learn dwelling*" (*GA* 7: 163/*PLT* 159, tm).

6

The Slight and Abiding Thing

The gathering of the fourfold is the thinging of the thing. The thing must be understood as being composed of these four aspects or relations of earth, sky, divinities, and mortals. When Heidegger names the fourfold, he is identifying the minimal essential traits of any thing whatsoever: that they are ungrounded, mediated, meaningful, and open to us. These four aspects come together in what we have been calling the *relational* thing, whereby this relationality is understood as the interface of a finite thing with its beyond. The fourfold thus names the finite thing. The aspects of the fourfold are the essential characteristics of things, the criteria (or rules) for the thing's abiding. To say that the fourfold is gathered "in" the thing is to say that things are defined by how they are disposed in these various relations, each thing differently each time.

The gathering of the fourfold is the thinging of the thing. Without this thinging, there is no thing. There is a thing when the fourfold gathers; this coalescence is its thinging. The thing does not precede its thinging, because the thing is precisely this gathering of the four, this relation. As such, as a relation, this thinging overflows the thing and cascades through world. The world thus begins with the fourfold: "We name the appropriating mirror-play of the single fold of the earth and sky, divinities and mortals the world" (*GA* 79: 19/18). Thing and fourfold, thing and world, the thing is caught up in both these relations—its very thinging draws it away from any presumed solidity and integrity, any locatable self-identity.

But what does it mean to say that the fourfold is gathered in this way? Each of the four is implicated in the essencing of the other. The earth is involved with sky, divinities, and with mortals, and such is so for each in turn. Each only is what it is by participating in this. So the earth provides the shine of the sensible and it provides this precisely by withdrawing its ground. This groundless appearing is of the earth. But the shine of the thing could not appear were it not for the medium through which it streaks. Whatever appears like that is not self-contained, but moves past itself requiring a receptive medium in so doing. This medium is the sky. But again, the sky can only offer this mediation if it itself is nothing stable and present; the sky must be complicated with temperatures, humidities, clouds and stars, darkness, light, twilight, and more besides. The groundless existence that unfurls into the sky is always marked by its exposure to what lies beyond it and this marking is the play of meaning. The divinities ensure that no loss goes unremarked, that there is meaning even in absence, and that there is thus no utter absence at all. This ungrounded, mediated, and marked situation is one of finite existence. For the thing to thing there must be beings that are defined by their limits, finite beings, mortals. For the thing to thing there must be death, meaningful death upon the earth where it bleeds into sky. Each of the four thus coalesce in the emergence of finite existence.

For such a finite thing, the fourfold prevent the encapsulation essential to self-identity (and the fact that identity has an essence, properly understood, i.e., that identity *essences*, already gives us reason to deny its self-sameness). Each of the four displays a refusal of purity and closure. With the earth, we find a thinking of withdrawn ground, a withdrawal that is coincident with the gleam of things. In sky, there is a chiaroscuro of presence and absence and a multifarious texturing of all appearances. The divinities withdraw and leave us their hints. The mortals are defined by the death they can never possess. All of these withdrawals and retreats, all of this non-belonging and dispossession converge, paradoxically enough, in an instance of relation, the thing. Only through these vacillations, distant contacts, and tenuous bonds can the thing extend itself into the relations that will sustain it and provide it with its purchase in the world.

The thing is consequently a nodal point for the assembly of the four. There is no fourfold if it is not instantiated and incorporated. As Heidegger says of mortal dwelling, "the mortals would never be able to accomplish this if dwelling were only a residence upon the earth, under the sky, before the divinities, and with the mortals" (*GA* 7: 153/*PLT* 149, tm). If dwelling were simply the agglomeration of these relational directions, it would not take place. The traction for it would be missing and the four would simply slip past each other. Instead, as Heidegger continues, "dwelling is far rather and always already *a residence with the things*. Dwelling as protecting preserves the fourfold in that with which the mortals reside: *in the things*" (*GA* 7: 153/*PLT* 149, tm, em). The fourfold *needs* to be instantiated in the things. Dwelling does not happen in the abstract; it is a way of being in a world of things, a way of being among the things. Dwelling is thus always a "building" (*bauen*), always tied to the production or tending of things: "*Insofar as it preserves the fourfold in the things*, dwelling, as this preserving, is a building" (*GA* 7: 153/*PLT* 149, tm, em). The four must be gathered into things and preserved there if there is to be any dwelling whatsoever, any space upon the earth, under the sky, before the divinities, and with the mortals, i.e., if there is to be world.

As we have noted, this gathering is nothing stable. That a fourfold would have to be gathered already entails that it is nothing pre-existent and at the ready. The thing is nothing substantive, something its very thinging already ought to make clear. Instead of the self-possessed, stolid object, the thing is a grouping, and what is peculiar to a gathering of this sort is precisely its spacing, the rifts between the parties joined. These seams of the thing allow its pieces to belong together, to be sure, but these seams also prevent a complete amalgamation of the pieces into an integral whole. In this sense—and this is the utmost consequence of all the atomic bombs never detonated in the world—everything is *disintegrated* in advance.

When we think the thing via the fourfold, i.e., as disintegrated, "we are met by the thing as thing" (*GA* 79: 20/19). To think the relations of things is to let them reach us and for us to hear their appeal. By encountering things in this way, "we are, in the strict sense of the word, conditioned [*Be-Dingten*]" (*GA* 79: 20/19). We are involved with these things, be-thinged (*bedingt*), as it were. The privilege of the modern subject is precisely its isolation from the world, its imperviousness, its disconnection and extricability from the things around it. To not insist on our privileged independence from the world, but instead to accept our place among the things, to give credence to the appeal of things, is to become humble before the modesty of things. In Heidegger's words, in thinking the thing, "we have left the arrogance of everything unconditional [*Unbedingten*] behind us" (*GA* 79: 20/19).

Even in the 1930s, in *The Question Concerning the Thing*, a certain modesty lies at the heart of the very question of the thing. The philosopher who would ask the question concerning the thing is subject to ridicule. Like Thales in the *Theaetetus*, the philosopher's head is in the clouds, overlooking the things around him, questioning them, and leading to a sudden fall into a well. Such oversight provokes the laughter of the servant girls. The philosopher's response to this light-hearted derision is not retributive. Instead, "we have apparently learned something from the laughter of the servant girl. She thinks we should first look about at all that surrounds us" (*GA* 41: 7/7, tm). Ridicule enjoins us to move closer to the things, and, to be sure, "we remain exposed to the laughter of the servant girls" (*GA* 41: 8/8, tm). Ultimately, what we come to see is that philosophy must open itself to ridicule. As Heidegger explains, "perhaps we are already close to falling into the well, in any case the servant girls are already laughing; and what if only we ourselves are these servant girls" (*GA* 41: 27/27, tm). Perhaps this would mean that our own servile attitudes prevent us from seeing the thing for what it is, opting instead to see it as a tool, for example, to be used in our servile chores. More than twenty years later, Heidegger will return to the image of the *Theaete-tus*, this time not to caution us against a fall, but rather to provoke one: "Mortal thinking must let itself down into the dark depths of the well if it is to see the stars by day" (*GA* 79: 93/89). The modesty that forswears independent integrity falls upon an entry into mediation, a vision of the inapparent stars by day.

Apart from the ridicule of the servant girls, this modesty can be found in the fourfold, too, where no one component can be isolated from the others, not even in our thinking. In the inaugural depictions of the fourfold, the presentation of each member ends with something of a refrain addressing this interrelation. Taking the earth as representative, in the lecture version of "The Thing" from December 1949, we hear that "when we say earth then we already think, in case we are thinking, the other three along with it from the single fold [*Einfalt*] of the fourfold" (*GA* 79: 17/16). By the time of its publication, however, this has changed to read "when we say earth, then we already think the other three along with it from the single fold of the four" (*GA* 7: 179/*PLT* 176, tm).[1] The lecture voices a worry over whether we are actually thinking (*What Is Called Thinking?* is only a year and a half away). Presumably, the published version entails that if we talk of the earth in Heidegger's sense, then we are already demonstrably thinking. By the time of "Building Dwelling Thinking" in 1951, the worry has shifted: "When we say earth then we already think the other three along with it, but we do not yet consider the single fold [*Einfalt*] of the four" (*GA* 7: 151/*PLT* 147, tm). Taken together, we see a concern as to whether or not we are thinking, and even if we are thinking, a concern over whether we are still failing to consider the four in their simple unity. We might think the four members together, but the link between them remains thought-provoking.

Heidegger is explicit in "The Thing" as to how *not* to understand the interrelation of the four. As he cautions, "the united four are already suffocated in their essence when one represents them only as individuated actualities which are grounded through one another and are to be explained in terms of each other" (*GA* 79: 19/18). The members of the fourfold are so tied to each other that to think them as separated, *even if only to mutually ground them in one another*, is to misconstrue their delicate relation. The four are neither groundable nor explicable, insofar as both of these functions presuppose a stable basis upon which the grounding occurs or back to which the explanation leads. Instead, and not surprisingly, Heidegger will speak of the gathering of the fourfold in more active terms as a "fouring" (*Vierung*), to wit: "The unity of the fourfold is the fouring" (*GA* 79: 19/18). It is this unity, however, that we must diligently pursue further. Is this unity something that encompasses and contains the four? Do the four simply join together into the unity of their fouring? Heidegger rejects both of these options, observing, "the fouring does not happen in such a way that it encloses the four and as this enclosure only comes to them belatedly. Just as little is the fouring limited to the four, once again present at hand, merely standing next to each other" (*GA* 79: 19/18). The belonging together of the four cannot be construed in terms of a containment, especially not when this is understood as happening to four present at hand entities. The four members of the fourfold do not precede it, they belong to it and only are what they are through their participation in it. In construing the four as simply together we think an amalgam, but not the thing, and certainly not its seams. But this is precisely Heidegger's task, to think the thing by its seams, i.e., in all its disintegrity.

To do so means attending to the vulnerability of things, and this in at least three ways. First, in regards to the very manner of the four-fold's coalescence, Heidegger thinks this strange assembly in terms of a "mirror-play" (*Spiegelspiel*) of the four. Held together by nothing more than a play of reflections, the thing must be understood in terms of an inherent ex-propriation. This distinguishes the Heideggerian sense of a reflective mirror-play from all dialectical speculation. Second, as the ex-propriation of the thing undermines any claims to a self-reliant persever-ance of the thing, the thing is consequently *slight* (*gering*). But it is slight with a slightness that bestows a great pliancy and receptivity to the thing. Third, along with this slightness of the thing, the thing is fleeting. Its constitution as a gathering prohibits any long term existence. The thing abides (*weilt*), but only for so long and only for a while (*Weile*). Things are *ephemeral* upon the earth and under the sky. Nevertheless, it is these same things that are said to "gesture" world, and the world that is said to "grant" these things. The differentiation (*Unter-Schied*) between thing and world is just so fine. The disintegration of things is simultaneously the very creation of the world.

§21. Mirror-Play and Speculation (Hegel)

Toward the close of "The Thing," Heidegger explicitly takes up the ques-tion of the interrelation between the members of the fourfold. He desig-nates the relation a mirroring (*spiegeln*). Here at the heart of the thing, at its core, would be found no stable center or substantive foundation.

Instead there is a spacing, a chasm of belonging. The four belong to each other by reaching across this chasm, and this reach is construed in terms of reflection.

The sense of reflection operative here, however, must be distinguished from reflection as it has functioned in the history of philosophy, particularly in the work of Hegel where reflection makes up the speculative movement of the dialectic. Reflection as a return to self is the crux of subjectivity; it comprises the subject's sheer adherence to itself, its very unity qua subject. In "Hegel and the Greeks" (1958), Heidegger describes the Hegelian movement of subjectivity as "proceeding from the thesis, advancing to the antithesis, going over into the synthesis, and, from out of this synthesis as the whole, the return to itself of the positing posited. This course gathers the whole of subjectivity into the unfolded unity of subjectivity" (*GA* 9: 431/326). The movement over and back, the reflection of the subject, its self-reflection, makes Hegelian dialectic a matter of speculation: "Dialectic is speculative in this manner. For *speculari* means detecting, catching sight of, apprehending, com-prehending" (*GA* 9: 431/326). The speculation of dialectics is a seeing of oneself in the other whereby this reflection is detected, apprehended, and ultimately comprehensively retrieved and assimilated into the unity of subjectivity (its interior).

For Heidegger this means that Hegelian speculation is grounded in a thinking of opposition: "Hegel's way of characterizing speculation becomes clearer if we notice that, in speculation, what is at stake is not only the apprehending of unity, the phase of synthesis, but in the first instance and always the apprehending 'of opposites' as opposites. This requires apprehending the shining of opposites against one another and in one another" (*GA* 9: 431/326). Speculation is thus the movement of the dialectic whereby what exists opposes itself to itself in order to retrieve itself from its alienated state: "*speculari* (*speculum*: mirror) receives its conclusive definition from this self-re-flecting shining or mirroring" (*GA* 9: 431/326, tm). The mirroring of speculation is a reflection of the self to the self as it stands over against its reflection. So construed, "speculation is the positive whole of that which 'dialectic' is meant to signify here: not a transcendental, critically restrictive, or even polemical way of thinking, but rather the mirroring and uniting of opposites as the process of the production of spirit itself" (*GA* 9: 431/326). Speculation names a productive relation.

Heidegger's reading is worked out a few years earlier, in the 1955–56 seminar *On Hegel's Logic of Essence*. In the seminar, Heidegger remarks that "reflection is, for Hegel, the essence in its absolute self-movement" (*GA* 86: 442). The self-movement in question is that of oppositional alienation and retrieval. Heidegger describes the movement of this re-flection, in a somewhat jumpy manner, by inquiring into the nature of being's return to itself from alienation. He writes: "*To what extent does 'being' recollect itself* [erinnert sich; enter into itself]; to the extent that being—is objectivity—at first—[i.e.] the most extrinsic of the immediate for representing—; as *opposed* [Gegen]—it [objectified being] is already directed towards the interior of representing—is latent reflection—[and thus] in that it goes to this *in itself*—it becomes essence [i.e., being in and for itself]" (*GA* 86: 441). In other words, for the empty abstraction of "being" to become concretized as "essence," there must be reflec-tion. But this reflection trades precisely on a thinking of opposition and counter-position—it still remains committed to the over-against, the *Gegen-*, of the object, the *Gegenstand*. The speculative thinking of reflec-tion presupposes this: "Reflection is a returning [*das Rückkehren*]; as such it presupposes that from which it returns" (*GA* 86: 441). The ultimate re-return of spirit is a movement inside, an *Er-innerung*, a recuperation and reclamation of an alien outside that was first posited by spirit itself. As such, through the speculative oppositional structure of dialectics, there is no encounter with the alien, always only with the self's appearance in the foreign, an appearing that must be retrieved and recollected within spirit itself.

In a 1956–57 seminar entitled *Conversation with Hegel on the Issue of Thinking*, the last session of which was included in *Identity and Differ-ence* (1957) as "The Onto-Theological Constitution of Metaphysics," Hei-degger identifies the speculative as a "*positio*," a positing, going on to note how the oppositional structure of this positing ultimately revolves around a conception of being:

> to say it in one | *speculative proposition:*
> "The beginning | *is* | the result–
> the finite | *is* | the in-finite
> the true | *is* | the truth
> the "is"—"*the floating middle* [die schwebende Mitte]" (*GA* 86: 505)

Heidegger's reference here is to the "Preface" of the *Phenomenology of Spirit*, where Hegel writes that the "conflict between the general form of a proposition [i.e., the separation expressed in S is P] and the unity of the Notion which destroys it is similar to the conflict that occurs in rhythm between meter and accent. Rhythm results from the floating middle and the unification of the two."[2] The syncopation of rhythm plays the regularity of meter against the spontaneity of accent. For Hegel it would be the middle of the two, the "is," that carries them without being reducible to either meter or accent. Heidegger sees this as the key to Hegel's philosophy as a whole, as noted in the protocol to the seminar: "The speculative 'is' in the propositions 'the beginning is the result' and 'the result is the beginning' points to something that never lands upon one side or the other, but rather in the 'is' keeps to the floating middle. If we think the beginning in its speculative nature from here, then we do not consider it as what lies before others or as what will be left behind at some point, rather we think the method as the authentic content and thus have arrived into the whole of Hegel's philosophy" (*GA* 86: 865).

But owing to the oppositional antagonisms of the dialectical method, Hegel cannot think being in its transitional nature, as Heidegger points out in "The Onto-Theological Constitution of Metaphysics." He can only construe it as either full or empty: "Hegel thinks being in its emptiest emptiness, thus at its most universal. He thinks being at the same time in its finished completed fullness" (*GA* 11: 65/*ID* 56, tm).

Given this, Hegel's oppositional, speculative claim concerning the beginning being the result is ultimately the arch traditional notion of a metaphysical (divine) *causa sui*. Hegel brings the ontological conception of being as the most universal together with the theological conception of god as the highest being into one, a thinking that Heidegger terms onto-theology, finding that "the unity of this one is of such a sort that what is last in its way grounds the first and the first in its way the last" (*GA* 11: 68/*ID* 61, tm). Hegelian thought is the cause of itself.

In sum, we could say that Hegel did not know how right he was. The oppositions he proposes do orbit around a conception of being, of the "is," and it is this "is" that is generative of the oppositions surrounding it. But Hegel does not go far enough in determining this "is": "The issue of thinking is thus for Hegel self-thinking thought as being circling within itself [*das in sich kreisende Sein*]" (*GA* 11: 62/*ID* 53, tm). Comparing this to Heidegger, what is mirrored back for Heidegger is not mirrored *in* to anything, but instead *out* to what lies *between* these oppositions, in the midst and middle (*Mitte*) of them. The medium of this middle offers a suspending (floating) support to what appears. This thought is at the crux of the Heideggerian conception of mirroring in "The Thing."

Against Hegelian speculative dialectics, what Heidegger wants to propose is not an objectifying reflection of oneself into the other. Heideggerian mirroring dispenses with all thought of original and copy, and thus of the self-objectification of reflection. It does not presuppose its own binary counterpart, nor is its other the other of the self, i.e., an other first posited by that self. More, the Heideggerian mirror does not serve to retrieve the self as it lies outside of itself, in alienation. There is no inward movement whereby the alienated self is re-collected, retrieved, and reconciled, ushered back into the safety and security of an interior. Instead, Heideggerian mirroring is expropriative, not recuperative. It is a thinking of relationality without *relata*, or at least without *relata* that could exist independently outside this relationship.

At the center of the thing we find just such a mirroring. It is presented in a dizzying passage of reflection and appropriation, one that rewards close reading:

> Each of the four in its way mirrors the essence of the remaining others again. Each is thus reflected in its way back into what is its own within the single fold [*Einfalt*] of the four. This mirroring is no presentation of an image. (*GA* 79: 18/17)

Each of the four mirrors the essence of the others. We might first take this to mean that each of the four *resemble* each other in some "structural" manner and by this account thereby "mirror" each other as well. But the resemblances of the four are not the issue here, and the thought of resemblance must be kept at bay if we are to think this mirroring at the crux of the thing.

By mirroring the others, each is reflected. A is a mirror for B, as well as for C and D. But B here is itself a mirror for A (as are C and D), as each of the four mirrors the others. Because of this, the reflection of A from B gives A back to itself, to "what is its own." But this reflection from B is not a reflection solely of A. Insofar as A is a mirroring of the other three, what it receives back from B will be the reflection of its own triple mirroring. And B, too, will offer to A not just A, but B, the reflection of A, C, and D. And so too for B, C, and D. What we are given to think here is a mirroring without original. Each of the four gives itself to the others and receives back from the others what it has given of itself. Even this still says too much and presumes an independent existence of the parties, that there even could be an A at all. What is mirrored back to A as its own is its own mirroring of mirrors B, C, D.

> Lighting up each of the four, this mirroring appropriates the essence of each to the others in a simple bringing into ownership [*einfältige Vereig-nung*]. In this appropriating-lighting way, each of the four reflectively plays with each of the remaining others. (*GA* 79: 18/17)

What each member is, is nothing given. Or rather, it is nothing preestablished because it is precisely something given, something that must be received. I am brought into ownership of myself by being given myself from the others. (This is the force of the *"ver"* in *Vereignung*.) The reflecting of a mirroring that is itself reflective means that identity and propriety are nowhere to be found within a subject. Rather what one is truly lies outside of oneself, right in the midst of this dazzling array of reflective relations. Heidegger terms it a play, another striking contrast with the Hegelian labor of the dialectic:

> The appropriative mirroring releases each of the four into what is its own, while binding the ones so released to the single fold [*Einfalt*] of their essential reciprocality.
> The mirroring that binds into this space of freedom is the play that entrusts each of the four to the others by the folded support of this bringing into ownership. (*GA* 79: 18/17)

By appropriating what is mirrored back, each member is allowed to be what it is, i.e., just this interrelation with the others. What is a member's "own" is nothing that it would possess outright, but instead something that must be appropriated. But even this appropriation cannot be a sheer interiorization. Rather, where the parties to this appropriation are themselves already mirrored out past themselves, the result is not a containment of the self, but its entry into what Heidegger here terms a "space of freedom" (*das Freie*). The movement of belonging found among the elements of the fourfold brings with it a kind of spatialization. To be what it is, each party is nothing independent, to be sure, but each party is not even something self-identical. Each is always already inculcated in a reciprocal movement of appropriation essential to what it is, giving and receiving itself. This exteriority of the member—that it would be a mirroring reflection in the first place—allows it to belong in the "single fold" of a reciprocity among the four. The single fold (*Einfalt*) thus names a uniting connection, the relation of self-reflection, though not in any interiorizing way. The relations of mirroring go over and back, connecting A with B as well as B with A. The unity at stake (the *ein-* of the *Einfalt*) is nothing other than this over and back, or this "fold" of relational identity (unity), a relation that belongs, properly speaking, to neither party alone, is never the possession of just one or the other, but which first brings each to the other and does so precisely as what is ownmost to each (their own is this relating and nothing more, a point we previously considered in terms of "bearing"). There is no discrete or isolated member. To be itself, each is shoved out past itself, to be with others. Heidegger's language could not express this outward movement more strongly:

> None of the four insists on its separate particularity. Each of the four within this bringing into ownership [*Vereignung*] is much

> more expropriated [*enteignet*] to what is its own. This expropriative
> bringing into ownership [*enteignende Vereignen*] is the mirror-play of
> the fourfold. From it is entrusted the single fold of the four. (*GA* 79:
> 18/17–18)

Because what is one's own is found within the single fold that joins the
four, what is one's own is nothing simply received. One's own is not something merely appropriated, but simultaneously expropriated as well. To
belong to this fold and thereby to be what one is requires not keeping
to oneself, but exhausting oneself in a movement of expropriation. The
mirroring out is expropriative, but only on this non-identity of self can
any appropriative movement be found. Not in the sense that the appropriation would reconcile the expropriated—rather it receives it back
multiplied by the reflections of the others. Each member must expro-
priate itself in order to receive itself back as having reflected the other.
Bringing expropriation together with appropriation should keep us from
thinking identity as anything internalized. Rather what is one's own takes
place outside oneself, in the stretch of relation between appropriation
and expropriation.[3] Identity happens through this tensed belonging that
creates its own "free space." All belonging is consequently a belonging to
this freedom. All belonging is spaced. This is ultimately what the mirror
play gives us to think. A belonging that is sustained expropriatively and
thereby allows what belongs to move past itself in a manner that opens
a region, even a world. The expropriative mirror play lets there be world:
"we name the appropriating mirror-play of the single fold of the earth
and sky, divinities and mortals the world. . . . The fouring essences as the
worlding of world" (*GA* 79: 19/18).

The reciprocity of this movement is what leads to its determination
as a circling, a circling that lets the four be together:

> The collected essence of the mirror-play of the world, ringing in this
> way, is a circling [*das Gering*]. In the circling of this playfully-mirroring
> ring, the four nestle [*schmiegen sich*] into their united essence and
> nonetheless each respectively into its own essence. Supple [*schmiegsam*]
> in this way, they join pliantly [*fügsam*] and worldingly the world. (*GA*
> 79: 19/18)

The ring joins by letting each maintain its own identity while participating in the unity of the four, its circling. Were the four to lose themselves,
there would be no ringing, just static homogeneity. The play of circling
emerges out of an appropriation that brings each party into the ownership of itself precisely through its relational contact with others. Through

this negotiation, the four come to nestle into their relational essencing. The delicacy of Heidegger's language here, that the four would "nestle" and be "supple," indicates the relationality of the four, where no part insists or asserts itself unilaterally or one-sidedly, but each is exposed to and informed by the others. The relationality of the four, their gleaming past themselves, reaches out in a joining of world. Because at its core, the thing is nothing more than this play of mirrors—because at its core there is no core—the thing leaves off the stolid, sober seriousness of the substantive. The thing is not armored or weighed down, but supple, pliant. The thing is slight.

§22. The Slightness of Things

Heidegger's thinking of the slightness of the thing stands at odds with the tradition of thought that would confine the thing to the solidity of rigid bounds. Such self-contained, self-aggrandizing things exist as if they were extractable from the world. But this we know is impossible. The relations through the world first give the thing to itself. The slightness of the thing simply names its permeability to relation. It is not so thick or heavy as to foreclose relations. Rather, things suffer slightness on account of their relational character (the world abrades). Diaphanous, membraneous, sheet-like, slight, such are the things of the world. Things are so slight as to dance.

a. The Round Dance

The four that gather together in the mirror play of the fourfold keep the thing from closing in on itself. The reflections that join the four together in the thing "dance." The four belong together as partners in a dance. The dance that Heidegger names—the dance that is constitutive of the very things of the world—is the *Reigen,* a folk round-dance.[4] The circling nature of this *Reigen* is of first importance for considering the belonging together of the four. Indeed, for Heidegger, it even illuminates the event of appropriation itself. In a passage toward the end of "The Thing" (following shortly upon the passage discussed above) we read:

> The mirror-play of world is the round-dance of appropriation [*der Reigen des Ereignens*]. For this reason the round-dance does not hug the four like a hoop. The round-dance is a ring [*der Ring*] that rings by its play as a mirroring. (*GA* 79: 19/18)

The ring of the round-dance is no receptacle that would contain the four within it. Such a conception would require that the four exist independently of each other, present-at-hand for their subsequent collection within the hoop. Such a conception would likewise require that the hoop be an enclosure, like a pen. Heidegger emphatically rejects both of these. While the round-dance is a gathering of the four, it is not an externally imposed one. The dance emerges from the mirroring whereby each element is already reflected out into the others and reflected back to itself precisely as commingled with the other four. In this way the round-dance serves as a figure of appropriation—each of the four can only be what it is through its reflection of and by the others. Each goes beyond itself in relating to the other, and each of these others is already touched by the radiance of the others as well.

> Appropriating [*Ereignend*], it [the ring of the round-dance] lights up the four in the gleam of their single fold. Gleaming, the ring everywhere openly brings the four into the ownership [*vereignet*] of the riddle of their essence. (*GA* 79: 19/18)

The ring lights up (*lichtet*) the four as gleaming. This gleam radiates out of each party, bringing it into contact with the others, and reflecting it back to the first. This contact is the uniting interface of the single fold. The ring itself is nothing more than this mutual implication. And for Heidegger this is appropriation. I am what I am by receiving myself from the other. But what I receive from the other is never purely me. What I receive from the other is likewise not assimilated by me into a stronger self. Rather, and as we have seen, the appropriation of myself is at the same time an expropriation. Whatever does not kill me makes me weaker, weakens the border keeping me from the world. Who I am is expropriatively determined. This non-possession at the heart of identity is the "riddle" of all essencing. In essencing, I expose myself to what I receive of the world. This reception is determinative of myself, though simultaneously shaped by that self. It is nothing I simply assert, nor something I simply receive. For what something is is nothing pre-given; each must be brought into the ownership of itself, precisely by this gleaming movement of expropriative appropriation.

The round-dance is thus a way of being together, and it is intimately connected to the notion of the slight that we are concerned with here. In the 1959 lecture "Hölderlin's Earth and Sky," Heidegger follows Hölderlin's hymn "Greece" in thinking the round-dance as part of an initiatory rite. It is found at the beginning of a new relation, a wedding. But this is likewise an initiation into thinghood for the slight. The lines guiding

Heidegger's analysis concern how the round-dance gets underway at a wedding, how it lets begin:

> But as the round-dance [*der Reigen*]
> comes to the wedding,
> to the slight [*Geringem*] can also come
> a great beginning[5]

Heidegger notes the strangeness of the parallel here, with the dance presented as the great and the wedding as what is slight, rather than what one would more readily expect, that the wedding would be the great event and the dancing just a minor addition. But the slightness that Heidegger has in mind is an ability to receive. The slight is the exposed, the addressable. Something can come to the slight. If the wedding is the slight in this sense, it could be said to participate in the arrival of the great, to make way for it. For this slight wedding, then, "insofar as something other comes to it, the wedding remains referred to what comes" (*GA* 4: 172/197, tm). The wedding qua slight is precisely this openness to the coming of the round-dance, a reception of the great. There would be nothing great were it not in some manner received, borne, suffered, withstood, welcomed, greeted, invited, prepared for, remarked, or needed. As Heidegger writes, the wedding "even belongs in the coming"; more, "it itself is what comes" (*GA* 4: 172/197, tm). Since the wedding only is what it is through its reception of the other, the coming of the other gives the wedding to itself, letting it be what it is qua recipient. The wedding is dependent upon, or "referred to," the coming of the round-dance in order to be the wedding. In the coming of the dance, the wedding is made wedding.

The greatness of the round-dance is the access it provides to the infinitude of relationality. The dance keeps the four distinct and prevents their collapse into homogeneity, keeps them separate yet syncopated to one another, rhythmically and physically entwined despite the distances between them. In fact, the dance is nothing other than the mutual articulation of this spacing. For this reason, the round-dance is "great" and a "beginning," if we bear in mind that things "begin" at their limits, and that only as delimited in this way may a thing relate to others beyond it. Relationality is the greatness that comes to the slightest of things.

In the 1959 lecture, Heidegger initially connects this round-dance with the gods and thematically traces the round-dance back to the Ancient Greeks (pace the Grimms, who etymologically trace it back to middle High German): "The round-dance is the Greek *choros*, the festive, singing dance that celebrates the god" (*GA* 4: 174/198). But this relation to the gods alone is not enough to make the dance "great." No, if the round-dance comes to the wedding, it does not do so solely as an opening to the gods. Rather, as Heidegger is at pains to explain, "what comes is not the god taken on its own. What comes is the whole in-finite relation in which, along with the god and the human, the earth and sky belong" (*GA* 4: 175/200, tm). Relationality does not come in pieces. It corrodes all pretensions to self-standing independence. What comes in the round-dance of the wedding is relationality itself: "The wedding is the whole of the intimacy of: earth and sky, human and gods. It is the festival and celebration of the in-finite relation" (*GA* 4: 173/197, tm).

Because relationality is mediation and not anything objective, it cannot have a stable self-same presence, but must come. Coming (*Kommen*) and arriving (*Ankommen*) enjoy a special valence with Heidegger. They name a way of non-present essencing. They are both involved in Heidegger's thinking of sending and giving, as well (what comes and arrives is the given, we might say, in order to flag the moment of withheld non-presence in all coming and arriving).[6] As something that comes, the round-dance is understood as "the emergent beginning of the great dispensation [*Geschick*]" (*GA* 4: 174/199, tm). And we know that whatever is sent entails a holding back, the holding back that allows for the emergence of this dispensation. The beginning can only let begin by itself withdrawing, by granting the space of a beginning, by withdrawing itself to allow the spacing of relationality to take place. This is the lure of the dance. The "beginning" is not an untapped reserve upon which the thing could draw to replenish itself—the beginning is precisely what exceeds the thing and gives it to the world, to relation. This is likewise the invitation of the dance. The round-dance names the relational connectivity of all that is in its arriving. As Heidegger explains, "we are unable to exhaust the riches of this word 'round-dance,' spoken in simple reserve. For it names richness [*Reichtum*] itself, namely *of that which would like to come*" (*GA* 4: 174/199, tm, em).

The round-dance names the coming of relation, not the coming of any particular party, but the coming of the medium or middle (*Mitte*) of relationality. As Heidegger explains, "the middle, which is named such due to its mediation, is neither the earth, nor the sky, neither the god, nor the human" (*GA* 4: 163/188, tm). The middle is no particular component that arrives at the wedding, but the bond of the wedding itself. It is a jointure that each party has to be able to receive, but without entirely internalizing. Each of the four must participate in this middle without taking it up so completely as to annul it. As relation, as medium, the middle itself is nothing that could appear on its own: "The middle, however, *is* as what joins and disposes in mediating [*das mittelnd Fügende und Verfügende*]. Sparing its own appearing, it is the joint of the relations of the four" (*GA* 4: 179/203, tm). No middle can appear in isolation, no medium is empty.

The middle that is named here is the same middle misconstrued by Hegel in his own thinking of mediation. Heidegger referred to the "floating middle" of the *Phenomenology of Spirit* (§61) in the Hegel seminar of 1956, identifying this middle with the speculative "is," and implicitly contrasting this with being understood in terms of expropriative appropriation, i.e., with the event (*Ereignis*). The Hegelian insistence on beginning with opposition means that the circularity of the round-dance is undermined from the outset. Where there should be expropriation and play, there is "being circling within itself" (*GA* 11: 62/*ID* 53, tm). This leads Heidegger to briefly note in the seminar, "with Hegel the *squaring of the circle!* [*die* Quadratur des Kreises]" (*GA* 86: 509). The expropriative dimension of the coming of the middle in the round-dance is overlooked. The circle is cordoned off, squared (now truly "enframed"). Against this squaring of the circle with Hegel there is Heidegger's own apparent squaring, indeed, the presumably four-sided square of the fourfold itself (a point against the translation of *Geviert* as "quadrate"). A note to the same seminar addresses this directly:

> *The Squaring of the Fourfold* [Die Quadratur des Ge-Vierts] not containing the absolute circle within itself—as something classified and subordinated—but rather: letting free into what has-been [*ins Gewesen*]—i.e. *letting come!* (GA 86: 508)

The round-dance of the fourfold is to be considered directly against the circling of the absolute circle in Hegel, i.e., the appropriative oppositional dialectic of being's speculative self-identity in reflection. As we have seen, the difference lies in the expropriative nature of the middle that comes and allows what is to stretch out beyond itself, rather than be retrieved and contained in a reconciliation of opposition.

b. The Slight (*das Geringe*)

The name for what is able to exist in this way, as participant in the round-dance, is the slight. For there to be a wedding, there must be a coming, and for there to be a coming, there must be something receptive, i.e., permissive yet resilient. The slight is what is able to receive this great beginning, withstand its attraction, and thereby enter the "in-finite" relation. The slight is what it is precisely through this inceptual relationality: "the coming of the great beginning first brings about the slight in its slightness [*das Geringe in sein Geringes*]" (*GA* 4: 175/200, tm).

To understand how this relationality could be called something slight, Heidegger notes that "slight [*Gering*] is the emphatic word for 'nimble' [*ring*], which means the easy, supple, flexible [*das Leichte, Geschmeidige, Fügsame*]: the small in distinction to the great. But small [*klein*] originally means 'fine' and precious, as the word *Kleinod* [little jewel] still says" (*GA* 4: 173–74/198, tm). The "slight" (*Gering*) therefore should not be understood in terms of the negligible or insignificant (*geringfügiges*), nor as something depreciatory (*geringschätzig*), though these senses are not unrelated to the nature of the slight. It is part of its being to be easily overlooked and construed in these disparaging ways (just as it is part of the being of the thing to be threatened by standing reserve). Heidegger explains that the depreciative understanding of the slight misses the phenomenon in question: that of the slight's ability to relate beyond itself and participate in greatness (in the wedding, in the great beginning). The disparaging view begins from a thought of reconciled totality and wholeness, the fullness of self-enclosed identity, and then determines the slight as what lacks this fullness. But Heidegger is not concerned with such one-sided misunderstandings of the slight "in the sense of what is of little value [*des Geringschätzigen*]. For what blossoms in an impoverished place will indeed stand as 'great.' The slight first becomes slight, becomes the precious [*zum Kostbaren*], which is the last to be enjoyed [*zu kosten*], in the coming of the great beginning. This comes, however, in the manner of the round-dance" (*GA* 4: 173–74/198, tm). The slight is precious, is singular, and this due to its inherently relational nature. As such it is able to receive the coming of the great beginning, *relationality*. "Hölderlin's Earth and Sky" thus gives us to think the slight as what is capable of receiving without appropriating, and returning to "The Thing," it is in just these terms that Heidegger now casts it:

> Supple, lithesome, malleable, pliant, light [*Schmiegsam, schmiedbar, geschmiedig, fügsam, leicht*], this is called in our old German language *ring* and *gering*. As what is slight about the ring [*das Gering des Ringes*], the mirror-play of the worlding world ringingly releases [*entringt*] the united four into their own pliancy, the nimbleness of their essence [*das Ringe ihres Wesens*]. From out of the mirror-play of the circling of the nimble [*des Gerings des Ringen*] there takes place the thinging of the thing. (*GA* 79: 19–20/18–19)

The malleability of the thing is its ability to adapt to its environs, or rather, the thing's malleability is due to the reciprocity established between thing and environs. Each marks the other and bears the other. Each thing bears the world, we might say, but each is in turn borne aloft by that world, the medium in which all these things surface. This malleability, then, leads Heidegger to characterize the thing as slight and nimble. He takes recourse to the Old High German senses of these terms, *ring* and *gering*, in order to emphasize the connection between this slightness and adaptability of things with his discussion of the round-dance and the mirror-play of the fourfold. The appropriative-expropriative mirroring of the four was understood as a "circling" (*Gering*). It named the way in which each member of the fourfold remained itself through a joining with the others. This way of being oneself as party to others was described in terms of a suppleness. This supple, malleable, pliant, and therefore compliant thing is slight (*gering*). Made slight by the expropriative circling of its essence, the thing is likewise nimble (*ring*), i.e., responsive to what comes, even (like the wedding visited by the round-dance) "referred" to the coming of this. As Heidegger notes toward the close of the lecture, "in accordance with this circling, the thinging itself is slight [*gering*] and the thing that each time abides is nimble [*ring*], inconspicuously pliant in its essence" (*GA* 79: 21/20).

The thinging of the thing is thus this doubled movement whereby each element of the fourfold joins with the others while retaining its distinction from the others. Or rather, each one achieves its distinction from the others only through its implication among the others. This is the logic of the *Einfalt*, the single fold that gathers the four together (and why the translation of *Geviert* as "fourfold," too, is misleading). In the circling around this non-center of the thing, the four splay themselves onto the middle, a middle or medium that is only able to receive them because it, too, is nothing fully given, but something that comes—otherwise it would brook no passage. The thing complies with what comes, complies with its medium, and complicates the world. This is its slightness.[7]

In the mid-1970s, in sketches for what was intended to be an introduction to his *Collected Edition* with the general title *Legacy of the Question of Being* (*Vermächtnis der Seinsfrage*), Heidegger takes up this conception of the slight in a brief gathering of notes aptly entitled "The Slight" (*Das Geringe*). Here the idea of compliance, i.e., the supple receptivity of the thing for what comes, is presented as a relation of "sanctioning" (*Befugnis*).[8] Examining Heidegger's remarks in this short text should help us understand the way in which the slight relates to a world (or in the language of the text, to the "sanctioning region") that lies beyond it. The opening section of the text, for example, reads:

The Slight [das Geringe]

The Negligible [Das Gering-fügige]

ambiguous
but naming much

> to be thought in terms of the sanctioning-region [*Be-fugnis-Gegend*]
>
> *
>
> The greatness of the slight
>
> *
>
> The slight [*Ge-Ringe*]: the gathering
> of the bringing-into-ownership [*Vereignis*] of all things
> to themselves.[9]

The term "sanctioning-region" here brings together the thought of an authority, one who disposes from a position of superiority, with the idea of a jointure (*Fug*) or articulation. Indeed, as Heidegger notes, one of the synonymous terms for the slight, the "negligible," is constructed upon this notion of jointure (the slight joint, *Gering-fügige*). The *Befugnis* would name the need for compliance with any authoritative directive. Such compliance, however, simultaneously undermines any pretention to sovereign authority or utter exclusion, since the directive requires this compliance to hold sway. We should note here that the ultimate directive for Heidegger, the authority over the sanctioning (but this authority is itself only authorized through compliance with its sanctions) is being: being understood as given, i.e., as beyng. This beyng that is sent to us, arrives to us, is always coming to us, and we are called on to comply. Our compliance is the adoption of a receptivity to what lies beyond us, one that situates us in a relationship with coming. For this reason, authorization is spaced and Heidegger speaks of a "sanctioning region." As something sent, the sanction of this sanctioning region is something that is equally held back from us. This withholding, as we have repeatedly seen, is itself a granting and what makes possible the extension of what is given. The space that is stretched apart by the reach of this sent sanction is the spacing of the "sanctioning-region." The sanction is indissociable from this reservation or withholding.

It is only a small step from this to understand that what comes to us in the sending is precisely the marker of a withholding, all that is given or sent is so marked. The task of the thinker is to attend to this withholding:

> *To more questioningly question—*
> means: *to become more hearing for* that
> which is addressed to us: i.e. for the
> *withholding* [Vorenthalt] of the sanctioning-region
>
> more hearing: more pliant [*fügsamer*] in the pre-
> paration for belonging
> to *the slight*[10]

In the reception of this withholding, we ourselves become more pliant and through this pliancy are able to belong to the slight things around us. To understand what is outside of us as something not at our disposal— as withheld—and to see the evidence of withholding as the very things themselves is to take the things as granted, as stretched and slight, read-ied for relation. The thought of compliance is ultimately the thought of the givenness of being—that it must be received and that this very recep-tion undermines the independence of authority (hypostasized being). The compliant being is the slight, the thing, the thinging of which im-plicates the fourfold.

The fourfold that sets in play the thinging of the thing does so in such a way that the thing is desubstantialized, made centerless in order to participate in the mediation of the middle. The fouring of the four allows the thing entry to what lies beyond it. Thinging in this way, the thing *implicates* a beyond, where to implicate means to relate to some-thing so essentially as to belong together with it in the simplicity of the single-fold (*Einfalt*), a transpartitional limit of separation and contact. The thing that things via the mirror-play of the four has adapted itself to the sanctioning-region, is tied to its withholding bestowal. It is this adaptation to the sanction that renders the thing slight, as we have en-deavored to show.

Some twenty-five years prior, the lecture "The Thing" concludes with a thought that could stand as the distillation of all that we have struggled to articulate here: "Only what is slight of world ever becomes a thing" (*GA* 79: 21/20).

§23. The Thing Abides

The slightness of the thing is not solely a matter of its malleability to en-ter into relation with the sending of being (the givenness of world). Or rather, this malleability cannot be construed solely in "synchronic" terms, but must be understood "diachronically" as well. The sending of being is history. The thing as slight is from the outset exposed to the coming of this history, i.e., is temporal or historical. For Heidegger there is a par-ticular kind of temporality that attends such things, an explicitly finite temporality, that of abiding (*weilen*). The thing abides.

This notion of abiding (*weilen*) and tarrying (*verweilen*) arises in Heidegger's thinking of the 1940s. To be sure, the notion of *Jeweiligkeit* ("awhileness") plays a critical role in the early 1920s during the period of fundamental ontology where it indicates the temporalized particularity of the individual Dasein. By the time of *Being and Time*, however, it largely disappears in favor of *Jemeinigkeit* (mineness).[11] Indeed, in *Being and Time*, the idea of *Verweilen*, a tarrying or lingering (or "letting abide"), has something of a negative connotation, being associated with a disengagement from the world that then regards it only in terms of the present-at-hand:

> In order for knowing to be possible as determining by observation
> what is present-at-hand, there must first be a deficiency of having to
> do with the world and taking care of it. In refraining from all production, manipulation, and so on, concern [*das Besorgen*] places itself in
> the only mode of being-in which is left over, in the mode of just lingering alongside . . . [*das Nur-noch-verweilen bei . . .*] . . . In this *'residing'*
> [Aufenthalt]—as a refraining from all manipulation and use—the
> *perception* of what is present-at-hand takes place. (*GA* 2: 82–83/*SZ*
> 61–62, tm)

In the 1930s, too, *weilen* plays a very limited role. It is largely absent from the notebooks of the period, such as the *Contributions*, and while it appears in the 1934–35 Hölderlin course *Hölderlin's Hymns: "Germania" and "The Rhine,"* it is not thematized as such. Indeed, the hymn "The Rhine" features lines that will be of no small importance to Heidegger's later understanding of *weilen*. In the thirteenth stanza we read:

> Humans and gods then celebrate [*feiern*] the bridal festival [*Brautfest*],
> Every living being celebrates it,
> And balanced [*ausgeglichen*]
> For a while [*eine Weile*] is fate [*das Schicksaal*].[12]

In the 1934–35 course itself, these lines receive practically no discussion. It is only in the very last section of that course that we are told the celebration by humans and gods of the "bridal festival" can last "only for a while" (*GA* 39: 289).

With the 1940s, however, the while (*Weile*) emerges as a central term in Heidegger's thinking, specifically in the treatments of Hölderlin's hymn "Andenken" ("Remembrance")—in both the 1941–42 lecture course *Hölderlin's Hymn "Remembrance"* and the 1943 treatise "Remembrance"—as well as in the 1946 essay "Anaximander's Saying." In thinking the while with Hölderlin and abiding in Anaximander, Heidegger begins to lay out the temporal parameters for the thinging of the thing in the years ahead.

a. The While of the Festival (Hölderlin)

Heidegger's comments on "abiding" in the "Remembrance" readings take up the notion of the "festival" presented in Hölderlin's "The Rhine" as cited above. According to Hölderlin's poem, the festival is the "bridal festival" of humans and gods. Heidegger makes clear in the essay that festival (*Fest*) is to be rigorously distinguished from celebration (*Feiern*). Celebrating is "a becoming-free for what is unusual of the day," but when this is understood merely as a holiday (*Feiertag*) from the work week, then "the celebrating, which exhausts itself only in the cessation of work, has of itself nothing which it could celebrate and is thus not essentially a celebration" (*GA* 4: 103/126, tm). Again, mere disengagement from work (or one's projects) is not enough to experience a new way of being of things. Cessation of work on its own does not provoke celebration. Rather, as Heidegger states, the celebration is "solely determined by that which it celebrates," a positive determinant rather than a cessation (*GA* 4: 103/126, tm). And for Heidegger that positive determinant "is the festival [*Fest*]" (*GA* 4: 103/126). Not just any festival, but, following Hölderlin, a bridal festival, a marriage, between humans and gods. What the festival celebrates, then, is the forging of a bond.

The festival celebrates a relationality capable of bringing together what is most unlike, the humans and the gods. Each party must be open to the relationship that comes to them. Neither party can be the possessor of the relationship (something true of all relations). The gods and humans alike stand similarly exposed to the coming of this relation. When we think coming in terms of the arriving of something "sent" (*geschickt*) then we are once again in the province of the historical (*geschichtliche*). For this reason, Heidegger claims, "the festival is for Hölderlin the ground and essence of history [*der Geschichte*]" (*GA* 52: 92). In the lines from the poem cited above, what is sent is fate (*Schicksal*). Consequently, to be historical is to be exposed to the sending of fate: "All standing in fate [*im Schicksal*] is historical [*geschichtlich*]" (*GA* 52: 92). Gods and humans alike are exposed to fate and celebrate this bond at the wedding.

The while is the time of this bonding. The bond is historical by definition, drawing as it does each of the parties out past their bounds. The bond thus entails an exposure not just to the other, but to fate more broadly, to what comes. (Exposure is always exposed in this way.) This fate is said to be "balanced," as the lines from "The Rhine" would have it— "and balanced / for a while is fate"—and this equilibrium is the nature of bonds that last "a while." In the lecture course devoted to "Anden-ken," Heidegger explains the equilibrium in terms of an equivalence in essencing between apparently conflicting parties where each is left to be itself. But in a relation that could be said to prefigure the mirror-play of the fourfold previously discussed, what each one is is a movement out to the other:

> The true equilibrium [*Ausgleich*] places the parties of the conflict back into the equivalence [*Gleiche*] of their essencing. Equilibrium means that everything is brought equi-inceptually [*gleichanfänglich*] into the calm of its essence and is carried out from there so that from out of this essential calm it receives the strength to recognize the counter-essence and also to find itself entirely for the first time in such a recognition. But to-find-oneself is never an obstinate insisting-upon-oneself-alone, but rather a going over [*Hinübergehen*] from out of one's own to what is foreign of the other and a coming here [*Herübergehen*] from out of this recognized foreign into one's own. Equilibrium is going over and coming here, is transition [*Übergang*]. (*GA* 52: 86)

Fate is balanced when the parties participate in the harmony of a mutual exposure to what comes. An existence defined by this coming and going is transitional and balanced. This kind of surrender to the other is the bond of love celebrated in the bridal fest.

A year later, in the essay "Remembrance," a new dimension is added to this thought of balance. The bridal fest is no longer understood simply as wedding and relation, but also as a birth: "The *bridal festival* [*Brautfest*] is the contact between humans and gods, those for whom the birth emerges that stands between the humans and gods and endures this 'between'" (*GA* 4: 103/126, tm). The birth that attends the wedding of humans and gods is itself neither human, nor God, but demigod (*Halbgott*). As neither one nor the other, the demigod corporealizes the bond of the bridal fest, giving it its traction in the world. The equilibrium of fate, the event of the "while," is now cast as condition for the birth of a being that lives the relation between humans and gods, but is essentially "unlike" either:

> The essence of the demigod, however, is to hold together that which is *unlike* [*das* Ungleiche] both the gods and humans. To be this unlike, neither like the sky nor the earth, requires the essence that is allotted to the demigod. To preserve this is the destinal. Fate thus finds its equilibrium only when the unlike essences as the unlike. Here the equilibrium is no forced equivalence in the distinctionless, but rather an equalizing letting reign of the different in their difference. The equilibrium is not the dissolution of the different, but rather their (the gods' and the humans') return into their own essence. In such a return is grounded

the remaining of the unlike. When this remains, only then is there that while in which fate can purely linger [*verweilen*]. (*GA* 4: 105/128–29, tm)

Equivalence is now less about each party being left to its own than the birth of a new figure from out of the relation. It is the middle figure that holds open the difference between the others, the "unlike" parties. Thinking the relation between the unlike as held open by the demigod means that it is not simply the demigod that is born of this relation, for if to be human and to be divine are both to be open to something beyond one's bounds (provisionally termed "fate"), then it is only where the demigod endures that this relational essence of both humans and gods comes to light. It is not simply that the humans and gods give birth to the demigod at the bridal feast, but rather that the demigod likewise gives birth to the gods and humans themselves. This is what it means to be between (to "bear" it): that the supposedly antipodal, the parties of conflict, are born out of the between; the between does not derive from the separation of two independent or indifferent entities.

The participation endemic to the bridal fest, that celebration whereby each is allowed to be itself through a relation to the others, is nothing lasting. It lasts only for "a while." This is so much as to say that one cannot simply "be" in the between. The between—and this is ultimately what is celebrated in the bridal festival—is nothing one could occupy as a self-identical entity or agent. It cannot endure like something stable or present-at-hand; "this while cannot be measured by a clock" (*GA* 52: 103). It is simply not itself enough to last for more than just a little while. All relations are this way, however enduring they might seem. Heidegger explains the rarity of this while in the lecture course: "Fate is balanced for a while. Otherwise and most of the time, it is thus unbalanced: humans and Gods along with those who prepare for and interpret their encounter in regards to the sending and what is fateful in it, these all find themselves for the most part not within the fateful" (*GA* 52: 93). For the most part, we do not participate in this relationship. In the essay, which gives greater emphasis to the role of the demigods than the lecture course does, Heidegger notes that the nature of these demigods depends on a relating to the unlike, to the gods and the humans. But where gods and humans seek to avoid relation and remain among themselves as themselves, the between that the demigod is supposed to open gets closed off instead. Heidegger observes that "through the bifurcating greed for unity [i.e., each party seeking to be itself independent of the others], however, the between is destroyed that the demigod is supposed to hold together. The open of this between is closed" (*GA* 4: 104/128, tm). As a consequence, it is no fault of any particular party that the balancing of fate occurs only for "a while." The "greed" for unity is endemic to all that relates, indeed it is a condition of relationality itself (that there be closure). It is constitutive of the nature of the while qua relational field. What enters the while, what abides, does so at the price of lasting duration.

Still it is important to note that the while is fleeting because it is transitional. Its ephemeral nature is nothing derogatory or negligible. For this reason, we miss what is essential to the while when we construe it negatively against the standard of the eternal. The inherent "finitude" of the while, we might say, is negated in conceptualizing it as subordinated to the lasting. In a section of the lecture course entitled "The Temporal Character of the 'While' and the Metaphysical Concept of Time" Heidegger explains that, "for the sort of thinking that reckons upon effects [or on a "non-festive securing of the stability (*Bestandsicherung*) of the actual" per the essay version (*GA* 4: 105/129, tm)] and that measures the actuality of these only in terms of their duration [*Dauer*], the while appears as a brief duration. The while is reckoned as what is merely temporary [*Zeitweilige*]. As something fleeting and tenuous [*Bestandlos*] it is subordinated to the lasting and continual [*dem Dauernden und Fortwähren-den*]" (*GA* 52: 103). The "lasting and continual" is thus taken as the standard against which all else is measured. But the while cannot be thought starting from an infinite duration. Indeed, as transitional, "the while is neither finite nor infinite. It abides *before* these measures" (*GA* 4: 106/129, tm). When we construe the finite and infinite oppositionally, then the while is that "between" from out of which their opposition emerges, and thus neither one nor the other (it is "in-finite," as we shall see). The while is the time of this between, the time of the relationality that the between allows, the time of its transitioning.

The while is a time of transition, that is to say, of coming. As such, it is the time of mediation and, in Heidegger's Hölderlin readings, this means that it is the time of the holy, the medium par excellence. Heidegger can thus write that "to such a while, first blessing it in its essence, the holy comes" (*GA* 4: 106/129, tm). But Heidegger will also think this holy not simply as something sent to us (as our fate, for instance), but instead as the origin of that sending as well, as in the remark that "the holy . . . is the dispensing of fate [*das Schicken des Schicksals*]" (*GA* 4: 104/128, tm).[13] But the two ultimately say the same: the holy is the coming itself, the connection established between the dispensation and the dispensed (what abides). We remain in contact with the sender through the sending. To do so we must be able to receive and this means that what is sent must be apportioned to us.

Heidegger follows Hölderlin in thinking the sending that is apportioned to us as a greeting. The whole festival as the bonding of the unlike is an abiding in this while of greeting: "The festival is the event of greeting [*Ereignis des Grußes*] in which the holy gives greetings and appears in greeting [*grüßt und grüßend erscheint*]" (*GA* 4: 105/128, tm). But to be greeted by this greeting is to be reachable by it, to be extended toward it. And this means being more than oneself, beyond oneself. The holy that greets does not impose itself upon the greeted; instead the holy remains at a distance from the greeted. As such, the greeting of the holy is a kind of "letting be": "What is first dispensed [*Geschickte*] from the holy is the festival. What is festive of the festival has its determining ground in the *holy*. The holy lets the festival be the bridal festival that it is. *Such an allowing of what essences to essence in its essence is the original greeting*" (*GA* 4: 104–5/128, tm, em). The while as time of the holy is thus the time in which things are let be. It is the time of a greeting, and what appears in the festival is defined by the arrival of this greeting.

The abiding things that stay a while are thus never simply here; they originate from this greeting and remain tied to it, are hailed (greeted and made hale) by it. The hail of the holy leaves them inceptual and singular. Heidegger thinks these two qualities together in terms of the while. As he explains, "that which lasts briefly from the perspective of calculation, can nevertheless outlast all the 'and-so-forth' of mere continuation [*Fortdauerns*], after the manner of the inceptual [*anfänglichen*], i.e. of a remaining that essences *from out* of the beginning [*dem Anfang*] and *back into it*" (*GA* 52: 104). For something to essence out of the beginning and likewise back into it means that this something is not disconnected from that beginning at all, but tied to it *essentially* (per our discussion of rivers in chapter two, "Waters [*Gewässer*]"). What so essences brings the beginning with it (is hailed by it), because the beginning is what gives it to the world in the first place. What essences for a while, in the while, as something that is sent, sustains a relation to the "beginning" in its stretching out to us from it. The beginning is thus inseparable from the while: "The beginning remains in that it is each time a while" (*GA* 52: 94). The while is now the time of beginning, the time for what is sent and dispensed. What is so sent never fully arrives into presence-at-hand, but remains on the way, remains coming, remains in contact with its origin. Only in this way can it be arriving and only as arriving can it last for a while: "everything that comes has its arrival only in the while" (*GA* 52: 104).

The time of the while is the time for things that remain connected to their beginning. But this connection is one that is forged through exposure, i.e., through an essential connection to what lies beyond one's bounds, through a departure from the beginning. This connection means that what one is is nothing directly present. One becomes a relation. And since one is not completely there to begin with, the thing that remains in contact with its beginning is not available for evaluative assessment and thus not available for replacement by an ersatz of equal value. The relation is not completely assessable in this regard. Otherwise put, what essences in the while is singular. Indeed, "the singular is 'only' as the inceptual. Every beginning is singular" (*GA* 52: 94). What begins hails from non-beginning and remains in touch with this as it is born singularly into the whiling world. As Heidegger explains, "in the while, the singular has an appropriate sort of remaining, one from out of the singularity of its inceptual essencing" (*GA* 52: 104). The time of the while is the time for this singular relationality: "the highest and authentic remaining is not persistence in the continuation of the and-so-forth, but rather the while of the singular" (*GA* 52: 93). Heidegger's Hölderlin readings give us to think the while as the time of arriving, i.e.. the time of what is inceptual and singular.

Heidegger terms the manner of thinking such an inceptual singularity "remembrance" (*An-denken*), and in so doing further distinguishes himself from Hegel. Remembrance must be distinguished from a calling up of something past: "such *remembrance* cannot be the mere making present of something past [*eines Vergangenen*]" (*GA* 4: 96/119, tm). Rather, where things are understood relationally, as what comes, there can be nothing simply past in this way: "*remembrance* [Andenken] would be indeed a remembrance, but one that remembers what comes. Granted that this *remembrance* thinks ahead, then a thinking-back likewise cannot remember something 'past' [*Vergangenes*], which is the ever staunch irrevocable. The 'remembrance' [*Denken an*] of what comes can only be the 'remembrance' of what has-been [*das Gewesene*], by which name we understand, in distinction to what is only past, that which is still distantly essencing" (*GA* 4: 84/109, tm). What is past still concerns us (*geht uns an*) as something that has-been (*das Gewesene*). Remembrance is a way of thinking that breaks with the thought of an isolated, discrete, and "present" being. But this does not mean it thinks what is simply past. Instead, it thinks what comes to us, whether past or futural: "Because this thinking thinks rememberingly [*andenkend denkt*] and never merely represents the present-at-hand, it must at the same time remember what comes" (*GA* 52: 165). In fact, once we accept relationality, there is a deeper union to be seen between what has-been and what is to-come: "When the remembering of what has-been allows this its essencing and does not disturb its reigning through a hasty settling on something present, then we discover, in its return [*Rückkunft*] into *remembrance*, that what has-been swings out beyond our present and comes upon us as something futural [*ein Zukünftiges*]. Suddenly remembrance must think what has-been as something not-yet-unfolded" (*GA* 4: 100/123, tm). Remembrance (*Andenken*) is our way of thinking the non-presence of things, not from out of the past, but from where they begin their presencing (*An-wesen*), from this "*An-*" itself.

In thinking things in this way, remembrance does not confine them to their bounds, but lets them stream forth through world. Whereas for Hegel the speculative movement of the absolute is an internalization, *Erinnerung*, a recollecting of its essential self within an interior (the rescue of itself from alienation and exteriority), for Heidegger the expropriative dimension of existence places that self outside of itself. Not in a memory, but in remembrance. The *Andenken* lecture course makes this clear (without adhering strictly to the terminological distinction we have introduced between *Andenken* and *Erinnern*):

> this is one of the secretes of "remembrance" [*An-denkens*] which we otherwise name "recollection" [*Erinnerung*]. This thinking ahead [*Hin-denken*] goes forth to what has-been and abandons the present. Indeed in this thinking ahead, what has-been comes to those thinking ahead from the oncoming direction [*Gegenrichtung*] at the same time. But not only in order to now somehow remain standing as something present, namely, as something present from a presentification. If we allow what is recollected the whole of its essence and nowhere disturb its reign, then we discover how, in its return, what is remembered does not stop at all in the present, so as to be, as something still presentified, merely a replacement for what is past. What is recollected swings itself away over our present and stands suddenly in the future. (*GA* 52: 54)

Hegel and Heidegger differ in their understanding of mirroring; between speculation and mirror-play what is at stake is the nature of identity itself. For Hegel it is recollected and interiorized, for Heidegger remembered and expropriated. The while as the time of arriving and not of self-presence can only be thought in remembrance.

b. Abiding Each Time Together (Anaximander)

If Heidegger's Hölderlin readings of 1941–43 emphasize the temporal nature of the while (*die Weile*), as a time of the bond (festival) and of arriving, then the Anaximander reading shortly thereafter (1946) gives us the beings that will populate that while, beings that "abide" (*weilen*).[14] Heidegger's reflections on abiding are found in a close reading of one of Anaximander's fragments.[15] The traditional rendering of this fragment, in Kathleen Freeman's translation of Diels and Kranz, runs:

> The Non-Limited is the original material of existing things; further,
> the source from which existing things derive their existence [*hê genesis*]

is also that to which they return at their destruction [*tên phthoran*], according to necessity; for they give justice and make reparation to one another for their injustice, according to the arrangement of Time [*tou chronou*].[16]

Heidegger, however, agrees with Burnet that the front portion of the fragment is of later introduction.[17] Diels and Kranz's text is taken from Simplicius, who himself is relying on a long lost version from Theophrastus, but Diels and Kranz fail to provide the true beginning of the citation—they begin their citation too soon. The talk of genesis and corruption is a later addition, something derived from the conceptual repertoire of Aristotle. As Kirk, Raven, and Schofield note, "the use of the abstracts *genesis* and *phthora*, well established in Peripatetic but not (from the other extant evidence) in Presocratic vocabulary, suggests that these belong to Theophrastus. The sentiment, too, looks Peripatetic: it is a close restatement of one of Aristotle's basic dogmas about the primary substance of the physical monists, 'all things are destroyed into that from which they came-to-be' (*Phys.* 3.5, 204b33)."[18] Consequently Kirk, Raven, and Schofield's edition of the fragment runs:

> . . . some other *apeiron* nature, from which come into being all the heavens and the worlds in them. And the source of coming-to-be for existing things is that into which destruction, too, happens, "according to necessity; for they pay penalty and retribution to each other for their injustice according to the assessment of Time," as he describes it in these rather poetical terms.[19]

The genuine wording of Anaximander is thus the portion given in quotation marks. But Heidegger carries the argument one step further: "Whoever is persuaded to strike out the part of the text found dubious by Burnet cannot retain the usually accepted closing part either" (*GA* 5: 341/257). If talk of *genesis* and *phthora* is anachronistic and overtly conceptual, so too is the talk of *chronos* that concludes the fragment. For Heidegger, then, the original wording of Anaximander is thus:

> . . . *kata to chreôn· didonai gar auta dikên kai tisin allêlois tês adikias.*

> . . . according to necessity; for they pay one another penalty and recompense for their injustice. (Cited at *GA* 5: 341/257, tm)

Editing the fragment in this way, Heidegger seeks to remove the metaphysical framework in which the fragment has come to be understood. By deleting the peripatetic anachronisms from the fragment, Anaximander's "poetical terms," as Simplicius calls them, are given their full scope in their attempt to address what Heidegger calls "the riddle of being" (*GA* 5: 344/259, tm). Anaximander does so through a thinking of abiding.

While Anaximander's attempt was elided by the subsequent effort to bring his statement into conformity with the teachings of Aristotelianism, what is evinced there is nonetheless an attempt to come to grips with the ephemeral, fleeting character of beings: "the claim [*Spruch*] speaks of that which, coming forth, arrives into unconcealment, and having arrived here, departs from this in going away" (*GA* 5: 343/258, tm). The oppositional language of genesis and corruption fails to capture this transitional movement. As Heidegger explains, "whatever has its essence in arriving and departing, we would more readily name the becoming and passing, i.e. the fleeting, but not the extant [*das Seiende*]; for we are long accustomed to opposing being to becoming, just as though becoming would be nothing and would likewise not belong to being, which for a long time now we only understand as mere perpetuation [*Beharren*]" (*GA* 5: 343/258, tm). Heidegger's goal is to discover this Ancient Greek experience of being prior to its conceptual formulation in Plato and Aristotle. To do so will require breaking with the opposition of being and becoming, even of being and nothing, as these have been construed. In short, Heidegger seeks to understand the meaning of *to on*, or, given his view that "with Plato and Aristotle the words *on* and *onta* confront us as conceptual terms" (*GA* 5: 344/259, tm); what he seeks to understand is *to eon*, the being, plural *ta eonta*, i.e., the being as it was known still earlier, at the time of Homer. Without retracing all of Heidegger's moves in this lengthy essay, we will take up the issue where it first intersects with our concerns for abiding, in the consideration of the *eon* as something present or rather something presencing (*das Anwesende*).

Simply put, abiding is what Anaximander proposes for the way that beings are. Beings abide. This notion of abiding is thus meant to evade the metaphysical strictures of sheer opposition manifest in the twin notions of genesis and corruption. Now what presences in its abiding need not be present, strictly speaking. That is to say, what is present, *das Anwesende*, might well be abiding contemporaneously with us, *gegenwärtig*, but it might also be non-contemporaneously abiding, *ungegenwärtig*, though in either case it is still something presencing. As Heidegger points out, "indeed, *eonta* is also what is past [*das Vergangene*] and what is to come [*das Zukünftige*]. Both are a way of something presencing [*des Anwesenden*], namely of non-contemporaneous presencing [*ungegenwärtig Anwesenden*]" (*GA* 5: 346/261, tm). The distinction between the present and the absent is no longer so cut and dry. Heidegger emphasizes that "what essences non-contemporaneously is the absent [*das Ab-wesende*]. As this it remains essentially related to what presences contemporaneously, insofar as it either comes forth into the region of unconcealment or goes away from this. Even what is absent is something present and, *as* something absent from out of this, presences in unconcealment" (*GA* 5: 347/261, tm). Even absence is a way of presencing (and thus what is past is never over and done with, but rather something that has-been). Even absence must leave its mark in the region of unconcealment and thus "present" itself.

And here the notion of abiding first arises: "The Greeks also poignantly name what is contemporaneously presencing *ta pareonta*; here *para* means 'with' [*bei*], namely coming-with [*beikommen*] into unconcealment" (*GA* 5: 346/261, tm). What presences does not ever presence alone. Instead it enters into unconcealment "with" others, fitting itself into the world alongside them and in contact with them. To do so, what presences must be open to relationships, indeed must be able to "come" into the world at all, and this means that it cannot be an object (*Gegenstand*). Thus Heidegger clarifies that:

> The "gegen" [against] in "gegenwärtig" [contemporaneous] does not
> mean over-and-against a subject, but rather the open region [*Gegend*]
> of unconcealment into which and within which what comes-with lingers
> [*das Beigekommene verweilt*]. Accordingly, "contemporaneous" as a char-
> acteristic of *eonta* means so much as: arriving into the while [*der Weile*]
> within the region of unconcealment. (*GA* 5: 346/261, tm)

What enters unconcealment does so as a "coming-with." This is possible only where the being is not yet understood to be an object over and against a subject. Such an object is insulated and contained. It does not come with anything else (and if it comes with a subject, it only does so because the two, subject and object, are metaphysically identical qua substances). Here, however, the being is understood as inherently relating to others, to being "with" them and "lingering." What lingers in the while does so with others. As Heidegger explains, "everything essences together, one brings the other with it, one lets the other proceed. . . . *Ta eonta* names the united multiplicity of what abides each time [*des Je-weiligen*]. So construed, everything that presences in unconcealment presents itself to every other, each according to its manner" (*GA* 5: 350/263–64, tm). What abides is with others.

This lingering with others is not confined to lingering with other contemporaneous beings. Instead, what is present remains in contact with absence as well. This is due to the ephemeral nature of abiding. Abiding is defined by an arriving into unconcealment. But to *arrive* is to come and we have repeatedly noted how coming, like giving, is always tied to a withholding as well. Simply put, what is arriving is not all here, can never be "all here" because what the arriving thing is is nothing complete in this manner, but instead is a relation to a beyond. Abiding is arriving, but this also means it is a departing, a movement out of unconcealment into concealment. Abiding is transitory on both ends, into and out of unconcealment. As such, the transitional nature of abiding eludes categorization as either present or absent, and instead troubles these oppositions themselves. What abides as neither present nor absent cannot last long. Abiding is the way of being in the while. To be neither present nor absent is to abide.

> What is contemporaneously present each time abides [*weilt jeweils*]. It lingers [*verweilt*] in coming forth and going away. Abiding is the transition from coming to going. What presences is something that each time abides [*das Je-weilige*]. Abiding transitionally, it yet abides in coming forth and already abides in going away. What is each time abidingly present [*das jeweilig Anwesende*], contemporaneously, essences from out of absence. This is to be said of whatever authentically presences, something that our customary conceptions would like to exclude from all absence. (*GA* 5: 350/263–64, tm)

What abides is transitional, yet one thing, but already another. As transitional, what is present is always this interface with the absent, so much so that the essential nature of this contact disrupts any purported separation between the two, between presence and absence, however much this might ruffle our customary conceptions (especially of the past). Another way to say this would be that what abides does so in the "between."

Heidegger pursues this thought of the bond between what abides in considering the role of *adikia* in the fragment to be one of jointure (*Fuge*). As traditionally understood, *adikia* is the injustice for which the particular beings must pay penalty and make restitution. Heidegger refuses to think *adikia* in such moralistic and punitive terms. Instead, *adikia* "names the fundamental trait of what is present" (*GA* 5: 354/266). It means that "something is out of joint [*aus den Fugen*]" (*GA* 5: 354/267). But this in turn means that "jointure [*die Fuge*] must belong to presence as such together with the possibility of being out of joint" (*GA* 5: 354/267). What abides is always and ineradicably opened toward relations, is inherently relational. This means that what presences is always already "joined" to everything else in its presencing.[20]

The way in which each being relates to the others and thereby supports it in its presencing lies at the heart of what Heidegger understands Anaximander's fragment to report. This reciprocity of jointure is thought via the notion of *tisis*. Each being gives *tisis* to the others, Anaximander says, and this has traditionally been understood in terms of recompense or a penalty that is paid by each to the other. Heidegger breaks with all of this in his thinking of *tisis*, which he understands as a "prizing" or "esteeming" (*schätzen*) and as an "attending" (*achten*) to what one so esteems. This leads to thinking *tisis* in terms of a showing of respect (*Rücksicht*) from one to the other, where this respect is an allowing of the other to be what it is, qua relational entity: "those abiding each time [*die Je-Weiligen*] let each one belong to the other: respect one another" (*GA* 5: 359/271, tm). Heidegger turns then to the Middle High German term *ruoche* (a cognate of the outmoded English word "reck" found today only in its negative form, as "reckless") for articulating this sense of *tisis. Ruoche* consequently "names solicitude [*Sorgfalt*], care [*die Sorge*]. It tends to something so that another might remain in its essencing" (*GA* 5: 360/271, tm). As Heidegger states, "giving respect [*Ruch*, "reck"] from one to the other is how what is each time abiding as something present abides at all" (*GA* 5: 361/272, tm). To abide is to support the other in the jointure of being and to let oneself be so supported: "what abides each time is precisely in the jointure of its presencing" (*GA* 5: 355/267, tm). How then can Anaximander say that what presences is "out of joint"? More, how can this be the "fundamental trait" of all that presences?

To begin with, it is to be noted that the picture of the between we have painted here is still not mediate (or "between") enough. It would stand as a self-contained separate order of presencing, something utterly distinct from the closure of presencing that is operative in the technological standing reserve, and, to a slightly lesser degree, in modern metaphysical conceptions of objectivity. The between can never be conceived as a separate order of being, a region that we would one day ultimately attain and therein subsequently live out a fulfilled existence, etc. Heidegger is just as little utopic as he is nostalgic in this regard. There is no distinct order of existence to be found anywhere, whether in the past amid the Greeks or in some future amid things and the fourfold. Instead, presencing is always contested.

What needs to be noted in the second place, however, is that this contestation of presencing does not arise from anywhere other than presencing itself, as the demise endemic to the while qua finite and arriving. Were the case otherwise, we would inadvertently return to the view of separate orders of being, rather than coming to see being itself as differentiated (a point to which we shall return). In the reading of Anaximander, this tension is thought in terms of the "perpetuation" or "insistence" (*beharren*) of beings. The insistence of beings is a revolt against the transitory nature of the while. This rebellion in being (on the part of being) manifests itself in a rejection of the transitional character of the while in the futile quest for the enclosure of a totality that would have no outside and thus would remain as it was, being what it is, unexposed (internal). We could see it as a kind of perverse *conatus* or a progenitor of the will to power. Whatever the case, Heidegger finds this insistence operative even in the thought of Anaximander, giving the lie to so many naïve interpretations of Heidegger as longing for a return to the pristine age of the Greeks, or more specifically the "Pre-Socratics," an age somehow ontologically superior to our own. This insistence of being is nothing unique to our own age, we might now say, but a character of being itself, of presencing as such, an ineluctable condition of all appearing. Heidegger writes:

> Indeed, as something present, that which each time abides [*das Je-Weilige*], precisely this and only this, can at the same time stay in its while. What arrives can even persist [*bestehen*] in its while, solely so as to remain more present in the sense of something constant [*des Beständigen*]. What each time abides insists [*beharrt*] on its presencing. In so doing it detaches itself from its transitional while. It drapes itself in the obstinacy of insistence [*des Beharrens*]. It no longer tends to what else is present. It fixates on the constancy [*Beständigkeit*] of continuation [*Fortbestehens*], as though this were a lingering. (*GA* 5: 355/267–68, tm)

What threatens abiding is an insistence on self-sufficient isolation. Against tending to others, against relationality, there is a drive to continuation of the self-same. This is the way in which beings are "out of joint." They are out of joint and in "disjointure" (*Un-Fuge*): "Essencing in the jointure of the while, what presences departs from this and, as what is each time abiding, is in the disjointure [*Un-Fuge*]. Everything that abides each time stands in disjointure" (*GA* 5: 355/268, tm). What presences, in other words, is out of joint. It is out of joint by being indisposed to relations with what lies beyond it (the others, the world). In language that prefigures his concern over the standing reserve (*Bestand*), Heidegger writes that what essences in the disjointure (or "out of joint") seeks to reify itself into sheer constancy and self-sameness:

> The disjointure [*Un-Fuge*] consists in that what each time abides [*das Je-Weilige*] seeks to harden the while in the sense of turning it into something merely constant. Thought in terms of the jointure of the while abiding as insisting is a revolt into sheer perseverance [*bloße Andauern*]. In presencing itself, which each time lets what is present abide in the

> region of unconcealment, constancy [*die Beständigung*] arises [*steht . . . auf*]. Through this insurrection [*Aufständische*] of the while, what each time abides consists of [*besteht . . . auf*] mere constancy. What is present then essences without and against the jointure of the while. (*GA* 5: 356/268, tm)

The beings that seek to exist for themselves reify themselves against the others, they are "respectless toward one another" from out of the "quest for insistence that reigns in abiding presencing itself" (*GA* 5: 359/271, tm). What lingers for only a little while is inculpated in the quest for something more lasting and enduring, and this inherently so. There could not be an abiding without this. The slight is drawn to the poles that emerge from it, a dwindling into absence or a reification into presence. Neither allows for the mediacy of abiding.

Insistence pursues abiding. And yet the respectlessness with which each insistent being cordons itself off from the others is never final. Heidegger notes that Anaximander's claim "does not say that what is each time abidingly present [*das jeweilig Anwesende*] loses itself in disjointure" (*GA* 5: 356/268, tm). More, "what abides each time is not dissolved into mere respectlessness. Respectlessness even urges these into perpetuation [*Beharren*], so that they still presence as something present. What presences as a whole is not shattered into solely respectless individuals and is not dispersed into the tenuous [*Bestandlose*]" (*GA* 5: 359/271, tm). To be out of joint is not to be nothing. What would be out of joint must still exist. Indeed, it comes out of its jointure precisely by trying too hard to exist, by seeking to close itself off from the world that gives it its existence in the first place. Respectlessness can be seen as a kind of ingratitude in this way, one that belongs to essencing itself. Part of its finitude is this incapacity to give complete thanks. But such a thanks would only ever cancel whatever debt would be so repaid. And this would mean, in the case of the beings and things we are concerned with, that the thing would lose its very thinging in the process. It would surrender its openness. To give thanks completely is to give no thanks at all. It is again simply to seek an isolated insistence upon oneself, detached from all claims and obligations to others. If this is considered a kind of justice, *dikê*, this cancellation of all debt to others (of all relationality), then beings must be out of joint, for justice must now be otherwise construed precisely in terms of a remaining in and out of a jointure with these others.

This is true not least of all because beings receive their being from being and therefore must be inclined to its arriving. For Anaximander, *to chreôn* is the law governing the dealings of beings. Or, rather, as Heidegger provocatively translates it, "need" names the way in which being relates to beings. In another vocabulary, it names the coming of the great to the slight. *Chreôn* names the relationality of being itself, where presencing and what is present are no longer construed as independent parties even if ontologically locked in some symbiotic relation. Heidegger emphasizes the relational nature of the term:

> presencing as such may evince such a relation to what presences that presencing is spoken of *as this relation*.
>
> The early word of being, *to chreôn*, names such a relation. (*GA* 5: 365/275, tm)

Beings are not in being, they are *needed* by being. And these beings themselves are *in need of* being. Need is the connection between them. One way to think the character of this need is provided to us by etymological reflection on Anaximander's operative term. Etymologically, *to chreôn* is derived from *chraomai*, typically meaning "to use," which is itself related to *hê cheir*, the hand.[21] As Heidegger explains, "*chraô* ['I use'] at the same time means: to place in someone's hands, to hand over and thus hand out, to let something over [*überlassen*] so as to belong to someone. Such a handing out, however, is of the sort that this letting over is kept in hand, and with it that which is let over" (*GA* 5: 366/276, tm). To the question of how does being come to what abides, the answer is through a mutual surrender and handing over. There is a handing into unconcealment of a presencing that through its relational connectivity is handed out beyond itself. In handing over, there is likewise an ineluctable retention per the logic of giving that we have seen Heidegger deploy across these pages. What is handed over, in other words, is never fully released (what abides can never "dissolve itself" or "lose itself" in disjointure or constancy, as we have seen)—a connection is always retained. In considering the divinities, we spoke of this in terms of a "receiving back" (see "The Meaning of the Divine" in chapter 4). Here it is a *guarding*: "*To chreôn* is then the handing in [*Einhändigen*] of presencing, a handing in that hands out [*aushändigt*] presencing to what presences, and thereby retains what presences as such precisely in hand, i.e. guarded [*wahrt*] in presencing" (*GA* 5: 366/276, tm). Nothing is ever let go completely by the guarding hand.

To chreôn names the way beings are held in being. Need "hands out limits" and in so doing it "sends the limits of the while to what is each time abidingly present" (*GA* 5: 368/277, tm). What Anaximander gives us to think is beings at their limits, where being differentiates from beings, though only so as to extend its need of beings in relationality.

To think the being at its limit, to think it as *abiding*, as Anaximander does, as Heidegger does, is to think it in terms of a relational connectivity. It is to think the being at its limit: "The jointure of the while finishes and delimits [*be-endet und be-grenzt*] what presences as such a thing. What is each time abidingly present, *ta eonta*, essences at the limit (*peras*)" (*GA* 5: 368/277, tm). This is lost the moment such a being is conceptualized. The concept contains what it conceptualizes, whereas the relationality of what abides is precisely its appeal to us. The claim (*Spruch*) of Anaximander is the appeal (*An-spruch*) of the world, and as such exceeds the bounds of any easy conceptualization. Instead it reaches to claim us, to implicate us in its appearing. The conceptual armature of genesis and corruption could not capture the fleeting nature of what abides in the while. "Grasping together (*concipere*), in the manner of representational concepts, is held in advance as the sole possible way to think being as such . . . It remains completely forgotten that the supremacy of the concept and of the interpretation of thinking as a conceiving already rests, and only so rests, upon the unthought, because unexperienced, essence of *on* and *einai*" (*GA* 5: 334/252, tm). The unthought essence of these is precisely what Anaximander's fragment lets us approximate and in so doing it offers us a different way to think. Where the conceptual reigns supreme, there is no abiding, there is only containment and opposition.

What is called for, then, is another way of thinking. A thinking that would start from the limit and think relationality from there. It would break with the guiding oppositions of being and becoming (where the former is construed as mere persistence and the latter as a non-existence), of generation and corruption, of presence and absence. Heidegger sees this way of thinking as a way of converting our understanding of the forgetting of being from an inadvertent lapse of memory into a constitutive event of being's sending. His name for this conversional thinking is one that we have already encountered in our considerations of the "while" in the readings of Hölderlin: it is "remembrance" (*Andenken*): "Only when we historically experience what is unthought of the forgetting of being as what is to be thought, and have thought what has long been experienced at its longest in terms of the dispensation of being, may the early word [*to chreôn*] perhaps make its address through a later remembrance [*Andenken*]" (*GA* 5: 365/276, tm).

What presences (*das Anwesende*) is always an arriving (*Ankunft*) for a while in the while. As what comes to us (*kommt uns an*), what presences can concern us (*geht uns an*). We respond to this concern, come in contact with it, when we think the being at its interface with being, when we "remember" (*andenken*) the being, i.e., think it no longer in terms of presence and the present, but let it be "non-present," more than the conceptually captured present, more than the real, an arriving. Remembrance, *An-denken*, is a thinking that takes its start "right at" (*an*) the limit, right at the *an* differentiating being and beings. *Andenken* is a finite thinking of what abides.

Anaximander's fragment is ultimately a remembrance of abiding. Freely rendered it reads: ". . . in terms of the need between being and beings, offering relation (jointure) and respect to one another, even from out of disjointure." No pure abiding, but jointure, and this even where out of joint—or rather, *on account of this being out of joint*. Approached in remembrance, we are reached by this address (*Anspruch*). The reading of Anaximander concludes with some thoughts on how we are "out of joint" when it comes to the thinking of the thing: "The human is on the verge of pouncing upon the whole of the earth and its atmosphere, of ripping out the concealed reign of nature in the form of forces in themselves and subordinating the course of history to the planning and ordering of a government of the earth. The same rebellious human is not in position to simply say that which *is*, to say *what* this *is*, that a thing *is* [*das ein Ding* ist]" (*GA* 5: 372/280–81, tm).

c. Abiding, Appropriating, Essencing

With the work of the mid-1940s, the notion of abiding was well prepared for its emergence into Heidegger's thinking of the fourfold at the decade's end. Indeed, abiding is the very thinging of the thing itself. It takes place when the fourfold is let abide (*verweilt*, in Heidegger's transitive usage of the term). What lingers (*verweilt*, intransitively used) is exposed to the worlding of the world. Heidegger is clear in "The Thing" that this lingering is no indifferent perduring: "to be sure, lingering is now no longer the mere perpetuation [*Berharren*] of something present-at-hand. Lingering appropriates. It brings the four into the light of what is their own" (*GA* 79: 12/11). Appropriating here is an acceptance of relation, a countervailing move to the insistence of being that we encountered in "Anaximander's Saying," where beings sought to isolate and encapsulate themselves against relation. To abide in the while is to relationally appropriate. This appropriation is not a simple taking possession, for appropriation is not an increase in the self-same, but an exposure to what is beyond oneself such that what one is comes to be defined by this contact with the other. The other is made my "own" through an appropriation that does not take possession (and thus the other is not "my" own). Instead, appropriating lets abide, lets there be this relation whereby my essence is now on the part of another, my essencing this relating. *Ereignen* is less an appropriating and more a non-possessive contact with what is most one's own (the world, the beyond, the while, the holy, the medium).

In the thing, then, what is gathered "appropriatingly gathers itself . . . so as to let the fourfold abide" (*GA* 79: 13/12). The appropriation of an abiding is called a "gathering," i.e., a bringing into relation.

It brings near: "The thing things. By thinging, it lets the earth and sky, divinities and mortals abide. By letting abide, the thing brings the four in their remoteness near to each other" (*GA* 79: 17/16). Such a relating qua gathering is at the essence of the thing, of a jug, for example: "this manifold and simplistic gathering is the essencing of the jug" (*GA* 79: 13/12). Essencing is appropriating as a gathering into relation. But this can only take place where the thing is understood as exposed (abiding) and since this exposure will ineluctably and essentially tie the thing to its surroundings, essencing can only take place where there is the medium for such abiding, where there is a while. "The essence of the jug," Heidegger writes, "is in a while [*Weile*]" and we should understand this at its fullest sweep to mean that there is no jug, there are no things, without this while (*GA* 79: 13/12).

The thing needs its while, but the while just as much needs its thing: "Thinging gathers. Appropriating the fourfold, it gathers the fourfold's while [*dessen Weile*] each time into something that abides: *into this or that thing*" (*GA* 79: 13/12, em). There could be no while without each time something abiding (a *Je-Weiliges*). There is no abiding in the abstract. It always is conditioned and be-thinged (*bedingt*).[22] The while is the medium of what abides and insofar as there is likewise no medium without something mediated (the thing brings its medium with it), there is no while without something whiling, abiding, lingering, without things.

And things there are. The lecture "The Thing" concludes with a sudden blossoming of things. It demonstrates the richness and diversity of abiding:

> The thing is nimble [*ring*]: jug and bench, footbridge and plow. But
> a thing is also, after its manner, tree and pond, stream and mountain.
> Things are, each abiding [*je weilig*] thing-like in its way, heron and deer,
> horse and bull. Things are, each abiding thing-like after their manner,
> mirror and clasp, book and picture, crown and cross. (*GA* 79: 21/20)[23]

Abiding has another name: thing. Abiding implicates a beyond by instantiating itself liminally in a medium, through a material exposure, we might say. And mortals, too, are similarly thinglike, though the passage does not say it. (Earlier in the lecture, Heidegger had cited Meister Eckhart referring to God as a thing or *dinc*; see *GA* 79: 15/14.) What is thing-like of mortals is their residing (*aufhalten*). Mortals abide in residing, in dwelling. In more than one sense, then, all these things abide *for a while.*

The temporality of abiding as a relation to the while offers a time that would not simply contain the abiding thing, but would be influenced by it, fitted to it. Such a time would not be an empty form, as Fink points out to Heidegger in their *Heraclitus* seminar of 1967. Because it only comes to what receives it, this time is an "apportioned" time:

> FINK: The time that the fire allows, by apportioning [*zumißt*] time to things, is no empty form of time, no medium separated from a content, but, to a certain extent, time along with its content.
>
> HEIDEGGER: Of the time thus given, one must say: it abides each time [*sie jeweiligt*]. It is not a container in which things appear distributed; rather, time as apportioned is already related to what each time abides [*Jeweiliges*]. (*GA* 15: 99/58, tm)

It is apportioned to what abides, the abiding thing open to its while (the reception of this apportioned time). When Fink adds that this time would be apportioned "to the individual [*auf Individuiertes*]," Heidegger quickly replies, "let us leave individuals to the side" and by now it is clear why (*GA* 15: 99/58, tm). Individuals are incapable of receiving. The capacity to receive the great, i.e., the greatness of relational expropriative liminal identity, involves a move beyond individuation. What abides each time (*je-weiligt*) is "what it is not" or is "nothing at all," where "is" still identifies an abstract being, trapped outside the world. The "individual" is not its beyond; what abides is, and essentially so (if this still needs to be said). What abides each time is open to receiving its time, the while. Its openness is likewise an openness to the coming world. The disaggregation of the thing into the four is the same opening to relationality, the same abiding, that lets there be world. For this reason Heidegger will speak of the abiding thing as a "gesture" of world.

§24. Thing as Gesture of World

The mirror-play of the fourfold that gathers the four together likewise spaces them apart. This spaced gathering of the four must be instantiated and this instantiation is the thing. The spaced gathering of the four keeps this instantiated thing from closing in on itself, releasing it instead to world. This spaced gathering of the four is consequently the thinging of the thing. Thinging in this way, the thing surrenders any pretensions to objectivity and rests in its own delimited nature as thing. The thing is consequently slight, receptive to what comes, apportioned to it. Its slightness can be understood temporally, too, as an abiding that lasts for only a little while. But that little while is necessary if there is to be any abiding at all, any thinging, and therefore also any world. The fourfold that assembles at the thing does not gather around an inert pole; rather the fourfold collects itself into a relational interface, one that opens onto world: "The four are a reciprocity, inceptually-uniting. The things let the fourfold of the four linger with each other [*bei sich verweilen*]. This collective letting-abide is the thinging of the thing. We name the uniting fourfold of the sky and earth, mortals and divinities, lingering in the thinging of the thing: the world" (*GA* 12: 19/*PLT* 197, tm). The thing is thus intimately connected with world.

Heidegger will think this relation at the time of the fourfold not simply as something on the part of the thing, but a movement on the part of the world as well. It is both a gesturing and a granting. The relation so articulated is a line of difference, but not a difference (*Differenz*) that would run between isolated parties; rather it is a *differentiation* (*Unter-schied*) that first gives each to the other: "Differentiation [*der Unter-Schied*] lets the thinging of the thing rest in the worlding of the world. Differentiation expropriates the thing into the calm of the fourfold. Such expropriating does not rob the thing of anything. Rather, it first lifts the thing into its own: that it lets world abide" (*GA* 12: 26/*PLT* 203, tm). To think the thing in its relation to world is to think this "singular" differentiation of thing and world (*GA* 12: 22/*PLT* 200, tm).

a. Gesture and Granting

Because of their inherently relational nature (and thanks to the fourfold), the abiding things implicate a world beyond them. They not only implicate it, but, following Heidegger, they un-fold it: "Thingingly the things un-fold [*ent-faltet*] the world in which they abide and thus are each time abiding [*je die weiligen sind*]" (*GA* 12: 19/*PLT* 197, tm). The simple (*einfach*) and guileless (*einfältig*) things develop the world, unfurling it while providing it with pleats and folds of their own, complicating it. In so doing, things bear the burden of the world so unfolded. Things are the executioners of world, they carry it out: "In their thinging, the things carry out [*tragen . . . aus*] the world" (*GA* 12: 19/*PLT* 197, tm). They are not inert items in an indifferent container, but are caught in a relation of carrying out, executing, or even of performing (*austragen*) world. As we saw in our earlier consideration of the earth, *Austrag* names an ungrounded relationship of co-constitution. The world is a performance of things, sustained and upheld by them.

But how do the things bear this world? Is all bearing the same? We already know that this is not the case. How a thing bears world is each time a distinct performance. Heidegger names it with a term we have also already encountered. Things bear world as gestures: "Our old language names carrying out [*Austragen*]: *bern, bären,* and thus the words 'to bear' [*gebären;* 'to carry,' 'to give birth'] and 'gesture' [*Gebärde*]. Thingingly, the things are things. Thingingly they gesture [*gebärden*] world" (*GA* 12: 19/ *PLT* 197, tm). Things bear the world as burden and as birth, i.e., inceptually. They gesture it.

By implicating a beyond, things gesture. The gesture is not confined to its performer—it is itself a performance. And this means it is always beyond what carries it out. Gesture is itself the transition into this "out." Gesture is the carrying, the carriage or bearing (comportment), of this transition beyond oneself. The things that gesture world hold it up. As we have seen in considering the hinting divinities, the bearing of gesture is a bearing that gives no ground, but instead is a "counter-bearing and conveying [*Entgegentragen und Zutrag*]," that is, gesture is an interface, as is the thing (*GA* 12: 102/*OWL* 19, tm). There would be no world without things. They are the pinions of world, the axes upon which it turns. The movement of the thing beyond itself effulges forth a space of relation. Relations stream away from things, through the cracks of the four, along the avenues of the four, billowing out from the thing. In so doing, these relations articulate world.

In this regard there is something initiatory about things. They let a world be born around them. They are not simply relations of intellectual affinity, but bodily instantiated meanings, connections, accidental alliances and tendencies, all of which push out the world that is being born around the thing. This is the generative character of relations. The demigod's birth attested to it earlier—now it is a matter of the world itself. The gesture of the thing is a birth of world into the world from amid the things. And as borne, the things themselves are born in their own giving birth to the world. Their birth is their youth, i.e., their closeness to their beginning, the medium that supports them. The thing abides as slight and this means it sustains and is sustained by a world of relations. To abide is to be caught up in gesture, to be liminally inclined. World keeps things from being isolated and frozen gesticulations, allowing them the sweep of their movement and course.

As we have repeatedly seen, there can be no appearance without a medium capable of supporting it, and the same holds true of the thing. The world itself is the medium of things. The world can no longer be construed as a container or totality in this regard. Indeed, Heidegger is clear in the "Language" essay that "the word 'world' is now no longer used in the metaphysical sense. It names neither the secularly conceived *universum* of nature and history, nor does it name the theologically conceived creation (*mundus*), nor does it mean solely the whole of what presences (*kosmos*)" (*GA* 12: 21/*PLT* 199, tm). Instead world must be understood with greater instantiation now in relation to the gesturing things. This relationship between thing and world "entrusts world to things and at the same time shelters the things in the radiance [*Glanz*] of world. This grants to the things their essence. Things gesture [*gebärden*] world. World grants [*gönnt*] things" (*GA* 12: 21/*PLT* 199, tm). The gesture of the thing that opens out onto world is not simply a gesture of offering; it is also a gesture capable of receiving, one capable of receiving this grant of world.

In tandem with the gesture of things, there is the granting of world. The thing asks and receives, the world is solicited and bestows, and the two do so together. The granting of world is no simple giving; rather this granting (*Gönnen*) is a sending of grace (*Gunst*), as etymology attests, and Heidegger makes the connection himself, speaking at times of the "gestures of things and the grace [*Gunst*] of world" (*GA* 12: 24/*PLT* 202, tm). The granting of grace was thematized by Heidegger a few years earlier in the 1943 lecture course *Heraclitus: The Beginning of Western Thinking*, where at issue is fragment 123, *physis kryptesthai philei*, traditionally rendered "nature likes to hide."[24] Heidegger takes up the notion of *philein* expressed there, and rather than understand this as "like" or "love," opts for a more periphrastic rendering as "to give grace [*die Gunst schenken*]" (*GA* 55: 128), to make a gift of one's grace, to bestow favor. But as Heidegger warns, "we understand grace here in the sense of an originary granting and affording [*Gönnens und Gewährens*], and therefore not in the mere accessory meaning of 'benefit' [*Begünstigen*] and 'patronage' [*Begönnern*]" (*GA* 55: 128). Granting, in other words, and per the world's granting of things, is not a simple equipping, outfitting, or supplying. Rather, as Heidegger points out, "the originary granting [*Gönnen*] is the affording [*Gewähren*] of that which is due to the other because it belongs to his essence insofar as it bears his essence. . . . through this granting the granted essence blossoms into its own freedom" (*GA* 55: 128). Since this originary granting is a giving to the other of what is already their own, it does not "benefit" the other in the sense of something that would additionally accrue to them. Rather, it first lets the other be the other, gives them the space to blossom into their own freedom, the spacing of their relations. But let us also not lose sight of the fact that what is so granted is something that "bears" (*trägt*) the essence of the other. I give, or rather "grant," to the other that which bears his/her essence. That is to say, I give the other to themselves, precisely as that which must be borne by another (me). I grant the other their relational essencing. In so doing, I do not make the other into anything he or she is not, nor do I make the other into what he or she is. Instead I let the other come forth in his/her freedom through this granting. As such, "granting is an ability to wait" (*GA* 55: 129). In waiting I do not demand full presence from the other (for if there were full presence, there could be no waiting), but instead let them come and be what they are as arriving.

If world grants things then this means that world gives the things what is their due qua essencing, thinging, and this is nothing other than the space of their relating. This spacing of world is what bears the things. The world that grants things also buoys them up in the interweaving of the relations running through it. The things that gesture world are granted by world so as to thing. They are supported by what they themselves carry out, they are *borne (getragen)*. In the Heraclitus course, the relation teased out of fragment 123 is thought in regards to being itself: "since long ago, what is called being [*Sein*] is in itself pervaded by a grace and a granting" (*GA* 55: 129). Seven years later, it is a matter of thing and world.

The interface of thing and world is the meeting ground (though it is groundless) of gesture and granting (the slight and the great). Each implicates the other in a manner we have already named that of "appropriation" (*ereignen*). To think the thing as the spaced gathering of the fourfold is to surrender claims to integrity and stolidity. Instead the implication of world is so great that Heidegger will speak of the "world-fourfold [*Welt-Geviert*]" so as to indicate the ineradicable connection between the fouring of the four and the worlding of the world, a connection that obviously runs through the thinging of the thing.[25] And to be sure, the same essay "Language" speaks not of the thing or the world alone, but names instead "thing-world and world-thing [*Ding-Welt und Welt-Ding*]" (*GA* 12: 26/*PLT* 203) so as to emphasize this ineradicable conjunction. Heidegger is explicit as to the dual appropriation operative in the interface between thing and world. It is a matter of what he terms "differentiation" (*Unter-Schied*): "For world and thing, the differentiation *appropriates* things into the gestures of world, *appropriates* world into the granting of things" (*GA* 12: 22/*PLT* 200, tm). The appropriation here is the effect of the exposure of thing to world. They cannot reside next to each other in isolated indifference—they already pervade the other and seep past themselves into the other (and this essentially, i.e., by dint of essence).

Differentiation names this seepage. Heidegger identifies it with the between, noting of things that "their gesturing of world is fulfilled from out of the grace of the world. Such things are sufficient for allowing the fourfold of the world to abide with them. The pure brightness of the world and the simple gleaming of things measure out [*durchmessen*] their between, the differentiation" (*GA* 12: 25/*PLT* 203, tm). The radiance of things and the brightness of the world together share between themselves a limit of differentiation. It remains for us to explore this interrelation a little further before concluding.

b. Differentiation and In-finitude

Heidegger's thinking of differentiation is a thinking of the productivity or generative capacity of limits. It is a thinking of the interfacial, of coordinate implication. Because the delimited always spills past itself, limitation is never isolating: "World and thing do not subsist alongside one another. They penetrate [*durchgehen*] each other" (*GA* 12: 21–22/ *PLT* 199). The limit can therefore not be thought in terms of the line or the linear. Limitation is never so thin as this. The limit already blossoms on both its sides, but in saying this we still resort to linear thought as though the line would not be surrounded on all sides—as though it would even have sides—and in every dimension by what surpasses it. A limit is nothing so widthless or slender. Limitation is not confined to a line somewhere, it permeates everything. Everything is at the limit and therefore in the between. The limit of delimitation is the expanse, the breadth, of a between.

This between is a space of relationality, of intimacy: "In this, the two measure out [*durchmessen*] a middle. In this they are united [*einig*]. As what is united in this way, they are intimate [*innig*]. The middle of the two is intimacy [*die Innigkeit*]. Our language names what is in the middle of two a between" (*GA* 12: 22/*PLT* 199, tm). Heidegger's sense of intimacy here, *Innigkeit,* is also a term for "interiority," an inside as opposed to an outside. But Heidegger takes this interior and exposes it, sends it out into the between. What stands so exposed, mediated by the middle of the between, is related. These connections across distance bring near and in so doing give birth to an intimacy between the near and the distant, an intimacy confined to the interior of neither and no one. Just such an intimacy across separation is voiced in this term *Innigkeit,* a term we should hear as both a conversion of the Hegelian notion of interiorization, *Er-innerung,* as well as a move away from the more austere sense of "being-in" found in *Being and Time.*

But for the intimacy of the between there must be those capable of such intimacy, disposed to such mediation. Such things are relationally pouring through the world, split onto the world, cut open. This cut runs through the thing exposing it, cutting it open to the sky. Any notion of integrity must be abandoned. What can be intimate are the cut open, the wounded. Being is the exposure of this wound, the beyond called together by this cut. The wounded thing is sensitive enough to receive what is granted, yet resilient enough to bear the world. The cut distinguishing thing and world runs "between" them: "The Latin language says: *inter.* To this corresponds the German *unter* [under, among]. The intimacy of world and thing is no conflation. Intimacy only reigns there where what is intimate, world and thing, purely distinguish themselves [*sich scheiden*] and remain so cut [*geschieden*]. In the middle of the two, in the between of world and thing, in their *inter*, in this among [*Unter-*] there reigns the cut [*der Schied*]" (*GA* 12: 22/*PLT* 199, tm). The cut of things neither annihilates them nor leaves them unscathed. In a different register we might call it a "weathering," a wearing away, but here it has the purity of a cut, a slice that exposes a surface, removing the integument (or perhaps it is even only a scratch). Only beings defined by this cut can be "in" anything, much less a between, and only in such a between can there be this intimacy (or even "interiority," properly understood, since there is no outside that does not mark itself on the inside).

Differentiation (*Unter-Schied*) is the cut (*Schied*) that moves among (*Unter*) things, or first lets there be an "among"—i.e., a relation between things—by cutting through the capsule of beings. Only beings so cut can be among one another. Returning to a thought from our considerations of the technological challenge to things, the thing is cut open like a part, not a piece. While the piece can stand alone, the part is always essentially the part of a whole. It is exposed to a whole beyond it. And as so exposed the thing is whole, or hale: cut open onto the holy, cut into mediation, bleeding through the between among things.

The cut of differentiation cuts among, and its productivity in this respect is that of exposing the thing to world. Differentiation is not a result of this distinction—it first performs it or carries it out (*austragen*). And this means that, as a limit, differentiation, too, is nothing restricted to a line, but is already spatialized into a between, a dimension. Differentiation as this limit carries out the interface between thing and world. That between is the dimension, nothing self contained but an apportioning to things, a fitting to them:

> differentiation is the dimension for world and thing. But in this case "dimension" also no longer means a district present at hand on its own within which this and that would be settled. Differentiation is *the* dimension, insofar as it apportions [*er-mißt*] to world and thing what is their own. Its apportioning first opens up the separated reciprocity [*Aus- und Zu-einander*] of world and thing. Such an opening is of the sort whereby differentiation here measures out [*durchmißt*] both of these. As the middle for world and things, differentiation metes out [*vermißt*] the measure [*Maß*] for their essencing. (*GA* 12: 23/*PLT* 200, tm)

The articulation of thing and world through this differentiation spaces itself into a dimension. It finds a standard (or rule) for the dimension precisely in the outline of the thing, the surface of its exposure. The dimension apportions this exposure to things by exceeding those things, by virtue of the fact that every line stands exposed, that there are no lines but only surfaces, or better "bodies," of interfacial exposure coalescing at the things themselves.

Through differentiation, the thing participates in the world's granting of things and the world participates in the thing's gesturing of world. The reciprocity of this "participation" is their differentiation, their co-implication. It is the name for a limit that does not isolate and that falls between the immersed and its medium. It is the buoyancy of the medium itself we might say, a mediation of being that provides the lift of a bearing: "Differentiation carries out the world in its worlding, the things in their thinging. In carrying these out, it bears them to one another. Differentiation does not mediate [*vermittelt*] after the fact, by tying world and thing to some middle to be produced from them. As the middle, differentiation first mediates [*ermittelt*] world and things to their essence, i.e. into their reciprocity, the unity of which it carries out" (*GA* 12: 22/*PLT* 200, tm). Gesture and granting differentiate a medium of worldly things, slight and abiding—or *infinite.*

But in what sense might things be infinite? The slight and abiding things, gesturing world and cut open to receive its granting, are never ending. As cut open they have had their ends excised from them. Where they are supposed to end, they gesture a world. The 1959 lecture "Hölderlin's Earth and Sky" says it best: they are in-finite: "In-finite [*Un-endlich*] means that the ends and sides, the regions of the relation, do not stand on their own, cut off [from relation] and one-sided. Rather, relieved of one-sidedness and of finitude [*Endlichkeit*], they belong in-finitely to one another in a relationship that they 'thoroughly' hold together from its middle" (*GA* 4: 163/188, tm). What cuts the thing open removes its ends from it, the ends that would encapsulate it. Relieved [*enthoben*] of these ends, the thing is now end-less and opened into a mediating relation held together not by poles that would stand outside it, but at its middle: "The middle, which is so called because it mediates, is neither the earth, nor the sky, neither the god, nor the human. The in-finite that is to be thought here is abysally distinct from the merely endless [*Endlosen*], which, on account of its uniformity [*Gleichförmigkeit*], allows for no growth" (*GA* 4: 163/188, tm). The in-finite as the manifold of relationality is not uniform, but modulated, mediated, different, and differentiated. It is exposed to a beyond into which it can grow and flourish. The uniform, on the contrary, would seek self-same perpetuation, an insistence allowing for no growth or change. And yet the endlessly uniform and the in-finite are not opposites; such a positioning would only make sense from the perspective of the uniformly one-sided and its operative dualisms. Rather, Heidegger says the two are "abysally distinct," which means neither opposed nor identical. But if there is an abyss between the in-finite and the endless—*between relationality and metaphysics*—then we already know that this abyss must be borne between them, separating them and relating them at once. Indeed, while it was Hegel whom Heidegger charged with oppositional thinking in his 1956 seminar cited in our discussion of speculation, nonetheless, in the 1959 Hölderlin reading Heidegger says in introducing his notion of the in-finite that "the determination '*in*-finite' is to be thought here in the sense of the speculative dialectic of Schelling and Hegel" (*GA* 4: 163/188). We shall return to this abyssal relation in the conclusion that follows. On the one side is totality, enclosure, and perpetuation of the self-same, while on the other there is "the 'tender relation' of earth and sky, god and human," a relation that itself "can become more in-finite [*un-endlicher werden*]" (*GA* 4: 163/188, tm). Because the in-finite is an issue of relationality, there is no limit that it can reach. Or, rather, it is always at its limits, all the way out to the limitless or unattainable (as we have seen in considering the reach of the dimension). There is always more to relate to, always a place to look up. Relationality never achieves closure, it just becomes more in-finite and more intimate: "For what is not one-sided can more purely shine forth [*zum Vorschein kommen*] from out of the intimacy [*Innigkeit*] in which the four just mentioned are held to each other" (*GA* 4: 163/188, tm). There is always more to expose; intimacy is found outside.

The expropriated mirror-play of the fourfold ungrounds the thing and renders it slight. The slightness of the thing means it only abides for a little while. But these things, slight and abiding, are the joists of the world we inhabit, the poles that stretch out the vault above upon the ground below. In gesturing world, these things are ineradicably meaningful. In dwelling, the mortals abide with these remarkable things. The infinite is an infinitude of things. What could bear to project the world? How weathered would one have to become to do so even in part? How much would one lose of oneself and how much would one be forced to retain? Where all that is unfolds from a limit, where being is relational, the barrier of that limit must be so worn away, so threadbare, so slight as to allow thing and world both their run through. Only with this can there be a gesture of world. The in-finite demands as much, that things be so raw and exposed. But in this it grants them place and meaning—*for a while*. The thinging of the thing is this expropriated, slight, abiding, gesturing of world.

There Have Never Been Things

Heidegger's thinking of the fourfold is a thinking of things. It names the dehiscence of the thing as it unfurls itself through world. In the foregoing analyses we have traced the components of the fourfold in order to show how they converge in the thinging of the thing. The thinging thing is resolutely finite, that is, relational (in-finite). Each component contributes to the constitution of just such a relational, finite existence.

The earth grounds the thing, but this ground is ultimately an abyss, nothing solid beneath one's feet. This abyss, however, is by no means an absence, but instead is what comes to appearance in the very radiant phenomenality and sense of the world itself. The ground of the thing is consequently nothing other than this "bearing" of sense, this appearing. The earth is stretched between a withholding (an abyss, *Ab-grund*, remaining away of ground) and a radiance (the shining forth of the sensible). This earth as stretched, or spaced, requires a medium through which to extend itself.

The sky provides this, receiving the earthly thing and distributing it across its variegated field. The sky opens the heavens around the thing, granting to such things the reverberation of their relations. The sky is thus nothing inert or stable, but constantly aflutter with the streaming of these relations. This thickened sky, replete now with the relations of all that appears, has its own texture and density that shifts from place to place. The reciprocal relations of things give the sky the tensile strength to buoy and support what appears in it. The mediation of the sky, however, can only last a little while. The shifting of the sky, its light and its dark, brings a measured time to things, a time that they themselves help bring about by receiving what is apportioned to them.

The situation of the earth and sky alone does not yet arrive at the full fledged thinking of mediation determinative of Heidegger's later thinking. One could still misconstrue this situation as one of containment. With the divinities, Heidegger provides the measure of the relation, the "logic" of mediation whereby all that appears, the arriving and the withdrawing, is marked by its exposure to this medium. The divinities name the fact that appearance is remarked, however destitute the times, and that even things bear witness. The divinities allow the unattainable to appear to us. There is no meaning without this (meaning is an ontological designation). The messengership of the divinities ensure that every relation is always marked and that meaning is the arriving of a relation beyond oneself.

Lastly, the thing would not thing if it could not reach the mortals, those beings defined by non-possession, those for whom this world is meaningful. Mortals dwell in their death. They exist. Relationality would not be relationality were it not able to reach them. If we are the mortals, then we are inculpated in the essencing of things, however much we might act to the contrary or refuse their appeal. What is most the mortal's own is nothing he or she might possess. Mortality is a shared endeavor, an accompanying of others across this world of things. The finite mortal is able to receive and support the world of appearing upon the earth, under the sky, before the divinities, and with others.

Heidegger's thinking of the fourfold thus provides a way of considering finite appearing as ungrounded, mediated, meaningful, and shared. As such, finitude is worldly, it is the creation of the world. The dehiscent things are understood to be gestures of our world. The thing gestures itself into a world that grants back to things this reception. It is a relation of bearing once again, or *Ereignis*: the two ultimately name the same. The tent of the world stakes itself on things. Heidegger's later thinking traverses this finite world opened here by the fourfold. The period of the fourfold is the fullest articulation of what we might call the *topos* of Heidegger's thinking, the landscape of his later thought.

And yet, for Heidegger, *there have never been things*. These pivotal gestures of world are yet to appear. A preparatory sketch for "The Thing" states it clearly: "Things are as though long gone and nevertheless they have never yet been *as things* [*sind sie noch nie* als Dinge *gewesen*]" (*GA* 79: 23/22). Heidegger attributes this in part to the manner of knowledge in the modern sciences. This has always encroached upon things in their thinging, whether under the reign of objectification and representation in modern natural science, or through a more technologically advanced atomic destruction, as we have seen. The thought is developed further in the lecture:

> Within its purview, that of objects, the compelling knowledge of science has already annihilated the thing as thing long before the atomic bomb exploded. The explosion of the atomic bomb is only the crudest of all crude confirmations of an annihilation of things that occurred long ago: confirmation that the thing as thing remains nullified. (*GA* 79: 9/8)

The published version of "The Thing" inserts a brief explanation at this point: "The thinghood of the thing remains concealed, forgotten. The essence of the things never comes to appearance, i.e. to language. The talk of an annihilation of the thing as thing means just this" (*GA* 7: 172/ *PLT* 168, tm). The annihilation of the thing is located in the forgetting of its essencing. For the moderns, this forgetting led to representational objectification, for the post-moderns, to circulative replaceability. In both cases, the thinging of the thing, its essencing, was overlooked. Rather than understand the thing as relationally implicating a beyond and as disaggregated, the thing was stalled in representation or sent circulating. And yet, if this annihilation is understood as a forgetting, then perhaps it may likewise be remembered—and we have considered "remembrance," *An-denken*, precisely in this light, as a thinking of the non-present thing that begins from its interface with a beyond, i.e., as a thinking that thinks the thing at its limit, its *An-*. Heidegger continues:

> The annihilation is so uncanny because it brings with it a twofold delusion. For one, the opinion that science, more so than all other experience, would encounter the actual in its actuality. Second, the pretence that the thing could just as well be a thing regardless of scientific research into the actual, which presupposes that there ever were essencing things at all. (*GA* 79: 9/8–9)

The annihilation of things is carried out by science via both its exclusive character—that it is held to be the only way to encounter "the real"—as well as its claims to objectivity—that this "real" would be independent of science's intrusion. Things are annihilated in favor of indifferent capsules that we may catalog and test from a position of non-interference à la Gyges. The history of things as well as the role of science and technology in that history is disregarded. Still, Heidegger is not trying to remove any technological influence from things, but to understand the technological as always already operative in the thing itself.[1] So much so, in fact, that we would do wrong to think of this relationship as one of incursion or challenge upon the thing issuing from somewhere outside it. The thing itself essences in this way. Technology is not external to the thing, lurking in dark corners and waiting to strike. The thing itself brings it with itself necessarily. Heidegger expands on the point:

> If the things had ever shown themselves as things, then the thinghood of the thing would have been evident. It would have laid claim to thinking. In truth, however, the thing remains obstructed as thing,

nullified and in this sense annihilated. This occurred and occurs so essentially that the things are not only no longer admitted as things, but the *things have not yet ever been able to appear as things at all.* (*GA* 79: 9/9, em)

It is not that science has somehow sullied our experience of the world, that we would otherwise dwell with things were it not for the technological commodification that is everywhere prevalent. Rather, things have never appeared as things at all. Not only have there never been things in the past, Heidegger is likewise not advocating that there ought to be things in the future, if we could just somehow manage to get out from under the oppressive grip of a technological society. In a letter appended to the published version of "The Thing," the 1950 "Letter to a Young Student," Heidegger is quite clear about this. In regards to the relationship between positionality and the interface between thing and world that we have presented in the above he writes: "In the dispensation [*Geschick*] of being there is no mere succession: now positionality, then world and thing" (*GA* 7: 186/*PLT* 183, tm). Instead, the thinking of thing and world—i.e., the thinking of the fourfold that *performs* this very interface—includes that of positionality, and essentially so. They are concurrent. Thing and world are not something to be achieved in the future, they are essencing now. There have not yet ever been things. There have ever been not-yet-things. The not-yet-thing is the only thing capable of the slightness that gestures a world.

To be sure, Heidegger takes pains to point out to the student that in the lecture "being is by no means opposed to no-longer-being and not-yet-being; these both belong themselves to the essencing of being" (*GA* 7: 184/*PLT* 181, tm). There have never been things because the thing is not something that could ever simply be. It is more relation than entity. The thing can only exist as something that comes, as an arriving, as essencing and thinging, *as not yet*, but never as some kind of accomplished thing. The thing is nothing to be, for if the thing were ever to be the thing, the world would stop.

As this not yet, the thing is arriving into a world that motions back to it in a granting. This granting brings the world to the thing. But the world that is brought in is the technologically dominated unworld of post-modernity. The letter to the young student is unequivocal that one cannot understand the thing without taking account of its technologized essence. In discussing the reception that the thing lecture has received in the context of the Bremen lecture cycle *Insight Into That Which Is*, Heidegger observes:

one very happily and attentively listens to the presentation of the essence of the jug, but right away closes one's ears when the talk is of objectivity [*Gegenständlichkeit*], the standing [*Herstand*] and provenance [*Herkunft*] of production [*Hergestelltheit*], when the talk is of positionality [*Gestell*]. But all this necessarily belongs to the thinking of the thing, a thinking which remembers [*denkt . . . an*] the possible arriving of world. Perhaps remembering [*andenkend*] in this way helps ever so slightly and inapparently [*im Allergeringsten und Unscheinbaren*] for such arrival to reach into the opened realm of the human essence. (*GA* 7: 186/*PLT* 183, tm)[2]

The thinking of positionality necessarily belongs to the thinking of the thing. What is brought to the thing by its very openness is a connection to its replacement. The thing would not be the thing were it not open to the point of self-destruction (disintegration). It has to welcome this. And what comes is the challenge to come forth and simply be what it is. And once the thing is what it is then it is immediately replaceable by what it is. And yet this replaceability is of its essence.

The thing is singular and we have argued this by virtue of the fact that the thing is not all there. The challenge to come forth would have the thing be exactly all there. But, paradoxically enough, the thing is not all there only thanks to this challenge that it be all there. For the thing to thing it cannot *be* the thing, it can only be *not yet the thing*, which is to say that it can be nothing self-contained and identifiable. If it were simply the thing it would not gesture the world, it would be contained in that world and seamlessly merge with it. The thing needs the technological challenge in order *to keep from being the thing*. And what this means is not that the thing's essencing is inhibited or obstructed by technology, but rather that its very essencing itself must be rethought apart from any residue of a sequentialist thinking whereby we would move out of positionality and into a new era of thing and world, ie., the fourfold (which is precisely the interface between these). Indeed, Anaximander already thought this in terms of the insistence of beings, to be what they are they must be drawn to their undoing—or their consummation, which is the same.

What this means is that the singularity of the thing is dependent upon its very replaceability. Singularity would be meaningless without replaceability as a counter concept, we might say, but the separation implicit in the "counter" of this concept already gives the lie to formulations of this kind. We are called on to think the thing starting from its essencing, not by means of a hasty conjunction of otherwise independent parties (thing and standing reserve, for instance, or fourfold and technology). Essencing is continual entry to the between, a constant delivery of more of oneself, a bringing to bear of what one withholds, an arriving tense with the challenge of its completion. And yet without this, no thing. *The same challenge that would reduce the thing to nothing simultaneously protects it from being anything.*

In considering this technological challenge to things in our introduction, we noted how both the standing reserve and the thing were in agreement in their rejection of objectivity. Now we see why. The thing *is* the standing reserve, or rather, they are the "same." Stated conversely, there is an essence of technology. And again, it is not the case that technological replacement is a possibility that may or may not befall a particular thing. Thinghood is constituted by replaceability. Essencing and singularity are nothing other than openness and vulnerability as expressed in this devastating challenge of technological replacement. If there were no threat to the thing in standing outside of itself, it would simply merge with the world. Otherwise phrased, despite all its efforts to establish a frictionless, circulating unworld for itself, technology only ever proves the ineluctable viscosity of world. Technology keeps the thing from merging with world and reifying itself there. Technology saves the thing.

If we wish to speak of a post-modern Heidegger, then, it no longer suffices to posit either the thing or the standing reserve as configurations surpassing objectivity. They themselves are one. In 1962 Heidegger speaks of a "Janus head" uniting technology and the event of appropriation, and this is precisely what he means (*GA* 14: 63/ *TB* 53). This new configuration of his thought—the *differentiation* between thing and world effected at the fourfold and shading into replacement—is so thoroughly relational as to inaugurate another beginning for Heideggerian thought. What the relation of thing and world presents, in other words, is no longer addressable in terms of a relation between being and beings, and this by Heidegger's own account. The differentiation (*Unter-Schied*) of thing and world cannot be thought in terms of ontological difference (*Differenz*). The fourfold converts (*verwindet*) ontological difference itself.[3]

These ideas come most clearly to the fore in Heidegger's very late thinking, in poems and notes from the mid-1970s. Here we encounter an overt concern with getting outside of the ontological difference and thinking otherwise. Before we turn to these late texts, we should first examine how the ground for this change is already being prepared at the time of the fourfold itself. In both the Bremen lectures of 1949 and the letter to Ernst Jünger, "On the Question of Being," of 1955—the "bookends" of the era of the fourfold, as it were, and the sixtieth birthdays of each thinker—there is already evinced a transformation of how we are to understand being. An attempt is made in both cases to mitigate its abstractive force.

In "The Danger," this unfolds in Heidegger's rumination on his claim that the world would be "the truth of the essence of being" (the space through which being radiates). In making such a claim, he says,

> we now characterize the world in respect to being. So conceived, world is subordinate to being, while in truth the essence of being essences from out of the concealed worlding of world. World is not one way of being and deferential to said being. Being has to own its essence from the worlding of world. This points out that the worlding of world is an appropriating [*das Ereignen*] in a still-unexperienced sense of this word. When world first properly takes place, then being, and along with it the nothing, vanish into worlding. Only when the nothing, in its essence from the truth of being, vanishes into this is nihilism overcome. (*GA* 79: 48–49/46–47)

The passage is rather cryptic, to be sure, but the distinction that it makes is a crucial one for our concerns. World is nothing subordinate to being. The situation is almost the opposite. The priority lies with the world. Being has to establish itself from within the world. The sense of being operative here seems to be one that is diametrically opposed to nothingness. It is the being of metaphysics, in other words, a thinking of sheer presence and absence. These would be abstractions, we might say, from the rich middle ground of the world, a world that is itself a between, i.e., nothing self-same and self-present, but an arriving and conductive medium of radiance. Were this worlding to take place—and let us note that if there have never been things, then there has likewise never been world, at least not yet—this worlding would undermine the ostensibly oppositional nature of being and nothingness by relationally contextualizing all that appears. As such, this opposition of being and nothingness would vanish before the worlding world. For Heidegger, this would be the only imaginable "overcoming" of metaphysics (Heidegger speaks of an overcoming here—nihilism is to be *überwunden*—but strictly speaking he would have to mean a conversion, *Verwindung*, of nihilism, not simply its discarding). Nihilism is not overcome by advocating for being over nothingness; nihilism is lodged in the very opposition between them, and picking one side over the other does nothing to change that. Instead, when being and nothing are no longer thought oppositionally, as we saw in considering the shrine of the nothing and the refuge of being (see "The Shrine of the Nothing, the Refuge of Being" in chapter five), the essencing "between" them can come to the fore and do so as worlding.

Only when our oppositional conception of nothingness is converted into a thinking of the between, of the world, will nihilism be "overcome."

The world that being and nothingness "vanish into" should be understood as a materially radiant medium of appearance. It loses any of the abstraction that might still cling to our conception of "being" *simpliciter* (the metaphysical sense of being at the very least).[4] But if we take Heidegger to the extreme on this point, then any sense of being "vanishes" into worlding. There would not be beings any longer, there would be things instead (or, more precisely, not yet things). With this transition, we enter the thinking of thing and world. At stake is the difference, or rather, differentiation between them.

What Heidegger thinks by differentiation is a non-oppositional relationality whereby the thing abides in the while of world. Differentiation cannot be thought of as an ad hoc connection established between two pre-existing parties. While such a connection can be termed a "relation," it cannot be one of need, where each party is essentially defined by the relation itself. Things *need* world and world *needs* things. But if this need is so essential, then there are no longer two to speak of here. Differentiation is consequently not about any parties that would be differentiated and otherwise independent. Instead, differentiation is a break from simple differences, or even "ontological" differences. Differentiation concerns the limit of relatability, the reciprocal, constitutive relation of need (*to chreôn*).

A similarly transformed understanding of being arises in "On the Question of Being," one of the four inaugural presentations of the fourfold. This letter is where Heidegger famously introduces the "crossing through" (*Durchkreuzung*) of being, a literal typographic striking through of the word "being." He does so explicitly in regards to the fourfold as a way of naming the converted "being" that is no longer being, but what we are calling instead "world." Heidegger speaks of it here in terms of a turning (*Zuwendung*) of being. Rather than maintaining itself in the aloofness of an indifferent concept, being now has turned to us, addressing us and dispensing itself to us. It concernfully approaches us, we have said. And similar to "The Danger," being vanishes into this other relation evinced by its turning. Heidegger writes:

> If a turning belongs to "being," and indeed in such a way that the latter resides in the former, then "being" dissolves into the turning. The latter now becomes that which is worthy of question, that in terms of which we henceforth think being, which has gone back and entered into its essencing. Accordingly, a thoughtful look ahead into this realm can write "being" only in the following way: being. (*GA* 9: 410–11/310, tm)

Rather than a present or absent being, we have a still legible cancellation, the marking of a loss. The situation is one we have addressed before in terms of the *enshrinement* of being ("The Shrine of the Nothing" in chapter 5). The crossed through being is posited and withdrawn simultaneously. It is given as erased. But its erasure is never complete. It remains legible—the loss of being announces itself in the crossing through and thus eludes oblivion. It is remarked.

There is thus an essential ambiguity to this marking whereby what is marked is the appearing of a concealment. Heidegger explains this in terms of a preventative and an indicative side of this crossing through. Concerning the former he writes:

> The crossing out of this word initially has only a preventive role, namely, that of preventing the almost ineradicable habit of representing "being" as something standing somewhere on its own, over against the human, that only occasionally comes to him. In accordance with this way of representing matters, it appears as though the human being is excepted from "being." However, he is not only not excepted, i.e. not only included in "being," but "being," in needing the human being, is obliged to relinquish this appearance of the for-itself. And this is why it is also other in essence than the representation of an inclusive concept might have it, even one that embraces the subject-object relation. (*GA* 9: 411/310, tm)

Being gives up its own independence in this conversion. It is not anything encapsulated, even if this capsule were to include everything (the "whole relation" as Heidegger says of Rilke; *GA* 5: 302/227). Being is not a capsule. But this is precisely why it is no longer being, but ~~being~~. Yet this negative formulation is only one aspect of this ambiguous crossing through. More positively construed, as indicative, the situation can also be thought in terms of the fourfold:

> From what has been said, however, the sign of this crossing through cannot be the merely negative sign of a crossing out. It points, rather, toward the four regions of the fourfold and their gathering in the place of this crossing through. (*GA* 9: 410–11/310–11, tm)[5]

The negative role of crossing out (*Durchstreichung*) could be said to be a defensive gesture facing against metaphysics. But the other face would be the surface of exposure that (from this limit) faces out beyond metaphysics, the face toward which being was turned in address of us. David Krell sketches the configuration of the fourfold and being here as follows:

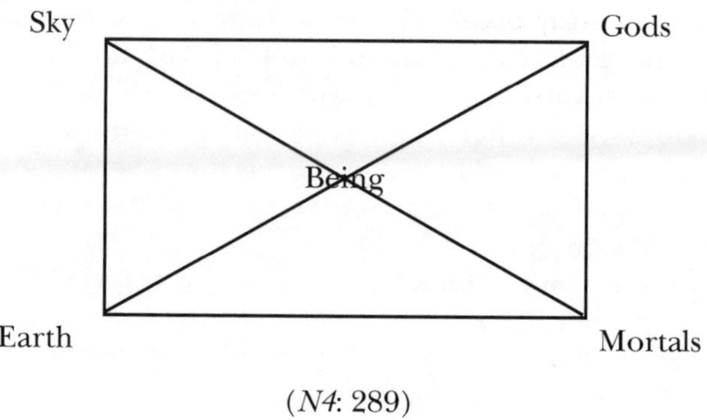

(*N4*: 289)

It is noteworthy that the crossed through being sits precisely where world would be in the fourfold schema of the Bremen lectures. B̶e̶i̶n̶g̶ is pronounced "world."

The modulation in the sense of being undertaken at the time of the fourfold leads to an antagonism with the notion of ontological difference, a notion often taken as synonymous with Heidegger's thinking as a whole, a notion that in the 1960s and 1970s he comes to explicitly reject.

Heidegger's reflections on the issue are perhaps most telling in the marginal notes to a particular passage of the Anaximander interpretation. Heidegger says in that text that "it is the issue [*Sache*] of being to be the being *of* beings" (*GA* 5: 364/274, tm). The marginal note here reads "reference to the ontological difference [*ontologische Differenz*]" (*GA* 5: 364 n.b/274 n.a, tm). The discussion continues regarding the way in which presencing has historically been overlooked and misconstrued as something present, as the highest or most universal of what is present, but as something present all the same. Heidegger comments that "the essence of presencing and with this the differentiation [*Unterschied*] of presencing from what presences remains forgotten. *The forgetting of being is the forgetting of the differentiation of being from beings*" (*GA* 5: 364/275, tm). The language has shifted from one sense of difference, *Differenz* ("difference") to another, *Unterschied* ("differentiation"), and not accidentally. The marginal note to the word "differentiation" in the above reads: "Differentiation [*der Unter-Schied*] is infinitely different from all being [*Sein*], which remains the being *of* beings. Thus it is unfitting to still give differentiation the name of 'being'—be it *with* y, be it without" (*GA* 5: 364 n.d/275 n.a, tm). As such, the thinking of differentiation (of thing and world) ceases to think ontological difference.

For Heidegger this occurs through exposure, something that comes to the fore in one of Heidegger's poems—or rather "thoughts" (*Gedachtes*) as he calls them to distinguish them from poetry (*Gedichte*) while simultaneously observing the similarity. In the thought entitled "Cézanne," the conversion of the ontological difference is addressed directly. In the first version from 1970 we read:

> In the late work of the painter, the twofold [*Zwiefalt*]
> of what is present and presence becomes simple [*einfältig*],
> "realized" and converted [*verwunden*] at once,
> transformed into a secretive identity. (*GA* 13: 223)

Realization would thus name the way in which what presences and its presencing lose their indifference to each other and are *converted* into a simplicity. This simplicity lies in an identity that is constitutively secretive (the secrets of its relations to the world). The simple exists relationally. The conversion (*Verwindung*) Heidegger considers is nothing other than an entry into mediation. There is no ready distinction between the thing that presences and its presencing. Each implicates the other. This relational existence is simple. The prose postscript to the 1974 version of the poem explicitly thinks this realization mediately, in terms of an appearing in a clearing:

> What Cézanne names *la realisation* is
> the appearing of what is presencing in the clearing
> of presence—in such a way, indeed, that the twofold of both
> is converted [*verwunden*] in the simplicity of the pure
> appearing of its image. (*GA* 81: 347–48)

The lines are obviously of great importance for understanding Heidegger's notion of the image. For our present purposes, however, it is enough to note that conversion into the simple is a mediated sensual appearing. Heidegger's thought continues (and what Heidegger refers to here as "overcoming" [*Überwindung*] is what we are calling "conversion" [*Verwindung*]; Heidegger uses both terms in "Cézanne," though neither in a metaphysical sense and drawing no evident distinction between them):

> For thinking, this is the question of the
> overcoming of the ontological difference between
> being and beings. The overcoming, however, is only
> possible when the ontological difference is first experienced as such
> and taken into consideration, which again can only occur
> on the basis of the question of being, as posed in *Being and Time*.
> Its unfolding requires an experience
> of the dispensation of being. The insight into this is first prepared by

> a walk along the field path, which finds its way into a simple saying
> in the manner of a naming of the outstanding,
> to which thinking remains exposed. (*GA* 81: 348)

Realization, the conversion of ontological difference does not just happen, it requires an experience of exposure. On the basis of the inquiry into being begun in *Being and Time*—but let us immediately add, on the basis of this, yes, but by no means limited to this, rather, only starting from this—we are to set out now on a path (get underway) that exposes us to the dispensation of being (*Seinsgeschickes*). In keeping with the Hölderlinian subtext, in this exposed encounter with nature we come away with a name. The exposure marks itself in the word, a word bestowed by what does not show itself, by something withheld, that nonetheless remarks itself in this name. This inscription, or "exscription," to borrow a term from Jean-Luc Nancy, is what we have regarded as the erosive or marking effect of the medium. (It crosses everything through, we might say.)[6]

The conversion of the ontological difference proposed here is now to be thought in terms of the fourfold. A marginal note to "The Onto-Theological Constitution of Metaphysics" in *Identity and Difference* (1957, the text read at the close of the seminar on Hegel's *Logic*), seems to stem from this same period of the mid-1970s (it is impossible to know for sure), employing some of the same language we have already encountered in "The Slight" (see "The Slight [*das Geringe*]" in chapter six). The text to which the note is appended is precisely concerned with difference and metaphysics. Heidegger contrasts two senses of being, that of being as ground or reason (*Grund*), per the thinking of metaphysics, and that of being as bearing, as we have discussed in considering the earth. The separation of these two senses, which nonetheless bears them together, is the work of performance, a carrying out (*Austrag*). Heidegger writes of this in the 1957 essay: "What is so named directs our thinking to a realm where it no longer suffices to speak the guiding words of metaphysics: being and beings, ground-grounded. For what these words name, what the manner of thinking that is guided by them conceives, stems from difference [*der Differenz*] as something different [*das Differente*]. The provenance of this can no longer be thought of within the scope of metaphysics" (*GA* 11: 77/*ID* 71, tm). Heidegger's point is that metaphysics is part of an opposition that is beholden to an opening of difference (though we would say here differentiation). Heidegger's later marginal note to this passage reads:

> No longer: to question after provenance—this at a dead end; rather:
> to let difference [*Differenz*] and transcendence go

> letting oneself into the "identity" of being and beings
> that is, however, to convert [*verwinden*] identity into the event of
> appropriation as the sanction of the fourfold [*das Ereignis als
> Befugnis des Ge-Vierts*]
> the thing—(*GA* 11: 77 n. 126)

The realization that Cézanne brought to image, the simplicity of that, is the same conversion moving from object to thing, or, more pointedly, from particular being (*Seiende*) to thing. Ontological difference converts at the fourfold. Identity is here likewise rethought, it is an appropriating, by which we would understand that identity lies in the relations that support a thing in its essencing, how it "appropriates" its place in the world, relating to what lies beyond it and contextualizing itself there. This relation of appropriation (the event of it) is determined as the "sanction" (*Befugnis*) of the fourfold.

We have already addressed this sanction in considering the thinging of the thing. Sanction named a compliance with a directive that was not simple obedience, but instead, through its compliance, first establishes the authority of the sanctioning authority (a "bearing" relation). At that time we considered how the authority in question is being and the sanction delivered to us and demanding compliance a particular dispensation (*Geschick*) of being. The conversion that is indicated in Heidegger's note is a transformation in our experience of identity—we now understand identity as beginning from this relation of appropriation, it is understood in terms of compliance. This compliance requires something slight. Conversion is consequently a conversion into "the event of appropriation as the sanction of the fourfold" (*GA* 11: 77 n. 126).

The collection of notes entitled "The Slight," almost exactly cotemporaneous with the later version of "Cézanne" (they can only be dated from 1973–75), again addresses the fourfold in its relation to ontological difference. In a particularly poignant note that synthesizes much of what we have considered above, Heidegger writes:

> *The Fourfold*
>
> as *the slight* in withholding [*im Vorenthalt*]
> (the conversion [*Verwindung*] of the *ontological difference*
> i.e., of what is proper to metaphysics
>
> The sanctioning-region

Withholding and fourfold[7]

Here the fourfold is joined by a line to the sanctioning-region (*Befugnis-Gegend*). As we know, the dispensing of the sanction is a giving that entails a withholding. The stretch between that withdrawal and that bestowal is the spacing of this "sanctioning-region," the space between arrival and donation. The fourfold needs this sanctioning-region because it is into this space that the fourfold radiates in the thinging of the thing. This compliance is expressly directed against the ontological difference as a hallmark of metaphysics, i.e., a thinking of purity, opposition, difference, concretion, and propriety. The fourfold's relation to the sanctioning region is a relation to withholding (since the sanction is given and thus stretched by a withdrawal). The exposure to this withdrawal leaves the thing slight. The slightness of the thing distinguishes it from the self-assured particular being of metaphysics. The fourfold would not simply expose the thing to an otherwise inert world. It opens the thing onto a world of withholding, a withholding that comes forth to it (*Vor-ent-halt*). It is a world wherein that withholding is likewise remarked. These marks are nothing other than the marks of the divinities, the hints and traces of a reign beyond/between presence and absence. The fourfold enters the thing into a world of meaning. But such an entry requires abandoning all difference in the name of differentiation, the ontological difference most of all.

There is no longer ontological difference. Being and beings are in compliance. Wondering about the abandonment of this figure, one might consider that ontological difference is a relation between quite related parties, being and beings. The very names could be seen to characterize the relation as one of possession or participation, and it is precisely this that Heidegger wishes to avoid. The names *world* and *thing* name a difference (differentiation), one could say, while *being* and *beings* name the sides of a relation. The fourfold attempts to name the interface of that relation itself, not to name the sides of it. Those "sides" would be called thing and world, were they ever separable from each other, were the *event* of them severable in this way. For this reason Heidegger writes on the next page that the slight is "this side of all that is abstract / and everything concrete."[8] The fourfold begins from relationality. It cannot be reached starting from the supposed relata of the relation, abstract/concrete, beings/being. In short and in conclusion, as a marginal note to the collection powerfully states:

> the fourfold
> no
> ontological difference[9]

Notes

Introduction

1. Egon Vietta, author of *Die Seinsfrage bei Martin Heidegger*, as cited in Petzet, *Stern zugehen*, 62/*Encounters*, 56. For more on Vietta, see Petzet, *Stern zugehen*, 107–10/*Encounters*, 100–2.

2. Letter to Dieter Sinn of August 24, 1964, cited in Sinn, *Ereignis und Nirwana*, 172, em. I am grateful to Richard Polt for drawing my attention to this reference. For Heidegger's thinking of the thing "in terms of the tradition," see my "A Brief History of Things: Heidegger and the Tradition." The Sinn letter also has the potential to shed some light on a perplexing claim from the 1951 seminar in Zürich. Here Heidegger is asked why his own thought is so bound up with the interpretation of texts. He replies that "an essential part of this arises from an embarrassment: because I am apprehensive to say directly what I could perhaps still say; for this reason I eschew this, because in today's age it would be immediately commonplace and thereby distorted. It is to a certain extent a defensive measure. In my 30–35 years of teaching, *I have only once or twice spoken of my own concerns* [*Sachen*]" (*GA* 15: 426, em). It is my contention in the following that Heidegger's "own concerns" here are those of the fourfold and the thing. This is at least in accordance with the claims of the 1964 letter just cited.

3. In considering the secondary materials addressing the fourfold and the thing in Heidegger's thinking, we should recall the hesitation of William J. Richardson, who remarks in addressing the fourfold (or "quadrate" as his text would have it) that "we do not feel obliged to solve the problem (if it can be solved)" (Richardson, *Heidegger*, 570). Richardson ultimately proposes taking earth and sky together as "nature," and reading this alongside the divinities and mortals as a recasting "of the trilogy that characterized classical metaphysics: God, man, 'world'" (Richardson, *Heidegger*, 572). The hesitation persists in regards to contemporary scholarship on the fourfold, insofar as discussions of it have been few and neither extended nor comprehensive. Of the discussions that do exist, Julian Young has an entry on "The Fourfold" in *The Cambridge Companion to Heidegger*. Young endeavors to understand the fourfold as ultimately offering an opposition between nature and culture as the crux of human dwelling. While the role of nature is surely an important one in the fourfold, construing the relation between divinities and mortals in terms of "culture" is quite limiting given the richness of Heidegger's account. Indeed, in "Sky and Earth

as Invariants of the Natural Life-world," Klaus Held notes that "this polarity [of sky and earth] belongs to the invariants of the human life-world, but one would understand it in a falsely naturalistic way, if one opposed it to culture as a work of human freedom" (Held, "Sky and Earth," 22). This is a danger for all who write on these matters. Young also tends to read the fourfold in terms of *Being and Time.* My tendency runs in the opposite direction, to let the fourfold be as radical and original a thought as possible, and this on its own terms. Perhaps the person who has said the most about the fourfold (though still not a great deal) is Graham Harman, who first takes up the notion in his book *Tool-Being: Heidegger and the Metaphysics of Objects.* Harman views the fourfold as a tension between concealment and revelation, on the one hand, and specificity and generality, on the other. This is a reading that is by his own admission not concerned with textual fidelity to Heidegger so much as promoting his own object-oriented philosophy. In his subsequent book, *Heidegger Explained,* where the goal is at least titularly one of explanation, Harman nonetheless repeats the same reading. Apart from how this construal functions in Harman's own philosophy, it lacks the specificity requisite for a full-fledged interpretation of the fourfold as I hope to provide in the pages that follow. Another author who has worked on the thematic of the fourfold is Jean-François Mattéi, author of "The Heideggerian Chiasmus" in Janicaud and Mattéi, *Heidegger: From Metaphysics to Thought.* In this text, Mattéi reads Heidegger as a thinker of chiasmic relation, one formulation of which is that of the fourfold. The focus is thus not on the fourfold as such but rather on a chiasmic structure that expresses itself throughout Heidegger's work as a whole. This creative interpretation is continued in Mattéi's subsequent book, *Heidegger et Hölderlin: Le Quadriparti,* which is not so much an interpretation of the fourfold as a creative conception of the political underpinnings of Heidegger's readings of Hölderlin and the question of a homeland (the fourfold is an instance of a "crossroads"). For both Harman and Mattéi, then, the agenda is not one of exegesis, but creative appropriation. My work attempts to show the creative dimension of Heidegger's own thought through strict interpretation and close reading of the texts themselves. While some of our sources are the same, my agenda is far more restricted.

4. While "The Thing" and "Building Dwelling Thinking" present the fourfold at its fullest and will serve as the guides for the interpretations that follow, two other early contextualizations of the fourfold are to be noted and will be drawn upon opportunely as the interpretations proceed: the lecture "Language" of 1950 and the letter to Ernst Jünger, "The Question of Being," from 1955. These four texts provide the fullest sense of how Heidegger conceives the fourfold.

5. See Heidegger, *Eine gefährliche Irrnis,* 15: "The lack of vision [*Blicklose*] in contemporary philosophy and its quest for 'theory' remains far distant from the inceptually determining and naming saying [*Sage*] of the simple relations of the fourfold."

6. After the 1949 lectures of *Insight Into That Which Is* ("The Thing," *GA* 79: 12/11, "The Danger," *GA* 79: 46/44, 57/54, and "The Turn," *GA* 79: 74/70, 77/73; the term does not appear in the second lecture, "Positionality"), Heidegger employs the term "Geviert" in "Language" (1950; *GA* 12: 19/*PLT* 197, *GA*

12: 20/*PLT* 199; cf. *GA* 12: 21/*PLT* 199 for "Welt-Geviert"), "Building Dwelling Thinking" (1951; *GA* 7: 152/*PLT* 148), the Jünger letter "On the Question of Being" (1955; *GA* 9: 411/311), the third lecture of "The Essence of Language" (1958; *GA* 12: 203/*OWL* 107; cf. *GA* 12: 200/*OWL* 104 for "Weltgevierts"), in the 1959 lecture "Hölderlin's Earth and Sky" (*GA* 4: 153/176, and cf. 162–163/187), in "Sprache und Heimat" (1960; *GA* 13: 178, 180), in the 1966–67 notes to the Heraclitus seminar with Eugen Fink ("Aus den Aufzeichnungen zu dem mit Eugen Fink veranstateten Heraklit-Seminar"), and in the 1973 Zähringen seminar (*GA* 15: 387/FS 73). This is a partial list of appearances for the term "Geviert" only. It does not take into account the many times that Heidegger speaks of humans and god, earth and sky, for example, nor the times where he speaks of the mortals without explicit reference to the fourfold (as in the 1951 essay "Logos").

7. Heidegger's thinking of the thing and its essential relation to technology has been largely lost on his English readership owing to editorial decisions of his early translators. In the Bremen lectures, the opening lecture is "The Thing" after which come the two technology essays ("Positionality" and "The Danger"). In *Vorträge und Aufsätze* (1954), there is a tripartite division, which opens with technologically relevant essays (including "The Question Concerning Technology," revamping material from the Bremen lectures), followed by the initial fourfold depictions ("The Thing" and "Building Dwelling Thinking"), and concluding with a section devoted to interpretations of the Greeks (partial summaries of the 1940s courses on Parmenides and Heraclitus). The Greek material is not in the service of a return to the Greeks, but in the interest of thinking historically. The Bremen lectures have only recently been translated into English (*Bremen and Freiburg Lectures: Insight Into That Which Is and Basic Principles of Thinking*). As to *Vorträge und Aufsätze*, what has been translated of it (the lecture "Was Heißt Denken?" has not been) is spread across five volumes of English translations (*The Question Concerning Technology; The End of Philosophy; Nietzsche*, vol. 2; *Poetry, Language, Thought*; and *Early Greek Thinking*, where it has been combined with material from other periods and other books. These compilations are all fine on their own, but the editorial decisions behind them nevertheless bury the essential connection between technology and the thinking of the thing.

8. "workshop-landscape," *Werkstättenlandschaft*, Ernst Jünger, SW 8: 224.

9. Cf. "Building Dwelling Thinking" (*GA* 7: 155/*PLT* 151), "The Thing" (*GA* 79: 13/12). The term also plays an important role in the contemporaneous "Logos" (*GA* 7: 225/*EGT* 70).

10. Not coincidentally, a recurrent example for Heidegger. See the 1936–38 *Contributions to Philosophy (from Enowning)* (*GA* 65: 339/268) as well as the 1945 *Country Path Conversation*, "Angchibasiê" (*GA* 77: 126–137/82–89).

11. I translate *Seyn* as "beyng" to distinguish it from *Sein* ("being"). The distinction between these is largely the work of the *Contributions*. Beyng names being as not only distinct from particular beings, but distinct even from traditional conceptions of "being" itself, as beyng is the withdrawal that grants beings, and being, in the first place (and metaphysical notions of "being" are only an abstraction from these abandoned beings).

12. I provide a fuller account of Heidegger's notion of essence in my "Contamination, Essence, and Decomposition: Heidegger and Derrida."

13. Hannah Arendt, "For Martin Heidegger's Eightieth Birthday," *HNS*, 207–17, 207.

14. Arendt, "Heidegger's Eightieth," 208.

15. Arendt, "Heidegger's Eightieth," 209.

16. Hugo Ott, *Martin Heidegger: A Political Life*, 335. The report itself is found on pages 336–41.

17. Cited in Ott, *Political*, 339.

18. Cited in Ott, *Political*, 340.

19. Petzet, *Stern zugehen*, 52/*Encounters*, 46.

20. For further details on the Heidegger-Gebsattel relationship, see my forthcoming "Heidegger's Breakdown: Health and Healing under the Care of Dr. V. E. von Gebsattel."

21. We could even mark the bounds of the most productive phase of this thinking of the fourfold by two sixtieth birthdays, those of Heidegger in 1949 and that of Ernst Jünger in 1955. Each contributed to the Festschrift of the other, Heidegger's contribution being "On 'the Line,'" republished as "On the Question of Being," wherein the fourfold is construed as intersection relations that cross through being itself. I return to this casting of the fourfold in the conclusion.

1. The Technological Challenge to Things

1. Heidegger will repeatedly insist that his thinking of the essence of technology be kept far from confusion with any "philosophy of technology." His concern here is to preserve the thought that there is an "essence" of technology. Philosophies of technology become enamored of devices and view technology as merely an assemblage of these. In "Positionality" he remarks that "by no means do we consider the essence of technology in order to construct the edifice of a philosophy of technology or even merely to outline such a philosophy. Technology essences as positionality. But what reigns in positionality? From where and how does the essence of positionality take place?" (*GA* 79: 45/43). Philosophies of technology are unable to see that technology *essences*, a key to Heidegger's understanding of technology in its relation to the thing. As early as the notebooks on technology from the 1940s, Heidegger observes that "in keeping with its point of departure, all 'philosophy of technology' is already a misjudgment of its essence" (*GA* 76: 294).

2. In these references to "constancy" (*Beständigkeit*) we find the first inklings of what will become the thinking of the standing reserve (*das Bestand*). The shift in the role of the term identifies the transformation in Heidegger's thinking in a nutshell. At the time of the *Contributions*, the notion of *Beständigkeit* is still indiscernible from objectivity. With the thinking of positionality in the late 1940s, the *Bestand* is anything but objective; instead it undergoes an endless circulatory replacement.

3. Similarly, the diagrams in sections 64 and 65 of the *Contributions* also

show the link between machination and lived-experience (*GA* 65: 130/102–3). Sections 61–68 detail the role of machination and lived experience in the *Contributions* as supplemented by the argument of "The Age of the World Picture."

4. On the metaphysical presuppositions of war, the modernism of Clausewitz, and Heidegger's conception of a war grown appropriate for a post-modern age, see my "Heidegger and Terrorism."

5. See Kulturverwaltung der Stadt Darmstadt, ed., *Ernst Barlach: Dramatiker, Bildhauer, Zeichner*, 5. The essay is later included as section 26 of "Overcoming Metaphysics," the *Gesamtausgabe* version of which includes a marginal note to the section number likewise dating it to "1939/1940" (*GA* 7: 90 n. i). There is an anomaly in the dating, however, in that both the *GA* version and the Barlachheft version of the essay cite the chemist Richard Kuhn as recipient of the Goethe Prize, a prize that was not awarded until 1942. In what follows, I will cite pages of "The Abandonment of Being and Errancy" from the more readily available *GA* 7 adoption (variances are minor).

6. Heidegger's essay "Nihilism as Determined by the History of Being," dating from 1944–46, likewise considers "a humanity become human material" (*GA* 6.2: 351/N 4: 242, tm, and *GA* 67: 247).

7. Heidegger, "Die Armut," *GA* 73.1: 881/"Poverty" 9, tm.

8. Heidegger explicitly wrestles with the notion of mobilization in a set of notes entitled "Important Remarks on 'Technology'" (*GA* 76: 325–32). One of these, entitled "Positionality [*Ge-Stell*] and Total Mobilization," consists of three critical remarks; first, that positionality conditions beings as a whole and thus the adjective "total" is unnecessary; second, Heidegger wonders whether thinking technology as mobilization still remains within the "instrumental" conception of technology; and lastly, he wonders about the reciprocal relation between the human qua worker and total mobilization, noting that Jünger fails to achieve an ontological purchase on this relation. In the notes entitled "Preparatory Studies to the Technology Lecture," Heidegger addresses the Jünger connection directly: "The essence of contemporary technology is positionality, not because it is mobilized, but rather the reverse. Because positionality, therefore mobilization" (*GA* 76: 342). All of these notes serve to show that Jünger's presence was operative even in the formulation of the lecture "The Question Concerning Technology."

9. In "The Question Concerning Technology," this challenge often seems to derive from a human attitude or comportment: "Only insofar as the human for his part is already challenged forth to expedite natural energy, can this ordering disclosure occur" (*GA* 7: 18/*QCT* 18, tm). In the Bremen lectures, however, the emphasis is more on what Heidegger terms a process of "conscription" (*Gestellung*) operative in the requisitioning of standing reserve itself, whereby all that this requisitioning encounters is enlisted and conscripted in the furthering of the standing reserve. It is an integral part of positionality: "The essence of technology is positionality. Positionality orders. It orders what is present through conscription. Positionality orders what is present into standing reserve" (*GA* 79: 40/38). The difference is perhaps clearest when Heidegger states "positioning occurs as a conscription [*die Gestellung*]. The demand for conscription is directed at the human. But within the whole of what presences, the human is not the only pres-

ence approached by conscription" (*GA* 79: 27/26). When conscription is omitted from the "Question Concerning Technology" lecture and publication, the question of a human privilege within positionality easily (though mistakenly) arises.

10. Heraclitus, *DK* 22 b 123/Freeman, *Ancilla*, 33.

11. The lecture course phrases it so: "The emergence into self-concealing grants grace" (*GA* 55: 131).

12. The marginal note refers to an exchange of letters between Heidegger and the classical philologist Hildebrecht Hommel, where Hommel writes in support of Heidegger's interpretation of the fragment (*DK* 22 b 123/Freeman, *Ancilla*, 33), citing a philological finding by Johansson whereby *philein* is traced to something equivalent to a possessive pronoun. The translation is thus Hommel's rendering of Johansson. For further details, see Friedrich-Wilhelm von Herrmann's editorial afterword to *Vorträge und Aufsätze* in the *Gesamtausgabe*, GA 7: 297–98.

13. Husserl, *Ding*, 49–50/*Thing*, 42.

14. Husserl, *Ding*, 50/*Thing*, 43, em.

15. Husserl, *Ding*, 55/*Thing*, 46, em.

16. Heidegger will think this unguarding in terms of a forgetting of that differentiation by means of which the thing would spill out into world (differentiation as the difference between concealment and unconcealment). Concomitant with this is thus a loss of world itself: "in thinging, the thing brings the world near and lets the world abide. If the thing, unguarded as it is, does not thing, then the world as world remains denied. In the unguarding of the thing there takes place the refusal of world" (*GA* 79: 47/45). A note connects this unguarding with the lack of differentiation: "Forgetting of differentiation: unguarding of the thing— refusal of world" (*GA* 79: 50 n. i/48 n. 9). A section of the technology notebooks entitled "How Does Technology Leave Difference (the Event) Unguarded?" confirms that technology "is the most extreme unguarding of the differentiation [*Ver-wahr-losung des Unter-Schiedes*]" (*GA* 76: 370).

17. See *GA* 79: 32/30–31, 65/61; *GA* 7: 20/*QCT* 19; *GA* 15: 388/*FS* 74, among others. The word is built like *Gemut* or *Gebirge*. Cf. the notes entitled "The *Essence* of Technology," where one reads "Positionality [*Gestell*] (like baying [*Gebell*], a barking [*bellen*] concentrated in itself)" (*GA* 76: 365).

18. In *The Cylinder: Kinematics of the Nineteenth Century*, Helmut Müller-Sievers situates Heidegger's remark here in a context of kinematic and rotational thought of the nineteenth century as a whole, with particular emphasis on the role of Reuleaux, whom Heidegger was reading during the composition of his technology notebooks.

19. On Hegel: "The completion of metaphysics begins with Hegel's metaphysics of absolute knowing as the will of spirit" (*GA* 7: 74/*EP* 89, tm). On Nietzsche: "we can never succeed in arriving at Nietzsche's philosophy proper if we have not in our questioning conceived of Nietzsche as the end of Western metaphysics" (*GA* 6.1: 8/*N1*: 10). On the connection between Hegel and Nietzsche, see *GA* 66: 281–86/249–54. Insofar as what is at stake in this discussion is in part the issue of negativity, see Dahlstrom, "Thinking of Nothing: Heidegger's Criticisms of Hegel's Conception of Negativity."

20. Hegel, *Logik, GW* 12: 133/*Science of Logic*, 711.

21. Hegel, *Logik, GW* 12: 133/*Science of Logic*, 711, tm. For more on the role of mechanism in the Logic, see James Kreines, "Hegel's Critique of Pure Mechanism and the Philosophical Appeal of the *Logic* Project."

22. Hegel, *Enzyklopädie, Werke* 8: 353/*Encyclopaedia Logic*, 274, addition to §195. Hegel's early Jena writings remain consistent with these later remarks from the *Logics*. See the 1802–3 *System of Ethical Life* (Hegel, *Schriften, GW* 5: 297/*System of Ethical Life*, 117–18) and the 1805–6 *Philosophy of Spirit* (Hegel, *Jenaer III, GW* 8: 243/*Philosophy of Spirit*, 139).

23. See Heidegger's remarks on the opening of the closed circle at the conclusion of *Basic Principles of Thinking, GA* 79: 175–76/165.

24. And this even for the Greeks; see Heidegger's comments on the need of *physis* for *technê* in section 38 l of *Basic Questions of Philosophy: Selected "Problems" of "Logic"* (1937–38), entitled, "*Technê* as the basic attitude toward *physis*, where the preservation of the wondrous (the beingness of beings) unfolds and is established. *Technê* maintains the holding sway of *physis* in unconcealedness" (*GA* 45: 177–80/153–55).

25. A parallel passage in "The Question Concerning Technology" four years later seems to mark a shift in Heidegger's view: "The air is imposed upon for the discharge of hydrogen, the soil for ore, the ore, for example, for uranium, and this for atomic energy, which can be unleashed for destructive or peaceful uses" (*GA* 7: 16/*QCT* 15, tm). It would seem now that destruction is not so necessary after all. Recalling Heidegger's comments on World War II, however, we can see here a coincidence to the opposition. As Heidegger explains, "as long as the contemporary meditation on the world of atomic energy, in all the seriousness of responsibility, only urges for—and thereby satisfies itself with—pursuing the peaceful use of energy, contemplation remains standing at the halfway point" (*GA* 79: 128/120–21). Peaceful uses and destructive uses make no difference at this point. To believe otherwise would be to succumb once again to the myth of a neutral technology.

26. *The Bhagavad Gita*, 11.12. The line likewise forms the title of Robert Jungk's 1956 book, *Heller als tausend Sonnen: Das Schicksal der Atomforscher*, the first published account of the Manhattan project where Robert Oppenheimer famously recalled these words upon the detonation of the first atomic bomb (Jungk, *Heller*, 206/*Brighter*, 198). Heidegger discusses an earlier work of Jungk's in the preparatory studies for his 1953 lecture "The Question Concerning Technology" at *GA* 76: 347.

27. "To be sure, atomic physics is experimentally and calculably of a different sort than classical physics. Thought in terms of its essence, however, it nevertheless remains the same physics" (*GA* 79: 43/41).

2. Earth, Bearing and Fructifying

1. Taminiaux compares the three versions of the text in "The Origin of 'The Origin of the Work of Art.'" Françoise Dastur's essay "Heidegger's Freiburg

Version of the Origin of the Work of Art" offers a focused reading of the second (*UK2*).

2. Gadamer, "Zur Einführung," 98.

3. The sky is understood as part of the earth in all three versions of "The Origin of the Work of Art" as well as in other works leading up to the fourfold; see *UK1*: 11/335 (air, light, dark, day, night), *UK2*: 26, *GA* 5: 28/21.

4. Heraclitus, *DK* 22 b 123/Freeman, *Ancilla*, 33.

5. The 1943 summer lecture course on Heraclitus, *The Beginning of Western Thinking: Heraclitus*, devotes over thirty pages to this fragment, with Heidegger translating it as "emerging grants grace to self-concealing" (*GA* 55: 139). In the 1967 Athens lecture, 'The Provenance of Art and the Determination of Thinking,"Heidegger translates it less provocatively as "it is characteristic of what arises from itself to conceal itself" (21). The 1969 seminar in Le Thor renders it "self-concealment is the innermost essence of the movement of appearing" (*GA* 15: 343/*FS* 46).

6. The second version of the Freiburg lecture is also the first to speak of the earth in terms of a bearing: "The tree and the grass, the eagle and the bull, the snake and the cricket first move into their distinctive figures and thus emerge as that which they are. This emergence the Greeks named *physis*. This means: the arising of itself and thereby stepping into the light. . . . This arising bears, encompasses, and runs through all things. It is the whole upon which and in which the human grounds his dwelling. We name it the *earth*" (*UK2*: 26). Given Heidegger's interest at the time in understanding the artwork's relation to a historical people, it is worth noting that the Nazi theorist Oscar Becker finds Heidegger's thinking to lack an adequate conception of "bearing." In "Race and Earth in Heidegger's Thinking During the Late 1930s," Robert Bernasconi shows how Becker criticized Heidegger's conception of Dasein in 1929 precisely for its inability to address the work of art. Becker proposed to remedy this through the introduction of "a para-existence in terms of which one can theorize a borneness in the sense of a 'being carried' (*Getragenheit*)" (Bernasconi, "Race and Earth," 51). The connection is striking, to say the least.

7. The first elaboration discusses a similar situation, but speaks of it only as a "grounding" (*UK1*: 20/344).

8. It is also why Heidegger will say that the *Austrag* is in harmony with *Ereignis* (cf. *GA* 11: 29/*ID* 21). "Bearing" names *Ereignis*; it is what holds beings to being.

9. A claim Heidegger repeats in a discussion of art: "Distress-lessness, the authentic distress," from "Die Unumgänglichkeit des Da-seins," 6.

10. Jean-Luc Nancy, "The Weight of a Thought," in *The Gravity of Thought*, 75–84.

11. Nancy, *Gravity*, 75.

12. Nancy, *Gravity*, 76.

13. Nancy, *Gravity*, 79.

14. And let us note that Heidegger's use of *Getier* (animals) here rather than the *Tierheit* considered throughout the 1929–30 *Fundamental Concepts of Metaphysics* lecture course surely complicates one of Derrida's criticisms of Hei-

degger's treatment of animality. Of this course, Derrida writes that "one will not be able to speak of the essence of animality in general unless—and although as his discussion progresses Heidegger cites many examples of animals—the categorization of all animals within a 'general essence of animality,' in spite of their differences (differences between lizard and chimpanzee, for example), remain beyond question" (Derrida, *Animal*, 154). For Heidegger, the non-homogenizing collection of singular animals named by *Getier* (as proposed within the fourfold) is surely distinct from the *Tierheit* (animality) of the 1929–30 course.

15. Trakl, "Ein Winterabend," *Dichtungen*, 102/*Poems*, 118, tm; cited at *GA* 12: 15/*PLT* 192.

16. For further elaboration of Heidegger's view of pain, please see my "Entering the World of Pain: Heidegger."

17. Trakl, "Heiterer Frühling," *Dichtungen*, 50/*Poems*, 66, tm; cited at *GA* 12: 58/*OWL* 181.

18. Trakl, "Heiterer Frühling," *Dichtungen*, 50/*Poems*, 66, tm; cited at *GA* 12: 59/*OWL* 182.

19. In *Stone*, an indispensible work for any thinking of stone, John Sallis writes "in itself the word *sense* houses the most gigantic ambivalence, indifferently coupling the difference between what is called the sensible, things of sense apprehended perceptually, *and* signification, meaning, a signified or intended sense . . . to differentiate between the two senses of sense presupposes the very differentiation that it would effect." Sallis, *Stone*, 13–14. Hegel notes in the *Aesthetics* that "'Sense' is this wonderful word which is used in two opposite meanings. On the one hand it means the organ of immediate apprehension, but on the other hand we mean by it the sense, the significance, the thought, the universal underlying the thing. And so sense is connected on the one hand with the immediate external aspect of existence, and on the other hand with its inner essence." Hegel, *Ästhetik, Werke* 13: 173/*Aesthetics*, vol. 1, 128–29.

20. Heidegger uses the same terminology he will later use in describing the earth within the fourfold to discuss the workings of the river: "How is the river supposed to be a river, that is, go streaming, if it were not before all else constantly arising? This streaming is each time a fully productive one—*building, nurturing, grounding*" (*GA* 39: 265, em).

21. A reliable recapitulation of the course, along with critical commentary, is found in William McNeill, "Life Beyond the Organism: Animal Being in Heidegger's Freiburg Lectures, 1929–30." See also Didier Franck's provocative essay "Being and the Living."

22. The text is replete with reservations about the proceedings. The task is to approach the issue of world through a comparison with the animal. The goal is simply to unfold a question about the nature of world, not to answer it (*GA* 29/30: 272/184). At the very outset Heidegger acknowledges that "it is difficult to determine even the distinction between man and animal" (*GA* 29/30: 265/179). His comparative procedure means that all his findings will be about how the animal appears *to us*. The thesis is "far from being a, let alone *the*, fundamental metaphysical principle of the essence of animality. At best, it is a proposition that follows from the essential determinations of animality, and moreover one

which follows only if the animal is regarded in comparison with humanity" (*GA* 29/30: 394/271). Consequently, "the thesis is misleading precisely with respect to the essence of animality itself" as "we ourselves have also been in view all the time, whether we wanted to be or not" (*GA* 29/30: 394/271, 395/272). It is not, nor is it meant to be, "an essential definition of animality" (*GA* 29/30: 349/240, tm). "Admittedly this is not said as though this were to represent the definitive clarification of the essence of animality beyond which there is no need to ask any further for all time" (*GA* 29/30: 378/260, tm). Indeed, even this comparative analysis is deemed "incomplete" (*GA* 29/30: 385/265). Ultimately, regarding the "essential organization of the organism," this is "still not adequately clarified" (*GA* 29/30: 396/273, tm). This is an astonishing amount of reservation, even for a thinker so deeply committed to preparation as Heidegger.

23. In regards to such "solicitation," Oliver is right to point out Heidegger's acceptance of the most invasive scientific research in regards to animals: "In the name of guarding and protecting the being of beings, he endorses dismembering them" (Oliver, *Animal Lessons*, 198). Her worry over Heidegger's embrace of scientific experimentation in his thinking of animality, despite his criticisms of technology—"Of course, Heidegger's criticisms of technology and techno-science are well known, which makes even stranger his use of high-tech experiments in zoology and biology to prove his point" (Oliver, *Animal Lessons*, 198)—is somewhat anachronistic, given that even the fledgling critique of technology as machination only first arises in 1936. None of this diminishes her larger ethical point, however.

24. A note from the late 1930s entitled "Animal-Plant" concludes with the implication that animals and plants should be understood as bearing "accordingly different phenomenological characters!" (*GA* 73.1: 414).

25. Grimm and Grimm, *Deutsches Wörterbuch*, s.v. "gediegen."

26. Angelus Silesius, "Ohne warum," book 1, sec. 289 of *Cherubinischer Wandersmann*, 39. English translation: "Without Why" in Angelus Silesius, *The Cherubinic Wanderer*, 54, tm. Cited at *GA* 10: 53/35.

27. Hebel, "Ideen zur Gebetstheorie" in *Werke*, 350–55, 350. Cited at *GA* 16: 521/*DT* 47. Heidegger cites the same passage in the 1955 "Hebel—The Friend of the House" at *GA* 13: 150/*HFH* 100.

28. For Nietzsche's claim see *KGW* 7.2: 269.

29. Maturation is the change bestowed upon us by our exposure to the world. We are graced with maturity. A 1944 sketch of an interpretation of Hölderlin's poem "Mnemosyne" (third version) entitled "Ripe are . . ." thinks the change of maturation as the beginning of a new time: "The previous history of gods and humans has run its course. The beings are exhausted and the relations to beyng [are] empty and undecided. In such times it is the time that another time begins. This maturation [*Zeitige*] is ripeness" (*GA* 75: 318). Maturation is the beginning of another time, another way of beginning. In a later essay on Stefan George, Heidegger writes that "Time brings to maturity [*Die Zeit zeitigt*]. Maturation means: ripening, letting emerge. What is mature [*Das Zeitige*] is the emerging of what has emerged [*das Aufgehend-Aufgegangene*]" (*GA* 12: 201/*OWL* 106, tm). Otherwise put, maturity is a connection with one's past, a bearing of that past upon the

present, such that what has been is nonetheless still emerging in one's present growth. In short, maturity is the exposing of what has been.

30. A radicalization of "*Homo sum: humani nil a me alienum puto*," Terence, *The Self-Tormentor*, line 77, which should literally say "I am human: nothing human is alien to me." And yet, understood relationally, everything we come in contact with is "human" or "humanized" by the very fact of our contact with it. Thus the second "human" is redundant and I have deleted it in the adapted form of the quotation included above. In the play, the context for the claim is nothing so metaphysical. It is used as an excuse for an old man's curiosity into his neighbor's affairs. Barsby's translation is "I'm human, and I regard no human business as other people's" (187).

31. On this point see Robert Harrison's *Gardens: An Essay on the Human Condition*.

32. It is not discussed in Elden's otherwise comprehensive look at the role of the animal in Heidegger's work ("Heidegger's Animals"), nor does it find its way into Agamben, Derrida (even when this exact text is the focus of his analysis, as in *Of Spirit*), Calarco, Lawlor (though his attention is more to the issue in Derrida's work than in Heidegger), or Oliver, to name only the most prominent commentators on this issue.

33. Calarco, *Zoographies*, 30.

34. Trakl, "Frühling der Seele," *Dichtungen*, 141/*Poems*, 160; cited at *GA* 12: 35/*OWL* 161.

35. Trakl, "Kindheit," *Dichtungen*, 79/*Poems*, 95; "An den Knaben Elis," *Dichtungen*, 84/*Poems*, 100, tm; cited at *GA* 12: 40/*OWL* 165.

36. Trakl, "Nachtlied," *Dichtungen*, 68/*Poems*, 85, tm; cited at *GA* 12: 40/*OWL* 166.

37. One of the arguments in Lawlor's *This Is Not Sufficient*, following Derrida, is that such gathering is denied to animals: "In any case, and this is the central point, animals do not have access to the 'as such' or gathering" (Lawlor, *Sufficient*, 50).

38. Trakl, "Passion," *Dichtungen*, 125/*Poems*, 142, tm.

39. Trakl, "Sommersneige," *Dichtungen*, 137/*Poems*, 155, tm, cited at *GA* 12: 39/*OWL* 164, tm.

40. Calarco views part of Derrida's concern with the animal to be that "working through the question of the animal at this level, at the level of proto-ethical exposure, will challenge the metaphysical grounding of modern ethics and politics and reorient thought along alternative lines" (Calarco, *Zoographies*, 119–20). We believe the observing recollection of the blue deer to have gone no small distance along these same lines, and this already within Heidegger's own work.

41. It has also turned rationality into unimaginative calculative planning. See "Overcoming Metaphysics" on the instinctual nature of planning (*GA* 7: 92–93/*EP* 105–6).

42. For Nietzsche's claim see *KGW* 6.2: 79 and 7.2: 121.

43. Grimm and Grimm, *Deutsches Wörterbuch*, s.v. "sanft."

44. Calarco, *Zoographies*, 30.

3. Sky, Weathering Medium of Appearance

1. See *GA* 39: 183, 215, and 289, among other places. An exception is a parenthetical mention at *GA* 39: 289, which seems a possible addition to the final section of the text.

2. This holds for the first draft of the essay as well; cf. *UK1* 11.

3. Hölderlin, "In lieblicher Bläue . . . ," *GSA* 2.1: 372.14–15/"In Lovely Blue," *Hymns*, 249, tm.

4. In the 1941–42 lecture course on Hölderlin's hymn "Andenken," the bridal celebration of humans and gods is likewise presented as initiatory. See *GA* 52: 69–70.

5. Klaus Held writes in "Sky and Earth" that "as the region for the weather the sky is an other form of region to the regions of the earth. Us human beings do not just have the sky 'over' us in a spatial sense, but also in the sense that the climatic changes which happen there have a dominance over us. Such domination commands our corporeal life: we are affected by the happenings in the sky to the extent to which we feel well in one type of weather and not in another" (34). Held understands climate precisely as that which bonds sky to earth.

6. For further considerations of the role of grace in Heidegger's texts around this time, see my "The Exposure of Grace: Dimensionality in Late Heidegger."

7. Hölderlin, "Aber die Sprache," *Sämtliche Werke*, historisch-kritisch Ausgabe, vol. 4: 237.

8. Hölderlin, "Wie wenn am Feiertage . . . ," *GSA* 2.1: 119.56–57/"As on a Holiday . . . ," *Poems and Fragments*, 394–99, 397.

9. Accordingly, Heideggerian thinking could be considered a kind of esoteric philosophy. The issue is forcefully pursued by Peter Trawny in his *Adyton: Heideggers esoterische Philosophie*.

10. Hebel, "Ideen zur Gebetstheorie" in *Hebels Werke*, 2: 350–55, 350. Cited at *GA* 13: 150/*HFH* 100.

11. This is the Clarendon translation of the passage by Hamlyn. When Empedocles says that light travels and "arrives" the Clarendon text reads for the latter word *gignomenou*, drawing on the support of many manuscripts. By this reading, Empedocles would be wrong to speak of the travelling and "of the coming to pass" of light in the between. The Oxford text by Ross, however, reads here *teinomenou*, which would have Empedocles wrong to speak "of the stretching" of light in the between (*De Anima*, ed. Ross, 418b22). Heidegger, perhaps, could agree to the condemnation of a final *arrival* here (favoring instead an *arriving*), but could only support a thought of color stretching across the between.

12. Aristotle generalizes the claim that vision requires a medium to hold for all the senses at *De Anima* 419 a 25, specifically addressing touch at 423 b 22, where flesh serves as its medium.

13. Cited in David Ross, *Aristotle*, 144.

14. Hölderlin, "In lieblicher Bläue . . . ," *GSA* 2.1: 372.01/"In Lovely Blue," *Hymns*, 249, tm.

15. The relationship between blue and depth is most forcefully presented by Wassily Kandinsky in *On the Spiritual in Art,* see esp. 177–81.

16. "Frühling der Seele," *Dichtungen,* 141/*Poems,* 160, tm.

17. Heraclitus, *DK* 22 b 57/Freeman, *Ancilla,* 28.

18. Hölderlin, "In lieblicher Bläue . . . ," *GSA* 2.1: 372.18/*Hymns,* 249, tm.

19. Hölderlin, "Heimkunft: An die Verwandten," *GSA* 2.1: 96.01–2/*Poems,* 275; cited at *GA* 4: 15/34, tm.

20. Understanding the "joyous" (*das Heitere*) as synonymous with what Hölderlin terms in his poem the "merry" (*das Freudige*); Heidegger: "What the cloud poetizes, the 'merry,' is the joyous" (*GA* 4: 16/35, tm).

21. Hölderlin, "Griechenland," *GSA* 2.1: 256.01/*Poems,* "Greece," 623, tm; cited at *GA* 4: 165/188.

22. Heidegger will go on to show that there are four such reverberations of destiny operative in Hölderlin's poetry. Not coincidentally they are those of the earth, the sky, humans, and gods. Heidegger explicitly names the fourfold in his introductory remarks to the 1959 Stuttgart reading of this lecture, eight days after its first presentation in Munich (*GA* 4: 153/176).

23. But cf. Sallis, *Force of Imagination*: "Scattered clouds (cumulus ones, for instance) display a certain depth in the form of voluminosity; as they run together with the sky, this depth of the clouds serves to accumulate, by contrast, the absolute depth (= absolution from depth) of the sky" (182). If, along with this "absolution from depth," the sky "offers no profiles whatsoever" and holds to an "utter immobility" (182), then it is the poetizing of the clouds that brings depth, perspective, and mobility to the sky. Perhaps there are no cloudless days for Heidegger (and likewise no starless nights).

24. Our conception here can thus be seen to respond to the worry of Michel Haar in a section of his *The Song of the Earth* entitled "Death, Clocks, and the Exclusion of 'Natural Time'" where Haar asks (seemingly against Heidegger): "Is it absurd to describe a significant encounter with the play of lights and shadows, with the sun, which would be independent of any care for what time it is, or at least if such a care were necessarily implied in the experience of temporality, which would have no relation to work that must be done, to some concern, apparently an obsession in all these analyses [of time and clock-time in the period of fundamental ontology]? Are there not shades in the lighting that indicate and make *known*—apart from any measure, expectation, or project—the *climate* of the hour?" (Haar, *Song,* 24). Haar's beautiful formulation of the "climate" of the hour is perfectly in keeping with the mediating conception of time we will present in what follows. His reservations about Heidegger's ability to accommodate such a thought of natural time should thus be confined to *Being and Time* and the texts of the period in question.

25. Husserl's 1934 manuscript "Foundational Investigations of the Phenomenological Origin of the Spatiality of Nature," likewise finds a necessity to the sky. Let us recall that Husserl does not think human life is somehow accidentally upon this earth: "We must not perpetrate the absurdity of then seeing human history, the history of the species anthropologically and psychologically within

the evolution of the individual and people, the cultivation of science and the interpretation of the world as an obviously accidental event on the earth which might just as well have occurred on Venus or Mars" (Husserl, "Räumlichkeit," 323/*Shorter*, 230). Indeed, Husserl will not even allow that human life could arise in multiple places at once. What it means to be human is to be of the earth: "But that does not mean that the moon or Venus could not just as well be conceived as primitive places in an original separation and that it is only a fact that the earth is just for me and our earthly humanity. *There is only one humanity and one earth*" (Husserl, "Räumlichkeit," 324/*Shorter*, 230, em). To be human, to be of this earth, for Husserl is thus to be under the sky: "But if the earth is constituted with animate organisms and corporeality, then the 'sky' is also necessarily constituted as the field of what is outermost, yet which can be spatially experienced for me and all of us—with respect to the earth-basis" (Husserl, "Räumlichkeit," 318/*Shorter*, 227–28). Perhaps Heidegger's thinking of the fourfold can be seen in a line with these later thoughts of Husserl's.

26. John Sallis arrives at a similar point in "Time Out . . ." when he notes that "originary time will always already (in an order no longer detachable from time) have begun to double itself, will always already have been contaminated by an outside, drifting toward something like the time of concern" (*Echoes*, 69).

27. Aristotle, *Physics*, 218 b 8–9.

28. See Heraclitus, *DK* 22 b 100/Freeman, *Ancilla*, 31.

29. On measure, cf. *GA* 55: 170–71.

30. The term is found in discussions of technology at the time of the fourfold. In the 1949 Bremen lectures, for instance, it is introduced in the concluding lecture "The Turn," where we hear talk of "the constellation in the essence of beyng. This constellation is the dimension in which beyng essences as the danger" (*GA* 79: 74–75/70). In the lecture "The Principle of Identity," from the 1957 cycle *Basic Principles of Thinking*, constellation comes to name the relation between the human and beyng, which is one of mutual positioning and challenging: "The claim that lets the being appear in planability and calculability, and which also challenges the human into requisitioning the beings that thereby appear, this claim constitutes the constellation in which we reside. The whole essence of the modern technological world is determined by this" (*GA* 79: 124/116). Heidegger emphasizes this mutual positioning or placing (*stellen*) in a notebook of the time (entitled "Important Remarks on 'Technology'") by writing "the *con-stellation* [*die* Kon-Stellation]" (*GA* 76: 329). By the time that this lecture, "The Principle of Identity," made it into published form as part of *Identity and Difference* (1957), Heidegger was growing skeptical of the term. A note to the text at its first mention reads: "instead of 'constellation': Coordination [*Zu-Ordnung*]—*Disposition* / Bringing into what belongs [*das Gehörige*]," and the supplementary materials to *Identity and Difference* (*Beilage* II) include the following remark: "The talk of the 'constellation of being and human' is insufficient, if being and human are each taken by themselves and then (one does not know in which region) are put together.—better: '*belonging*-together'" (*GA* 11: 42 n. 30, *GA* 11: 99). For a reading of the role of the constellation in Heidegger's thinking, see Rojcewicz, *Gods and Technology*, 178–82.

31. Rojcewicz discusses the mention of constellation here in "The Question Concerning Technology" to show that Heidegger is referring to both stars and planets (which are literally "wandering stars," as when Heidegger refers to the earth as the "errant star [*Irrstern*]" in "Overcoming Metaphysics"; *GA* 7: 96/*EP* 109, tm). Rojcewicz argues that "what Heidegger means by the term 'constellation' is what in astronomy is called an 'appulse,' the 'driving-toward' each other of two heavenly bodies. The appulse of two planets is, of course, merely an apparent drawing near. They seem to approach one another only from our vantage point." Rojcewicz, *Gods and Technology*, 179. For our reading, no such merely apparent drawing near will do (especially if an underlying unchanged reality is presumed).

32. This "one" ringing should be understood as Heidegger prescribes in the "Language in the Poem" essay two years prior, where it names "that uniting [*Einende*] which unites from out of the gathering blueness [*Bläue*] of the spiritual night" (*GA* 12: 74/*OWL* 195, tm), i.e., the jointure of the medium, as we have seen.

4. Divinities, Hinting Messengers of Godhood

1. These texts and others from the period have been assembled in vol. 16 of the *Gesamtausgabe*. English translations of the *Der Akademiker* articles, "Contributions to *Der Akademiker*," can be found in Brainard, Jacobs, and Lee, eds., *Heidegger and the Political*, 486–519.

2. It should be noted that Nietzsche, too, recognized the difficulties in simply proclaiming God dead. The madman who makes such a pronouncement claims that he has "come too early," that his time "is not yet," for example. Nietzsche, *Fröhliche Wissenschaft*, §125, *KGW* 5.2: 143/*Gay Science*, 181–82. And even earlier in *The Gay Science*, the task of posthumously killing God is announced: "God is dead; but given the way of men, there may still be caves for thousands of years in which his shadow will be shown.—And we—we still have to vanquish his shadow, too." Nietzsche, *Fröhliche Wissenschaft*, §108, *KGW* 5.2: 158–60/*Gay Science*, 167. Heidegger could nevertheless still see in this the imposition of an eternal task, indeed, an eternally recurring one.

3. Hölderlin, "Rousseau," *GSA* 2.1: 13.30–32/*Poems*, 125.

4. For the etymological discussion that follows, see Grimm and Grimm, *Deutsches Wörterbuch*, s.v. "winken" and *Oxford English Dictionary*, s.v. "wink."

5. See *Identity and Difference*: "Er-eignen heißt ursprünglich: er-äugnen, *d.h.* er-blicken, im Blicken zu sich rufen, an-eignen" (*GA* 11: 45/omitted from English translation) a derivation reiterated in a post-1959 marginal note to the essay "The Way to Language": "Er-eignen—Er-äugnen, Er-Blicken, Er-Blitzen" (*GA* 12: 253, n. b). A parallel claim is to be found in "The Overcoming of Metaphysics" as well, "er-äugnet, d.h. er-blickt" (*GA* 7: 98/*EP* 110, tm).

6. "Rousseau," *GSA* 2.1: 13.30–32/*Poems*, 125.

7. Cf. *GA* 66: 237, where "a denial [*Verweigerung*] is opened which is the hint of beyng itself."

8. Cf. *GA* 65: 384/303: "what withholds itself does so in a hesitant way and

thereby grants [*schenkt*] the possibility of bestowal [*Schenkung*] and appropriation [*Ereignung*]." Within the *Contributions*, Heidegger considers such giving in terms of ripeness, a notion whose importance we have already addressed. See *GA* 65: 410/325, tm: "In such an essencing of hinting, beyng itself comes to its ripeness [*Reife*]. Ripeness is the preparedness for bringing forth a fruit and bestowal [*Verschenkung*]"; and *GA* 65: 400/317, tm: "Fruit and accident [*Zufall*], onset [*Anfall*] and hint."

9. The last God is tied to such waiting, the waiting that is likewise, as we have seen, a hardening against hints: "The end is the incessant 'and so forth' from which the *last*, as the most primordial [*Anfänglichste*], has withdrawn right from the beginning and for the longest time. The end never sees itself; instead, it considers itself the completion and will therefore be least ready and prepared either to await, or to experience, what is *last*" (*GA* 65: 416/329).

10. The same point is made again in "A Dialogue on Language." Since hints illuminate a trace of presence in the heart of absence, they demand "the widest region in which to swing," this region is found in hesitation, and hesitation, for its part, "occurs truly when slowness is borne through modesty" (*GA* 12: 113/ *OWL* 27–28, tm).

11. Such a logic prohibits any pronouncement on the existence or non-existence of God and the gods as long as both presence and absence (*Anwesen* and *Abwesen*) remain understood substantially, rather than on the (non)basis of the trace (cf. *GA* 9: 350–351/266–267 and the therein cited *GA* 9: 159 n. 56/123 n. 62). Instructive in this regard is Thurner: "Theism and atheism . . . have no meaning since they pose themselves only within the frame of theo-*logic*," a logic for which "the alternatives of theism and atheism also already harbor a definite determination with respect to the Being-, i.e., temporal-character, of the divinities" (Thurner, "Gott und Ereignis," 98). This temporal character is that of "*pure* presence, or absence," and in the judgments of such a theo-logic, "only mere presence, or absence, can come to expression in the affirmation, or denial" (Thurner, "Gott und Ereignis," 98). From a different perspective, Jean-Luc Nancy in "On a Divine *Wink*" can proclaim that "such is the divine truth of the *Wink*: it stems from the fact that there is no wink *of* god, but that the god *is* the wink. He does not do it, he winks himself there." Nancy, *Dis-Enclosure*, 119. A similar thought is already operative in Nancy's "Sharing Voices" some twenty-three years earlier: "The divine is what gives itself, what divides itself in voice and in *hermeneia*: it is what signifies 'en-thussiasm.' In this sense, the divine, or god himself, *is* enthusiasm." Nancy, "Sharing Voices," 237.

12. For further consideration of the last God in his coming, its relation to eschatology, and a comparison of this with Hegel's notion of temporality, see Peter Trawny, "The Future of Time: Reflections on the Concept of Time in Hegel and Heidegger."

13. We might think this gathering of gesture (*Gebärde*) etymologically as *Ge-bären*, the collection of *bären*, where this term, as the 1950 essay "Language" explains, names precisely a "bearing." Heidegger writes, "our old language names carrying-out [*Austragen*]: *bern, bären*, from this the words 'to bear' [as of children; *gebären*] and 'gesture' [*Gebärde*]" (*GA* 12: 19/*PLT* 197, tm).

14. For ruminations on the ethical dimension of gesture and the hand in particular, see Derrida, "Heidegger's Hand (*Geschlecht* II)" and Kleinberg-Levin, *Gestures of Ethical Life*, 204–74.

15. The idea of a salvation through hints concludes Heidegger's 1970 poem entitled "Hints": "The more intrusive the calculator, / the more measureless the society. / The rarer the thinking, / the lonelier the poetizing. / The more needful the intimating, / intimating the distance / of saving hints" (*GA* 13: 222).

16. The angels of this sort, however, must be opposed to those of Rilke's thoughtful poetry, as will be shown in the following chapter. See "The Metaphysical Completion of the *Animal Rationale*" in chapter 5.

17. Hölderlin, "Dichterberuf," *GSA* 2.1: 46–48/*Poems* 176–181.

18. According to Kisiel, "here, for the very first time, Heidegger clearly coopts the neo-Kantian term 'facticity' for his own unique technical use." Kisiel, *Genesis*, 136.

19. We now know this to be incorrect. The term arises at the conclusion of Heidegger's first Freiburg lecture course from the war-emergency semester of 1919, *The Idea of Philosophy and the Problem of Worldview*, in the closing section that is itself entitled "hermeneutical intuition" (*GA* 56/57: 116–17/89–90). Here we read that "the empowering, living experience of lived experience . . . is an understanding, hermeneutical intuition" (*GA* 56/57: 117/89, tm). This link between understanding and hermeneutics will stay with Heidegger through *Being and Time*.

20. The difficulty was already broached in the 1923 course: "Should it now turn out that *to be* in the mode of *self-covering* and self-veiling belong to the *being*-character *of being* which constitutes the object of philosophy, and indeed not in an accessorial sense but in accord with its being-character, then the category of 'phenomenon' will become a truly earnest matter. The task involved—making it a phenomenon—will become phenomenological in a radical sense" (*GA* 63: 76/60, tm).

21. In "The Way to Language" (1959), Heidegger ponders how "*to bring language as language to language*," noting that at first "the formula points to a web [*Geflecht*] of relations in which we ourselves are included. The undertaking of a way to speech is woven into a kind of speaking which intends to uncover speech itself in order to present it as speech and to put it into words in the presentation—which is also evidence that language itself has woven us into the speaking" (*GA* 12: 230/*OWL* 112, tm). This involvement that we find here with language is again a "hermeneutical" one, as our treatment of the message in what follows will demonstrate. As such, and once again, this hermeneutical implication should not be thought in terms of a circle. Heidegger objects to those who would cast this relation in such terms, those who would construe "this involuted relation as a circle—an unavoidable yet meaningful circle. The circle is a special case of our web of language. It is meaningful, because the direction and manner of the circling motion are determined by language itself, by a movement within language. We might learn the character and scope of this movement from language itself, by entering the web" (*GA* 12: 231/*OWL* 113). This abandonment of the circular conception of understanding, language, meaning is indissociable

from the newfound concern for the thing and a more "materialist" or "ontic" thinking of the fourfold.

22. In making these claims, I am in agreement with the recent thinking of Thomas Sheehan on the role of meaning in Heideggerian thought. Sheehan argues that "Heidegger's key terms 'being itself' and 'the being of beings' come from a *pre*-phenomenological metaphysics of objective realism," while Heidegger himself "understood *Sein* phenomenologically, that is, within a reduction from *being* to *meaning*" (Sheehan, "The Turn," 83). Without effecting this reduction, Sheehan claims, "one risks slipping back into the incoherent tendency to think of 'being' as objectively out there" (Sheehan, "Facticity and *Ereignis*," 51). He proposes that by means of "an emphatically phenomenological-hermeneutical way of reading Heidegger, the *Da-sein/Sein* correlation is transformed into the *Da-sinn/Sinn* conjunction" (Sheehan, "Astonishing!," 3). In the thinking of the messengerial proposed in what follows above, an attempt is made to break with the view of being as "objective" and as unqualifiedly "present" in favor of a thinking of the relational reach of beings. Only such beings can concern us (*gehen uns an*), and they do so by coming to us, by relating to us (issuing to us and appearing to us as an "issue" calling for response). Richard Polt objects that Sheehan's view omits the excess of being from its account of meaning (see Polt, "Meaning, Excess, and Event," 32–38). It is my hope that articulating the way in which meaningfulness is ontologically located in a way of being of things themselves would satisfy both sides of this debate—that of meaning and of being—though ultimately I find myself in agreement with Sheehan on the identity of the two.

23. The 1923 course *Ontology: The Hermeneutics of Facticity* provides a far richer account of the history of the term. It begins by noting that, while the etymology is "obscure," the term is "related to the name of the God *Hermês*, the messenger of the gods" and the source for the "original" meaning of the term is Plato, with Heidegger following the *Ion* in stating "a *hermêneus* is one who communicates, announces and makes known, to someone what another 'means,' or someone who in turn conveys, reactivates, this communication, this announcement and making known" (*GA* 63: 9/6). Subsequent discussions concern the use of the term in Aristotle, Philostratus, Thucydides, Philo, Aristeas, to name only the Greek sources consulted.

24. For a discussion of the relation between *Einfalt* and *Einfach* in Heidegger, see my "Simplicity and Relation: Remarks on Heidegger's 1963 Dedication to Char."

25. Sheehan notes that "That fact that sense-making *can* be taken away from each of us at any moment is what Heidegger means by mortality . . . Mortality and first-order *hermêneia* are two sides of the same human coin. Mortality lets us make sense of . . . and in fact *requires* us to do so if we don't want to die" (Sheehan, "Facticity and Ereignis," 47).

26. In the 1953 lecture "The Question Concerning Technology," where we read, "all that essences endures. But is enduring only a continuing on? [. . .] If we more thoughtfully consider what authentically endures, and perhaps solely endures, then we are permitted to say: *Only what is granted endures* [Nur das

Gewährte währt]. *What endures inceptually from out of the dawn is what grants* [das Gewährende]" (*GA* 7: 32/*QCT* 31, tm; cf. *GA* 7: 32–34/*QCT* 31–33).

27. A few years later, in 1939, sobriety (*Nüchternheit*) is identified as the fundamental mood corresponding to an experience of the holy: "Sobriety is the ever ready fundamental attunement of preparedness for the holy" (*GA* 4: 77/98, tm).

28. See Heidegger's 1945 text "*Die Armut*" ("Poverty") and associated notes for elaboration of the references, *GA* 73.1: 871–84.

29. In this regard, and despite Heidegger's own linking of the holy to the clearing of being, it nonetheless misses the mark to see here a refinement and reaffirmation of the ontological difference, as some commentators have contended. Kovacs, for instance, in *The Question of God in Heidegger's Phenomenology* claims that "it does become clear through these considerations (the Holy, the poet, the God, gods, 'nature,' men) that Heidegger is trying to unwrap the nature of the ontological difference" (167), finding Heidegger's reflections on the holy as the adoption of a "new vocabulary," part of a "new way of 'saying' (*Sagen*) the onological difference and the meaning of Being" (169). All would depend on how one understands difference and, further, Heidegger's subsequent abandonment of the ontological difference as a trope of his thought. Karsten Harries's 1966 essay "Heidegger's Conception of the Holy" offers a more nuanced view of the holy in regards to the ontological difference, finding that "to be such messengers, the gods ["divinities"] must bridge the *ontologische Differenz*," ultimately concluding that "Heidegger's understanding of poets and gods does not provide a satisfactory account of mediation" (Kovacs, *Question of God*, 182). Hopefully our analysis not just of the divinities, but of the fourfold as a whole, shows the error of this early conclusion.

30. Hölderlin, "Gestalt und Geist," *GSA* 2.1: 321.01/*Hymns*, 223, tm.

31. For further discussion of the role of coming in *The History of Beyng*, see my "The Coming of History: Heidegger and Nietzsche Against the Present."

32. While Ben Vedder is one of the few commentators who actually addresses Heidegger's thinking of the fourfold in regards to his views on divinity, we must nevertheless take our distance from his claim in *Heidegger's Philosophy of Religion* that "the holy indicates a condition of the possibility for the appearing of the divine" (234) for the reasons given above.

33. In 1974's "Der Fehl heiliger Namen" ("The Lack of Holy Names"), Heidegger speaks of the provenance (*Herkunft*) of this "lack" as "the forgetting of being" (*Seinsvergessenheit*; *GA* 13: 235). This thought of an "origin" in forgetting is entirely in keeping with the above.

34. Hölderlin, "Der Ister," *GSA* 2.1: 192.71–72/*Poems*, 517.

35. The same point is found at the close of "The Western Conversation," a 1946–48 conversation devoted to Hölderlin's "Ister" hymn. Commenting on this same passage concerning the concealed and unknowable doings of the river, Hölderlin's poetry is said to "encounter the concealed and know most purely the unknowable" (*GA* 75: 194). This knowledge and this encounter, this touching of the concealed, is its own preservation.

36. See Danner, *Das Göttliche*, 99.

37. On the relation between grace and exposure, see my "The Exposure of Grace: Dimensionality in Late Heidegger."

38. A paraphrase of Terence; see note 30 in chapter 2. Sheehan expresses the same thought in his claim that "being is always *'ad hominem'*" (Sheehan, "Facticity and *Ereignis*," 68).

5. Mortals, Being-in-Death

1. See, for example, ". . . poetically dwells man . . . ," "The human essences as the mortal" (*GA* 7: 200/*PLT* 219, tm) and "The Danger," "The human is not yet the mortal" (*GA* 79: 56/54).

2. See von Herrmann, *Wege ins Ereignis*, 224 and 227, 249 and 384, 351, 353, 101–102.

3. See Ernst Jünger, "Die totale Mobilmachung," *Betrachtungen zur Zeit*, 131–32/"Total Mobilization," 130–31.

4. Ernst Jünger, *Der Arbeiter*, 93; *Betrachtungen*, 165/*On Pain*, 23.

5. Jünger, "Über den Schmerz," *Betrachtungen*, 158/*On Pain*, 16, tm.

6. Jünger, "Über den Schmerz," *Betrachtungen*, 162/*On Pain*, 19–20.

7. Jünger, *Arbeiter*, 181.

8. Jünger, *Arbeiter*, 224.

9. Rilke, *Die Sonnete an Orpheus*, 2.13, *Werke* 1: 760/*Orpheus*, 85. On nature as a force, see Rilke, "Schwerkraft," *Werke* 2: 179/"Gravity," *Selected*, 271. The improvised verse (editorially titled "Für Helmuth Freiherrn Lucius von Stoedten") is found at Rilke, *Gedichte*, 2: 261.

10. See *GA* 5: 279/*PLT* 101, *GA* 9: 323/246.

11. In the *Ister* lecture course Heidegger notes that "a thoughtless throwing together of my thinking with Rilke's poetizing has already become cliché," and to repudiate this he points to Rilke's understanding of "the open" which is "at best the complete opposite" of what Heidegger thinks (cf. *GA* 53: 113 n. 2/91 n. 2, see also 113–114/91–92). A semester later, in the *Parmenides* lecture course (*GA* 54), Heidegger's irritation has escalated into something of a fervor. He insists that Rilke's notion of the open is by no means identical with what is meant by *alêtheia* and repeats this claim at least six times in the space of ten pages! Important formulations of this disagreement for the present context: "Rilke knows and suspects nothing of *alêtheia*, no more than Nietzsche does" (*GA* 54: 231/155), "yet the 'open' according to the word of Rilke and the 'open' thought as the essence and truth of *alêtheia* are distinct in the extreme, as far apart as the beginning of Western thought and the completion of Western metaphysics— and nevertheless they precisely belong together—the same [*das Selbe*]" (*GA* 54: 230/154).

12. The letter to a Russian reader asking about the eighth elegy is found in Betz, *Rilke in Frankreich*, 289–91; the quotation is from 291. Heidegger's citation of this is at *GA* 5: 285/*PLT* 108.

13. Rilke, *Duineser Elegien*, 8, *Werke* 1: 715, 716/*Selected*, 193, 195, tm.

14. Rilke, ". . . Wenn aus des Kaufmanns Hand," *Werke* 2: 182; cited at *GA* 5: 314

15. While Heidegger performs no single reading of the *Übermensch*—according to Michel Haar, he offers eight at the least ("The Ambivalent Unthought of the Overman and the Duality of Heidegger's Political Thinking")—the vacillation between the views expressed in the *Nietzsche* lectures and essays of the 1930s–1940s and the thought articulated in the work of the 1950s (*What is Called Thinking?* and "Who is Nietzsche's Zarathustra?") is perhaps more a testament to the decisive, essentially ambiguous role of the *Übermensch* than to any fundamental shift in Heidegger's thought of Nietzsche.

16. Nietzsche, *Also Sprach Zarathustra*, 2.12, *KGW* 6.1: 143/*Thus Spoke Zarathustra*, 114.

17. Nietzsche, *Wille zur Macht*, §582, 396, in the notebooks from Fall 1885–Fall 1886 at *KGW* 8.1: 151/*Will to Power*, 312.

18. Nietzsche, *Wille zur Macht*, §1067, 697, in the notebooks from June–July 1885 at *KGW* 7.3: 338–39/*Will to Power*, 550.

19. See John Sallis, "Nietzsche's Platonism," for a thematic survey of Nietzsche's complex relation to Plato and Platonism, and "Twisting Free—Being to an Extent Sensible" (*Echoes*, 76–96) for a critical account of Heidegger's reading of that relationship.

20. In the view of Reiner Schürmann, humanity prior to the metaphysical reversal must be overcome because that humanity "is the type that underestimates"; see *Being and Acting*, 200. This underestimation prevents a total willing, and finds its most traditional source in the underestimation of the body in the history of philosophy: "It is the underestimation of the body that has inhibited the consummation of the will into will to power, an underestimation that reverses the overestimation of the soul or the spirit over the body. [. . .] the overman appears when the double control over the self (will) and over the world (its stabilization in the eternal return) abolishes the preëminence of representational reason over body" (Schürmann, *Being and Acting*, 200–1).

21. Nietzsche, *Jenseits von Gut und Böse*, §62, *KGW* 6.2: 81/*Beyond Good and Evil*, 75.

22. Also, "'Body' is the name for that figure of the will to power in which the latter is immediately accessible, because constantly persevering, to the human as the 'subject' so distinguished" (*GA* 6.2: 270/*N3*: 223, tm).

23. A note to the manuscript at this point emphasizes this abandonment of being, "released from the refusal of differentiation into the unguarding—from here: the *Übermensch*" (*GA* 50: 51 n. 3).

24. Nietzsche, *Also Sprach Zarathustra*, Vorrede §10, *KGW* 6.1: 21/*Thus Spoke Zarathustra*, 25.

25. Michel Haar is very able and ready to point out any inadequacy or insufficiency he may see in Heidegger's reading of the *Übermensch*: "Heidegger, who thought out so proudly the concept of earth, here assimilates two meanings of the concept which in Nietzsche are distinct: the earth as the rehabilitated realm of the *sensible* ('the Overman will be the meaning of the earth') and the earth as planet condemned to exploitation in the expressions 'the government of the

earth' or, particularly, 'the Masters of the earth'" (Haar, "Overman" 121). But are these two meanings really distinct? Is it not the case, rather, that exactly the reha-bilitated realm of the sensible (if by "rehabilitated" one means *herausgedreht*, then the term "earth" here is appropriate) and the exploited planet (here one should say "desert") are the same (*das Selbe*) in being the reverse of each other? Is this not Heidegger's thought of *Ereignis* and the same essential ambiguity or unde-cidability that necessitates the eight readings of the *Übermensch* in the first place?

26. Sallis *Echoes*, 84.

27. Sallis, "Twisting Free—Being to an Extent Sensible," 78–79.

28. Exactly what relation then exists between the thought of *Being and Time* and the thought of mortality from the period of the fourfold is a point of debate among scholars. The opinion of John Sallis, for example, that "all the later dis-courses [of death] serve constantly to confirm the earlier analysis by reinscribing it within contexts that otherwise decisively exceed that of *Being and Time*" (Sallis, "Mortality and Imagination," 135), must be brought into conjunction with that of Werner Marx, according to whom "the meaning of Heidegger's later deter-mination of 'dying' cannot be derived from the existentiales in *Being and Time*" (Marx, *Measure*, 99).

29. It is found in Laertius, *Lives of Eminent Philosophers*, 10.121–135. The Greek text is available in a Loeb edition edited by R. D. Hicks (vol. 2). A more recent translation is found in *The Epicurus Reader*, ed. and trans. Brad Inwood and L.P. Gerson. I will cite the English from this latter text. The saying here is found at 10.124 in Laertius, and *Epicurus Reader*, 29.

30. Laertius, *Lives*, 10.125; *Epicurus Reader*, 29.

31. Dastur, *Death*, 43.

32. This is in complete agreement with Derrida's claim that "there is no scandal whatsoever in saying that *Dasein* remains immortal in its originary being-to-death, if by 'immortal' one understands 'without end' in the sense of *verenden*." Derrida, *Aporias*, 39–40. Derrida himself had quoted Poe's Valdemar, "*I am dead*," at *Speech and Phenomena*, 1.

33. The transformation in the thinking of modality that attends the anal-ysis of death in *Being and Time* emerges again in the *Contributions to Philosophy*, in discussions of the splitting or cleaving (*Zerklüftung*) of being. In the *Contribu-tions*, Heidegger will speak of being-towards-death as the "collision of necessity and possibility," noting that "only in such spheres can it be surmised what truly belongs to that which 'ontology' treats as the pale and vacuous *jumble* of 'modali-ties'" (*GA* 65: 283/222). When understood more vividly and fully, the emphasis falls upon the belonging together of the traditional philosophical modalities: "Refusal as the essencing of beyng is the highest actuality of the highest possi-bility *as* possibility and is thereby the first necessity [*Notwendigkeit*]. Da-sein is the grounding of the truth of this most simple cleaving" (*GA* 65: 294/232, tm). Not surprisingly, the sections of the book immediately following turn directly to the question of being-toward-death.

34. Marx, *Measure*, 111–12. Werner Marx's essay *"Die Sterblichen"* (first pub-lished in 1979) was later slightly revised for inclusion as a chapter in his 1983 book, *Gibt es auf Erden ein Maß? Grundbestimmungen einer nichtmetaphysischen Ethik,*

translated as *Is There a Measure on Earth? Foundations for a Nonmetaphysical Ethics.* References to this text will be from the English translation.

35. Dastur, *Death: An Essay on Finitude,* 82.

36. Found also in the published version of "The Thing" at *GA* 7: 180/ *PLT* 176, tm. The claim is repeated nearly verbatim in both "Building Dwelling Thinking" (with emphasis added to the "as," at *GA* 7: 152/*PLT* 150, tm), and in ". . . poetically dwells man . . ." (with "Being able to die" replacing "Dying" at *GA* 7: 200/*PLT* 222, tm). In "The Essence of Language" we read "The mortals are those who are able to experience [*erfahren können*] death as death. The animal is not capable of this [*vermag dies nicht*]" (*GA* 12: 203/*OWL* 107, tm).

37. In the lecture "What Is Called Thinking?" we read that "what is called, for example, swimming, we never learn through a treatise about swimming. What swimming means is told to us only through a leap into the river. We thereby first familiarize ourselves with the element wherein swimming must move about" (*GA* 7: 138).

38. We can take this notion of a being-in-death, specifically the "in" of it, as a further consequence of Heidegger's move away from a philosophy of transcendence, even when understood in terms of ekstasis, to one of a "standing in" or "instancy." The "Introduction to 'What Is Metaphysics?'" stems from the same year as the Bremen lectures, 1949, and puts the matter thus: "The ecstatic essence of existence is therefore still understood inadequately as long as one thinks of it as merely a 'standing out,' while interpreting the 'out' as meaning 'away from' the interior of an immanence of consciousness or spirit. For in this manner, existence would still be represented in terms of 'subjectivity' and 'substance'; while, in fact, the 'out' ought to be understood in terms of the 'outside itself' of the openness of Being itself. The stasis of the ecstatic consists—strange as it may sound—in standing-in [*Innestehen*] the 'out' and 'there' of unconcealedness, which prevails as the essence of Being itself. What is meant by 'existence' in the context of a thinking that is prompted by, and directed toward, the truth of Being, could be most felicitously designated by the word 'in-standing' [*Inständigkeit*]. We must think at the same time, however, of standing-in the openness of Being [*Innestehen in der Offenheit des Seins*], of sustaining this standing-in (care), and of enduring in what is most extreme [*Ausdauern im Äußersten*] (being toward death); for together they constitute the full essence of existence" (*GA* 9: 374/284). Heidegger's thinking requires that the opposition of outside and inside be abolished, where either option precludes the mediation of this renewed understanding of "being-in." For an overview of Heidegger's shifting relation to transcendence and the shift from ekstasis to instancy, see "Consciousness and Dasein: The Question of *Ekstasis,*" chapter 6 of Raffoul, *Heidegger and the Subject,* 140–65.

39. At the opening of *What Is Called Thinking?* (1951) this is put thus: "The human can think insofar as he has the possibility [*Möglichkeit*] for this. However this possible would not yet be concealed from us insofar as we are capable of it [*es vermögen*]. For we are capable of only that which we like [*mögen;* with which we "affiliate"]. But we like on the other hand truly only that which for its part itself likes us and indeed in our essence, in that it addresses our essence as that which holds us in our essence" (*GA* 8: 5/3, tm).

40. Again the lecture "What Is Called Thinking?": "The human can think insofar as he has the possibility for this. Yet this possible would be not yet sheltered from us in that we are capable of it. For to be capable of something means: to allow something entry alongside us, in accordance with its essence, to ardently protect this entrance. Indeed we are capable of always only that which we like, something to which we are devoted, in that we allow of it. In truth, we like only that which each time in advance on its own likes us and indeed likes us in our essence, in that it inclines itself to this. Through this inclination our essence is taken into its claim. The inclination is address. The address speaks to us in our essence, calls us forth into our essence and thus holds us thus in this" (*GA* 7: 129).

41. A similar thought is voiced at the end of the lecture "What Is Called Thinking?" where Heidegger states "for this reason our thinking has not yet arrived in its element" (*GA* 7: 143). A marginal note to the word "element" here found in Heidegger's 1967 edition of the text reads "the 'element'—the event of appropriation" (*GA* 7: 143 n. u).

42. See the *Oxford English Dictionary*, s.v. "shrine," and Grimms' *Deutsches Wörterbuch*, s.v. "Schrein."

43. Ariès, *Hour of Our Death*, 168.

44. Ariès, *Hour of Our Death*, 168, 172.

45. Ariès, *Hour of Our Death*, 171–72.

46. Sallis, *Echoes*, 136.

47. For a general history of tree-coffin burial see Philipp Weiß, "Eine kleine Geschichte des Sarges," in Zentralinstitut und Museum für Sepulkrakultur, ed., *Vom Totenbaum zum Designersarg*, 10–22, and Karl Zimmerman, "Bemerkungen zur Geschichte der Holzsargbestattung," in Zimmerman, *Baumsarg und "Totenbaum,"* 28–36. Interestingly, coffin burial was forbidden in some areas and highly taxed in others due precisely to its lengthening of the decay process; cf. Joachim Diefenbach and Reiner Sörries, "Pestsarg und Ausschüttruhe: Kurzer Abriß der Entwicklung des Holzsarges," in Zentralinstitut und Museum für Sepulkrakultur, ed., *Vom Totenbaum zum Designersarg*, 37–42, 37, and Zimmerman, *Baumsarg und "Totenbaum,"* 28–29. Zimmerman also provides a helpful history of textual references to death-trees (including citations from J.P. Hebel), "Schriftenquellen zur Baumsargbestattung und zum Mundartbegriff '(Toten)Baum,'" in Zimmerman, *Baumsarg und "Totenbaum,"* 54–81.

48. Heidegger specifies the kind of craft that is able to produce such a farm house, "a craft which, itself sprung from dwelling, and which still uses its tools and frames as things [*noch als Dinge*], built the farmhouse" (*GA* 7: 162/*PLT* 158, tm).

49. Adam Scharr mentions Pius Schweitzer as leader of the hut's construction with some reservation, basing his observation on a tourist sign near the hut (Scharr, *Heidegger's Hut*, 54 and 118 n. 36). There is no such reservation on the part of Heidegger himself, who says in a private 1947 obituary for Schweitzer that "25 years ago, in accordance with the plans of our mother, the carpenter Schweitzer built the hut from out of an experienced sense for the soil and water, for the tree and the wind" (*GA* 16: 428). He repeats as much in the 1966 homeland speech cited above, saying that they were referred to Schweitzer in 1922 to build a hut that would be "a place of concentration for work and a place of proximity to

nature for the family" (*GA* 16: 642). Following their consultation with him, "Pius Schweitzer thus built the hut. . . . He not only had an exceptional natural sense for the right measure and for the simple beauty of everything that he planned and built. He was also always reliable [*zuverlässig*] and exact in the work itself" (*GA* 16: 642).

50. We should note that while the shrine is not named in the related essays "Building Dwelling Thinking" and ". . . poetically dwells man . . . ," this is not to say that the thought of preservation is far from Heidegger's mind concerning this topic. To begin with, in ". . . poetically dwells man . . . ," after naming the mortal to be the one who is able to die, who enables death as death, Heidegger goes on to say that the mortal dies continually, "so long as he dwells" (*GA* 7: 200/*PLT* 219). This is only two months after "Building Dwelling Thinking," where again the claims are found that mortals are the ones who are able to die and that the mortals are in the fourfold (i.e., are mortals) insofar as they dwell (*GA* 7: 152/ *PLT* 148). But "Building Dwelling Thinking" goes further in explaining exactly what this dwelling is: "The mortals dwell in the manner that they preserve [*schonen*] the fourfold in its essence" (*GA* 7: 152/*PLT* 148, tm). When Heidegger does not name death's shrine, he nonetheless emphasizes its preservative, care-taking, saving (*schonende*) function.

51. In the 1950 lecture "Language," Heidegger notes that "in death is gathered the highest concealment [*Verborgenheit*] of being. Death has already overtaken [*überholt*] every dying" (*GA* 12: 20/*PLT* 198, tm).

52. Marx, *Measure*, 105.

53. Marx, *Measure*, 110, tm.

54. Heidegger, "Das Ding," in Bayerische Akademie der schönen Kunst, ed., *Gestalt und Gedanke* 1: 128–48.

55. It is not only the shrine that is tied to the secret, but the refuge as well. In the same 1954 volume, *Vorträge und Aufsätze*, the essay "Moira," first published there, concludes with the thought that "the essence of the mortals is called into attentiveness to the behest [*das Geheiß*] which beckons them to come into death. As the most extreme possibility of mortal Dasein, death is not the end of the possible, but rather, the highest refuge [*Ge-Birg*] (the gathering sheltering) of the secret of calling disclosure" (*GA* 7: 261/*EGT* 101, tm). While we will turn to the relation between mortals and language shortly, here mortals are understood as those who respond to a behest and in so doing enter into death. The response to the call is this very entry into the medium of death. Death is the name of the refuge (*Ge-Birg*) understood as a gathering together (or concentrating, *versammelnde*) of sheltering (*Bergen*). Death provides refuge for the secret of a kind of disclosure that occurs through calling (a *rufende Entbergung*).

56. For a fuller treatment of Heidegger's thinking of the secret at this time, see my "Die Politik des geheimen Deutschland. Martin Heidegger und der George-Kreis."

57. Derrida, *Gift of Death*, 58.

58. "the thinking of community as essence . . . assigns to community a *common being*, whereas community is a matter of something quite different, namely, of existence inasmuch as it is *in* common, but without letting itself be absorbed

into a common substance. Being *in* common has nothing to do with communion, with fusion into a body, into a unique and ultimate identity that would no longer be exposed." Nancy, *Inoperative Community,* xxxviii.

59. Derrida, *Gift of Death,* 80.

60. Derrida, *Gift of Death,* 69.

61. Derrida finds the secret essentially unknowable, noting in *The Gift of Death* that, "if my secret self, that which can be revealed only to the other, to the wholly other, to God if you wish, is a secret without reflexivity, one that I will never know or experience or reappropriate as my own, then what sense is there in saying that it is 'my' secret, a secret 'of mine,' or in saying more generally that a secret *belongs,* that it is proper to or belongs to some 'one,' or to some *other* who remains some*one*? It is perhaps there that we find the secret of secrecy, namely, that there is no knowledge of it and it is there for no one. A secret doesn't belong, it can never be said to be at home or in its place. Such is the *Unheimlichkeit* of the *Geheimnis"* (92).

62. Hölderlin, "Seit ein Gespräch wir sind," from the poem "Versöhnender, der du nimmergeglaubt," third version, *GSA* 2.2: 137.50/*Poems,* 451.

63. On this, see Sheehan: "Our ability to deal with anything we encounter, our capacity to make sense of it, entails that the thing must have already entered the realm of language—that is, the realm of meaning" (Sheehan, "Facticity and *Ereignis,*" 43).

64. One might also consult, in this connection, the comments made in the second lecture of *Basic Principles of Thinking* (1957), where Heidegger returns to Hölderlin's hymn "Mnemosyne," which had guided his introductory remarks in the 1946 lecture "What Are Poets For?" (see *GA* 5: 270–71/201). In this later context Heidegger observes that "it is the mortals who reach sooner into the abyss, therefore they are the ones who dwell in the refuge of death and are thus able to die. An animal cannot die; it comes to an end. This may go along with the fact that the animal cannot think. Thinking lives by an elective affinity with death" (*GA* 79: 114/107).

65. Marx, *Measure,* 124.

66. Dastur, *Death,* 83.

67. Sallis, *Echoes,* 137.

68. Agamben, *Language and Death,* xi, 86–87.

69. The English translation omits this passage from the translated text; see *OWL* 91 n.

70. In "The Way to Language" (1959), Heidegger explains the line from the "Letter" thus: "It [language] is the protection [*Hut*] of presencing, insofar as the shining of this remains entrusted to the appropriating showing of the saying. Language is the house of being because, as saying, language is the mode of appropriation [*die Weise des Ereignisses ist*]" (*GA* 12: 255/*OWL* 135, tm).

71. The lecture "The Essence of Language" (1957–58) concludes with thoughts explicitly relating these views back to the fourfold: "As the world-moving saying, language is the relation of all relations [*das Verhältnis aller Verhältnisse*]. It relates [*verhält*], sustains [*unterhält*], reaches [*reicht*], and enhances [*bereichert*] the

contraposition of the world-regions, holds and protects them, in that it itself—saying—keeps to itself [*an sich hält*].

"Keeping to itself in this way, language reaches us [*be-langt uns*] as the saying of the world's-fourfold [*des Weltgeviertes*]" (*GA* 12: 203/*OWL* 107, tm).

72. "Whatever we meet, we meet under the rubric of 'is manifest as,' i.e., 'is accessible as' and therefore 'is meaningful as.' We can make sense of whatever we meet (even if only interrogatively), and if we cannot make any sense of something, we cannot meet it. We are condemned to ur-*hermêneia*" (Sheehan, "Astonishing!," 16).

73. Cf. Derrida: "there is no scandal whatsoever in saying that *Dasein* remains immortal in its originary being-to-death, if by 'immortal' one understands 'without end' in the sense of *verenden* [to come to an end]. . . . At least from this angle and as *Dasein*, I am, if not immortal, then at least imperishable" (*Aporias*, 39–40).

74. See, for example, the "Rettungen des Horaz," "Rettung des Hier. Cardanus," "Rettung des *Inepti Religiosi* und seines ungennanten Verfassers," and the "Rettung des Cochläus aber nur in einer Kleinigkeit" in Lessing, *Sämtliche Schriften*, vol. 5: 272–367.

75. Cited in Ariès, *Hour of Our Death*, 109.

76. Ariès, *Western Attitudes*, 38.

77. Ariès, *Hour of Our Death*, 310.

6. The Slight and Abiding Thing

1. The first appearance of "The Thing" in *Gestalt und Gedanke* of 1950 is identical on this point to both the Neske single edition of *Vorträge und Aufsätze* (1954) and its *Gesamtausgabe* adoption (2000).

2. Hegel, *Phänomenologie des Geistes*, *GW* 9: 43/*Phenomenology of Spirit*, §61, 38, tm.

3. In *The Face of Things*, Silvia Benso remarks that "this oneness (*Einfalt*) is not unity (*Einheit*), but rather a preservation and unfolding of the differences of its participants. Possibly in spite of Heidegger's own intentions, the nearing of the Fourfold brought about by the thinging of things discloses a form of alterity comparable to, although necessarily not identical with, the otherness which Lévinas retraces in persons, but is unwilling to recognize in things, and which Heidegger does not thematize as alterity, neither in persons, nor in things, because uninterested in the thematization of ethical otherness" (114). Perhaps the role of expropriation that we have delineated could be thought in terms of this desired recognition of an alterity in things.

4. According to Grimms' dictionary, the *Reigentanz* (or *Reihentanz*; French, *la Ronde*) is a folk dance that accompanies singing, rather than instrumentation alone. The Grimms also note that the circling of the *Reigen* can be more of a celebratory procession than a dance. Grimms' *Wörterbuch*, s.v. "*Reigentanz*."

5. Hölderlin, "Griechenland," zweite Fassung, *GSA* 2.1: 256.18–21/*Poems*, 623; cf. *GA* 4: 171–72/195–96, tm.

6. A note to "The Onto-Theological Constitution of Metaphysics" sets up a constellation of relations around this point:

Letting presence—as presencing—letting
letting: sending: giving: appropriating—(*GA* 11: 72 n. 102)

7. See also the discussion of the salvatory (*das Rettende*) in the closing pages of "The Question Concerning Technology." After noting that we are "not yet" saved, Heidegger remarks that, "we are there upon summoned to hope in the growing light of what saves," asking, "how can this happen?" (*GA* 7: 34/*QCT* 33, tm). His answer is in keeping with what we have stated above: "Here and now in what is slight [*im Geringen*], that we may tend what saves in its growth [*in seinem Wachstum hegen*]. This includes that we always hold before our eyes the most extreme danger" (*GA* 7: 34/*QCT* 33, tm).

8. Heidegger, *Das Geringe*, 16.

9. Heidegger, *Das Geringe*, 16.

10. Heidegger, *Das Geringe*, 17.

11. On this shift in Heidegger's determination of Dasein, see Kisiel, *Heidegger's Way*, 49, van Buren, *The Young Heidegger*, 283, and Raffoul, *Heidegger and the Subject*, 220–23. The course where *Jeweiligkeit* is most prominent is the summer semestser 1923 course *Ontology: Hermeneutics of Facticity*, as well as the 1924 lecture "The Concept of Time." In van Buren's translation of the course, *Jeweiligkeit* is rendered as "awhileness" or as the "awhileness of temporal particularity." His footnote 9 to the translation provides a fine discussion of the cluster of terms around *weilen* that are operative in the course. See *Ontology: Hermeneutics of Facticity*, 108–11.

12. Hölderlin, "Der Rhein," *GSA* 2.1: 147.180–83/"The Rhine," *Poems*, 441; cited at *GA* 39: 283.

13. It is a greeting in that it is directed at us and concerns us. In the 1946–48 dialogue "The Western Conversation," Heidegger returns to these same lines from Hölderlin's hymn "The Rhine" regarding the balancing of fate in order to distinguish between "dispensing" (*schicken*) and "sending" (*senden*), precisely in regard to how they concern us. The "fateful" (*das Schickliche*), we are told, "is a festive word" of Hölderlin's poetry (*GA* 75: 90). It is to be distinguished from a "postal mailing [*Postsendung*]" (*GA* 75: 91). "In dispensing [*Schicken*]," as the older interlocutor explains, "there lies something more decisive than in sending [*Senden*]" (*GA* 75: 93). The younger conversation partner finishes the point: "what is dispensed [*das Geschickte*] does not simply come to us [*geht uns . . . zu*], rather it *concernfully approaches* us [*geht uns an*]" (*GA* 75: 93). The older man concludes, "dispensing would thus be a letting draw near from out of the distance" (*GA* 75: 93). The entire discussion is instructive, see *GA* 75: 90–96, 106–14.

14. We now know that Heidegger planned a full-length lecture course on the Anaximander fragment for 1942, *Der Spruch des Anaximander* (*GA* 78). Without entering into a full comparison between the course and the published text, the course contains passages both provocative and relevant for thinking further into the "while." Among these: "Presencing is essentially a while, i.e. it is not only for a length of time, but rather is this while itself" (*GA* 78: 136); "The while is the

authentic jointure [*Fuge*] of withstood transition" (*GA* 78: 172); "Time is the whiling [*Erweilnis*] of the presencing of what presences" (*GA* 78: 198).

15. Anaximander, *DK* 12 b 1/Freeman, *Ancilla*, 19.

16. Freeman, *Ancilla*, 19.

17. Heidegger follows more proximately Franz Dirlmeier in this ("Der Satz des Anaximandros von Milet," 377), whom Heidegger cites in the references to his text, noting "I agree with the delimitation of Anaximander's text, though not with the basis on which it is done" (*GA* 5: 376/286).

18. Kirk, Raven, Schofield, *Presocratic Philosophers*, 118.

19. Kirk, Raven, Schofield, *Presocratic Philosophers*, 118.

20. Heidegger thinks this jointure as a way of uniting: "What is present belongs together in the unity [*im Einen*] of presencing, where, in its while, everything present reciprocally presences abidingly with the others. . . . there reigns in presencing as such the reciprocal-abiding [*Zueineander-Weilen*] of a concealed gathering" (*GA* 5: 353/266, tm). We have discussed this unity in treating of the meaning of the divine (see "The Meaning of the Divine" in chapter four) in terms of the Heraclitean conception of the *Hen* and Heidegger does not fail to make that connection here: "Therefore Heraclitus, catching sight of this gathering-uniting and disclosive essencing in presencing, named the *Hen* (the being of beings) the *Logos*" (*GA* 5: 353–54/266, tm). Heidegger goes much further toward the essay's end, where we read that "The *energeia*, that Aristotle thinks as the basic trait of presencing, of the *eon*, the *idea*, that Plato thinks as the basic trait of presencing, the *Logos* that Heraclitus thinks as the basic trait of presencing, the *Moira* that Parmenides thinks as the basic trait of presencing, the *Chreôn* that Anaximander thinks as what essences in presencing, name the same. In the hidden richness of the same, the unity of the uniting one, the *Hen*, is thought by all of these thinkers in their own way" (*GA* 5: 371/280, tm).

21. Passages such as these lead Derrida to worry over an anthropocentrism in Heidegger's thinking, one oriented around the privileging of the hand. See Derrida, "Heidegger's Hand (*Geschlecht* II)." What Heidegger describes in the treatment of Anaximander is essentially no different from what we have already considered in regards to the hand and gesture in "The Extra-Linguistic: Hint and Gesture," chapter 4. Human privilege would be centered around this privileging of the gesture. Without wishing to diminish the importance of the problematic, we shall see in the following section ("Thing as Gesture of World") that Heidegger explicitly grants to things a gesturing, indeed the very gesturing of world itself. In sum, any privilege of the hand is the privilege of gesture and gesture is no privilege of the human. Things gesture world. Gesture is a necessary consequence of finite materiality and mediation.

22. "The things condition [*be-dingen*] the mortals. This now says: The things visit each time [*jeweils*] the mortals especially [*eigens*] with world" (*GA* 12: 20/*PLT* 197–98, tm).

23. Mortals (and plants) are explicitly mentioned in the talk of abiding found in the Anaximander essay. There the *eonta* are named "all that presences, that essences in the manner of what each time abides [*des Je-weiligen*]: Gods and

humans, temples and cities, sea and land, eagle and snake, tree and bush, wind and light, stone and sand, day and night" (*GA* 5: 353/266, tm).

24. Heraclitus, *DK* 22 b 123/Freeman, *Ancilla*, 33.

25. On *Welt-Geviert*, *GA* 12: 21/*PLT* 199, see also the concluding pages of the 1957–58 George interpretation, "The Essence of Language," where the term plays an important role in thinking the overcoming of opposition as a move to cut a path (*Be-wëgung*) into nearness, *GA* 12: 200–4/*OWL* 104–8).

Conclusion. There Have Never Been Things

1. Even with the Greeks; again see *GA* 45: 177–80/153–55 on the role that *technê* plays in bringing about the blossoming of *physis*.

2. At the time of the letter, June 1950, Heidegger had delivered the full *Insight Into That Which Is* lecture cycle twice, once in Bremen in December 1949 and again at Bühlerhöhe resort and sanatorium in March 1950. Heidegger delivered the first lecture of the cycle alone under the title "On the Thing" at the Bavarian Academy of Fine Art in Munich on June 6, 1950. As the young student's letter is dated June 18, 1950, it would seem to be to this later reading that he is responding. And yet, in his response discussing the reception he mentions "positionality," something that does not appear in the thing lecture proper. Thus we can take Heidegger's remarks to concern the audience response to the whole cycle of *Insight Into That Which Is*.

3. The second half of the yet to be published volume 99 of the *Gesamtausgabe*, one of the "black notebooks" (*schwarze Hefte*), promises insight into this relation. It is entitled *Four Notebooks II: Through Ereignis to Thing and World*. The title is in keeping with my contention that the emergence of the thing/world relation in Heidegger's post-war thinking marks a move past the works of his middle period, which focused on the articulation of *Ereignis*.

4. One can still wonder about the role of beyng in all this—whether, for example, it would now be thought as that which grants the world in the first place. In this case, beyng would not send being (*Sein*) so much as world.

5. Heidegger adds a text reference to three of the essays in the second division of *Vorträge und Aufsätze*, "Building Dwelling Thinking," "The Thing," and ". . . poetically man dwells . . . ," essays we have considered at some length in the above.

6. Jean-Luc Nancy, "Exscription," *Birth to Presence*, 319–40. It is not only this term that I borrow from Nancy. So much of the thought that has motivated this work as a whole arose from engagement with his thinking of sense.

7. Heidegger, *Das Geringe*, 20.

8. Heidegger, *Das Geringe*, 21.

9. Heidegger, *Das Geringe*, 21.

Bibliography

For a complete explanation of the abbreviations used for works by Heidegger and others, see page xv.

Works by Martin Heidegger

Heidegger *Gesamtausgabe*

Heidegger, Martin. *Gesamtausgabe.* 102 vols projected. Frankfurt Am Main: Vittorio Klostermann, 1975–

GA 2   *Sein und Zeit.* Edited by Friedrich-Wilhelm von Herrmann. 1977. Translated by Joan Stambaugh as *Being and Time,* revised by Dennis J. Schmidt. Albany: State University of New York Press, 2010. Cited by the single edition pagination of "*SZ*" below.

GA 3   *Kant und das Problem der Metaphysik.* 5th ed., enlarged. Edited by Friedrich-Wilhelm von Herrmann. 1991. Translated by Richard Taft as *Kant and the Problem of Metaphysics.* Bloomington: Indiana University Press, 1997.

GA 4   *Erläuterungen zu Hölderlins Dichtung.* 2nd ed. Edited by Friedrich-Wilhelm von Herrmann. 1991. Translated as *Elucidations of Hölderlin's Poetry* by Keith Hoeller. Amherst, NY: Humanity Books, 2000.

GA 5   *Holzwege.* 7th ed. Edited by Friedrich-Wilhelm von Herrmann. 1994. Edited and translated by Julian Young and Kenneth Haynes as *Off the Beaten Track.* Cambridge: Cambridge University Press, 2002.

GA 6.1   *Nietzsche I.* Edited by Brigitte Schillbach. 1996.

GA 6.2   *Nietzsche II.* Edited by Brigitte Schillbach. 1997.

GA 7   *Vorträge und Aufsätze.* Edited by Friedrich-Wilhelm von Herrmann. 2000.

GA 8   *Was Heißt Denken?* Edited by Paola-Ludovika Coriando. 2002. Translated by J. Glenn Gray as *What is Called Thinking?* New York: Harper & Row, Publishers, 1968.

GA 9   *Wegmarken.* 3rd ed. Edited by Friedrich-Wilhelm von Herrmann. 1996. Translated as *Pathmarks.* Edited by William McNeill. Cambridge: Cambridge University Press, 1998.

GA 10   *Der Satz vom Grund.* Edited by Petra Jaeger. 1997. Translated by Reginald Lily as *The Principle of Reason.* Bloomington: Indiana University Press, 1994.

GA 11   *Identität und Differenz.* Edited by Friedrich-Wilhelm von Herrmann. 2006.

GA 12 *Unterwegs zur Sprache.* Edited by Friedrich-Wilhelm von Herrmann. 1985.

GA 13 *Aus der Erfahrung des Denkens.* Edited by Hermann Heidegger. 1983.

GA 14 *Zur Sache des Denkens.* Edited by Friedrich-Wilhelm von Herrmann. 2007. Translated by Joan Stambaugh as *On Time and Being.* New York: Harper & Row, Publishers, 1972.

GA 15 *Seminare.* Edited by Curd Ochwadt. 1986.

GA 16 *Reden und andere Zeugnisse eines Lebensweges.* Edited by Hermann Heidegger. 2000.

GA 17 *Einführung in die phänomenologische Forschung.* Edited by Friedrich-Wilhelm von Herrmann. 1994. Translated by Daniel O. Dahlstrom as *Introduction to Phenomenological Research.* Bloomington: Indiana University Press, 2005.

GA 24 *Die Grundprobleme der Phänomenologie.* 2nd ed. Edited by Friedrich-Wilhelm von Herrmann. 1989. Translated by Albert Hofstadter as *The Basic Problems of Phenomenology.* Revised ed. Bloomington: Indiana University Press, 1982.

GA 27 *Einleitung in die Philosophie.* Edited by Otto Saame and Ina Saame-Speidel. 1996.

GA 29/30 *Die Grundbegriffe der Metaphysik: Welt—Endlichkeit—Einsamkeit.* 2nd ed. Edited by Friedrich-Wilhelm von Herrmann. 1992. Translated by William McNeill as *The Fundamental Concepts of Metaphysics: World, Finitude, Solitude.* Bloomington: Indiana University Press, 1995.

GA 39 *Hölderlins Hymnen "Germanien" und "Der Rhein."* 2nd ed. Edited by Susanne Ziegler. 1989.

GA 41 *Die Frage nach dem Ding: Zu Kants Lehre von den transzendentalen Grundsätzen.* Edited by Petra Jaeger. 1984. Translated by W. B. Barton, Jr., and Vera Deutsch as *What Is a Thing?* Chicago: Henry Regnery, 1967.

GA 42 *Schelling: Vom Wesen der menschlichen Freiheit.* Edited by Ingrid Schüßler. 1988. Translated by Joan Stambaugh as *Schelling's Treatise on the Essence of Human Freedom.* Athens, OH: Ohio University Press, 1985.

GA 44 *Nietzsches metaphysische Grundstellung im abendländischen Denken: Die ewige Wiederkehr des Gleichen.* Edited by Marion Heinz. 1986.

GA 45 *Grundfragen der Philosophie: Ausgewählte "Probleme" der "Logik."* 2nd ed. Edited by Friedrich-Wilhelm von Herrmann. 1992. Translated by Richard Rojcewicz and André Schuwer as *Basic Questions of Philosophy: Selected "Problems" of "Logic."* Bloomington: Indiana University Press, 1994.

GA 47 *Nietzsches Lehre vom Willen zur Macht als Erkenntnis.* Edited by Eberhard Hanser. 1989.

GA 50 *Nietzsches Metaphysik; Einleitung in die Philosophie—Denken und Dichten.* Edited by Petra Jaeger. 1990.

GA 52 *Hölderlins Hymne "Andenken."* 2nd ed. Edited by Curd Ochwadt. 1992.

GA 53 *Hölderlins Hymne "Der Ister."* 2nd ed. Edited by Walter Biemel. 1993. Translated by William McNeill and Julia Davis as *Hölderlin's Hymn "The Ister."* Bloomington: Indiana University Press, 1996.

GA 54 *Parmenides.* 2nd ed. Edited by Manfred S. Frings. 1992. Translated by André Schuwer and Richard Rojcewicz as *Parmenides.* Bloomington: Indiana University Press, 1992.

GA 55 *Heraklit.* 3rd ed. Edited by Manfred S. Frings. 1994.

GA 56/57 *Zur Bestimmung der Philosophie.* 2nd ed. Edited by Bernd Heimbüchel. 1999. Translated by Ted Sadler as *Towards the Definition of Philosophy.* New York: Continuum, 2008.

GA 59 *Phänomenologie der Anschauung und des Ausdrucks. Theorie der philosophischen Begriffsbidldung.* Edited by Claudius Strube. 1995. Translated by Tracy Colony as *Phenomenology of Intuition and Expression.* New York: Continuum, 2010.

GA 63 *Ontologie: Heremeneutik der Faktizität.* 2nd ed. Edited by Käte Bröcker-Oltmanns. 1995. Translated by John van Buren as *Ontology—The Hermeneutics of Facticity.* Bloomington: Indiana University Press, 1999.

GA 64 *Der Begriff der Zeit.* Edited by Friedrich-Wilhelm von Herrmann. 2004.

GA 65 *Beiträge zur Philosophie (Vom Ereignis).* 2nd ed. Edited by Friedrich-Wilhelm von Herrmann. 1994. Translated by Richard Rojcewicz and Daniela Vallega-Neu as *Contributions to Philosophy (Of the Event).* Bloomington: Indiana University Press, 2012.

GA 66 *Besinnung.* Edited by Friedrich-Wilhelm von Herrmann. 1997. Translated by Parvis Emad and Thomas Kalary as *Mindfulness.* New York: Continuum, 2006.

GA 67 *Metaphysik und Nihilismus.* Edited by Hans-Joachim Friedrich. 1999.

GA 69 *Die Geschichte des Seyns.* Edited by Peter Trawny. 1998.

GA 73.1 *Zum Ereignis-Denken.* Edited by Peter Trawny. 2013.

GA 73.2 *Zum Ereignis-Denken.* Edited by Peter Trawny. 2013.

GA 75 *Zu Hölderlin. Griechenlandreisen.* Edited by Curd Ochwadt. 2000.

GA 76 *Leitgedanken zur Entstehung der Metaphysik, der neuzeitlichen Wissenschaft und der modernen Technik.* Edited by Claudius Strube. 2009.

GA 77 *Feldweg-Gespräche.* Edited by Ingrid Schüßler. 1995. Translated by Bret W. Davis as *Country Path Conversations.* Bloomington: Indiana University Press, 2010.

GA 78 *Der Spruch des Anaximander.* Edited by Ingeborg Schüßler. 2010.

GA 79 *Bremer und Freiburger Vorträge.* Edited by Petra Jaeger. 1994. Translated by Andrew J. Mitchell as *Bremen and Freiburg Lectures: Insight Into That Which Is and Basic Principles of Thinking.* Bloomington: Indiana University Press, 2012.

GA 81 *Gedachtes.* Edited by Paola-Ludovika Coriando. 2007.

GA 86 *Seminare: Hegel—Schelling.* Edited by Peter Trawny. 2011.

GA 90 *Zu Ernst Jünger.* Edited by Peter Trawny. 2004.

Heidegger in Single Editions

SZ *Sein und Zeit.* 17th ed. Tübingen: Max Niemeyer Verlag, 1993.

UK1 "Vom Ursprung des Kunstwerks: Erste Ausarbeitung." Edited by Hermann Heidegger. *Heidegger Studies* 5 (1989): 5–22. Translated by Markus Zisselsberger as "Of the Origin of the Work of Art (first elaboration)." *Epoche* 12: 2 (Spring 2008): 329–47.

UK2   "Vom Ursprung des Kunstwerkes." In *De L'Origine de L'œvre d'Art. Première Version (1935)*, edited and translated by Emmanuel Martineau, 20–54. Paris: Authentica, 1987.

"Aus den Aufzeichnungen zu dem mit Eugen Fink veranstateten Heraklit-Seminar." *Heidegger Studies* 13 (1997): 9–14.

"Das Ding." In *Gestalt und Gedanke* 1, edited by Bayerische Akademie der schönen Kunst, 128–48. Munich: Verlag von R. Oldenbourg, 1951.

Das Geringe. Martin Heidegger Gesellschaft. Jahresgabe 2010. Stuttgart: Offizin Scheufele, 2010.

"Eine gefährliche Irrnis." Martin Heidegger Gesellschaft. Jahresgabe 2008. Stuttgart: Offizin Scheufele, 2008.

"Die Unumgänglichkeit des Da-Seins ('Die Not') und Die Kunst in ihrer Notwendigkeit (Die bewirkende Besinnung)." Edited by Friedrich-Wilhelm von Herrmann. *Heidegger Studies* 8 (1992): 5–12.

"Zur Überwindung der Aesthetik: Zu 'Ursprung des Kunstwerks.'" Edited by Friedrich-Wilhelm von Herrmann. *Heidegger Studies* 6 (1990): 5–7.

Der Ursprung des Kunstwerkes. Stuttgart: Reclam, 1995.

Heidegger in English Translation

CT   *The Concept of Time.* English–German Edition. Translated by William McNeill. Oxford: Blackwell Publishers, 1992.

DT   *Discourse on Thinking.* Translated by John M. Anderson and E. Hans Freund. New York: Harper & Row, Publishers, 1966.

EGT   *Early Greek Thinking: The Dawn of Western Philosophy.* Translated by David Farrell Krell and Frank A. Capuzzi. New York: Harper & Row, Publishers, 1975.

EP   *The End of Philosophy.* Translated by Joan Stambaugh. New York: Harper & Row, Publishers, 1973.

HFH   "Hebel—Friend of the House." Translated by Bruce V. Foltz and Michael Heim. *Contemporary German Philosophy* 3 (1984), 89–101.

HMT   *Heidegger: The Man and the Thinker.* Edited by Thomas Sheehan. New Brunswick, NJ: Transaction Publishers, 2010.

HS   With Eugen Fink. *Heraclitus Seminar 1966/67.* Translated by Charles H. Siebert. Tuscaloosa, Alabama: The University of Alabama Press, 1979.

HNS   *Martin Heidegger and National Socialism: Questions and Answers.* Edited by Günther Neske and Emil Kettering. Translated by Lisa Harries. New York: Paragon House, 1990.

ID   *Identity and Difference.* Translated by Joan Stambaugh. New York: Harper & Row, Publishers, 1969.

MSC   "Messkirch's Seventh Centennial." Translated by Thomas Sheehan. *Listening* 8 (1973), 40–57.

N1   *Nietzsche: The Will to Power as Art.* In *Nietzsche*, vol. 1–2. Edited and translated by David Farrell Krell. San Francisco: Harper & Row, Publishers, 1991.

N2   *Nietzsche: The Eternal Recurrence of the Same.* In *Nietzsche,* vol. 1–2. Edited and translated by David Farrell Krell. San Francisco: Harper & Row, 1991.

N3   *Nietzsche: The Will to Power as Knowledge and Metaphysics.* In *Nietzsche,* vol. 3–4. Edited by David Farrell Krell. Translated by Joan Stambaugh, David Farrel Krell, and Frank A. Capuzzi. San Francisco: Harper & Row, Publishers, 1991.

N4   *Nietzsche: Nihlism.* In *Nietzsche,* vol. 3–4. Edited by David Farrell Krell. Translated by Frank A. Capuzzi. San Francisco: Harper & Row, Publishers, 1991.

OWL   *On the Way to Language.* Translated by Peter D. Hertz. New York: Harper & Row, Publishers, 1971.

PLT   *Poetry, Language, Thought.* Translated by Albert Hofstadter. New York: Harper & Row, Publishers, 1971.

"Poverty." Translated by Thomas Kalary and Frank Schalow. In *Heidegger, Translation, and the Task of Thinking: Essays in Honor of Paris Emad,* edited by Frank Schalow, 3–10. Dordrecht: Springer, 2011.

QCT   *The Question Concerning Technology and Other Essays.* Translated by William Lovitt. New York: Harper & Row, Publishers, 1977.

"Contributions to *Der Akademiker.*" Translated by John Protevi. In *Heidegger and the Political,* edited by Marcus Brainard, David Jacobs, and Rick Lee. Special issue, *Graduate Faculty Philosophy Journal* 14:2–15:1 (1991): 481–519.

Abbreviated Works by Other Authors

DK   Diels, Hermann, and Walther Kranz, eds. *Die Fragmente der Vorsokratiker.* 19th ed. 3 vols. Zürich: Weidmann, 1996.

GSA   Hölderlin, Friedrich. *Sämtliche Werke.* Große Stuttgarter Ausgabe. 15 vols. Edited by Friedrich Beißner. Stuttgart: W. Kohlhammer Verlag, 1943–1985.
    GSA 2.1 (1951): *Gedichte nach 1800.*

GW   Hegel, Georg Wilhelm Friedrich. *Gesammelte Werke.* Edited by Rheinisch-Westfälischen Akademie der Wissenschaften. Hamburg: Felix Meiner Verlag, 1968–.
    Vol. 5. *Schriften und Entwürfe (1799–1808).* Edited by Manfred Baum and Kurt Rainer Meist, with Theodor Ebert. 1998
    Vol. 8. *Jenaer Systementwürfe III.* Edited by Rolf-Peter Horstmann, with Johann Heinrich Trede. 1976.
    Vol. 9. *Phänomenologie des Geistes.* Edited by Wolfgang Bonsiepen and Reinhard Heede. 1980.
    Vol. 12. *Wissenschaft der Logik. Zweiter Band: Die subjektive Logik oder die Lehre vom Begriff.* Edited by Friedrich Hogemann and Walter Jaeschke. 1981.
    Vol. 20. *Enzyklopädie der philosophischen Wissenschaften im Grundrisse.* Edited by Udo Rameil, Wolfgang Bonsiepen, and Hans Christian Lucas. 1992.

KGW   Nietzsche, Friedrich. *Werke: Kritische Gesamtausgabe.* Edited by Giorgio Colli and Mazzino Montinari. Berlin: Watler de Gruyter, 1967–.

KGW 5.2 (1973). *Idyllen aus Messina. Die Fröhliche Wissenschaft. Nachgelassene Fragmente: Frühjahr 1881 bis Sommer 1882.*
KGW 6.1 (1968). *Also Sprach Zarathustra: Ein Buch für Alle und Keinen (1883–1885).*
KGW 6.2 (1968). *Jenseits von Gut und Böse. Zur Genealogie der Moral (1886–1887).*
KGW 7.2 (1974). *Nachgelassene Fragmente. Frühjahr bis Herbst 1884.*
KGW 7.3 (1974). *Nachgelassene Fragmente. Herbst 1884 bis Herbst 1885.*
KGW 8.1 (1974). *Nachgelassene Fragmente. Herbst 1885 bis Herbst 1887.*

Other Works

Agamben, Giorgio. *Language and Death: The Place of Negativity.* Translated by Karen E. Pinkus with Michael Hardt. Minneapolis: University of Minnesota Press, 1991.

Angelus Silesius. *The Cherubinic Wanderer.* Translated by Maria Shrady. New York: Paulist Press, 1986.

———. *Cherubinischer Wandersmann.* In *Sämtliche Poetische Werke,* edited by Hans Ludwig Held, vol. 3: 5–220. Munich: Carl Hanser Verlag, 1949.

Ariès, Philippe. *The Hour of Our Death: The Classic History of Western Attitudes Toward Death Over the Last One Thousand Years.* Translated by Helen Weaver. New York: Vintage Books, 2008.

———. *Western Attitudes Toward Death: From the Middle Ages to the Present.* Translated by Patricia M. Ranum. Baltimore: The Johns Hopkins University Press, 1974.

Aristotle. *The Complete Works of Aristotle.* Edited by Jonathan Barnes. 2 vols. Princeton: Princeton University Press, 1984.

———. *De Anima.* Edited and translated by W. D. Ross. Oxford: Oxford University Press, 1961.

———. *De Anima Books II, III.* Edited and translated by D. W. Hamlyn. Oxford: Clarendon Press, 1968.

———. *On the Heavens.* Edited and translated by W. K. C. Guthrie. Cambridge, MA: Harvard University Press, 1986.

———. *Physica.* Edited by W. D. Ross. Oxford: The Clarendon Press, 1950.

———. *The Physics.* Edited and translated by P. H. Wicksteed and F. M. Cornford. 2 vols. Loeb Classical Library. Cambridge, MA: Harvard University Press, 1934.

Benso, Silvia. *The Face of Things: A Different Side of Ethics.* Albany: State University of New York Press, 2000.

Bernasconi, Robert. "Race and Earth in Heidegger's Thinking During the Late 1930s." *Southern Journal of Philosophy* 48 (2010): 49–66.

Betz, Maurice. *Rilke in Frankreich: Errinerungen, Briefe, Dokumente.* Vienna: Herbert Reichner Verlag, 1938.

The Bhagavad Gita. Edited and translated by Laurie L. Patton. New York: Penguin, 2008.

Calarco, Matthew. *Zoographies: The Question of the Animal from Heidegger to Derrida.* New York: Columbia University Press, 2008.

Dahlstrom, Daniel O., ed. *Interpreting Heidegger: Critical Essays.* Cambridge: Cambridge University Press, 2011.

———. "Thinking of Nothing: Heidegger's Criticisms of Hegel's Conception of Negativity." In *A Companion to Hegel,* edited by Stephen Houlgate and Michael Baur, 519–36. Malden, MA: Blackwell, 2011.

Danner, Helmut. *Das Göttliche und der Gott bei Heidegger.* Meisenheim am Glan: Verlag Anton Hain, 1971.

Dastur, Françoise. *Death: An Essay on Finitude.* Translated by John Llewelyn. London: The Athlone Press, 1996.

———. "Heidegger's Freiburg Version of the Origin of the Work of Art." In *Heidegger Toward the Turn: Essays on the Work of the 1930s,* edited by James Risser, 119–42. Albany: The State University of New York Press, 1999.

Davis, Bret W., ed. *Martin Heidegger: Key Concepts.* Durham, UK: Acumen, 2010.

Derrida, Jacques. *The Animal That Therefore I Am.* Edited by Marie-Louise Mallet. Translated by David Wills. New York: Fordham University Press, 2008.

———. *Aporias.* Translated by Thomas Dutoit. Stanford: Stanford University Press, 1993.

———. *The Gift of Death and Literature in Secret.* 2nd ed. Translated by David Wills. Chicago: The University of Chicago Press, 2008.

———. "Heidegger's Hand (*Geschlecht* II)." Translated by John P. Leavey, Jr., and Elizabeth Rottenberg. In *Psyche: Inventions of the Other,* edited by Peggy Kamuf and Elizabeth Rottenberg, 2:27–62. Stanford: Stanford University Press, 2008.

———. *Of Spirit: Heidegger and the Question.* Translated by Geoffrey Bennington and Rachel Bowlby. Chicago: The University of Chicago Press, 1989.

———. *Speech and Phenomena: And Other Essays on Husserl's Theory of Signs.* Translated by David B. Allison. Evanston: Northwestern University Press, 1973.

Diefenbach, Joachim, and Reiner Sörries. "Pestsarg und Ausschüttruhe: Kurzer Abriß der Entwicklung des Holzsarges." In *Vom Totenbaum zum Designersarg,* edited by Zentralinstitut und Museum für Sepulkrakultur, 37–42.

Dirlmeier, Franz. "Der Satz des Anaximandros von Milet." *Rheinisches Museum für Philologie (neue Folge)* 87 (1938): 376–82.

Elden, Stuart. "Heidegger's Animals." *Continental Philosophy Review* 39 (2006): 273–91.

Epicurus. *The Epicurus Reader: Selected Writings and Testimonia.* Edited and translated by Brad Inwood and L. P. Gerson. Indianapolis: Hackett Publishing Company, 1994.

Franck, Didier. "Being and the Living." Translated by Peter T. Connor. In Cadava, 135–47.

Freeman, Kathleen. *Ancilla to the Pre-Socratic Philosophers: A Complete Translation of the Fragments in Diels, Fragmente der Vorsokratiker.* Cambridge, MA: Harvard University Press, 1966.

Gadamer, Hans-Georg. "Zur Einführung." In *Der Ursprung des Kunstwerkes* by Martin Heidegger, 93–114. Stuttgart: Reclam, 1995.

Grimm, Jakob, and Wilhelm Grimm. *Deutsches Wörterbuch.* 33 vols. Munich: Deutscher Taschenbuch Verlag, 1984.

Guignon, Charles, ed. *The Cambridge Companion to Heidegger.* 2nd ed. Cambridge: Cambridge University Press, 2006.

Haar, Michel. "The Ambivalent Unthought of the Overman and the Duality of Heidegger's Political Thinking." Translated by Madeleine Dobie. *Graduate Faculty Philosophy Journal,* 14: 2–15: 1 (1991), 109–36.

———. *The Song of the Earth: Heidegger and the Grounds of the History of Being.* Translated by Reginald Lilly. Bloomington: Indiana University Press, 1993.

Harman, Graham. *Heidegger Explained.* Chicago: Open Court, 2007.

———. *Tool-Being: Heidegger and the Metaphysics of Objects.* Chicago: Open Court, 2002.

Harrison, Robert. *Gardens: An Essay on the Human Condition.* Chicago: University of Chicago Press, 2008.

Hebel, Johann Peter. *Hebels Werke in vier Teilen.* Part 2: *Hochdeutsche Dichtungen—Religiöse Schriften.* Edited by Adolf Sütterlin. Berlin: Deutsches Verlagshaus Bong & Co., 1910.

Hegel, G. W. F. *The Encyclopaedia Logic: Part I of the Encyclopaedia of Philosophical Sciences with the Zusätze.* Edited and translated by T. F. Geraets, W. A. Suchting, and H. S. Harris. Indianapolis: Hackett Publishing Company, 1991.

———. *Aesthetics: Lectures on Fine Art.* Translated by T. M. Knox. 2 vols. Oxford: Oxford University Press, 1975.

———. *Phenomenology of Spirit.* Edited and translated by A. V. Miller. Oxford: Oxford University Press, 1977.

———. *Science of Logic.* Translated by A. V. Miller. Atlantic Highlands, NJ: Humanities Press, 1993.

———. *The Philosophy of Spirit (1805–6).* Translated by Leo Rauch. In *Hegel and the Human Spirit: A Translation of the Jena Lectures on the Philosophy of Spirit (1805–6) with Commentary,* edited by Leo Rauch, 83–183. Detroit: Wayne State Press, 1983.

———. *System of Ethical Life and First Philosophy of Spirit.* Edited and translated by H. S. Harris and T. M. Knox. Albany: State University of New York Press, 1979.

———. *Werke.* Theorie-Werkausgabe. Edited by Eva Moldenhauer and Karl Markus Michel. Frankfurt: Suhrkamp, 1970.
Vol. 8: *Enzyklopädie der philosophischen Wissenschaften im Grundrisse (1830).*
Vol. 13: *Vorlesungen über die Ästhetik I.*

Held, Klaus. "Sky and Earth as Invariants of the Natural Life-world." Translated by Felix à Murchadha. In *Phänomenologische Forschungen. Sonderband: Phenomenology of Interculturality and Life World,* edited by Ernst Wolfgang Orth and Chan-Fai Cheung, 21–41. Freiburg: Karl Alber, 1998.

Hobbes, Thomas. *Leviathan.* Edited by Richard Tuck. Cambridge Texts in the History of Political Thought. Cambridge: Cambridge University Press, 1996.

Hölderlin, Friedrich. *Poems & Fragments.* 3rd ed. Edited and translated by Michael Hamburger. London: Anvil Press Poetry, 1994.

———. *Hymns and Fragments*. Edited and translated by Richard Sieburth. Princeton: Princeton University Press, 1984.

———. *Essays and Letters on Theory*. Edited and translated by Thomas Pfau. Albany: The State University of New York Press, 1988.

———. *Sämtliche Werke. Historisch-kritisch Ausgabe*. Vol. 4: *Gedichte 1800–1806*. Edited by Norbert von Hellingrath. Berlin: Propyläen Verlag, 1923.

Husserl, Edmund. *Ding und Raum. Vorlesungen 1907. Husserliana*. Vol. 16. Edited by Ulrich Claesges. The Hague: Martinus Nijhoff, 1973. Edited and translated by Richard Rojcewicz as *Thing and Space: Lectures of 1907*. Dordrecht: Kluwer Academic Publishers, 1997.

———. "Grundlegende Untersuchungen zum phänomenologischen Ursprung der Räumlichkeit der Natur." In *Philosophical Essays in Memory of Edmund Husserl, Eine gefährliche Irrnis* edited by Marvin Farber, 307–25. New York: Greenwood Press, 1968. Translated by Frederick Kersten as "Foundational Investigations of the Phenomenological Origin of the Spatiality of Nature." Peter McCormick and Frederick A. Elliston, eds., *Husserl: Shorter Works*, 213–21.

———. *Husserl: Shorter Works*. Edited by Peter McCormick and Frederick A. Elliston. Notre Dame: University of Notre Dame Press, 1981.

Janicaud, Dominique, and Jean-François Mattéi. *Heidegger: From Metaphysics to Thought*. Translated by Michael Gendre. Albany: State University of New York Press, 1995.

Jünger, Ernst. *On Pain*. Translated by David C. Durst. New York: Telos Press Publishing, 2008.

———. *Sämtliche Werke*. Vol. 7: *Betrachtungen zur Zeit*. Stuttgart: Klett-Cotta, 1980.

———. *Sämtliche Werke*. Vol. 8: *Der Arbeiter*. Stuttgart: Klett-Cotta, 1981.

———. "Total Mobilization." Translated by Joel Golb and Richard Wolin. In *The Heidegger Controversy: A Critical Reader*, edited by Richard Wolin, 119–39.

Jungk, Robert. *Heller als tausend Sonnen: Das Schicksal der Atomforscher*. Stuttgart: Scherz & Goverts Verlag, 1956. Translated by James Cleugh as *Brighter than a Thousand Suns: A Personal History of the Atomic Scientists*. London: Victor Gollancz, 1958.

Kandinsky, Wassily. *On the Spiritual in Art*. Translated by Peter Vergo. In *Complete Writings on Art*, edited by Kenneth C. Lindsay and Peter Vergo, 119–219. New York: Da Capo Press, 1994.

Kant, Immanuel. *Critique of Pure Reason*. Edited and translated by Paul Guyer and Allen W. Wood. Cambridge: Cambridge University Press, 1998.

Kirk, G. S., J. E. Raven, and M. Schofield. *The Presocratic Philosophers*. 2nd ed. Cambridge: Cambridge University Press, 1983.

Kisiel, Theodore. *The Genesis of Heidegger's "Being and Time."* Berkeley: University of California Press, 1993.

———. *Heidegger's Way of Thought*. Edited by Alfred Denker and Marion Heinz. New York: Continuum, 2002.

Kleinberg-Levin, David Michael. *Gestures of Ethical Life: Reading Hölderlin's Question of Measure After Heidegger*. Stanford: Stanford University Press, 2005.

Kovacs, George. *The Question of God in Heidegger's Phenomenology*. Evanston: Northwestern University Press, 1990.

Kreines, James. "Hegel's Critique of Pure Mechanism and the Philosophical Appeal of the *Logic* Project." *European Journal of Philosophy* 12:1 (2004): 38–74.

Kulturverwaltung der Stadt Darmstadt, ed., *Ernst Barlach: Dramatiker, Bildhauer, Zeichner*. Darmstadt: Verlag von Eduard Stichnote, 1951.

Lawlor, Leonard. *This Is Not Sufficient: An Essay on Animality and Human Nature in Derrida*. New York: Columbia University Press, 2007.

Laertius, Diogenes. *Lives of Eminent Philosophers*. Translated by R. D. Hicks. 2 vols. Cambridge, MA: Harvard University Press, 1995.

Lessing, Gotthold Ephraim. *Sämtliche Schriften*, vol. 5. Edited by Karl Lachmann and Franz Muncker. Stuttgart: G. J. Göschen'sche Verlagshandlung, 1890; reprinted, Berlin: Walter de Gruyter, 1968.

Marx, Werner. *"Die Sterblichen."* In *Nachdenken über Heidegger: Eine Bestandsaufnahme*, edited by Ute Guzzoni, 160–175. Hildesheim: Gerstenberg Verlag, 1980.

———. *Gibt es auf Erden ein Maß? Grundbestimmungen einer nichtmetaphysischen Ethik*. Hamburg: Meiner, 1983. Translated as *Is There a Measure on Earth? Foundations for a Nonmetaphysical Ethics* by Thomas J. Nenon and Reginald Lilly. Chicago: University of Chicago Press, 1987.

Mattéi, Jean-François. *Heidegger et Hölderlin: Le Quadriparti*. Paris: Presses Universitaires de France, 2001.

———. "The Heideggerian Chiasmus." In Janicaud and Mattéi, *Heidegger: From Metaphysics to Thought*, 39–150.

McNeill, William. "Life Beyond the Organism: Animal Being in Heidegger's Freiburg Lectures, 1929–30." In *Animal Others: On Ethics, Ontology, and Animal Life*, edited by H. Peter Steeves, 197–248. Albany: State University of New York Press, 1999.

Mitchell, Andrew J. "A Brief History of Things: Heidegger and the Tradition." In *Paths in Heidegger's Later Thought*, edited by Günter Figal, Diego D'Angelo, Tobias Keiling, and Guang Yang. Bloomington: Indiana University Press, forthcoming.

———. "The Coming of History: Heidegger and Nietzsche Against the Present." *Continental Philosophy Review* 46 (2013): 395–411.

———. "Contamination, Essence, and Decomposition: Heidegger and Derrida." In *French Interpretations of Heidegger: An Exceptional Reception*, edited by David Pettigrew and François Raffoul, 131–50. Albany: SUNY Press, 2008.

———. "Entering the World of Pain: Heidegger." *Telos* 150 (Spring 2010): 83–96.

———. "The Exposure of Grace: Dimensionality in Late Heidegger." *Research in Phenomenology* 40 (2010): 309–30.

———. "Heidegger and Terrorism." *Research in Phenomenology* 35 (2005): 181–218.

———. "Heidegger's Breakdown: Health and Healing under the Care of Dr. V. E. von Gebsattel." *Research in Phenomenology*, forthcoming.

———. "Die Politik des geheimen Deutschland. Martin Heidegger und der George-Kreis." *Existentia* 23:1–2 (2013): 41–64.

———. "Simplicity and Relation: Remarks on Heidegger's 1963 Dedication to Char." *Mantis: A Journal of Poetry and Translation* 7 (September 2008): 45–51.

Müller-Sievers, Helmut. *The Cylinder: Kinematics of the Nineteenth Century.* Berkeley: University of California Press, 2012.

Nancy, Jean-Luc. *The Birth to Presence.* Translated by Brian Holmes and others. Stanford: Stanford University Press, 1993.

———. *Dis-Enclosure: The Deconstruction of Christianity.* Translated by Bettina Bergo, Gabrial Malenfant, and Michael B. Smith. New York: Fordham, 2008.

———. *The Gravity of Thought.* Translated by François Raffoul and Gregory Recco. Atlantic Highlands, NJ: Humanities Press International, 1997.

———. *The Inoperative Community.* Edited by Peter Connor. Translated by Peter Connor, Lisa Garbus, Michael Holland, and Simona Sawhney. Minneapolis: University of Minnesota Press, 1991.

———. "Sharing Voices." In *Transforming the Hermeneutical Context: From Nietzsche to Nancy,* edited by Gayle L. Ormiston and Alan D. Schrift, 211–59. Albany: State University of New York Press, 1990.

Newton, Isaac. *The Principia: Mathematical Principles of Natural Philosophy.* Edited and translated by I. Bernard Cohen and Anne Whitman with Julia Budenz. Berkeley: University of California Press, 1999.

Nietzsche, Friedrich. *Der Wille zur Macht: Versuch einer Umwertung aller Werte.* Edited by Peter Gast with Elisabeth Förster-Nietzsche. Afterword by Walter Gebhard. Stuttgart: Alfred Kröner Verlag, 1996.

———. *Beyond Good and Evil: Prelude to a Philosophy of the Future.* Translated by Walter Kaufmann. New York: Vintage Books, 1989.

———. *The Gay Science.* Translated by Walter Kaufmann. New York: Vintage Books, 1974.

———. *The Will to Power.* Translated and edited by Walter Kaufmann and R. J. Hollingdale. New York: Vintage Books, 1968.

———. *Thus Spoke Zarathustra.* Translated by Walter Kaufmann. New York: Modern Library, 1995.

Oliver, Kelly. *Animal Lessons: How They Teach Us to Be Human.* New York: Columbia University Press, 2009.

Oxford English Dictionary. 2nd ed. 20 vols. Oxford: Oxford University Press, 1989

Petzet, Heinrich Wiegand. *Auf einen Stern zugehen. Begegnungen mit Martin Heidegger 1929 bis 1976.* Frankfurt: Societäts-Verlag, 1983. Translated by Parvis Emad and Kenneth Maly as *Encounters & Dialogues with Martin Heidegger.* Chicago: The University of Chicago Press, 1993.

Plato. *Phaedo.* Translated by Eva Brann, Peter Kalkavage, and Eric Salem. Newburyport, MA: Focus Publishing, 1998.

———. *The Republic of Plato.* 2nd ed. Translated by Allan Bloom. New York: Basic Books, 1968.

———. *Ion.* Translated by Paul Woodruff. In *Plato: Complete Works,* edited by John M. Cooper, 937–49. Indianapolis: Hackett Publishing Company, 1997.

Polt, Richard. "Meaning, Excess, and Event." *Gatherings: The Heidegger Circle Annual* 1 (2010): 26–53.

Raffoul, François. *Heidegger and the Subject*. Translated by David Pettigrew and Gregory Recco. Atlantic Highlands: Humanities Press International, 1998.

Richardson, William J., S.J. *Heidegger: Through Phenomenology to Thought*. 4th ed. New York: Fordham University Press, 2003.

Rilke, Rainer Maria. *Sämtliche Werke*. Vol. 1, *Gedichte: Erster Teil*. Edited by Rilke-Archiv with Ruth Sieber-Rilke and Ernst Zinn. Frankfurt am Main: Insel Verlag, 1987.

———. *Sämtliche Werke*. Vol. 2, *Gedichte: Zweiter Teil*. Edited by Rilke-Archiv with Ruth Sieber-Rilke and Ernst Zinn. Frankfurt am Main: Insel Verlag, 1987.

———. *The Selected Poetry of Rainer Maria Rilke*. Edited and translated by Stephen Mitchell. New York: Vintage International, 1989.

———. *Sonnets to Orpheus*. Translated by Edward Snow. New York: North Point Press, 2004.

Risser, James, ed. *Heidegger Toward the Turn: Essays on the Work of the 1930s*. Albany: State University of New York Press, 1999.

Rojcewicz, Richard. *The Gods and Technology: A Reading of Heidegger*. Albany: State University of New York Press, 2006.

Ross, David. *Aristotle*. London: Routledge, 1995.

Safranski, Rüdiger. *Martin Heidegger: Between Good and Evil*. Translated by Ewald Osers. Cambridge, MA: Harvard University Press, 1998.

Sallis, John. *Echoes: After Heidegger*. Bloomington: Indiana University Press, 1990.

———. *Force of Imagination: The Sense of the Elemental*. Bloomington: Indiana University Press, 2000.

———. "Nietzsche's Platonism." In *Nietzsche: Critical Assessments*, vol. 4, *Between the Last Man and the Overman: The Question of Nietzsche's Politics*, edited by Daniel W. Conway with Peter S. Groff, 292–302. New York: Routledge, 1998.

———, ed. *Reading Heidegger: Commemorations*. Bloomington: Indiana University Press, 1993.

———. *Stone*. Bloomington: Indiana University Press, 1994.

———. "Twisting Free—Being to an Extent Sensible." In *Echoes: After Heidegger*, 76–96. Bloomington: Indiana University Press, 1990.

Scharr, Adam. *Heidegger's Hut*. Cambridge, MA: MIT Press, 2006.

Schelling, F. W. J. *Philosophical Investigations into the Essence of Human Freedom*. Translated by Jeff Love and Johannes Schmidt. Albany: State University of New York Press, 2007.

———. *Über das Wesen der menschlichen Freiheit und die damit zusammenhängenden Gegenstände*. Edited by Thomas Buchheim. Hamburg: Felix Meiner Verlag, 1997.

Schürmann, Reiner. *Heidegger: On Being and Acting: From Principles to Anarchy*. Translated by Christine-Marie Gros with Reiner Schürmann. Bloomington: Indiana University Press, 1987.

Seneca. *Epistles 1–65*. Translated by Richard M. Gummere. Loeb Classical Library. Cambridge, MA: Harvard University Press, 1996.

Sheehan, Thomas. "Astonishing! Things Make Sense!" *Gatherings: The Heidegger Circle Annual* 1 (2010): 1–25.

————. "Facticity and *Ereignis.*" In *Interpreting Heidegger: Critical Essays,* edited by Daniel O. Dahlstrom, 42–68.

————. "'Let a hundred translations bloom!' A Modest Proposal about *Being and Time.*" *Man and World* 30: 2 (1997), 227–38.

————. "The Turn." In *Martin Heidegger: Key Concepts,* edited by Bret Davis, 82–101.

Sinn, Dieter. *Ereignis und Nirwana: Heidegger—Buddhismus—Mythos—Mystik. Zur Archäotypik des Denkens.* Bonn: Bouvier Verlag, 1991.

Steeves, H. Peter. *Animal Others: On Ethics, Ontology, and Animal Life.* Albany: State University of New York Press, 1999.

Taminiaux, Jacques. "The Origin of 'The Origin of the Work of Art.'" In *Reading Heidegger,* edited by John Sallis, 392–404.

Terence. *The Self-Tormentor.* In *The Woman of Andros, The Self-Tormentor, The Eunuch,* edited and translated by John Barsby, 171–303. Loeb Classical Library. Cambridge, MA: Harvard University Press, 2001.

Thurner, Rainer. "Gott und Ereignis—Heideggers Gegenparadigma zur Onto-Theologie." *Heidegger Studies* 8 (1992): 81–102.

Trakl, Georg. *Dichtungen und Briefe, historische-kritische Ausgabe.* 2nd enlarged ed. Edited by Walther Killy and Hans Szklenar. Salzburg: Otto Müller Verlag, 1987.

————. *The Poems of George Trakl.* Translated by Margitt Lehbert. London: Anvil Press Poetry, 2007.

Trawny, Peter. *Adyton: Heideggers esoterische Philosophie.* Berlin: Matthes & Seitz, 2010.

————. "The Future of Time: Reflections on the Conception of Time in Hegel and Heidegger." Translated by Andrew Mitchell. *Research in Phenomenology* 30 (2000): 12–39.

van Buren, John. *The Young Heidegger: Rumor of the Hidden King.* Bloomington: Indiana University Press, 1994.

Vedder, Ben. *Heidegger's Philosophy of Religion: From God to the Gods.* Pittsburgh: Duquesne University Press, 2007.

Vietta, Egon. *Die Seinsfrage bei Martin Heidegger.* Stuttgart: Curt E. Schwab, 1950.

von Herrmann, Friedrich-Wilhelm. *Wege ins Ereignis: Zu Heideggers "Beiträge zur Philosophie."* Frankfurt am Main: Vittorio Klostermann, 1994.

Vycinas, Vincent. *Earth and Gods: An Introduction to the Philosophy of Martin Heidegger.* The Hague: Martinus Nijhoff, 1961.

Weiß Phillip. "Eine kleine Geschichte des Sarges." In *Vom Totenbaum zum Designersarg,* edited by Zentralinstitut und Museum für Sepulkrakultur, 10–22.

Wolin, Richard, ed. *The Heidegger Controversy: A Critical Reader.* Cambridge, MA: MIT Press, 1993.

Young, Julian. "The Fourfold." In Charles Guignon, ed., *Cambridge Companion to Heidegger,* 373–92.

Zentralinstitut und Museum für Sepulkrakultur, ed. *Vom Totenbaum zum Designersarg: Zur Kulturgeschichte des Sarges von der Antike bis zur Gegenwart.* Kassel: Arbeitsgemeinschaft Friedhof und Denkmal, 1993.

Zimmerman, Karl. *Baumsarg und "Totenbaum": Zu einer Bestattung unter dem Berner Münster. Acta Bernensia* XI. Bern: Verlag Stämpfli, 1992.

Index

abandonment: of being, 27, 33–36, 168–
69, 323n11; and devastation, 68–69;
and hints, 121, 168; and machination, 26, 28; as opening to relation,
27, 69, 168

abiding (*weilen*), 278–306, 348–49; in
abandonment, 168; as arriving,
290; in the between, 290; of clouds,
142–43; of divinities, 208; and dwelling, 251; and lingering, 279, 289–90,
292, 293, 296; as opening to relations, 290, 294; as plural, 290–91;
and *te onta*, 295; of the thing, 13, 49,
259, 263, 296–99, 306; vs. genesis
and corruption, 295; for a while,
161, 263

ability (*vermögen*), 190, 223–31, 254–55,
343n36; and being in an element,
190, 228; capable of only what we
like, 343n39; to die, 212–13, 223–24,
227, 254, 345n50; to guard the essence, 230; to receive, 272, 298. *See
also* affiliate (*mögen, philein*); enable;
Heraclitus: *physis kryptesthai philei*

abyss: and aether, 135–36; as between,
121; earth as, 71, 74, 76, 79, 95–96;
as groundless ground, 81; and meaning, 206; and mortals, 346n64; not
absence of ground, 76; between relationality and metaphysics, 306; as
remaining away of ground, 79, 307

aether, 134–38; and abyss, 135–36; and
clouds, 144, 162; as element, 197;
and godhood, 190; as joyous, 135

affiliate (*mögen, philein*), 39, 228–30, 237,
343n39. *See also* Heraclitus: *physis
kryptesthai philei*

Agamben, Giorgio, 243, 331, 346

age, the (*das Alter*), 22–23; as autumn of
life, 22; and ripening, 160; as sixty, 22

an- (prefix), 70, 285–86, 295, 309

Anaximander, 279, 286–88, 290–96, 311,
316, 348n14

angels: and time, 161; as gods, 202; of the
house, 161; as messengers, 175–76;
require the joyous as medium,
175–76; Rilke's, 203, 217–20, 222; of
the year, 161

animal, 32, 72–74, 87–88, 107–14, 211–
23; behavedness of, 98–100; belongs
to between, 114; and death, 113,
212, 343n36, 346n64; drive and ratio
the same, 216; as gentle, 111; *Getier*
vs. *Tierheit*, 328n14; and instinct,
32, 98, 215–16, 331n41; as poor in
world, 88, 90, 98; reservations in
analysis regarding, 329n22; in Trakl,
109; as wild, 111. See also *animal rationale*; blue: deer; *zôon logon echon*

animal rationale, 32, 107, 111, 168, 203,
211, 213–18, 221–23, 241. See also
zôon logon echon

annihilation, 8, 28, 35, 155, 222, 234; or
consummation, 200; impossibility
of, 129, 207; of the thing by science,
65–66, 308–10; vs. devastation, 68;
would bring relief, 69

anthropocentrism, 107, 113–14, 349n21

Arendt, Hannah, 19, 324

Ariès, Philippe, 232, 254

Aristotle, 55, 85, 136–37, 145, 148–49,
287–88, 332, 334, 338, 349

arriving: and greeting, 166; as abiding
and departing, 290; as beings, 77;
as darkness, 65; of gods, 197, 203,
253–54; of the great, 272–73; and

Milton, John, 154
mirror play, 9, 259, 263, 267–70, 275–76, 298, 306; vs. Hegel, 286
moon, 117, 145, 149, 155–56, 158–59, 225, 252, 334; as friend of house, 158
mortals, 9, 211–58, 260, 297, 343n36, 345n50, 346n64, 349n22; always plural, 212; always underway, 13; and *animal rationale*, 213–23; being-in-death, 227–31, 308; dwelling of, 249–58, 306, 308; endlessly dying, 251; human as not yet, 113, 231; language and, 241–49; no interiority, 92, 241; participate in worlding, 73, 88; as replacing name Dasein, 118, 211

Nancy, Jean-Luc, 82–83, 239, 318, 328, 336, 346, 350
Natorp, Paul, 176–77
nature, 87, 90, 93, 96–97, 115, 159, 318; animals, 107–15; challenged, 39; and holy, 192–93; loves to hide, 38, 75, 80; and mechanism, 55; no longer an object, 37; plants, 97–107; rivers and waters, 93–97; stones, 89–93; and technology, 47, 50, 64. *See also* time: natural time
Nietzsche, Friedrich, 30, 34, 55–56, 68, 105, 111, 163, 203, 214–16, 220–23, 250, 323, 326, 330–31, 335, 339–41; overcoming, 64, 130–31, 171, 188, 196, 215, 222–23, 313, 317, 325, 331, 335, 350; Übermensch, 20, 203, 220–22, 341–42; will to power, 30–31, 34, 51, 56, 220–22, 292, 341; Zarathustra, 20, 56, 220–22, 341
night, 117–18, 153–54, 155–59, 198, 333n23, 335n32; as blue, 139–40; and day, 8, 145–46, 150, 252; midnight, 197; to protect the night, 253; as seamstress, 157; stars of, 117, 155–59, 166, 252, 259, 262, 335n31
no longer: beyng no longer present, 169, 223; depths no longer dark, 142; energy no longer tied to countries, 67; gods no longer here, 197, 203; language no longer human property, 92; light no longer a clearing, 65; mourning and, 210; no longer being, 315; no longer at home not yet at destination, 108; no longer human, 231; no longer objects, 37, 40, 44, 47, 50, 61; no longer onto-logical difference, 320; no longer present at hand, 13, 17; no longer signs, 97; and setting, 155; things no longer merely technological, 257; things no longer things, 310, 312. *See also* not yet
not yet: abandonment not yet complete, 169; death not yet present, 224–25; gods not yet here, 200; human not yet the mortal, 113; no longer at home not yet at destination, 108; not yet annihilated, 207; not yet arrived, 203; not yet arriving God, 171; not yet extinguished traces, 210; not yet healed, 201; not yet represented enough, 30; not yet ripe, 103; not yet saved, 348n7; not yet the mortal, 230–31, 235–36, 241, 258, 340n1; not yet things, 310–11, 314; not yet thinking, 174, 344n40, 344n41. *See also* no longer

Oliver, Kelly, 330n23, 331n32
ontological difference: 9, 187, 312, 316–20, 339n29
Ott, Hugo, 19, 324

peace, 33–36, 68–69, 129, 256
Petzet, Heinrich, 20, 321, 324
plants, 87–89, 97–107, 136, 218, 330n24, 349n23; Hebel on relation to human, 136; Nietzsche on relation to human, 105
Plato, 55, 85, 120, 132, 183, 206, 215, 288, 338, 341, 349
poetry, 75, 136; belongs to between, 114, 135; clouds as poets, 142–44; as exposed, 129–30; and flown gods, 139–40, 163; as friend, 158; and hints, 165, 167, 337n15; names holy, 195; poetic word, 195–97, 199; poetizing relations, 97, 142; as thickened (*verdichtet*), 125, 136, 249, 307; unknown god as measure of, 124, 202
Polt, Richard, 321, 338